W9-BXC-984

Advance Praise for *Website Optimization*

"Andy King has drawn attention to the inherent synergy between search engine marketing and web page performance. Andy is a thought leader and genuinely understands the complexity of website optimization. The depth of research and experience in this book is astonishing. This book is a must-have for best practices to optimize your website and maximize profit."

> — Tenni Theurer, Engineering Manager, Yahoo! Exceptional
> Performance

"Thoughtful and rich in examples, this book will be a useful reference for website designers."

> — Vint Cerf, Internet pioneer

"Andy King has done it again! His latest book will help make your website better, faster, and more findable. This is destined to become the definitive guide to web optimization."

> — Peter Morville, author of *Ambient Findability* and coauthor of
> *Information Architecture for the World Wide Web*

"*Website Optimization* brings together the science, the art, and the business of Internet marketing in a complete way. From persuasion paths to search engine algorithms, from web page load performance to pay-per-click campaign management, and from organic search ranking metrics to multivariate testing, this book is a resource that goes from soup to nuts."

> — Jim Sterne, emetrics.org

"Andy King has distilled years of research and experience into a cohesive approach designed to get maximum value from your website. The book explains what measurable objectives to focus upon to increase website traffic and improve the value of the experience to your customers and your bottom line. Andy King provides a comprehensive set of concrete, practice-oriented principles, strategies, experimental methods and metrics illustrated with clear studies that provide the know-how to achieve your objectives. To me, as a researcher, what is particularly impressive is how all of this is backed by scientific studies and how the approach is rooted in experimental techniques and quantifiable metrics for engineering the best website possible."

> — Peter Pirolli, PARC Research Fellow and author of *Information
> Foraging Theory*

"I've never met anyone who didn't want more traffic, sales, or leads to their website. This is the first book to cover optimization from high-level concepts down to code-level details. WSO will guide you through the world of SEO and Pay Per Click to bring you more traffic, and breaks down the many things you can do to your website to make sure your visitor takes action. The first step, though, is for you to take action and do the things WSO tells you to do and buy this book."

— Bryan Eisenberg, bestselling author of *Call to Action* and *Always Be Testing*

"Andy has combined theoretical best practices with real-world examples, making *Website Optimization* a 'must read' for anyone who cares about their site's technical quality. As someone who has worked optimizing some of the largest websites in the world, everyone who cares about site performance has something to learn from this book."

— Ben Rushlo, Senior Manager of Keynote Performance Consulting Services

Website Optimization

Other resources from O'Reilly

Related titles

Ambient Findability
Building Scalable Web Sites
CSS: The Definitive Guide
Designing Web Navigation
Google Advertising Tools
High Performance Web Sites

Information Architecture for
  the World Wide Web
Subject to Change
Web 2.0: A Strategy Guide
Web Performance Tuning:
  Speeding Up the Web

oreilly.com

oreilly.com is more than a complete catalog of O'Reilly books. You'll also find links to news, events, articles, weblogs, sample chapters, and code examples.

oreillynet.com is the essential portal for developers interested in open and emerging technologies, including new platforms, programming languages, and operating systems.

Conferences

O'Reilly brings diverse innovators together to nurture the ideas that spark revolutionary industries. We specialize in documenting the latest tools and systems, translating the innovator's knowledge into useful skills for those in the trenches. Visit *conferences.oreilly.com* for our upcoming events.

Safari Bookshelf (*safari.oreilly.com*) is the premier online reference library for programmers and IT professionals. Conduct searches across more than 1,000 books. Subscribers can zero in on answers to time-critical questions in a matter of seconds. Read the books on your Bookshelf from cover to cover or simply flip to the page you need. Try it today for free.

Website Optimization

Andrew B. King

O'REILLY®

Beijing · Cambridge · Farnham · Köln · Sebastopol · Taipei · Tokyo

Website Optimization
by Andrew B. King

Copyright © 2008 Andrew B. King. All rights reserved.
Printed in the United States of America.

Published by O'Reilly Media, Inc., 1005 Gravenstein Highway North, Sebastopol, CA 95472.

O'Reilly books may be purchased for educational, business, or sales promotional use. Online editions are also available for most titles (*safari.oreilly.com*). For more information, contact our corporate/institutional sales department: (800) 998-9938 or *corporate@oreilly.com*.

Editor: Simon St.Laurent		**Indexer:** Lucie Haskins	
Production Editor: Rachel Monaghan		**Cover Designer:** Karen Montgomery	
Copyeditor: Audrey Doyle		**Interior Designer:** David Futato	
Proofreader: Rachel Monaghan		**Illustrator:** Jessamyn Read	

Printing History:

July 2008:	First Edition.

 This book uses RepKover™, a durable and flexible lay-flat binding.

ISBN: 978-0-596-51508-9

[M]

Table of Contents

Part II.   Web Performance Optimization

Foreword

"How do we make our website better?"

I've been answering that question for 15 years and had to write eight books on the subject to lay it all out. But I could not have written this book.

"What should we measure on our website?"

I've been answering that question for eight years and had to write a book on the subject, create a category-dominating conference, and start a professional association to lay it all out. But I could not have written this book.

I wrote about strategy and philosophy. I blazed a trail of logic and common sense, bringing marketing and technology together in the service of customer centricity and increased profitability. At least that's what I told myself.

I spouted opinion, conjecture, perspective, and punditry. To others, I said that this was a Brave New World and that although the jury may be out, the insight was obvious. I created 10,000 PowerPoint slides showing the good, the bad, and the ugly in an attempt to diminish the quantity and grief of aggravating encounters with electronic brochures laden with bad electronic penmanship.

When pressed for examples and case studies, I pointed to the newness and shininess of the art and practice of Internet marketing and declared that companies that had a clue and had figured out best practices were not talking. It was all too secret sauce and competitive edge to give away to potential competitors.

Today, we not only have examples, but we also have experiments and documentation. The result is scholarship.

One of the things that sets *Website Optimization* apart from the articles, white papers, blogs, books, and pundits is that it taps all of those to deliver a well-considered, well-researched, well-organized treatise on how to get the most out of your online investment.

This book brings philosophy, strategy, and tactical advice together, dressed up like avuncular guidance but incorporating a decade of emergent research. It lays out all the issues to consider and cites seminal sources. When you come across a passage that intrigues or something you need to implement right now, you can follow the thread to the source, drill down, and dive deep.

But that's just one of the things that sets this book apart. The other is its scope.

The history of online marketing started with the technology. Business people first had to understand what the Internet was and how it worked—technically. Then came the difficult task of understanding Internet culture. The gift economy, *Permission Marketing, The Cluetrain Manifesto,* and the desire of web surfers to share and commune all had to be assimilated and folded into marketing programs and web development efforts. But something was lost along the way: marketing. Good old-fashioned advertising, marketing, and sales skills that have been around since John Wannamaker invented the price tag.

A whole generation of web designers, information architects, and customer experience engineers missed those classes in school and haven't been in their careers long enough to have absorbed the lessons that those who did not grow up with their own domain names have lived and breathed for generations.

Those who can code Cascading Style Sheets (CSS) in their sleep and use Twitter to update their Facebook friends about the most viral YouTube videos are not familiar with phrases such as "unique sales proposition," "risk reversal," and "solution selling." They are in need of this book.

Those who remember three-martini lunches on Madison Avenue are still uncomfortable with link equity, *robots.txt* files, and Google analytics page tags. They need this book.

Website Optimization brings together the science, the art, and the business of Internet marketing in a complete way—if you'll excuse the expression, in a *textbook way.* From persuasion paths to search engine algorithms, from web page load performance to pay-per-click campaign management, and from organic search-ranking metrics to multivariate testing, this book is a resource that goes from soup to nuts.

My advice? Do not read this book. Spend a day scanning this book with a pad of yellow sticky notes at hand. You will repeatedly find topics that you want to explore in depth—passages you will want to read again and pages you will take to the copy machine to spread liberally around your company.

Website Optimization is the book that will help you make the case to your boss—and her boss—for more resources to help you make the most of your online investment.

How do you make your website better? Start on page 1.

—Jim Sterne

Jim Sterne is an international speaker on electronic marketing and customer interaction. A consultant to Fortune 500 companies and entrepreneurs, Sterne focuses his 25 years of experience in sales and marketing on measuring the value of the Internet as a medium for creating and strengthening customer relationships. Sterne has written eight books on Internet advertising, marketing, and customer service, including *Web Metrics: Proven Methods for Measuring Web Site Success*. Sterne is the producer of the annual eMetrics Marketing Optimization Summit (*http://www.emetrics.org/*) and is the founding president and current chairperson of the Web Analytics Association (*http://www.WebAnalyticsAssociation.org/*).

Preface

"We've had a website for years now, but it hardly pays for itself."

"Our site's pulling in more than 30% of our revenue, at a far lower cost than our other venues."

There's a world of difference between these two very real Internet experiences. Yet they provide a window into the landscape of web survival that plays out daily. Success is the result of a multitude of adaptations to this constantly changing environment. The fate of companies worldwide is at stake, yet few players grasp the full scope of the problem. Fewer still can clearly and thoroughly articulate its solution: website optimization.

Ultimately, website optimization (WSO) is about maximizing the (usually financial) return on a website investment. Research shows that attaining that ultimate goal is dependent upon fulfilling a set of known benchmarks, including making the site easier to find, easier to use, faster, more aesthetically pleasing, cheaper to run, and more compelling. Site stakeholders need accurate resources that spell out best-in-class, proven strategies and methods to reach those benchmarks, and thereby attain success.

I wrote this book to fill this need. By reading it, you will learn a comprehensive set of optimization techniques for transforming your website into a more successful profit-generation machine. You'll save money by shifting your marketing budget from hit-or-miss mass marketing to highly targeted, online marketing with measurable results.

WSO will teach you how to engage more customers by making your site more compelling and easier for search engine users to find. Part I, *Search Engine Marketing Optimization*, will teach you how to use natural search engine optimization (SEO), pay-per-click (PPC) advertising, and conversion rate optimization (CRO) to boost your site's visibility and convert browsers into buyers. Part II, *Web Performance Optimization*, will help you optimize your HTML, Cascading Style Sheets (CSS), multimedia, and Ajax to improve response times and reliability. You will learn that these two components of WSO have synergistic effects; faster sites convert more users, save money on bandwidth bills, and even improve potential search engine rankings, while search-friendly sites built with standards-based CSS are faster and more accessible.

Taken as a whole, WSO is a discipline of efficiency. Optimal search marketing makes the most of advertising budgets by boosting rankings, click-through rates (CTRs), and landing-page conversion rates. Optimum website performance makes the most efficient use of limited bandwidth and short attention spans. You'll learn how to achieve an important key to website success: balancing aesthetic appeal with responsiveness, while delivering a persuasive message.

The secrets to successful sites are contained in these pages. This book breaks ground by gathering disparate and seemingly unrelated disciplines under one marquee: website optimization. If you master the techniques that you'll find here, you will achieve website success.

Who Should Read This Book

This book is intended for three distinct groups:

- Web marketers
- Web developers
- Managers (project managers, business managers, site owners, etc.)

Different parts of the book are designed for these different audiences.

Web Marketers

For web marketers, this book assumes the following:

- You have some familiarity with SEO and the terminology thereof.
- You know what PPC, CPC, CTR, and ROI stand for and how they work.
- You understand that improving conversion rates is important to website success.
- You are comfortable with using metrics to guide your decision making.

Web Developers

Web developers will find it helpful to have an understanding of:

- HTML
- CSS rule syntax and the principles behind the separation of presentation from content
- JavaScript programming
- Server-side scripting and modifying server configuration files

This book does not assume that you are an expert in all of these areas, but it does assume that you are able to figure these things out on your own, or that you can consult other resources to help you follow the examples. Server-side examples are generally done in PHP or text-based server configuration files. The figures (most of which are reproduced in color) as well as key code examples and chapter summaries are available on this book's companion website:

> http://www.websiteoptimization.com/secrets/

Managers

Managers need not be versed in all of the prerequisites just described, but we assume that you have some familiarity with SEM and the process of website development. Managers will probably want to spend more time on the book's first two chapters on SEO best practices, as well as on Chapter 5, to find out how to make the most of existing traffic. The introduction to Part II of the book shows how the psychology of performance, the size and complexity of web pages, and response time guidelines have changed over time. Finally, this book expects that Internet terms and phrases are familiar so that you can follow along with the examples provided.

How This Book Is Organized

This book has 10 chapters and consists of two parts, each focusing on different yet synergistic aspects of WSO: SEM and web performance. It is not necessary to read the book sequentially, although some chapters build on previous chapters (e.g., Chapters 2 and 4).

Part I, *Search Engine Marketing Optimization*, which comprises the first five chapters of the book, is for web marketers who want to increase the visibility and conversion rates of their sites. Part II, *Web Performance Optimization*, composed of the next four chapters, is designed for web developers who want to speed up their sites. Chapter 10 bridges the two topics. It explains how the effects of search engine marketing and web performance tuning can be quantified and optimized.

Part I

Part I, *Search Engine Marketing Optimization*, explains how to use best-practice techniques to boost the search engine visibility and conversion rate of your website. It consists of the following:

Introduction to Part I, *Search Engine Marketing Optimization*
Briefly explores the behavior of users as they interact with search engine result pages, and how tight, front-loaded headlines and summaries help to improve natural referrals and PPC conversions for search result pages.

Chapter 1, *Natural Search Engine Optimization*
Shows best practices for improving organic search engine visibility, as well as how to overcome the most common barriers to high rankings. The chapter demonstrates the 10 steps you can take to achieve high rankings, including writing optimized title tags, targeting specific keywords, and building popular inbound links. You'll learn how to "bake in" keywords, as well as the importance of using your primary keyphrase.

Chapter 2, *SEO Case Study: PhillyDentistry.com*
Demonstrates the benefits of natural SEO and best-practice WSO techniques. In this chapter, you'll see how CRO, credibility-based design, natural SEO, and a dash of PPC were used to increase the number of new clients for a business by a factor of 47.

Chapter 3, *Pay-per-Click Optimization, written by the team at Pure Visibility Inc.*
Explains how to boost the ROI of your paid-search advertising campaigns. You'll learn how to become a successful PPC optimizer by developing targeted campaigns based on profit-driven goals. Through ad copy, auction bids, and landing-page optimization, you will maximize CTRs and increase conversions within a set budget.

Chapter 4, *PPC Case Study: BodyGlove.com, written by the team at Pure Visibility Inc.*
Demonstrates best-practice PPC and CRO techniques. In this example, PPC and landing-page optimization increased conversions by more than 600%.

Chapter 5, *Conversion Rate Optimization, written by Matt Hockin and Andrew B. King*
Reveals the top 10 factors to maximize the conversion rate of your site. You'll learn how to use persuasive copywriting and credibility-based web design to turn your website into a more efficient sales tool. Through benefit-oriented copy, applied psychology, and *source credibility*, you can persuade visitors to take positive action and increase their desire to buy. This chapter also shows how to craft a unique selling proposition, use risk reversal, and leverage value hierarchies to get visitors to act.

Part II

Part II, *Web Performance Optimization*, discusses how to optimize the response time of your website:

Introduction to Part II, *Web Performance Optimization*
Explores the benefits of high-performance websites and shows the effects of slow response times on user psychology. It provides perspective with average web page trends such as how the "speed tax" of object overhead dominates today's web page delays. You'll learn why the 8- to 10-second rule has diverged into the haves and have-nots as broadband has become more widespread. You'll also discover new response time guidelines based on the latest research.

Chapter 6, *Web Page Optimization*

Reveals how web page optimization is not only about raw speed, but also about managing the user's experience. We'll show you how to streamline your pages so that they download and display faster. This chapter offers the top 10 web performance tips as well as a list of common problems to avoid. It covers HTML optimization, minimizing HTTP requests, graphics and multimedia optimization, and loading JavaScript asynchronously with an emphasis on standards-based design.

Chapter 7, *CSS Optimization*

Reveals how to optimize and modularize your CSS to streamline your HTML by up to 50%. You will learn the top 10 tips for optimizing CSS, including shorthand properties and grouping, leveraging descendant selectors to replace inline style, and substituting CSS techniques for JavaScript behavior. This chapter also demonstrates how you can create CSS sprites, how to make CSS drop-down menus, how to use reset stylesheets, and how best to use CSS2.1 and CSS3 techniques.

Chapter 8, *Ajax Optimization, written by Thomas A. Powell*

Demystifies the emerging technology that is Ajax, and explores ways to optimize JavaScript code and make Ajax applications more robust. Optimized use of JavaScript updates portions of pages asynchronously, boosts interactivity, and increases conversion rates. This chapter features example code, criteria for evaluating Ajax libraries, pointers on parallelism, and the advantages of different data formats.

Chapter 9, *Advanced Web Performance Optimization*

Explores advanced server-side and client-side techniques for improving performance. Server-side techniques include improving parallelism, using cache control and HTTP compression, rewriting URLs, and using delta compression for RSS feeds. Client-side techniques include lazy-loading JavaScript, loading resources on demand, using progressive enhancement, and using inline images with data URIs to save HTTP requests.

Chapter 10

Chapter 10 bridges the topics covered in Parts I and II:

Chapter 10, *Website Optimization Metrics, written by David Artz, Daniel Shields, and Andrew B. King*

Illustrates the best metrics and tools for optimizing both search marketing campaigns and website performance. Here you'll learn the mantra "Data trumps intuition," how to use controlled experiments to compare website alternatives, how to maximize website success measures, and the importance of minimizing response time variability. This chapter also explains best-practice metrics such as *PathLoss* and *cost per conversion*, as well as presenting performance tools such as waterfall graphs and Pagetest to quash problems before they become trends.

Conventions Used in This Book

The following typographical conventions are used in this book:

Italic

> Indicates new terms, URLs, filenames, file extensions, and occasionally, emphasis and keyword phrases.

`Constant width`

> Indicates computer coding in a broad sense. This includes commands, options, variables, attributes, keys, requests, functions, methods, types, classes, modules, properties, parameters, values, objects, events, event handlers, XML and XHTML tags, macros, and keywords.

`Constant width bold`

> Indicates commands or other text that the user should type literally.

`Constant width italics`

> Indicates text that should be replaced with user-supplied values or values determined by context.

 This icon signifies a tip, suggestion, or general note.

 This icon indicates a warning or caution.

Using Code Examples

This book is intended to help you optimize your website. In general, you may use the code in this book in your programs and documentation.

You do not need to contact the publisher for permission unless you are reproducing a significant portion of the code. For example, if you are writing a program that uses several chunks of code from this book you are not required to secure our permission. Answering a question by citing this book and quoting example code does not require permission.

Incorporating a significant amount of example code from this book into your product's documentation *does* require permission. Selling or distributing a CD-ROM of examples from O'Reilly books *does* require permission.

We appreciate, but do not require, attribution. An attribution usually includes the title, author, publisher, and ISBN. For example: "*Website Optimization*, by Andrew B. King. Copyright 2008 Andrew B. King, 978-0-596-51508-9."

If you feel your proposed use of code examples falls outside fair use or the permission given here, feel free to contact us at *permissions@oreilly.com*.

How to Contact Us

Please address comments and questions concerning this book to the publisher:

O'Reilly Media, Inc.
1005 Gravenstein Highway North
Sebastopol, CA 95472
800-998-9938 (in the United States or Canada)
707-829-0515 (international or local)
707-829-0104 (fax)

On the web page for this book we list errata, examples, and any additional information. You can access this page at:

http://www.oreilly.com/catalog/9780596515089/

You can also download the examples from the author's website:

http://www.websiteoptimization.com/secrets/

To comment or ask technical questions about this book, send email to:

bookquestions@oreilly.com

For more information about our books, conferences, Resource Centers, and the O'Reilly Network, see our website at:

http://www.oreilly.com/

Safari® Books Online

When you see a Safari® Books Online icon on the cover of your favorite technology book, that means the book is available online through the O'Reilly Network Safari Bookshelf.

Safari offers a solution that's better than e-books. It's a virtual library that lets you easily search thousands of top tech books, cut and paste code samples, download chapters, and find quick answers when you need the most accurate, current information. Try it for free at *http://safari.oreilly.com*.

Credits

David Artz is Director of Optimization at AOL, LLC. His team's charter at AOL is to ensure that all experiences are optimized for speed, SEO, and browser accessibility. His team develops, maintains, and evangelizes a broad set of optimization tools, standards, and best practices that stretch across roles in design, development, and copywriting. Their innovative solutions have led to real results in page monetization for AOL.com, and their evangelism has paid off in lighter, more streamlined designs. Their ultimate goal is to infuse the optimization mindset and skillset into AOL's workforce and their outsourcing partners and help drive and track results, maximizing revenue by optimizing pages. He is currently living in the DC area with his Brazilian wife, Janaina, and dog, Ziggy. See also *http://www.artzstudio.com*.

Interactive Marketing is an Internet Marketing company founded by **Matt Hockin** of beautiful Bend, Oregon in 1997 (*http://www.interactivemarketinginc.com/*). Hockin's company helps business owners increase their sales by using website optimization strategies including conversion rate optimization, persuasive copywriting, and search engine marketing. In 1995, during the inception of e-commerce, Hockin gained a significant amount of his experience with Internet marketing while working with pioneers in the online marketplace such as John Audette's Multimedia Marketing Group, Inc. (MMGCO). He has worked on successful marketing and publicity campaigns for companies such as Intel, Art.com, and many others.

Thomas A. Powell is the CEO of PINT, Inc. (*http://www.pint.com/*), a web design and development agency with headquarters in southern California that has serviced corporations and educational institutions throughout the United States and Mexico since 1994. He is the author of numerous books on JavaScript, XHTML, site design process, and Ajax including *Ajax: The Complete Reference* (McGraw-Hill). Powell is a frequent instructor in web design, development, and programming languages for the University of California, San Diego Computer Science Department. His interest in site delivery optimization is well known, from his articles in *Network World* to his founding of Port80 software (*http://www.port80software.com*), a firm that develops numerous products for compression, caching, and code optimization used by developers worldwide.

Pure Visibility (*http://www.purevisibility.com/*) is an Internet marketing company based in Ann Arbor, Michigan, dedicated to growing businesses by connecting them to new qualified prospects online. Pure Visibility's Own Page One™ methodology starts with a commitment to understanding the distinctive positioning of each customer, and surfacing those qualities to receptive audiences through industry-leading, analytics-based processes. Dedicated to discovering industry needs—and innovating to fill them—Pure Visibility's combination of creativity, knowledge, and resolve to provide unbiased information on Internet strategies and techniques has earned it the rare combined status of both a Google Analytics certified consultant and AdWords-certified company.

Daniel Shields is the chief analyst and founder of Wicked Business Sciences in Fort Lauderdale, Florida (*http://www.wickedsciences.com/*). His company specializes in developing application measurement technologies to enhance function and increase metrics output from e-commerce web sites. He is frequently sought after for advanced multivariate testing services, strategic personalization analysis, and lab-based usability testing. He got his formal introduction to enterprise web analytics through CableOrganizer.com, where he was formerly manager of e-commerce initiatives.

Acknowledgments

This is my second book, the first being *Speed Up Your Site: Web Site Optimization* (New Riders). That book focused mainly on web performance. This book focuses on a broader set of issues in WSO, which is a combination of SEM optimization and web performance tuning.

For this book, I got a lot of help from many talented people. First, thanks to Louis Rosenfeld (*http://www.lourosenfeld.com*) for his help and early encouragement. I especially want to recognize and thank the chapter contributors: Matt Hockin of Interactive Marketing, Inc., who has been a tireless partner in our business, Website Optimization, LLC. Thanks also to chapter authors David Artz of AOL; Daniel Shields of Wicked Business Sciences; the team at Pure Visibility Inc. (namely, Catherine Juon, Linda Girard, Steve Loszewski [Chapter 3], Mark Williams [Chapter 4], Daniel O'Neil, Michael Beasley, Dunrie Greiling, and Edward Vielmetti); and Thomas A. Powell of PINT, Inc. David Artz also persuaded AOL to release Pagetest to the open source community. I am very grateful to them all.

I also want to thank Jim Sterne for his input and for writing the Foreword for this book. I'd like to thank my editors who helped: Robert Peyser, Devon Persing, Shirley Kaiser, and Wendy Peck. I'd like to thank my editor at O'Reilly, Simon St.Laurent, for guiding me through the process, answering all my questions, offering encouragement, and accepting my proposal in the first place.

The following people also helped me substantially in crafting this book, and I am grateful for their help: Samson Adepoju, Bill Betcher, Gregory Cowley, Micah Dubinko, Bryan Eisenberg, David Flinn, Dennis Galletta, Bradley Glonka, Dr. William Haig, Lawrence Jordan, Jean King, John King, Ronny Kohavi, Ryan Levering, Jem Matzan, Peter Morville, Eric Peterson, Stephen Pierzchala, Peter Pirolli, Ben Rushlo, Danny Sullivan, Jeni Tennison, Tenni Theurer, and Jason Wolf.

Finally, thanks to Paul Holstein of CableOrganizer.com for letting me borrow his web analyst, Daniel Shields, and for permitting me to reveal new metrics and site examples.

## PART I

Search Engine Marketing Optimization

Search engine marketing (SEM) is the process of using natural search engine optimization (SEO) and pay-per-click (PPC) advertising to increase the visibility of your website. To convert your newfound browsers into buyers and make the most of your advertising budget, SEM also includes conversion rate optimization (CRO). The chapters that follow will show you the best (and worst) practices for each of these topics, complete with case studies showing the techniques in action. First, let's explore how people behave when using search engines.

Search Behavior

To best optimize your website, it is important to understand how users interact with search engines. As you'll discover, searchers are selective in their viewing of search engine result pages (SERPs) and spend little time on each page browsing results.

SERP Viewing Statistics

Good search result placement is important because most searchers (92.5%) don't explore beyond the third page of search results.[1] In fact, about three-fourths don't look past the first page of results.[2,3] About 90% of searchers view only the first or second page of results. Yes, even on the Web the three most important elements of success are location, location, location.

---

[1] Jansen, B., A. Spink, and S. Koshman. 2007. "Web Searcher Interaction with the Dogpile.com Metasearch Engine." *Journal of the American Society for Information Science and Technology* 58 (5): 744–755.

[2] Ibid, 750. Found that 69.1% viewed the first SERP and 85.7% the second. Seventy-four percent is the average of 69.1% and Beitzel's 79%; 89.8% who viewed up to the second SERP is the average of 85.7% and Beitzel's 94%. Note that results are based on an analysis of Dogpile.com and AOL.com search logs.

[3] Beitzel, S. et al. 2006. "Temporal Analysis of a Very Large Topically Categorized Web Query Log." *Journal of the American Society for Information Science and Technology* 58 (2): 166–178. Found that 79% viewed until the first SERP and 94% the second. Beitzel analyzed the query logfiles of AOL.com for this study.

Click Patterns: Higher Is Better

Even within individual SERPs there are diminishing returns. During the initial search result view, higher SERP positions get measurably more attention, and consequently get more clicks than the lower positions (see Figure I-1).[4]

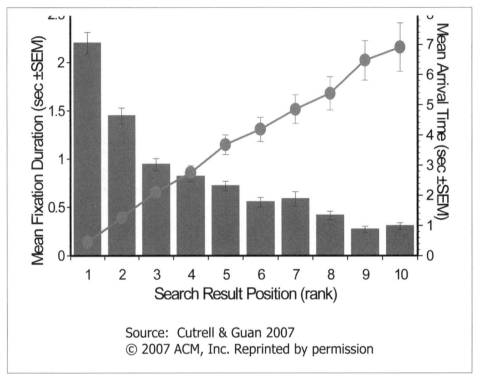

Figure I-1. View and arrival time versus search position (© 2007 ACM, Inc., reprinted by permission)

Although lower-ranked results still get some notice (especially upon subsequent page views), the lion's share of user attention and clicks are devoted to the first few results. This drop-off when attending to search results may be due to the perception of relevance for high-ranking results and information scent.

[4] Cutrell, E., and Z. Guan. "What Are You Looking For? An Eye-Tracking Study of Information Usage in Web Search." In *CHI 2007* (San Jose, CA: April 28–May 3, 2007), 407–416; *http://doi.acm.org/10.1145/1240624. 1240690.*

Prune Your Prose

For search results, brevity is the soul of success. Short attention spans necessitate terse verse that is front-loaded, especially in PPC advertising. Confronted with an average of 25.5 links per query result,[5] e-commerce users view the average search result for only 1.1 seconds.[6] The average view for a *natural* result is 1.3 seconds, with only 0.8 seconds spent on a sponsored result at the top. Sponsored results on the right are viewed for only 0.2 seconds on average.

Clearly, people spend little time reading search results. These findings show the importance of crafting compelling, front-loaded title and description meta tags, and PPC headlines and summaries that are designed for quick scanning.

Let the Optimization Begin

In the group of SEM chapters that follow, you'll learn how to address these issues. In Chapter 1, you'll learn best (and worst) practices to boost your rankings. Chapter 2 shows these SEO techniques in action. Chapters 3 and 4 do the same for PPC optimization, showing best-practice techniques to set up and optimize your PPC campaigns, with a case study showing how to execute these techniques within profit-driven goals. Chapter 5 shows how to optimize your landing pages with tight, persuasive copywriting and credibility-based design, and how to transform your website into a veritable lead-generating machine.

Finally, after Part II, *Web Performance Optimization*, Chapter 10 ties together the best metrics and tools that you can use to measure and optimize your SEM campaigns as well as your website performance to ensure your website's success.

---

[5] Jansen, B. 2007. "The comparative effectiveness of sponsored and nonsponsored links for Web e-commerce queries." *ACM Transactions on the Web* 1 (1): 25 pages. Analyzed search queries from Yahoo!, Google, and MSN.

[6] van Gisbergen, M.S. et al. 2006. "Visual attention to Online Search Engine Results." Checkit, *http://www.checkit.nl/pdf/eyetracking_research.pdf* (accessed February 24, 2008). Eye-tracked Google, MSN, Ilse, Kobala, and Lycos.

## CHAPTER 1

Natural Search Engine Optimization

"We're number one!"

That's the dream of site owners everywhere, as they seek to attain the highest search engine rankings for their sites. It's the Web's equivalent of having the best storefront location. The process of attaining those rankings is called search engine optimization (SEO).

The SEO process consists of two main components: *on-site* optimization and *off-site* optimization. On-site SEO focuses on three objectives: keyword-optimizing your content, effective content creation, and strategic cross-linking. Off-site SEO focuses on maximizing the number and popularity of inbound links with keywords that match your particular subject.

In the past, on-site optimization was enough to boost your website rankings. But the abuse of some meta tags and other SEO shenanigans such as invisible text and keyword stuffing[1] have forced search engines to weigh external factors, such as inbound links, more heavily than on-site optimization.

So, how do you achieve your SEO dream now? Today's successful SEO strategy requires a long-term approach with frequent postings, targeted content, and regular online promotion designed to boost inbound links—in short, a combination of off-site and on-site SEO.

The Benefits of SEO

A high ranking in search engine result pages (SERPs) has become a business necessity. High rankings have been found to increase the following characteristics:

---

[1] Keyword stuffing is a practice whereby keywords are "stuffed" within HTML elements too many times. "Too many" varies with each HTML element and search engine. For example, Google may flag more than three uses of the same phrase in an HTML title tag, but multiple keywords within body text is OK. In general, adopting an approach that uses natural, sentence-like titles and text is best.

- Site traffic (see Figure 1-1)[2]
- Perceived relevance[3]
- Trust[4]
- Conversion (to sales) rates

Figure 1-1 shows the effects of higher rankings. A Oneupweb study found that soon after the average client site appeared in the top 10 search result pages, both conversion rates and new traffic increased significantly. After one month on the first SERP, the average conversion rate rose 42 percentage points, and new traffic more than tripled. A similar effect was observed for sites appearing on the second and third result pages for the first time.

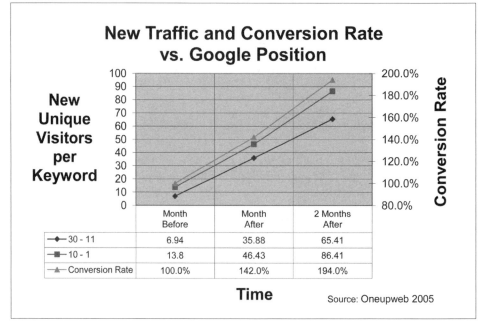

Figure 1-1. New traffic and conversion rate versus Google position

[2] Oneupweb. 2005. "Target Google's Top Ten to Sell Online." *http://www.oneupweb.com* (accessed February 19, 2008).

[3] Jansen, B.J. 2007. "The comparative effectiveness of sponsored and non-sponsored links for Web e-commerce queries." *ACM Transactions on the Web* 1 (1): 25 pages.

[4] Pan, B. et al. 2007. "In Google We Trust: Users' Decisions on Rank, Position, and Relevance." *Journal of Computer-Mediated Communication* 12 (3): 801–823. Most people click on the first SERP result.

Core SEO Techniques

Rather than using obscure jargon such as *search term vectors*, *web graph eigenvalues*, *click entropy*,[5] and *the Google similarity distance*,[6] in the following sections we'll simply describe the core techniques that we have found to actually work for clients.

First we'll expose some barriers that can harm or impede your rankings. Then we'll give you our top 10 guidelines for higher search engine visibility.

Common SEO Barriers

Certain website characteristics can harm or limit your potential search engine rankings. By avoiding these common SEO pitfalls, you can pave the way for higher search engine visibility.

Inadequate inbound links

One of the biggest problems with low-ranking websites is a lack of popular inbound links. Without a healthy number of high-quality links that point back to your site, you'll be at a disadvantage against a competitor who has more.

Other linking issues include links to flagged sites, overuse of parameters, improper redirects, lack of keywords, and generic link text. We'll explore link-related issues in "Step 10: Build Inbound Links with Online Promotion," later in this chapter.

Drowning in splash pages

Splash pages are usually graphically rich pages designed to impress visitors or to direct them to alternative views of content, such as high- or low-bandwidth versions of a site. A "Skip Intro" link on a web page implicitly says that the page isn't very important.

The problem with splash pages—whether they include "Skip Intro" links or not—is that they are a wasted opportunity. Splash pages usually reside at the top of a site's hierarchy. Pages that are higher in your site hierarchy tend to get more links and more traffic than pages that are lower in your hierarchy (see Figure 1-2).[7] If visitors must click and if search engines must crawl farther to reach the real home page (i.e., what should be your top-level index page), you've put up a barrier to success.

---

[5] Dou, Z. et al. "A Large-scale Evaluation and Analysis of Personalized Search Strategies." In *WWW 2007* (Banff, Alberta, Canada: May 8–12, 2007), 581–590.

[6] Cilibrasi, R., and P. Vitányi. 2007. "The Google Similarity Distance." *IEEE Transactions on Knowledge and Data Engineering* 19 (3): 370–383.

[7] Mandl, T. 2007. "The impact of website structure on link analysis." *Internet Research* 17 (2): 196–206. Higher is better. Figure reprinted by permission.

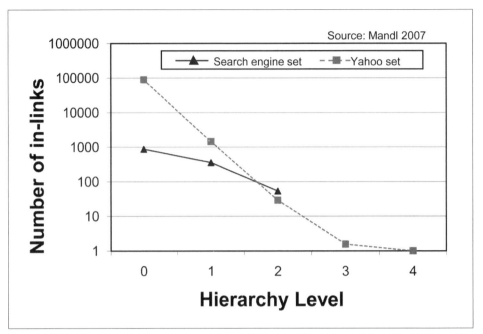

Figure 1-2. Relationship between average number of inlinks and position in hierarchy (© Emerald Group Publishing Limited, all rights reserved)

Flash fires

Flash is installed on nearly every computer (98%) that accesses the Internet.[8] This popularity has caused a conflagration of Flash gizmos on the Web. The problem with Flash is that search engines do not index it properly.

We recommend using Flash to enhance the user experience, not to create it entirely. So, a Flash news ticker or embedded hotel reservation system is OK, but creating your entire site in Flash is not OK.

Following is a Flash SEO trick from Flash expert Gregory Cowley (*http://gregorycowley.com/*).

> One technique you can use to make your Flash pages more SEO friendly is the two div trick. Use one div for the Flash movie, and the other with your HTML equivalent. Use JavaScript to hide the HTML DIV if the Flash plug-in is available, and the HTML is still available for search engines.
>
> This doesn't work in complicated multi-page sites though. The key to a multi-page site, however, is to have all your text in an XML file outside of Flash.

---

[8] Adobe Systems Inc. March 2008. "Flash content reaches 98% of Internet viewers." *http://www.adobe.com/products/player_census/flashplayer/* (accessed May 31, 2008). Adobe claims that more than 98% of users have Flash 8 or earlier installed in mature markets; 97.2% of the same group had Flash 9 installed.

This code requires a `FlashObject` class, available at *http://code.google.com/p/swfobject/*:

```
<div id="flashcontent">
    This is replaced by the Flash content if the user has the correct
    version of the Flash plug-in installed.
    Place your HTML content in here and Google will index it just as
    it would normal HTML content (because it is HTML content!)
    Use HTML, embed images, anything you would normally place on an
    HTML page is fine.
</div>
<script type="text/javascript">
    // <![CDATA[
    var fo = new FlashObject("flashmovie.swf", " flashmovie", "00", "300",
"8", "#FF6600");
    fo.write("flashcontent");
    // ]]>
</script>
```

To avoid the appearance of cloaking, be sure to not change the textual content between the two `div`s.

Unprofessional design

A first impression of your website can take only milliseconds[9] but will affect its long-term success. You wouldn't go on a date poorly groomed and with dirty fingernails, right? Don't make a similar mistake with your website. Having a professionally designed site is the most important factor for perceived web credibility. The higher the aesthetic quality of your site, the higher its perceived credibility will be.[10] Consumers are more willing to buy from (and presumably webmasters are more willing to link to) firms with well-designed sites.

What Is Professional Design?

Professionally designed sites share a number of traits, including a credibility-based logo and layout that conform to accepted and tested usability standards. They use a pleasing color scheme; persuasive copy that is benefit-oriented, error-free, and relevant to a target audience; relevant graphics to engage users; and meaningful markup that is easily updated—all wrapped up in a responsive, intuitively navigable package. To learn more about what constitutes a professionally designed site, see Chapter 5.

---

[9] Lindgaard, G. et al. 2006. "Attention web designers: You have 50 milliseconds to make a good first impression!" *Behaviour and Information Technology* 25 (2): 115–126.

[10]Robins, D., and J. Holmes. 2008. "Aesthetics and credibility in web site design." *Information Processing and Management* 44 (1): 386–399. The same content with a higher aesthetic treatment was judged to have higher credibility. Credibility judgments took, on average, 2.3 seconds.

Web credibility, valuable content, and useful tools are key factors that compel webmasters to link to you, and visitors to stay and spend money.

Fix your focus. Some sites do not focus specifically enough. A store that sells everything, or that wants to be the next Amazon.com, has a long, painful road ahead. Such a broadly focused site is unlikely to succeed in natural SEO and probably needs to advertise with pay-per-click (PPC). It's best to narrow your focus topically or geographically so that you have a better chance of ranking well and having higher conversion rates.

There is one exception to this rule, however. If you can optimize every individual product page (e.g., HP LaserJet 6MP printer replacement toner cartridge C3903), it is possible to rank highly for those very specific terms.

Obscure navigation

The navigation on your site should comprise text that is easily indexed and that wasn't created from graphical text, JavaScript, or Flash. Search engines can only index the text within your pages. They don't read text that is embedded in graphics or Flash movies, nor do they execute JavaScript. A reasonable compromise for image-based navigation is to include alternative text for images.

Give up graphics-based navigation. Macromedia Fireworks (now owned by Adobe) and Adobe ImageReady popularized the automatic slicing of graphics that made creating fancy navigation menus easy. Search engines don't read graphical text, however. By embedding your keywords in graphics, you lose a golden opportunity to bake your SEO directly into the information architecture of your site.

Junk JavaScript-only navigation. Avoid JavaScript-only navigation such as this:

```
<script src="/scripts/menunav.js" type="text/javascript">
```

Switch to list-based Cascading Style Sheet (CSS)-style menus or provide a text equivalent to your navigation elsewhere on the page for search engines to follow.

Duplicate content

Avoid exact or near duplicates of pages at different URIs. Although Google engineer Matt Cutts has said that there is no penalty for duplicate content, Google's own webmaster guidelines say "don't create multiple pages, sub-domains, or domains with substantially duplicate content."[11] Google generally tries to display the best version of a resource, but in rare cases it can penalize a site that appears to game the system with duplicate content.[12]

---

[11]Google. 2007. "Webmaster Guidelines." Webmaster Help Center, *http://www.google.com/support/webmasters/bin/answer.py?answer=35769* (accessed March 21, 2008).

[12]Google. 2007. "Duplicate content." Webmaster Help Center, *http://www.google.com/support/webmasters/bin/answer.py?answer=66359* (accessed March 26, 2008).

The use of duplicate titles and meta tags across too many pages on the same site can harm rankings. Duplicate content will confuse the Googlebot as to which page is authoritative, thereby diluting your PageRank among the various URIs. You can use the robots exclusion protocol to exclude duplicate content (see *http://www.robotstxt.org/ orig.html*).

On the other hand, creating mini sites, each with valuable content on a different topic related to your business, is one way around the two-URIs-per-domain limit to Google SERPs. Some companies buy domain names for each product or service, create and promote separate websites, and attain multiple top 10 spots on the first SERP. We don't recommend using this technique of creating multiple sites to crowd all of your competitors off the first SERP.

 Netconcepts.com believes that Google looks up domain registration information and accounts for it. If you register many sites, Google will know that they are all connected and will reduce the ability to pass link juice from one to another. See *http://www.news.com/8301-10784_ 3-9748779-7.html* for more information.

Ten Steps to Higher Search Engine Rankings

Let's boil down this entire process into 10 steps. To achieve high search engine rankings, you first need to find the right keyphrases to target. Then, create content around those keyphrases that is optimized with well-written titles, meta tags, headers, and body text. Finally, build inbound links and PageRank by tirelessly promoting your site.

Best Practices

We will discuss the 10 steps to follow to achieve higher search engine rankings shortly. While following the steps, keep these best practices in mind.

Deploy keywords strategically

SEO is a numbers game. Each web page can effectively target one or two phrases well. Rather than shooting for one keyphrase that ranks number one, strive to have many keyphrases that rank high. Overall, you'll get more leads because your keyword reach will be higher. Take advantage of the long tail of search query distribution by targeting very specific phrases (see Figure 1-3).

Reinforce the theme of your site

The theme of a web page should flow through everything associated with that page: the title tag, the headers, the meta tags (keywords and description tags), the content, the links, the navigation, and even the URI of the page should all work together.

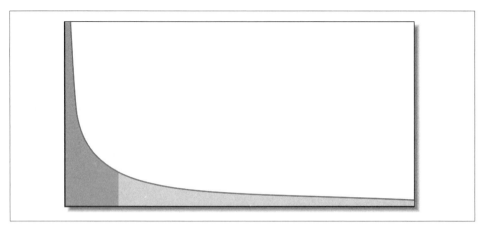

Figure 1-3. The long tail (picture by Hay Kranen/PD)

Playing the Long Tail

Given enough choice and a large population of consumers, search term selection patterns follow a power law distribution curve, or Pareto distribution. The first part of the curve contains 20% of the terms, which are deemed to be the most popular, and the rightmost long tail of the curve contains the remaining 80% of the terms, which are searched less frequently (as Figure 1-3 shows). With the widespread use of the Internet, targeting less popular terms has become a viable strategy. The more specific terms in the long tail can give you faster results and higher conversion rates.

Optimize key content

Search engines favor title tags, body copy, and headlines when ranking your site. They also prefer the meta description element for search result pages.

Optimize on-site links

You can map complex URIs to search-friendly URIs that include keywords and hide the technology behind your site to improve your rankings. To concentrate your Page-Rank, be selective regarding what resources you link to (e.g., avoid linking to flagged sites), and use the `nofollow` attribute.

Make it linkworthy

You have only one chance to make a first impression. Don't blow it with an unprofessional website. You are much more likely to get links when your site is professionally designed, with valuable, fresh content and useful tools. Make your site a focused beehive of activity.

Acquire inbound links

Search engines use external factors such as inbound links, anchor text, surrounding text, and domain history, among others, to determine the relative importance of your site. Most of your rankings in search engines are determined by the number and popularity of your inbound links.[13]

These concepts will come up again and again as you optimize for search-friendliness, and we'll discuss them in more detail shortly.

Step 1: Determine Your Keyword Phrases

Finding the best keyword phrases to target is an iterative process. First, start with a list of keywords that you want to target with your website. Next, expand that list by brainstorming about other phrases, looking at competitor sites and your logfiles, and including plurals, splits, stems, synonyms, and common misspellings. Then triage those phrases based on search demand and the number of result pages to find the most effective phrases. Finally, play the long tail by targeting multiword phrases to get more targeted traffic and higher conversion rates.

News Flash: SEO Competition Lengthens Campaigns

A few years ago, optimizing a site to rank high on search engines typically took four to six months for reasonably specific keywords. Now it can take from 6 to 12 months for many keyphrases to rank well because the Web has become more competitive.

Tools for keyword research

You can use Wordtracker's free keyword suggestion tool to research your keyphrases (see Figure 1-4). Wordtracker uses a database of queries from Dogpile.com and Metacrawler.com to estimate the daily search volume across all search engines. Check it out at *http://freekeywords.wordtracker.com*.

Wordtracker's free tool is limited, however, because it only shows search demand for phrases that contain the keywords that you enter. For more powerful keyword research, SEO professionals turn to Wordtracker's full service to perform keyword demand analysis and brainstorming. Visit *http://www.wordtracker.com* for more information on this service.

---

[13]Evans, M. 2007. "Analysing Google rankings through search engine optimization data." *Internet Research* 17 (1): 21–37. Inlinks, PageRank, and domain age (to some degree after the second SERP) help rankings. The number of pages did not correlate with higher rankings.

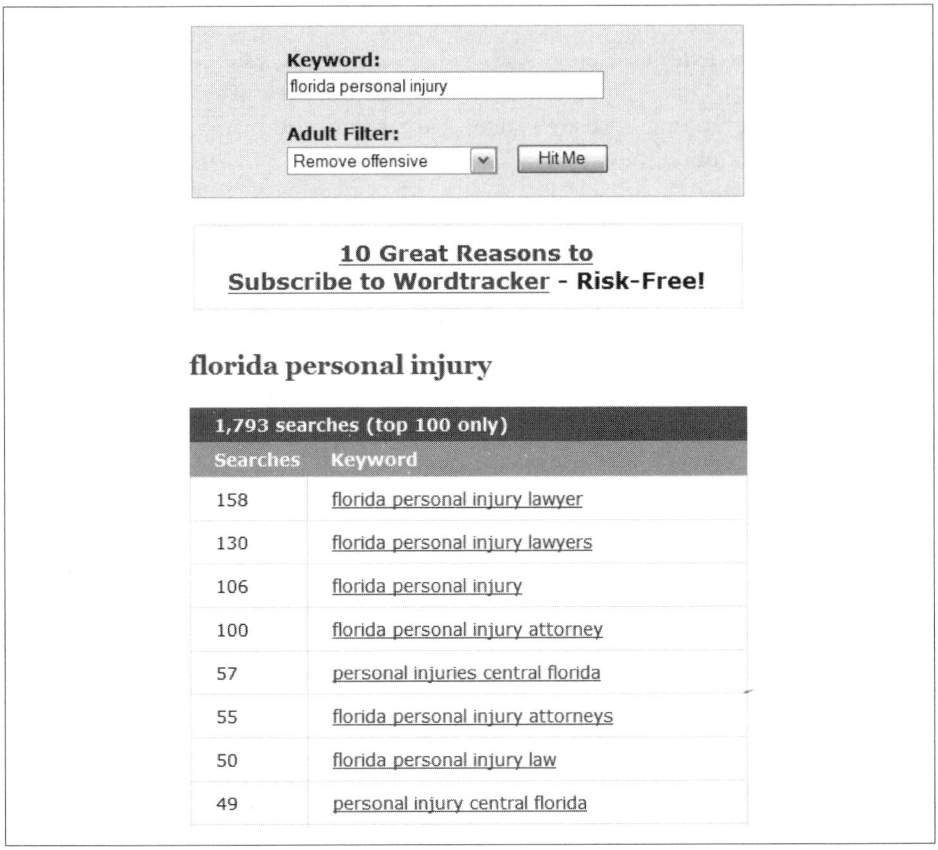

Figure 1-4. Wordtracker's free keyword suggestion tool

A fee-based web service, Wordtracker taps a large database of more than 330 million search terms from meta search engines. You can use it to brainstorm on keyphrases, determine search demand, and calculate the competitiveness of your keyphrases (for more information, see the upcoming "Wordtracker Keyword Research Tool" sidebar). Figure 1-5 shows an example of using Wordtracker to research keywords and optimize a site for a hypothetical personal injury lawyer in Florida. First, we enter the phrase "Florida personal injury" to find any related phrases culled from a thesaurus and meta tags of similar sites.

Clicking on any phrase in the left pane brings up the right pane with keyphrases sorted by search demand. You can add keywords to your master list by clicking on them in the right pane. Note how "Florida personal injury lawyer" is searched on more than "Florida personal injury attorney."

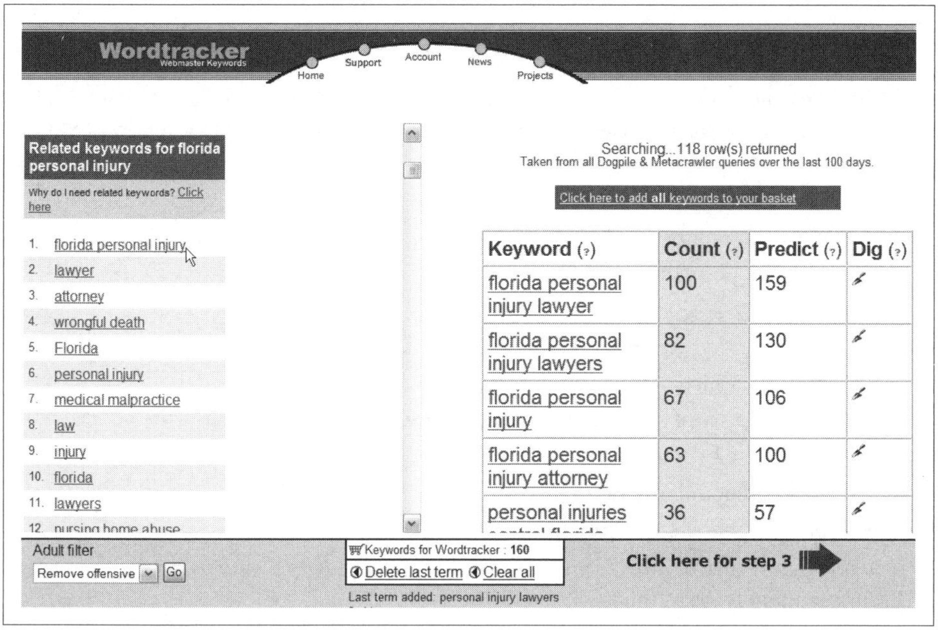

Figure 1-5. Building a keyword list with Wordtracker

Wordtracker Keyword Research Tool

You can use free online tools from Google and Yahoo! to determine search demand, but they are limited compared to Wordtracker. Used by SEO professionals and ambitious site owners, Wordtracker is a web service designed to streamline the process of keyphrase discovery. Wordtracker uses data from meta crawlers with more than 120 million searches per month, storing 100 days of searches to compile more than 330 million search terms, updated on a weekly basis. You can discover new keywords, search demand, and common misspellings. You can survey keywords and meta tags from other sites and perform competitive analyses. The keyword effectiveness index, or KEI, is a comparison of the number of searches and the number of web page results. Targeting high KEI phrases with adequate search volume gives you the best chance to rank quickly on particular terms by going where others aren't competing. Very Sun Tzu.

Find your primary keyphrase

Ultimately, you want to discover the *primary keyphrase* that accurately describes your overall business, product, or service but which still has adequate search demand. You'll use your primary keyphrase in your promotions to help boost your rankings.

Top Search Engine Ranking Factors

PageRank is not the only factor that Google uses to rank search results. Google uses more than 200 "signals" to calculate the rank of a page.[a] According to a survey of SEO experts, the top 10 most important factors include the following:[b]

- Keyword use in title tag
- Anchor text of inbound link
- Global link popularity of site
- Age of site
- Link popularity within the site's internal link structure
- Topical relevance of inbound links to site
- Link popularity of site in topical community
- Keyword use in body text
- Global link popularity of linking site
- Topical relationship of linking page

The top factors that negatively affect a search engine spider's ability to crawl a page or harm its rankings are as follows:

- Server often inaccessible to bots
- Content very similar to or duplicate of existing content in the index
- External links to low-quality/spam sites
- Duplicate title/meta tags on many pages
- Overuse of targeted keywords (indicative of stuffing/spamming)
- Participation in link schemes or actively selling links
- Very slow server response times
- Inbound links from spam sites
- Low levels of visitors to the site

[a] Sullivan, D. May 10, 2006. "Watching Google Press Day, Slides & Live Commentary." Search Engine Watch, *http://blog.searchenginewatch.com/blog/060510-123802* (accessed February 19, 2008).

[b] Fishkin, R., and J. Pollard. April 2, 2007. "Search Engine Ranking Factors Version 2." SEOMoz.org, *http://www.seomoz.org/article/search-ranking-factors* (accessed February 8, 2008).

Step 2: Sort by Popularity

Now that you've got an exhaustive list of keywords, sort them by popularity. Wordtracker does this automatically for you as you build your list (see Figure 1-6).

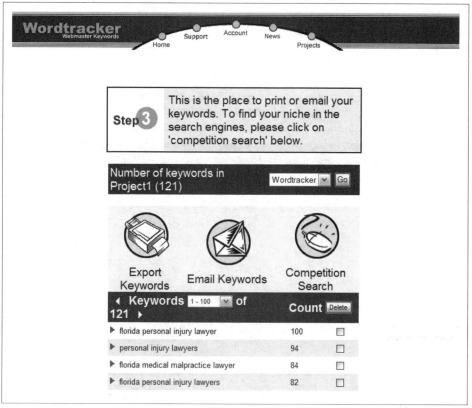

Figure 1-6. Sorting and pruning keywords in Wordtracker

If you click on Competition Search, Wordtracker performs a competitive analysis of the keywords in your master list. You can choose two major search engines to check at one time (see Figure 1-7).

Wordtracker calculates the keyword effectiveness index (KEI) for each phrase in your list. It also performs a search count and computes the number of result pages (see Figure 1-8).

In Figure 1-8, you can see that "homicide lawyer Orlando" has the highest KEI. Perhaps our hypothetical lawyer will steer clear of this type of case. The phrase "personal injury lawyers central florida" has a KEI of 84,100, and we could combine it with his hometown of Orlando.

You can also drill down with the keyword evaluator tool to quickly discover the KEI and search demand for your keywords (see Figure 1-9).

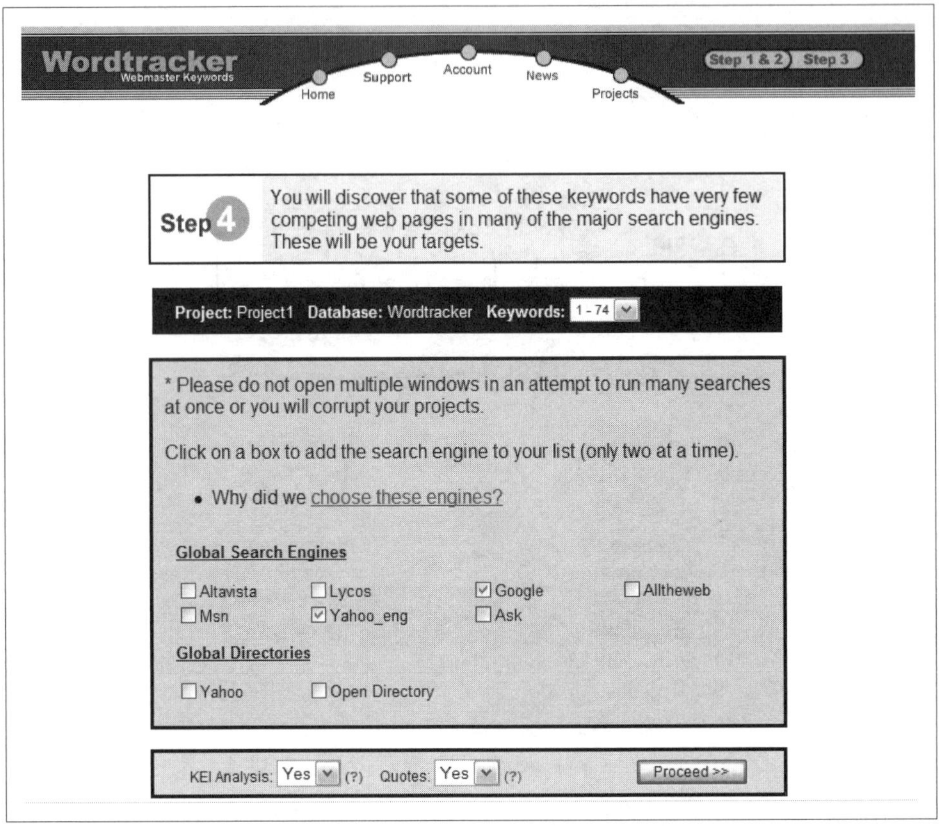

Figure 1-7. Choosing search engines to target for competitive analysis of keywords in Wordtracker

Step 3: Refine Keyword Phrases and Re-Sort

Next, refine your keyphrases by pruning out keywords that aren't related to your subject area, that are not specific enough, or that are ambiguous.

Right-size your keyphrases

The more specific you can get with your keyphrases, the faster you'll achieve high rankings and the better your conversion rates will be.

However, the longer the phrases you target, the lower the search demand will be. So, choosing the optimum number of words for each keyphrase is a trade-off between higher conversion rates and lower search demand. Conversion rates peak at about four terms,[14] whereas search demand peaks at two terms for all queries and three

---

[14]Oneupweb. 2005. "How Keyword Length Affects Conversion Rates." *http://www.oneupweb.com* (accessed April 14, 2008), 2.

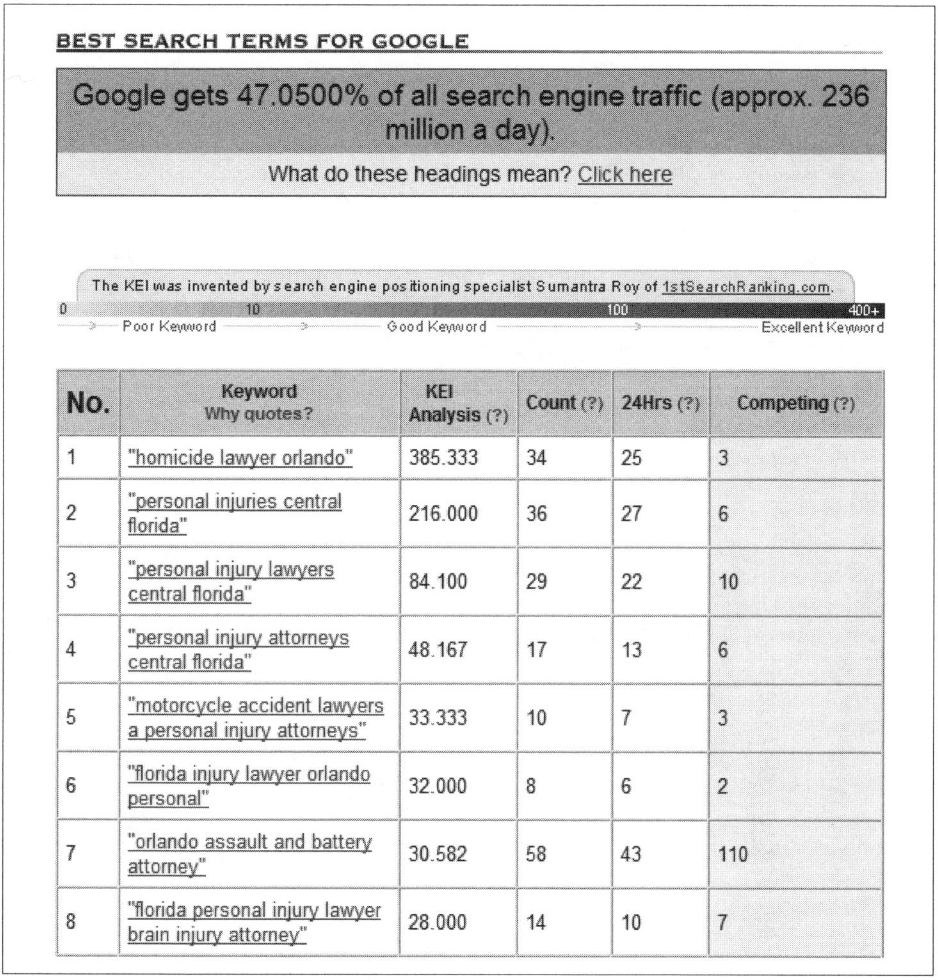

Google gets 47.0500% of all search engine traffic (approx. 236 million a day).

What do these headings mean? Click here

The KEI was invented by search engine positioning specialist Sumantra Roy of 1stSearchRanking.com.

0	10	100	400+
→ Poor Keyword	→ Good Keyword	→	Excellent Keyword

No.	Keyword Why quotes?	KEI Analysis (?)	Count (?)	24Hrs (?)	Competing (?)
1	"homicide lawyer orlando"	385.333	34	25	3
2	"personal injuries central florida"	216.000	36	27	6
3	"personal injury lawyers central florida"	84.100	29	22	10
4	"personal injury attorneys central florida"	48.167	17	13	6
5	"motorcycle accident lawyers a personal injury attorneys"	33.333	10	7	3
6	"florida injury lawyer orlando personal"	32.000	8	6	2
7	"orlando assault and battery attorney"	30.582	58	43	110
8	"florida personal injury lawyer brain injury attorney"	28.000	14	10	7

Figure 1-8. Keyword effectiveness index for Google in Wordtracker

terms for unique queries, according to Google.[15] Comparing conversion rates to search referrals, the optimum length of a keyphrase is slightly more than three words (see Figure 1-10).

For example, the term:

```
"lawyer"
```

is far too broad to target for someone hanging up his shingle in Orlando. A better approach would be to specify what type of lawyer:

```
"personal injury lawyer"
```

---

[15]Pasca, M. "Organizing and Searching the World Wide Web of Facts—Step Two: Harnessing the Wisdom of the Crowds." In *WWW 2007* (Banff, Alberta, Canada: May 8–12, 2007), 101–110. Google search statistics.

Your keyword list

☑ select ▾   🗑 delete ▾   💾 save ▾

	Keyword	Searches ▾	Predict	Google	Google KEI	Yahoo	Yahoo KEI
1	☐ florida personal injury lawyer	100	158	61,500 ⮌	0.16	270,000 ⮌	0.04
2	☐ florida personal injury lawyers	82	130	29,700 ⮌	0.23	78,400 ⮌	0.09
3	☐ florida personal injury	67	106	204,000 ⮌	0.02	580,000 ⮌	0.01
4	☐ florida personal injury attorney	63	100	31,300 ⮌	0.13	114,000 ⮌	0.03
5	☐ florida personal injury attorneys	35	55	34,400 ⮌	0.04	94,300 ⮌	0.01
6	☐ florida personal injury law	32	50	21,800 ⮌	0.05	42,600 ⮌	0.02
7	☐ personal injury central florida	31	49	405 ⮌	2.37	587 ⮌	1.64
8	☐ personal injury lawyers central florida	29	46	10 ⮌	84.10	498 ⮌	1.69
9	☐ florida keys personal injury attorney	29	46	7 ⮌	120.10	75 ⮌	11.21
10	☐ florida keys personal injury	26	41	401 ⮌	1.69	1,020 ⮌	0.66

Figure 1-9. Wordtracker's keyword evaluator tool

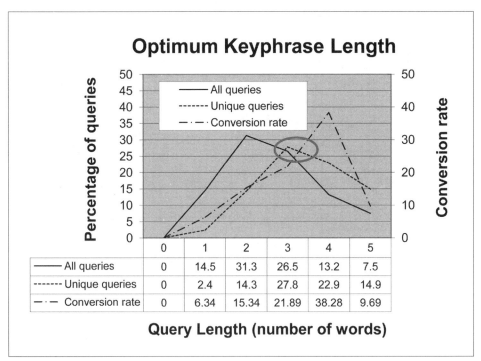

Optimum Keyphrase Length

Percentage of queries (left axis) / **Conversion rate** (right axis) vs. **Query Length (number of words)**

	0	1	2	3	4	5
—— All queries	0	14.5	31.3	26.5	13.2	7.5
------- Unique queries	0	2.4	14.3	27.8	22.9	14.9
—·— Conversion rate	0	6.34	15.34	21.89	38.28	9.69

Figure 1-10. Optimum keyphrase length—query length versus conversion rates

However, although the second phrase is more specific topically, it is still too broad for a lawyer based (and licensed) in a particular geographic area. An even better approach would be to target the city or state:

```
"Orlando personal injury lawyer" or "Florida personal injury lawyer"
```

Now you're talking. Unless you own LexisNexis Martindale-Hubbell (the firm that owns Lawyers.com and rates lawyers), targeting the type and the geographic location of your products or services is the most effective way to get high rankings.

After you've eliminated unrelated keywords and combined phrases, re-sort your list by popularity. The term "lawyer" was searched on a bit more than "attorney" in this case, so let's use the phrase "Orlando Florida personal injury lawyer" as our primary keyphrase.

Target multiple keyphrases

In addition to higher conversions, longer phrases also allow you to target multiple combinations of keywords and enable proximity hits. For example:

```
Orlando Florida personal injury lawyer
```

covers the following keyphrases:

```
Orlando personal injury lawyer
Florida injury lawyer
Orlando lawyer
Florida lawyer
Florida personal injury lawyer ...
```

Step 4: Write a Title Using the Top Two or Three Phrases

The title tag is the most important component of your web page for search engine rankings. Craft a natural, sentence-like title that describes the page content (or in the case of the home page, the entire site) using up to 15 words. Here is an example:

```
<title>Orlando Florida personal injury lawyer John Smith
serves the central Florida area as an injury attorney</title>
```

Keywords trump company name (usually)

Many companies put their company name at the beginning of every page title. A more search-friendly approach is to put your primary keyphrase up front and place your company name at the end of the title. That is, unless your company name is your primary keyphrase. So, this:

```
Smith & Jones - City Profession
```

becomes this:

```
City Profession - Smith & Jones
```

Usability-wise, Jakob Nielsen reports on an exception to this rule of de-emphasizing company names in headlines.[16] Front-load the company name when the link appears as

---

[16]Nielsen, J. March 3, 2008. "Company Name First in Microcontent? Sometimes!" Useit Alertbox, *http://www.useit.com/alertbox/microcontent-brand-names.html* (accessed March 24, 2008).

a hit on SERPs that are full of junk links, and when your company name is well known and respected.

You should craft a descriptive, keyphrased title with 10 to 15 words that flows well. Short titles limit your options for keywords and proximity hits, but long title tags are truncated by Google to display an average of 54 characters, according to a study by Alireza Noruzi.[17] Search engines continue to index well past this cutoff, however. Noruzi recommends that title tags be no longer than 10 words (60 characters), with the most important keywords listed first.

An experiment in stuffing

Attempting to stuff too many keywords into your title, or into other parts of your page, for that matter, can get you into trouble and drop your rankings.

To illustrate how to write good title tags, we tested how far we could go with an article about PDF optimization using then-new Adobe Acrobat 8, available at *http://www.websiteoptimization.com/speed/tweak/pdf/*.

Our original title tag was as follows:

```
<title>Optimize PDF Files - pdf optimization convert pdfs - Speed
Tweak of the Week</title>
```

As an experiment, we tried to stuff many related keyphrases into the title, phases that people search for the most. Google promptly dropped the article! Clearly, we went too far.

```
<title>Optimize PDF Files - pdf optimization tips, acrobat pdf
optimizer review, convert pdfs file optimizer tools</title>
```

After we rewrote the title tag to be more like a sentence, Google reinstated the article in its index (see Figure 1-11):

```
<title>Optimize PDF Files - tips on pdf optimization to compress
file size & optimizing pdf files - Acrobat 8 review</title>
```

Note that the article is about PDF optimization, but we also targeted Acrobat 8 review (for optimizing PDF files) in the title and description element. This example illustrates that you can go too far in optimizing your title tags, and that there can be an extremely fine line between overreaching with your titles and finding the perfect balance of pointed description and verbal thrift.

[17]Noruzi, A. 2007. "A Study of HTML Title Tag Creation Behavior of Academic Websites." *The Journal of Academic Librarianship* 33 (4): 501–506.

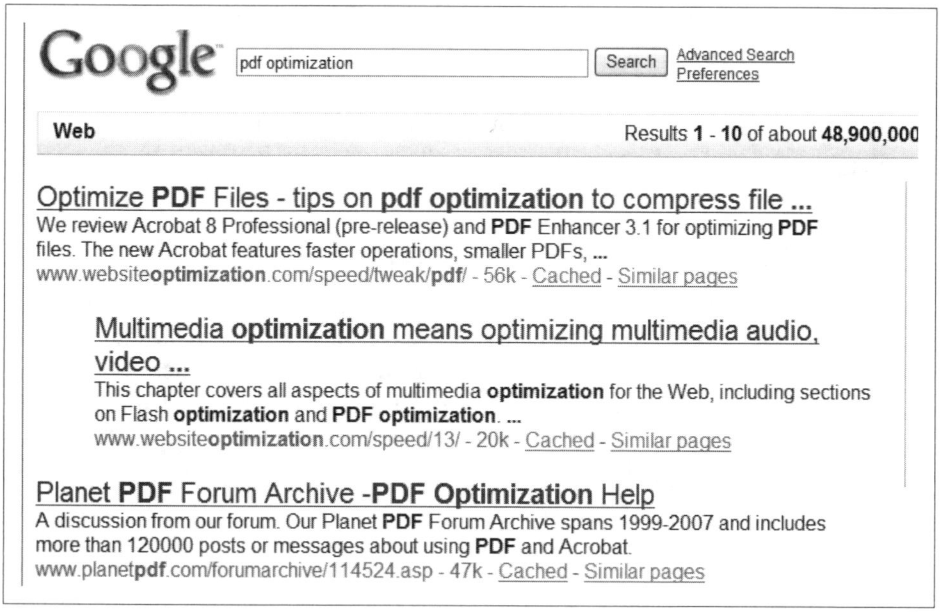

Figure 1-11. Google reinstating the PDF optimization article

Step 5: Write a Description Meta Tag

Although the importance of meta tags for search engine rankings has decreased, it is still important to write a good description meta tag because search engines prefer the description meta tag in their SERPs. If one doesn't exist, search engines create their description starting with the first content displayed on the page.

The description meta tag should be, at most, 250 characters long. For example:

```
<meta name="description" content="John Smith and Associates specialize
in representing personal injury victims of automobile accidents. Click
here for a free consultation with automobile lawyers in Orlando and
central Florida.">
```

Step 6: Write a Keywords Meta Tag

The keywords meta tag describes the content of the page at hand and should reflect keywords in the body text of the page. Create your keywords tag using your master keywords list and the visible words in your page. Although you can separate keywords with a comma or a space, omitting commas will give you more proximity hits between adjacent terms. Use lowercase text to better match search queries and for better compressibility. For example:

```
<meta name="keywords" content="orlando florida personal injury lawyer,
central florida personal injury attorneys, florida medical malpractice
lawyers, orlando injury attorneys, orange county automobile accident
attorney, personal injuries central florida, orlando law firm">
```

Avoid repeating your keywords in the same form more than three times. It is best to vary your terms using stems, plurals, splits, and misspellings.

 Avoid using the trademarks and brand names of other companies in your keywords. Legal precedent is on the side of the trademark owner. Instead, use terms that describe the overall topic of the target page.

Step 7: Make Search-Friendly Headlines

After title tags, headlines are the most important component of web pages for search engine rankings. Because search engines and screen readers key off structural headers for headlines (in HTML, h1 through h6), avoid fake structure where CSS or font tags are used to artificially simulate structural HTML. You can still use CSS, but instead of embedding style classes, simply define the look of your headers. For example, instead of this fake header:

```
<p class="fake-h1header">Orlando Florida Personal Injury Lawyer John Smith &amp;
Associates</p>
```

do this:

```
<style type="text/css">
<!--
h1{font:1.5em arial;}
-->
</style></head><body>
<h1>Orlando Florida Personal Injury Lawyer John Smith &amp; Associates</h1>
```

Include the primary keyphrase of your web page in the first-level header. Omit articles to give your headlines more impact. Headlines should compel search engines as well as users to read your content. You can use subheadlines to include additional keywords, benefits, and calls to action. For example:

```
<h2>Our Central Florida personal injury attorney services can help you
get the right settlement in the quickest amount of time. Here's how...</h2>
```

Write headlines that pop

Headlines appear in web pages as h1 through h6 tags, as well as in title tags and RSS entries matched with decks or short summaries; they are a form of *microcontent* that is read out of context in search results.[18] They should grab the attention of your users even after they read the first few words, but they still should accurately describe your page content with keywords used by searchers.

Here are some example headlines from CNN.com and MarketingSherpa.com:

Automotive fuel efficiency suddenly sexy
CNN's Allan Chernoff reports Americans are losing interest in gas guzzlers.

---

[18]Nielsen, J. September 6, 1998. "Microcontent: How to Write Headlines, Page Titles, and Subject Lines." Useit Alertbox, *http://www.useit.com/alertbox/980906.html* (accessed February 19, 2008).

```
http://www.cnn.com/video/#/video/us/2008/03/23/chernoff.gas.guzzlers.cnn
```

Landing Page Handbook: How to Lift Conversions Up to 55%
Newly updated and expanded for 20XX, MarketingSherpa's bestselling
Landing Page Handbook helps you raise conversions by up to 55% or
more for search, email, and ad campaigns for lead generation,
ecommerce, and even blogs.
http://www.sherpastore.com/RevisedLandingPageHB.html

The primary themes of the articles in question are placed right up front. HTML headlines should accurately describe the theme of the page or section using a keyphrase or two without keyword-stuffing, articles (*a*, *the*, etc.), or hype. The main header should describe the content of the page succinctly in 40 to 60 characters.

Keyphrase headlines early

To facilitate both scanning and the bias of search engines for prominence, place the keyphrases with which you want content to be found early in your headlines. As this headline is usually the link text for the page, you should include the primary keyphrase for the theme of your page in the text.

So, this expanded headline:

```
<a href="http://www.cnn.com/...">The Efficiency of Fuel Intake for the Internal
Combustion Engine in Automobiles has Abruptly Become Appealing</a>
```

becomes this:

```
<a href="http://www.cnn.com/...">Automotive fuel efficiency suddenly sexy</a>
```

Note how the primary keyphrase is placed first. Users quickly scan web pages as they forage for tasty morsels of information. They don't generally read everything. Also, RSS news aggregators sometimes truncate your headlines. Placing keywords earlier in headlines and titles thus gives them more weight.

 Keywords in h2–h6 headers correlated with higher rankings more than those in first-level headers (<h1>), according to one study.[19] Using keywords in first-level headings is still a best practice for drawing keywords in inbound links and user attention.

Step 8: Add Keywords Tactically

Include keywords in:

- The first couple of sentences of your visible text
- Headlines and subheadlines
- Links and anchor text

---

[19]Sistrix. May 2007. "Google Ranking Factors." *http://www.sistrix.com/ranking-faktoren/* (accessed March 26, 2008). Sistrix found that keywords in h1 headers did not correlate with higher rankings, but having keywords in h2–h6 headers did correlate. In German.

- Page URIs
- Filenames
- Alt text
- Indexable (text) navigation elements (not Flash, graphics, or JavaScript)

Here is an example of an opening paragraph for our Orlando lawyer scenario:

```
Introducing the Orlando personal injury attorney services by John
Smith & Associates, designed to help you get your life back together
and get you the maximum settlement possible.
```

Keyphrase anchor text

In an effort to glean the theme of your web pages, search engines look at the context of links pointing to and from your pages. One way to bake in your SEO is to strategically cross-link within your own site, using meaningful anchor text. Avoid using "Click Here" for your anchor text, unless, of course, you are talking about the perils of "click here." So, this:

```
For more information about our personal injury services <a href="/services.html">click
here</a>.
```

becomes this:

```
More information about our <a href="/services/personal-injury/">personal injury
services</a>
```

Another example is to bake in the company or site name within the Home tab. So, this:

```
<a href="/">Home</a>
```

becomes this:

```
<a href="/">Orlando personal injury lawyer home</a>
```

Buy keyphrased domain names

But why stop at navigation and page URIs? If possible, bake your keywords directly into your domain name. By incorporating your primary keyphrase into your domain name, you can guarantee that inbound links will contain your primary keyphrase, and make it more likely that the link text will contain your primary keyphrase. For example:

```
<a href="http://www.keyword1keyword2.com">Keyword1 Keyword2</a>
```

Sites that incorporate keywords into their domain name have been shown to have a higher position in SERPs, according to a 2007 study by Sistrix (see Figure 1-12).[20]

---

[20]Sistrix. "Google Ranking Factors." Sistrix found that keywords in hostnames correlated with higher rankings in SERPs, especially for positions 1 to 5.

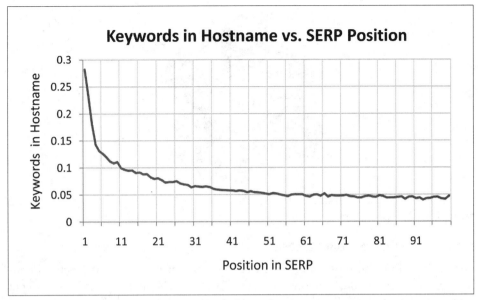

Figure 1-12. Hostname keywords versus search rankings

This effect may be due in part to inbound links and link text containing the target keywords. Avoid very long domain names containing keywords, however, because these make your listing look bad, and make it difficult to type. Ideally, acquire "your primary keyphrase dot com" (e.g., *primarykeyphrase.com*).

Step 9: Create Valuable Keyword-Focused Content

Content is still king on the Web. When they are ranking sites, search engines look for a lot of themed content about particular topics. Publishing a large amount of informative and valuable content that is keyword-optimized will give your site more chances to rank for different keywords, and will help your overall rankings (see Figure 1-13).[21]

If you happen to be a personal injury lawyer, mention the various injuries afflicting clients whom you have represented. If you are a realtor, mention the different cities and areas that you cover. Ideally, devote a page or section to each topic. Have an expert in the subject write compelling copy, or hire a copywriter to work with your marketing department.

Use a content management system (CMS) or blog to create high-quality content consistently. Reflect back what your visitors are searching on and what terms you want to target. It is ideal to target one main keyphrase per article or page. You want to create a large corpus of content about your subject area that will act as a kind of digital flypaper.

---

[21]Morville, P. June 21, 2004. "User Experience Design." Semantic Studios, *http://www.semanticstudios.com/publications/semantics/000029.php* (accessed February 9, 2008). Figure 1-13 used by permission.

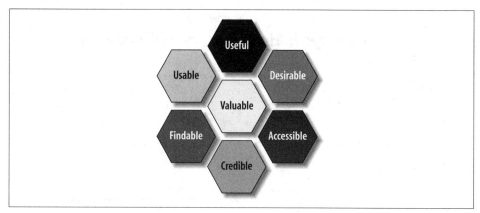

Figure 1-13. The user experience honeycomb

Sharpen your keyword-focused content

For on-site SEO, the most important website component is keyword-focused content. Your pages should be about something specific. The more specific you can get topically or geographically, the higher your conversion rates will be, and the faster you'll get results. Keyword-focused content is targeted at one *theme* or one keyphrase per page.

Avoid grouping all of your products or services into one page. Break up your content into key topics. For example, a lawyer who listed all of his services on one page:

```
http://www.example.com/services.html
```

would have one page for each of the following services:

```
Automobile accidents
Slip and fall
Traumatic brain injury
```

Creating a page for each major service—that is, an automobile accidents page, a slip and fall page, and so on—is a more search-friendly approach. Create separate pages that match your most popular queries as well as the services that you want to target:

```
http://www.example.com/services/automobile-accidents.html
http://www.example.com/services/slip-fall.html
http://www.example.com/services/traumatic-brain-injury.html
```

Create search-friendly URIs

One characteristic of a well-optimized site is the presence of search-friendly URIs. Search-friendly URIs include keywords related to the main subject of the page directly within the address of the page. Search-friendly URIs avoid numerical query strings that are semantically meaningless for search engines (and humans), but are typically found in database-driven CMS websites.

Search engines may follow one search parameter (e.g., *http://www.example.com/query?id=53*), but may balk at two or three.[22] Avoid using dynamic session identifiers in your URIs. A session ID is a unique string to link HTTP transactions within a particular domain. Without cookies, session IDs are passed in URIs. Search engines prefer permanent URIs that won't clog up their databases with duplicate content, create spider traps, or create 401 errors.

Here is an example URI with a session ID:

```
http://www.example.com/query.php?=53&sid=lit3py55t21z5v55vlm25s55
```

A better approach is to carefully design your information hierarchy, and "bake" your SEO keyphrases into the URIs of your site. By mapping keyword queries to database queries, you can include keywords in the URI of the page. So, instead of this:

```
http://wwww.example.com/index.php?cat=53
```

do this:

```
http://www.example.com/index?=photovoltaic+panels
```

Even better, remove all the variable query characters (?, $, and #):

```
http://www.example.com/photovoltaic+panels
```

By eliminating the suffix to URIs, you avoid broken links and messy mapping when changing technologies in the future. See Chapter 9 for details on URI rewriting. See also "Cool URIs for the Semantic Web," at *http://www.w3.org/TR/cooluris/*.

Write compelling summaries

In newspaper parlance, the description that goes with a headline is called a *deck* or a *blurb*. Great decks summarize the story in a couple of sentences, enticing the user to read the article. Include keywords describing the major theme of the article for search engines. Don't get too bogged down in the details of your story. Think "big picture."

Following are three examples, one each from CNN.com, Wired.com, and the *New York Times* website.

```
Man declared dead, says he feels "pretty good"

Zach Dunlap says he feels "pretty good" four months after he was
declared brain dead and doctors were about to remove his organs
for transplant.
http://www.cnn.com/2008/US/03/24/NotDead.ap/index.html

How Apple Got Everything Right By Doing Everything Wrong
```

---

[22]Spenser, S. July 23, 2007. "Underscores are now word separators, proclaims Google." CNET, *http://www.cnet.com/8301-13530_1-9748779-28.html* (accessed March 21, 2008). This summary of a talk given by Matt Cutts of Google includes query string information.

```
Apple succeeds by going against Silicon Valley wisdom, ignoring
business best practices, bucking the "don't be evil" ideals Google
has tried to uphold. Wired.com's Leander Kahney, author of the new
book "Inside Steve's Brain" (due out this spring) and the Cult of
Mac blog, explores why for Steve Jobs, the regular rules do not apply.
http://www.wired.com/techbiz/it/magazine/16-04/bz_apple

A New Tool From Google Alarms Sites

Google's new search-within-search feature has sparked fears from
publishers and retailers that users will be siphoned away through
ad sales to competitors.
http://www.nytimes.com/2008/03/24/business/media/24ecom.html
```

Well-written headlines and decks can increase your readership, shore up brand loyalty, and boost your rankings. Because your headlines and decks will be used and summarized by other sites from your RSS news feeds, the link text and deck keyphrases will increase the relevancy of these inbound links, thus raising your rankings accordingly.

Automatically categorize with blogs

Weblogs are an excellent tool that you can use in your SEO arsenal. To quickly build up themed content you can use automated categorization. By tagging and organizing your content, each time you post a new article the category pages will grow. Figure 1-14 shows an automated example using the Movable Type publishing platform.

Travel Blog

Book reviews (3)
Destinations (16)
Travel Photography (11)
Travel tips (13)

Figure 1-14. Example blog with categories

In Movable Type, each time you post a new article, select one or more categories to classify the article (see Figure 1-15).

To display the categories that you see in Figure 1-14, you can use the following minimalist code (include_blogs="3" signifies the third blog in the Movable Type installation):

```
<dl>
    <MTCategories include_blogs="3">
    <dt><a href="<$MTCategoryArchiveLink$>" title="<$MTCategoryDescription$>">
<$MTCategoryLabel$></a> (<CategoryCount>)
    </dt>
    </MTCategories>
</dl>
```

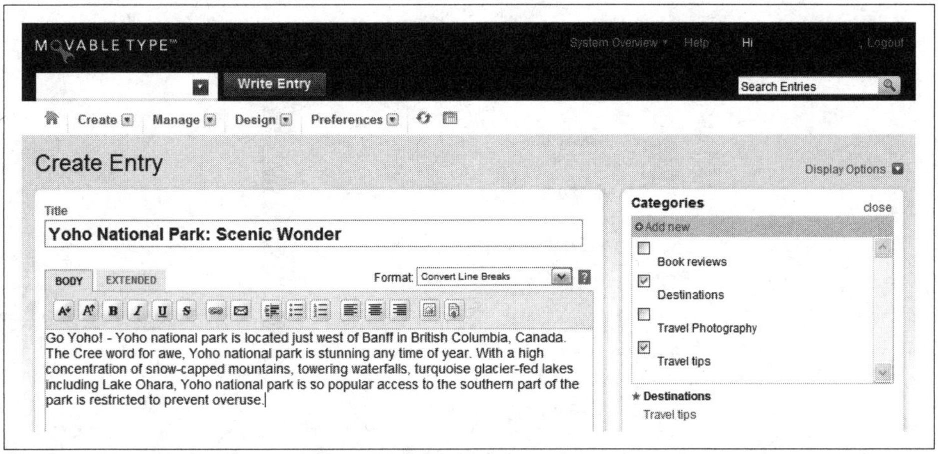

Figure 1-15. Creating an entry with categories in Movable Type

This code does not account for subcategories or categories with no entries, however. A more robust version of the category output code follows:

```
<div class="module-categories module">
  <h2 class="module-header">By Category</h2>
  <div class="module-content">
        <MTTopLevelCategories>
            <MTSubCatIsFirst><ul class="module-list"></MTSubCatIsFirst>
                <MTIfNonZero tag="CategoryCount">
                    <li class="module-list-item"><a href="<$MTBlogURI$>
<MTParentCategories glue="/"><$MTCategoryLabel dirify="-"$></MTParentCategories>"
title="<$MTCategoryDescription$>"><$MTCategoryLabel$></a> (<CategoryCount>)
                <MTElse>
                    <li class="module-list-item"><$MTCategoryLabel$>
                </MTElse>
                </MTIfNonZero>
                <$MTSubCatsRecurse$>
                    </li>
            <MTSubCatIsLast></ul></MTSubCatIsLast>
        </MTTopLevelCategories>
  </div>
</div>
```

Note that `dirify="-"` in the preceding code encodes the category value to a lowercase string with words separated by dashes. To add a subcategory to your blog, select your desired top-level category and then click on the plus sign on the right (see Figure 1-16).

Search engines favor category pages such as the ones listed earlier in Figure 1-14 because they are about a specific topic and are updated frequently. With blog software you don't have to create these pages; they appear automatically!

Figure 1-16. Adding a subcategory in Movable Type

Create tag clouds

Tag clouds are a list of keyphrases sized by popularity (see Figure 1-17). They expose your popular topics to search engines and users in an orderly way. Like a semantic site map, tag clouds make it easier to understand at a glance what your site is about.

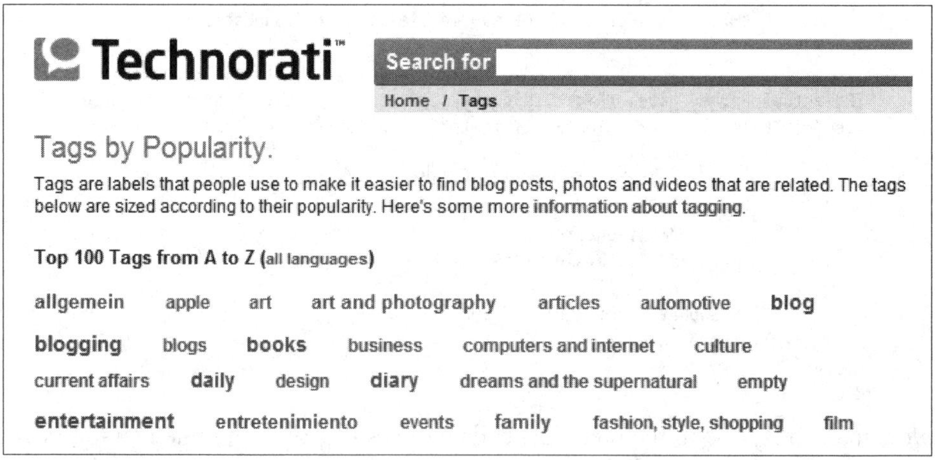

Figure 1-17. Sample tag cloud from Technorati.com

In Movable Type, you can create a tag cloud by using the tags feature. First, turn tags on in the Display Options dialog (see Figure 1-18).

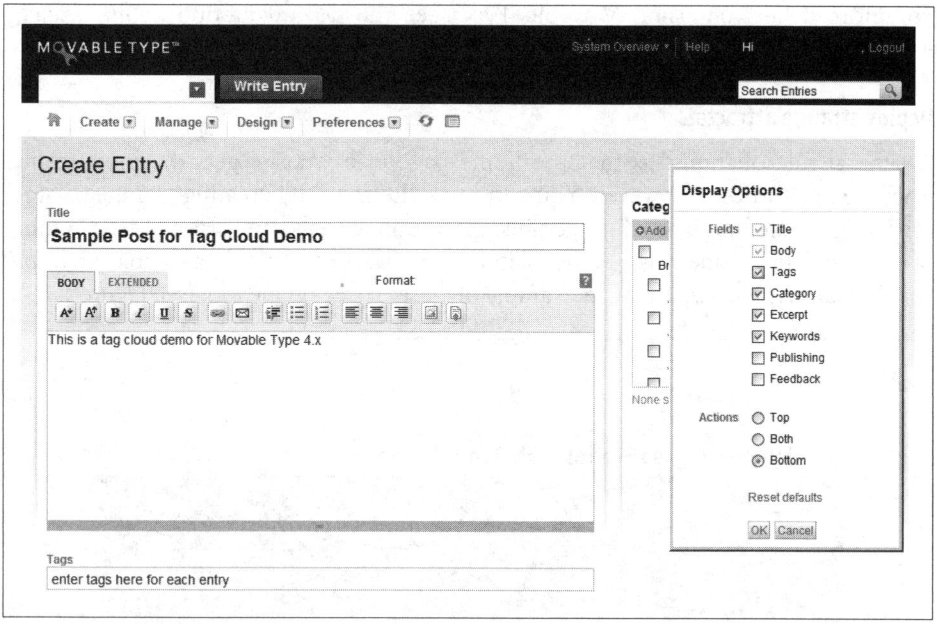

Figure 1-18. Turning on tags in Movable Type

Each time you create a new entry, tag it with the optional Tags field. Next, include the following code in a sidebar template to create a tag cloud from these tags:

```
<style type="css/text">
<!--
.rank-1{font-size:0.7em;}
.rank-2{font-size:0.8em;}
.rank-3{font-size:0.9em;}
...
-->
</style></head><body>
<MTIf name="main_index">
        <div class="widget-cloud widget">
            <h3 class="widget-header">Tag Cloud</h3>
            <div class="widget-content">
                <ul class="widget-list">
    <MTTags limit="20" sort_by="rank">
                    <li class="rank-<$MTTagRank max="10"$> widget-list-item"><a
href="<$MTTagSearchLink$>"><$MTTagName$></a></li>
    </MTTags>
                </ul>
            </div>
        </div>
</MTIf>
```

For more details on using Movable Type, see the documentation at *http://www. movabletype.org*.

Deploy strange attractors

A general rule of thumb is that the home page of a website gets the most traffic. There are exceptions, however. You can buck the trend by creating "strange attractors" to generate buzz and, thus, get links. Free online tools can garner a large number of links quickly. Babel Fish, a translator from AltaVista that is available at *http:// babelfish.altavista.com/*, is a good example of a useful free online tool (see Figure 1-19).

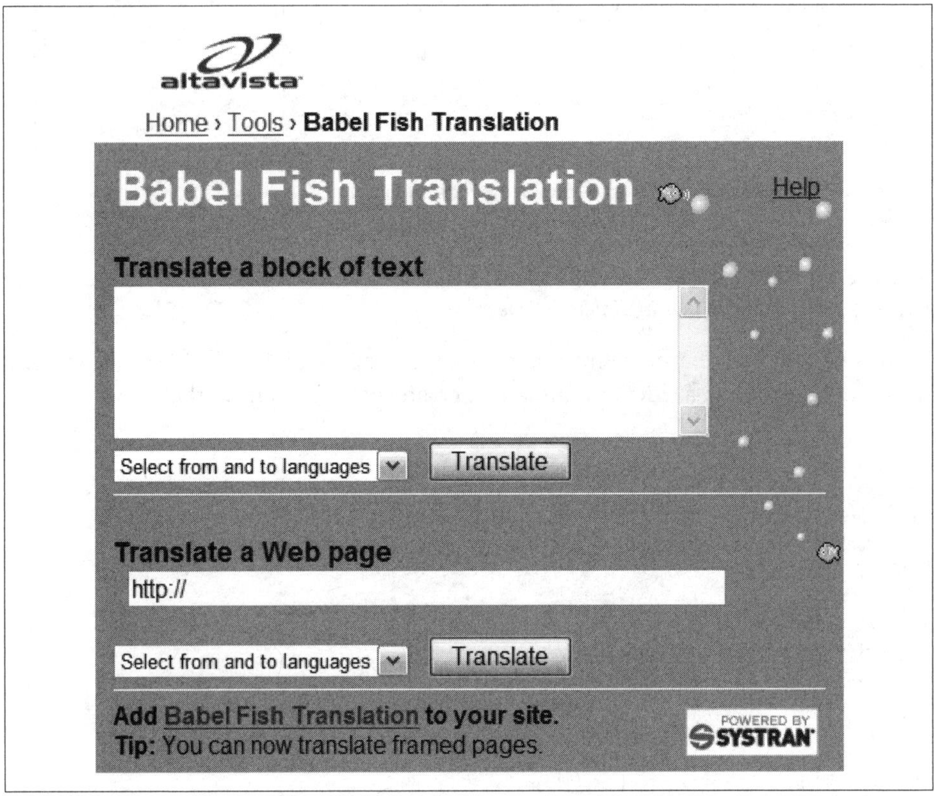

Figure 1-19. Babel Fish, a free language-translator tool

Free web-based tools, Flash configurators (such as a clothes colorizer, or a hotel reservation system/calendar), and Ajax mashups all are elements that wow your audience and provide compelling and useful services that are bound to help.

Step 10: Build Inbound Links with Online Promotion

Now that your website is keyword-optimized, it is time to build up your inbound links. Promoting your site to build more inbound links than your competitors, especially from high PageRank sites, is the most important way to increase your search engine rankings. Here are some techniques you can use to boost your inbound links to build up the buzz and rise above the noise:

- Use XML news feeds such as RSS and Atom to automatically syndicate your content to other sites.
- Register your feeds at news aggregators.
- Interview luminaries.
- Write articles on your most important topics for other sites, and have your bio link back to your website.
- Create useful tools.
- Publicize new content with press releases.
- Get listed in the major directories in the appropriate category:
  — *http://dir.yahoo.com*
  — *http://www.business.com*
  — *http://www.dmoz.org*
  — *http://botw.org*
- Get listed in industry directories and resource pages (e.g., the WorkForce.com Vendor Directory for HR software providers at *http://www.workforce.com/global/2007/vendormain07.htm*).
- Get links from industry websites and discussion forums (write articles, send press releases, post to forums, and use your link in signature files).
- Use "high-end" link exchanges, and partner with others in your industry and exchange links.

Press releases are an especially effective way to get guaranteed inbound links that say exactly what you want in the link text. Keep the newsworthy resources flowing, and follow up with search-optimized press releases to the online newswire sites such as PRweb.com, PRNewswire.com, and Businesswire.com. Spend the extra money to include link text for your URIs rather than using "naked" URIs for maximum Google juice.

Here is a sample press release:

Example.com Announces New E-Riser for HD Video Cameras

Example, a leading provider of [url=http://www.example.com/]HD video cameras and accessories[/url], is announcing the release of its essential new E-Riser product. The [url=http://www.example.com/E-Riser.htm]E-Riser[/url] is used in conjunction with other Example camera mounting components for adjusting a second set of rods to align matte boxes and follow focus units to cameras with high or low lens mounting.

Specifically, the E-Riser is an essential part of Example's kits for the RED ONE camera and the Letus35 Extreme Adapter. It also supports other camera gear such as the Follow-Focus and matte boxes.

The Example E-Riser attaches to a pair of standard 15mm rods…

Note the [url="..."/url] syntax, which specifies the keywords that are used in the press release link text. This level of control is not available from webmasters linking back to your site.

With regular promotion, most new sites take from 6 to 12 months to rank well on Google. They take slightly less time on Yahoo! and even less on MSN.

How to Get High-Ranking Inbound Links

To accelerate the process of getting high PageRank backlinks, invest in a professional design and newsworthy content. Create web-based tools to attract quality backlinks. Submit articles to prominent sites (or offline publications with websites) in exchange for a short bio linking back to your site. Register your RSS feeds and post quality content frequently. Get your press releases on the likes of PRWeb.com and PRNewsWire.com. Get yourself interviewed and interview luminaries. Pay for faster reviews to be included in popular directories such as Yahoo! and Business.com, and if necessary, buy text links (e.g., on Textlinkbrokers.com).

Leverage higher-ranking pages

Links from high PageRank sites carry more weight than links from low PageRank sites. In fact, Kenkai.com estimates that a PageRank 6 link is worth 125 PageRank 3 links, and a link from a PageRank 7 page is worth 625 PageRank 3 links, assuming relevant content (see Table 1-1).[23] So, links from sites with lots of quality inlinks are worth more to your rankings. Think quality, not quantity, when promoting your site. Strive to gather links from higher PageRank sites to boost your PageRank.

---

[23]Kenkai.com. "Google PageRank Table—Compare Pagerank Values." *http://www.kenkai.com/google-pagerank-table.htm* (accessed February 9, 2008).

Table 1-1. *Kenkai.com equivalent PageRank inlink estimates*

Inlink PageRank	Equivalent PageRank 3 inlinks
2	0.2
3	1
4	5×
5	25×
6	125×
7	625×

Don't dilute your PageRank

You can think of your own PageRank as a steeping pot of tea. The more links you get pointing to your site, the stronger the tea. The more links you place on your page, the weaker the tea (read PageRank) that will flow through each link. Placing lots of links in your pages actually dilutes the PageRank that is transferred to target pages. By being selective about whom you link to, you can transfer more "Google juice" to others and preserve your own supply. Danny Sullivan said this about outlinks and PageRank:

> Some people feel links off a page drain PageRank. Others more accurately say it means that the more links you have, the less powerful each of those links are, i.e., if you wanted to boost another page, linking to it from a page with fewer links on it means each of those links should carry more weight. But it's even more complicated than this, and the best advice for a site owner is to simply link out to any pages they feel a user will find appropriate.

There is one exception, however: the `nofollow` attribute, discussed later in this chapter.

Employ social networking and user-generated content

Talk to people in similar fields. Go to meetings and conferences. Send email to reporters, bloggers, and colleagues. Post media to Flickr and YouTube, add a page to Facebook, submit stories to Slashdot, and tag those stories on del.icio.us. Respond to Usenet and blog posts. In other words, use social networking to get your site out there. A link from one of these high PageRank sites drives a lot of traffic and is worth hundreds of links from lesser sites (refer back to Table 1-1).

A little preparation can increase your odds when submitting to news sites such as Slashdot, Digg.com, and Yahoo! Buzz because such sites have an extremely large user base that is equally critical to the site's effect. First, make sure you submit to the proper category. Submit only your most newsworthy content, because sites such as Slashdot are inundated with submissions. Be sure to follow the headline and deck writing guidelines in this chapter, as well as in Chapter 5. Finally, it helps if you have a story angle or address a current trend, and are relevant to the theme of the target site.

Additionally, enabling user-generated content can scale your business without requiring more staff members. Sites that illustrate this trend include Photo.net (the largest photography bulletin board), del.icio.us (rated bookmarks), and YouTube.com (videos).

Be leery of link exchange voodoo

Link exchanges must be done carefully to perform well. Recommending another doctor you know who does good work is fine, but recommending the entire medical community of the East Side is not.

Be very selective when choosing whom you link to. Link farms and doorway pages are never a good idea. You don't want to depend on another company for your traffic. You want your own pages to draw traffic directly to your site.

Pay for links

For some highly competitive keywords, it has become necessary to go beyond standard promotional techniques. Paid links are a form of advertising pioneered by the likes of Textlinkbrokers.com and Text-Link-Ads.com. These advertisers place text links on high PageRank sites for a fee. Unlike banner ads, which have no semantic value and often use redirects, paid links say exactly what you want them to say and link directly back to your site. Use the primary keyphrase of the page that you are promoting in your link text to build up the PageRank and the relevancy of your site.

Hurl harmful outlinks

Linking to some sites can actually have a *negative* effect on your rankings.

As part of its crawling process, Google follows links from your site to others, and penalizes the owner who links to sites that, according to Google's criteria, have misbehaved (see the upcoming sidebar, "The Google Sandbox and Penalty Box"). We discovered this when optimizing a site for a client in California. We thought we were doing everything right for him, but his rankings were still low after six months of intensive promotion. When we checked all the sites he was linking to (by looking for the dreaded gray PageRank bar in Google's toolbar), we found one site that Google didn't approve of.

After removing this link, his rankings improved. So, be careful whom you recommend on your website; it could come back to haunt you.

The Google Sandbox and Penalty Box

For a new site on a new domain, Google can delay ranking the site for months. Traditionally, this has meant that a new site couldn't seem to rank well for much beyond its own domain name. After a few months, Google decides that it can "trust" a new site and can let it rank for other things. This delay for new sites to be indexed is called the *Google Sandbox*. Google can also penalize sites that try to game the system. Although this has a similar effect, it is not the same thing because an older and even trusted site might get penalized (we call this the *Penalty Box*, which can cause a gray PageRank bar in Google's toolbar). To get out of Google's dog house, you need to remove the worst practices discussed in this section. After you've cleared your site with Google Webmaster Central (*http://www.google.com/webmasters/*), you can apply for inclusion again.

Use the nofollow trick. You can concentrate PageRank where you need it most with the nofollow attribute. Created to prevent blog comment spam, the nofollow attribute can be added to links that point to pages to which you don't want to refer Page-Rank, such as your privacy policy or help page. Google can't differentiate between blog and nonblog links and says that this practice is OK. Hammocks.com uses nofollow extensively on its site to concentrate its referred PageRank to flow to only those pages it wants to promote, as shown here:

```
<div class="cartText">
    <ul>
    <li class="pipe"><a rel="nofollow" href="http://www.hammocks.com/info/help.cfm">
Customer Service</a></li>
    <li class="pipe"><a rel="nofollow" href="http://www.hammocks.com/info/order-
tracking.cfm">Order Status</a></li>
    <li><a rel="nofollow" href="http://www.hammocks.com/cart/shopper.cfm"
id="cartImage">View Cart</a></li>
    </ul>
</div>
```

For more information on the nofollow attribute, see the HTML 5 draft at *http://www.w3.org/html/wg/html5/*.

Reduce risky redirects

Use page redirects with caution. Client-side redirects utilizing JavaScript and meta refresh redirects have been used for cloaking in the past, and search engines look for them. In general, avoid serving different content for users and search engine crawlers. If used improperly, temporary 302 redirects are potentially harmful to the rankings of your site.

Servers use HTTP status codes to tell the requesting agent that a resource has been moved (301, 302, and 307) or can't be found (404). The 301 HTTP status code tells the user agent that the resource has permanently moved to a new location. The 302 HTTP status code tells the agent that the move is temporary. For on-site redirects, there are cases in which a 302 temporary redirect makes sense. For example, */todays-menu.html* temporarily redirects to *monday.html, tuesday.html, wednesday.html*, and so on as the menu changes.

For off-site redirects, a permanent 301 redirect is the preferred method to avoid the possibility of link hijacking. However, some webmasters have reported that a hybrid approach works best for moving to a new, nonlinked domain. They temporarily use a 302 redirect to the new site, build up some links, and then change to a 301 redirect. Abrupt transitions from an old to a new site, coupled with a raft of new links to the new site, can cause your site to be penalized by search engines.

Google says that PageRank is handled properly for 301 redirects.[24] More recent data shows that Google is handing 302s more favorably.[25]

Permanent redirects. To redirect an old URI to a new URI, add the following lines to your *.htaccess* or *httpd.conf* file:

```
Options +FollowSymLinks
RewriteEngine on
RewriteRule ^oldpage.htm$ http://www.example.com/newpage.htm  [R=301,L]
```

Where possible, Windows users should use Internet Information Server (IIS) redirects, which are transparent to search engines. To redirect URIs on IIS, do the following:

1. Go to the Internet Services Manager and browse the website for which you want to do the redirect.

2. In the right pane, right-click on the file or folder you wish to redirect, and then click Properties.

3. Under the File tab, click the radio button labeled "A redirection to a URI".

4. Enter the target in the "Redirect to" text area.

5. Be sure to check the boxes labeled "The exact URI entered above" and "A permanent redirection for this resource".

6. Click on Apply.

Canonical URIs. Here is an example showing a permanent redirect to *www.example.com* of all URIs that do not start with "www". To create uniform URIs, add the following lines to your *httpd.conf* or *.htaccess* file in your *root* folder:

```
Options +FollowSymLinks
RewriteEngine On
RewriteBase /
RewriteCond %{HTTP_HOST} !^example.com$ [NC]
RewriteRule ^(.*)$ http://www.example.com/$1 [R=301,L]
```

where L indicates that this is the last rule and R signifies the return code it sends, which requires an argument.

This technique defaults to one canonical domain, to ensure uniform URIs and inlinks. It also permits flexibility for subdomains.

Note that redirecting an entire domain and then changing all the old links to new links can harm your rankings because of the large amount of new links to a new domain that must be re-indexed. A better approach is to use relative URIs and to not change URIs after the domain name is redirected.

[24]Boser, G. March 11, 2007. "Understanding the 301 redirect." SEO Buzz Box, *http://www.seobuzzbox.com/ understanding-the-301-redirect/* (accessed March 29, 2008).

[25]Cutts, M. January 4, 2006. "SEO advice: discussing 302 redirects." Mattcutts.com, *http://www.mattcutts.com/ blog/seo-advice-discussing-302-redirects/* (accessed March 29, 2008).

Measuring inbound links

The Marketleap.com link popularity tool is a good way to compare your site against others for inbound links (see Figure 1-20).

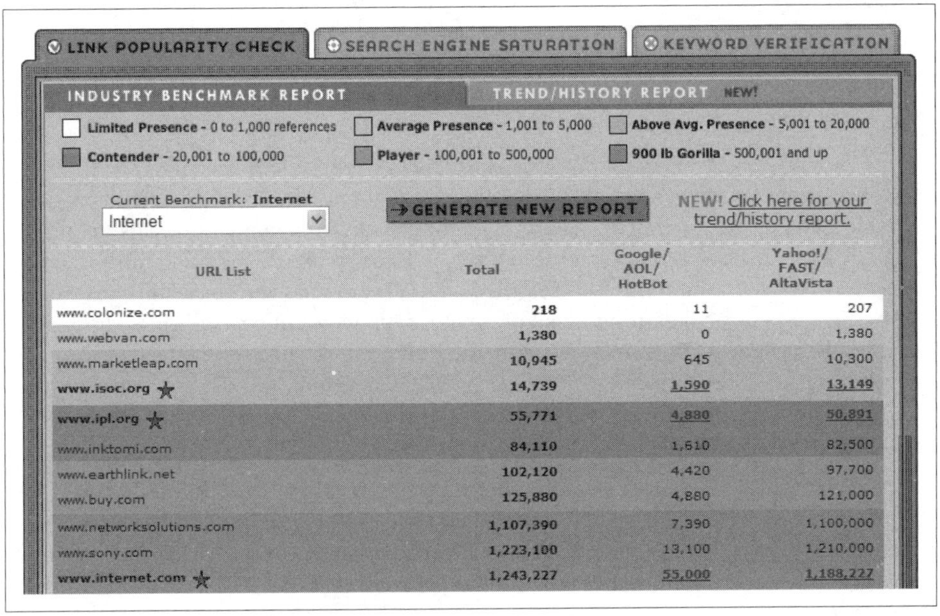

Figure 1-20. Marketleap's link popularity checker

You can also gauge the number of inbound links you have at Yahoo! or Google by typing `link:http://www.example.com`. To see how well your site is indexed, type `site:example.com` into Yahoo! or Google. If there are 1,000 pages on your site and only 50 are indexed, you've got a problem.

The Yahoo! Site Explorer tool at *http://siteexplorer.search.yahoo.com/* lets you access the information in Yahoo!'s database about your site's presence, including inbound links.

Summary

Natural SEO is the process of keyword-optimizing your site, creating targeted content, and promoting your website to boost inbound links and search engine rankings. If possible, bake keywords directly into your site with your domain name, URIs, navigation, and site hierarchy. First, use keyword research tools to discover the search demand and competition for phrases related to your business. Next, select a primary keyphrase based on these findings that is specific enough to convert, yet broad enough to draw enough traffic. Then customize your content and meta tags to the topic of each web page. Once your site is optimized with irresistible content and tools, tirelessly promote it to boost inbound links.

The Future of SEO: Metadata

In early 2008, Yahoo! announced that its web crawler would begin to process micro-formats and other forms of structured metadata, making it available to developers as a way to present richer search results.[a] For example, instead of a blue link and a plain text abstract, a search result for an electronic gizmo could contain a thumbnail of the device, its price, its availability, reviews, and perhaps a link to buy it immediately. The greater the percentage of search results that take advantage of metadata (from any search engine), the greater interest site owners have in structuring their sites accordingly.

Metadata generally means machine-readable "data about data," which can take many forms. Perhaps the simplest form falls under the classification of microformats,[b] which can be as simple as a single attribute value such as `nofollow`, described in more detail in "Step 10: Build Inbound Links with Online Promotion," earlier in this chapter. Another popular single-attribute microformat is `XFN`,[c] which allows individual links to be labeled as connections on a social graph, with values such as `acquaintance`, `co-worker`, `spouse`, or even `sweetheart`. A special value of `me` indicates that a link points to another resource from the same author, as in the following example:

```
<a href="myothersite.example.com" rel="me">Homepage</a>
```

Some microformats expose more structure, particularly to represent people and events and to review information, all of which can help make sites more presentable in seman-tic search engines. For example, a social network might expose a personal profile using hCard,[d] the microformat equivalent of the vCard address book standard:[e]

```
<div class="vcard">
  <h2 class="fn">John Q. Public</h2>
  <img class="photo" src="/images/jqp.jpg"/>
  <a class="URI" href="http://jqp.example.net">
    Personal Page
  </a>
  <div class="tel">+1-650-289-4040</div>
  <div>Email:
   <span class="email">jqp@example.net</span>
  </div>
</div>
```

Microformats are great for this sort of thing, but it is fairly easy for the structured data needs of a site to run beyond what's covered by a microformat specification.

RDF, the Resource Description Framework,[f] is (as the name suggests) a general frame-work for metadata not tied to any particular syntax or representation. The main concept mirrors that of a statement, often called a *triple* because it encompasses a subject (what you talk about), a predicate (some property of the subject), and an object (the value of the property). For example, in plain language one might say that "this book is written by Andy King," which demonstrates a subject, predicate, and object, respectively. By breaking down knowledge into small, statement-size chunks and using URIs to stand for resources and relationships between them, you can express nearly any fact or opinion imaginable.

—continued—

Quite a few different ways to embed RDF in web pages have been proposed, but the most popular one is called RDFa,[g] which defines a few additional attributes to be used in pages. The about attribute defines a subject, the property attribute defines a predicate, and the resource attribute defines an object, though to avoid having to repeat information already present, many existing XHTML elements also come into play. RDFa also makes broad use of CURIEs,[h] or Compact URIs, to make life easier for authors. The following short example shows how the statement mentioned previously could be encoded in a web page:

```
<div xmlns:dc="http://pURI.org/dc/elements/1.1/"
 about="http://www.oreilly.com/catalog/9780596515089">
  <span property="dc:creator">Andy King</span>
</div>
```

Soon, a significant amount of traffic from search engines will depend on the extent to which the underlying site makes useful structured data available. Things such as microformats and RDFa have been around in various forms for years, but now that search engines are noticing them, SEO practitioners are starting to take note, too.

---

a *http://www.techcrunch.com/2008/03/13/yahoo-embraces-the-semantic-web-expect-the-web-to-organize-itself-in-a-hurry/*

b *http://www.microformats.org*

c *http://gmpg.org/xfn/11*

d *http://microformats.org/wiki/hcard*

e *http://www.ietf.org/rfc/rfc2426.txt*

f *http://www.w3.org/RDF/*

g *http://www.w3.org/TR/rdfa-syntax/*

h *http://www.w3.org/TR/curie*

## CHAPTER 2

SEO Case Study: PhillyDentistry.com

In this chapter, we'll show you how to put into action the optimization techniques that you learned in Chapter 1 and the conversion techniques you'll learn in Chapter 5. To do so, we feature a case study that shows the benefits of natural search engine optimization (SEO).

Original Site

Dr. Ken Cirka, DMD, contacted us in mid-2004 seeking to boost the number of patient leads he was getting from his website. The original website had a simple, graphically rich design using stock images (see Figure 2-1).

Although it was visually appealing to humans, it was not appealing to search engines.

Through the lens of a Lynx viewer, the site looked like this:

```
Title=Dr. Ken Cirka, DMD

<alt text>
  Dr. Ken Cirka Center City Philadelphia dentist 1601 Walnut Street,
  Suite 1302 Philadelphia, PA 19102 215.568.6222
</alt text>

[1]drcirka@phillydentistry.com Center City Philadelphia dentist
[2][USEMAP:menu.gif]

<alt text>
  Center City Philadelphia dentist Center City Philadelphia dentist
  Center City Philadelphia dentist Center City Philadelphia dentist
  Dental Care for your lifestyle
</alt text>

[3]Meet the Doctor   |   [4]Hours & Location   |   [5]Services

            [6]drcirka@phillydentistry.com
```

```
[3] http://www.phillydentistry.com/doctor.html (meet the doctor)
[4] http://www.phillydentistry.com/hours.html (hours & location)
[5] http://www.phillydentistry.com/services.html (services)
```

Meta description=Five star service in dental care is abundant in Dr.
Cirka's cosmetic and general dentistry office in Center City Philadelphia.

Meta keywords=Dr. Ken Cirka, Ken Cirka Dentist, Philadelphia Dentist,
Philadelphia area dentist, Center City Philadelphia dentist,
cosmetic dentistry, gentle dentistry, Philadelphia dentistry, philly,
bleaching, dentist, dentistry, Philadelphia, dental,
Walnut Street, cosmetic, best, DDS, DMD, Dr., doctor, general, center
city, pennsylvania, veneers, porcelain, PA, good, Penn, spa,
evening, weekend

Figure 2-1. PhillyDentistry.com, circa June 2004

The site used keyword-rich image alt tags, but search engines give more weight to visible text such as headlines and body copy than they do to invisible text. In Dr. Cirka's original site, search engines could detect no body copy or headlines. They saw only alt and link text. The site was also opening up the business to spam; note that publishing a plain-text email address in your page will increase the amount of spam emails that you receive. It is best to use a contact form instead to avoid spam from spambots.

As a comparison to the earlier view, the HTML for the old home page began like this:

```
<HTML>
<HEAD>
<TITLE>Dr. Ken Cirka, DMD</TITLE>
<LINK REL="StyleSheet" HREF="/style.css" TYPE="text/css">
<meta name="Description" content="Five star service in dental care is abundant in Dr.
Cirka's cosmetic and general dentistry office in Center City Philadelphia.">
<meta name="Keywords" content="Dr. Ken Cirka, Ken Cirka Dentist, Philadelphia
Dentist,
Philadelphia area dentist, Center City Philadelphia dentist,
cosmetic dentistry, gentle dentistry, Philadelphia dentistry, philly, bleaching,
dentist, dentistry, Philadelphia, dental, Walnut Street, cosmetic, best, DDS, DMD,
Dr., doctor, general, center city, pennsylvania, veneers, porcelain, PA, good,
Penn, spa, evening, weekend">
</HEAD>

<BODY BGCOLOR="#006699" MARGINWIDTH=0 LEFTMARGIN=0 RIGHTMARGIN=0>
<center>
<table border=0 cellspacing=0 cellpadding=2 bgcolor=FFFFFF width=610>
<tr>
<td>
<table border=0 cellspacing=0 cellpadding=2 bgcolor=#006699 width=610>
<tr>
<td>
<table bgcolor="#ffffff" border="0" cellpadding="0" cellspacing="0" width=610>
<tr>
<td align="center" colspan=2>
<table border="0" cellpadding="0" cellspacing="0" width=610>
<tr>
<td><img src="images/small_ken_logo.gif" hspace=30 alt="Dr. Ken Cirka Center City
Philadelphia dentist"></td>
<td><img src="images/address.gif" width="194" height="61" border=0 alt="1601 Walnut
Street, Suite 1302 Philadelphia, PA 19102 215.568.6222" vspace=6><br>
```

```
<span class=arial><a href="mailto:drcirka@phillydentistry.com">
drcirka@phillydentistry.com</a></span></td>
<td align=right><img src="images/fower-3.jpg" width="114" height="150" border=0
alt="Center City Philadelphia dentist"></td>...
```

Few Indexable Keywords

The title tag, body copy, and headers are the most important factors in search engine rankings for on-site optimization. The description meta tag is of secondary importance for SEO rankings. The keywords meta tag and alternative text have little effect on rankings, but alt attributes do affect image searches.

You can see from Figure 2-1 and from the results of the search engine simulator that the original home page, which was made up almost entirely of graphics, offered little visible text to index. The title tag, "Dr. Ken Cirka, DMD," had no targeted keywords. There was no visible keyword text to index in the main body of the page. The only applicable keywords were in the description meta tag, the keywords meta tag, and the alt text for graphics.

First Redesign: Mid-2004

Dr. Cirka's primary goals were to increase appointment requests and to target more lucrative cosmetic dentistry services. Based on these goals, we developed a search engine strategy to optimize Dr. Cirka's site for higher visibility. An analysis of keyword queries in search engines revealed that most of Dr. Cirka's target audience searched for dentist philadelphia and cosmetic dentist philadelphia (see Table 2-1).

Table 2-1. Top keyword search demand for Philadelphia dentist

Frequency	Keyword query
1,125	dentist philadelphia
378	cosmetic dentist philadelphia
107	dentist implant philadelphia
105	dentist in philadelphia
73	dentist pa philadelphia

We also found that the site had few inbound links. As you learned in Chapter 1, off-site SEO such as inlinks is weighed more heavily than on-site SEO for high rankings. Based on our research, we advised the doctor to incorporate search-friendly best practices into his site. Dr. Cirka agreed. We launched the redesign of the site in June 2004 (see Figure 2-2).

Figure 2-2. PhillyDentistry.com first redesign, circa July 2004

Search Engine Optimization

Upon indexing Dr. Cirka's new home page, search engines saw the following:

```
Title=Cosmetic Dentist & Tooth Whitening in Philadelphia Pennsylvania PA

[1]Philadelphia Dentistry Dr Ken Cirka Logo
    1601 Walnut Street, Philadelphia PA [2]request appointment | [3]easy
                financing | [4]guarantee | [5]location
    [6]PHILADELPHIA DENTISTRY HOME | [7]DENTAL SERVICES | [8]SMILE GALLERY
                | [9]ABOUT DR CIRKA | [10]CONTACT

        Dr. Ken Cirka DMD, Philadelphia Dentistry

        Where dental care goes beyond your expectations

    Are you looking for a Philadelphia Dentist? Dr. Ken Cirka, DMD, can
    make you look younger... boost your confidence... and help you enjoy
                    pain-free chewing again!
```

Nothing conveys good health and enhances your smile more than clean, white teeth. So, take advantage of HUGE SAVINGS with our [11]Get Acquainted Specials including our [12]Free New Client Exam. [13]Click here »

COSMETIC DENTISTRY SERVICES
...

The redesigned site was much more search-friendly. It used text-based menus with keywords in the anchor text and in the URIs. The new site included service-specific pages optimized for one or two keywords, and prominently used his primary keyphrases (cosmetic dentist Philadelphia and Philadelphia dentist[ry]). The new title element targeted the phrase cosmetic dentist Philadelphia and tooth whitening Philadelphia:

<title>Cosmetic Dentist & Tooth Whitening in Philadelphia Pennsylvania PA</title>

Conversion Rate Optimization

In addition to SEO, the redesigned website also makes use of conversion rate optimization (CRO). For instance, you can also see the "baked-in" persuasive copywriting and SEO in action. Instead of "Home," the main navigation bar says "Philadelphia Dentistry Home" to squeeze in his primary keyphrase. The main header contains his primary keyphrase as well as his name, which people now search on:

<h1>Dr. Ken Cirka DMD, Philadelphia Dentistry</h1>

The tagline entices visitors to continue reading for more information:

Where dental care goes beyond your expectations

To grab your attention, the opening paragraph starts with a question and then moves right to the benefits of healthy, straight, and gleaming white teeth:

Are you looking for a Philadelphia Dentist? Dr. Ken Cirka, DMD, can make you look younger... boost your confidence... and help you enjoy pain-free chewing again!

The second paragraph and the rest of the page contain more services, benefits, and calls to action:

Nothing conveys good health and enhances your smile more than clean, white teeth. So, take advantage of HUGE SAVINGS with our [11]Get Acquainted Specials including our [12]Free New Client Exam. [13]Click here »

Free exams, discounts, specials, referral incentives, and even the directive "Click here" all work together to entice visitors to explore more of the site and to contact the office. The URIs are also keyword-optimized, with addresses such as *http:// www.phillydentistry.com/cosmetic-dentistry.html*.

Results

After eight months of promotion, Dr. Cirka's site rankings increased from nonexistent to number one on Google for both natural and pay-per-click (PPC) rankings for his primary keyphrase, philadelphia dentist (see Figure 2-3). Note that he was also second in Google local results for the same term.

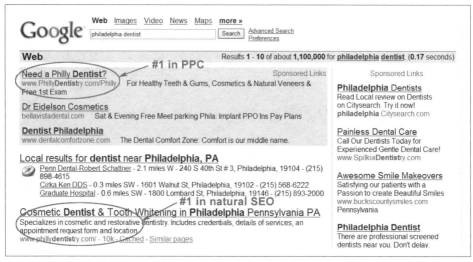

Figure 2-3. Google rankings for PhillyDentistry.com after website optimization

In eight months, Dr. Cirka went from gaining one new client per week from his website to gaining an average of nine new clients per week from his website. This nearly tenfold improvement was caused by three factors:

- Keyword optimization of his site
- A monthly promotion campaign to build inbound links
- Minimal PPC advertising

In the nine months after we first worked on his site, Dr. Cirka hired another dentist, added new staff members, and moved to a larger office to accommodate the influx of new patients.

Second Redesign: Late 2007

Dr. Cirka contacted us three years later to give his site a new look and to focus it on different services. Our new design for him incorporated best practices from Chapters 1, 5, and 6 (see Figure 2-4).

Figure 2-4. Second redesign of PhillyDentistry.com

Search engines saw the new home page like this:

```
Title=Philadelphia Dentistry by Dr. Ken Cirka - Cosmetic Dentist

* [1]philadelphia dentistry home
    * [2]dental services
        + [3]Tooth Whitening
        + [4]Zoom Whitening
        + [5]Porcelain Veneers
        + [6]Dental Crowns/Bridges
        + [7]InvisAlign
        + [8]Cerinate Lumineers
        + [9]NTI Tension Suppression
        + [10]Aesthetic Dentisty
        + [11]Cosmetic Dentistry
        + [12]Preventive Care
        + [13]Free Visit
    * [14]smile gallery
    * [15]success stories
    * [16]meet our staff
    * [17]contact
    * [18]request appointment
    * [19]easy financing
    * [20]guarantee
    * [21]location
```

[22]Dr Ken Cirka, Philadelphia Dentistry

Dr. Ken Cirka

1601 Walnut Street
Suite #1302
Philadelphia, PA
Call Now!
(215) 568-6222
Philadelphia Dentist Awards

Best Dentist...
2007: Dr. Cirka was awarded "Top Dentist" by the Consumers Research
Council ...

Dr Ken Cirka Logo

Dr. Ken Cirka, DMD - Philadelphia Dentistry
Healthy teeth and gums for life

Are you looking for a Philadelphia Dentist? Dr. Ken Cirka, DMD, can
make you look younger... boost your confidence... and help you enjoy
pain-free chewing again!

Nothing conveys good health and enhances your smile more than clean,
white teeth. So, take advantage of BIG SAVINGS with our [23]Get
Acquainted Specials including our [24]Free New Client Exam. [25]Click
here »

[26]Philadelphia Dentist Cosmetic Dentistry Cosmetic Dentistry Services

Do you have crooked, chipped or discolored teeth? Would you like a
"perfect" smile that makes you look great and feel confident? Dr.
Cirka is able to dramatically improve your smile in just 2 visits with
Cerinate Lumineers.
[27]Cosmetic Dentistry o [28]Learn more about Cerinate Lumineers o
[29]Tooth Whitening ...

To increase the number of phone calls we added two conversion builders: just below
the menu in the left column is an image of Dr. Cirka, above his address and phone
number. Studies have shown that people tend to click more on human faces.

We also placed Dr. Cirka's phone number along with a call to action in the upper-
right corner of the screen and integrated into the new logo.

It is important to avoid requiring your customers to make too many clicks. At
WebReference.com, we found that with each click a user is forced to make, about
50% of your traffic is lost. To help avoid this, we added a quick contact form on the
upper right to encourage more appointment requests.

Let Keywords Do the Work

For higher keyword prominence, the newest home page is ordered to place dental service links high up in the visible body code. The vertical menu on the left appears at the point where most users first begin to scan web pages. To boost credibility we placed Dr. Cirka's awards in the left column, and we included "Success Stories" in the left navigation menu to highlight testimonials from satisfied clients.

Also, note the new title tag optimized for Dr. Cirka's primary keyphrase:

```
<title>Philadelphia Dentistry by Dr. Ken Cirka - Cosmetic Dentist</title>
```

Naming your business with your primary keyphrase is a best practice that allows you to put your business name up front. This automatically front-loads your primary keyphrase to maximize the prominence of keywords.

The description meta tag does three things. It begins with Dr. Cirka's current primary keyphrase, philadelphia dentist; highlights his target services; and ends with a call to action:

```
<meta name="description" content="Philadelphia dentist Dr. Ken Cirka,
D.M.D. is an exceptional general and cosmetic dentist specializing in
cosmetic dentistry, porcelain veneers, dental crowns and implants,
tooth whitening, restorative dentistry and preventive care for healthy
teeth and gums. We are currently accepting new patients and referrals.
Call for a free consultation.">
```

The top-level heading tag is similar to the previous iteration:

```
<h1>Dr. Ken Cirka, DMD - Philadelphia Dentistry</h1>
```

The second-level header now targets Dr. Cirka's second target phrase, cosmetic dentist[ry]:

```
<h2><a href="cosmetic-dentistry.html"><img src="art/teeth.jpg" alt="Philadelphia
Dentist Cosmetic Dentistry" width="65" height="71" border="0" align="left">Cosmetic
Dentistry Services </a></h2>
```

Links are underlined and colored blue to improve usability and conversion rates. The text includes new persuasive copy for key pages to emphasize the services that Dr. Cirka wanted to target (cerinate lumineers and porcelain veneers).

Results

After the November 2007 redesign, PhillyDentistry.com referred an average of 47 new clients per week to the doctor's office, using a combination of natural SEO promotion and increased PPC advertising. This is an increase of more than 5.2 times over the previous design and an improvement of 47 times over the original site.

The traffic on PhillyDentistry.com went from tens to hundreds of visitors per day after the first redesign. Dr. Cirka was pleased with the results:

> The patient response from the website has been absolutely incredible! We are looking to expand our practice, including hiring more staff. Much gratitude and appreciation go to you and everyone from WSO who has helped us.

Summary

This case study shows how search-friendly design, CRO, and steady promotion to build inbound links can boost your visibility and significantly increase the number of new customers to your business. When we started this campaign, Dr. Cirka attracted most of his new clients from traditional offline advertising. After two website redesigns and monthly promotion, Dr. Cirka's practice is thriving due in large part to his website. This case study also shows the value of redesigning your site every few years. As your business changes with new products and services, upgrading your site will keep it current for your users' increasing demands.

Pay-per-Click Optimization

Pay-per-click (PPC) optimization is the process of improving keyword choice, ad copy, landing pages, and ad groups to boost the return on investment (ROI) of your search engine-based ad campaigns.

The advice in this chapter will help you rewrite your ad copy to boost click-through rates (CTRs), optimize landing pages to improve conversion rates, and organize ad groups to increase the overall effectiveness of your PPC advertising. These methods will generate more leads and sales, garner valuable market intelligence, and build brand awareness.

This chapter begins with a quick overview of terms and the basics, but it assumes a general understanding of PPC advertising. Then it reviews the differences among the advertising programs offered by the top three search engines. The rest of the chapter explores the details of PPC optimization with a strong focus on Google AdWords.

We recommend the following tips for effective PPC advertising:

- Choose appropriate, profit-driven goals.
- Target campaigns and keywords to the right audience.
- Set up ad groups with closely related, tightly themed keywords.
- Write ads that feature your keywords and the interests of potential visitors.
- Create goal-driven landing pages with clear calls to action that target your keywords directly and focus on the interests of potential visitors.
- Set bids to meet realistic, profit-driven goals.

That's PPC in a nutshell.

PPC advertising can be overwhelming at first. It has numerous options, complex targeting, and a variety of measurements. However, the main points are simple. If you target the right audience and do not spend more than you can afford, you will have a successful PPC campaign.

Pay-per-Click Basics and Definitions

The cycle of PPC optimization and management starts with goal setting. It then proceeds to a number of tasks: choosing keywords, creating ad groups, writing ad copy, creating landing pages, and making bids. The last step consists of continuously tracking and optimizing all of these elements to hone the targeting, message, and performance of your advertising (see Figure 3-1).

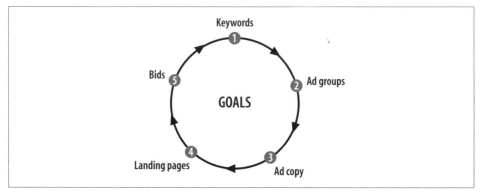

Figure 3-1. The cycle of PPC optimization

When setting up an ad campaign, you'll choose keywords, on-page ad location, language, and network settings to aim your campaign at your "target" searchers. Thus, when someone searches in the right location, using the language and keywords that you specify, the search engine will show your ad. The location of your on-page ad is determined by several factors: your bid, the relevance of the query to your ad, the past performance of the matched keyword, and the past performance of your account.

Ads are sometimes called *creatives*. Although PPC advertising spans several formats, including text, images, video, local businesses, and mobile text, this chapter will focus on the most common type, *text ads*.

Ad groups are the sets of keywords and keyword phrases that you can manage as a unit.

Landing pages are the destinations for the ads. This is where the user lands after clicking on the ad. In practice, landing pages can be expanded to include a larger group of pages that work together to convert visitors to buyers. Such larger page groups are sometimes called *conversion funnels*. These pages need to have information relevant to the incoming keywords and clear calls to action to motivate the visitor to act to fulfill the goal of the campaign.

Bids are often called *maximum costs per click* (or *maximum CPCs*). The bid you submit for a keyword is the most you will pay to get traffic. PPC programs use a type of auction that is like a second-price sealed bidding system with private values. These types of auctions are difficult to bid successfully because you usually have incomplete information.

The Pay-per-Click Work Cycle

The rhythm of work on PPC is cyclical, but the amount of effort spent on each part of the cycle changes over the duration of the work. For new PPC campaigns, what takes the most time are keyword generation, grouping, and bidding. In later stages, landing page refinement becomes the primary focus (see Figure 3-2).

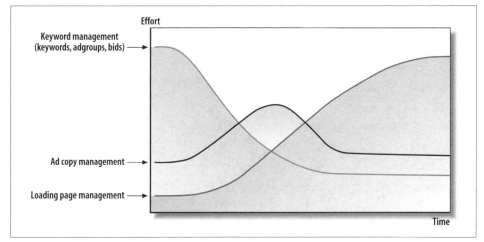

Figure 3-2. The pattern of effort over time for PPC management

Bids and targets are critical elements. Big changes to a campaign will require changes to bidding and targeting. Unless there are huge mistakes in meeting the needs and expectations of visitors, ads and landing pages will typically have a smaller effect on a campaign. Improving the performance of PPC requires accurate tracking of campaigns and comparison of CTRs, CPCs, conversion rates, and costs per conversion.

Common Problems with Pay-per-Click Optimization

The most common mistakes made when optimizing a campaign are:

- Not taking large enough samples
- Not providing a controlled environment
- Not using the most appropriate metrics to gauge success

It can sometimes take months before you can accumulate enough data to decide what is working best. Some short campaigns do not receive enough conversions to get adequate optimization data. When you are experimenting with ads and landing pages, remember to allow sufficient campaign time to acquire the data you are trying to measure.

Google, Yahoo!, Microsoft, and Everybody Else

There are many vendors of PPC advertising. Of vendors offering the greatest reach (and likely the greatest click-through), Google AdWords delivers the most, Yahoo! Search Marketing (YSM) is second, and Microsoft adCenter is third. Smaller programs exist, some boasting a higher ROI than that of the large vendors. Of these, Ask.com, Kanoodle, and MIVA are quite reputable.

Although advertisers may choose smaller vendors to save money, there can be drawbacks:

- They don't drive as much traffic.
- Possible savings can be reduced by the increased cost of campaign management time.
- Some don't have adequate safeguards against click fraud.

According to eMarketer, Google received 75% of U.S. paid search advertising and Yahoo! received 9% (*http://www.emarketer.com/Reports/All/Emarketer_2000473.aspx*). This chapter will focus on the clear leader in reach, Google AdWords, and will compare and contrast it with the two runners-up: YSM and Microsoft adCenter. The most important differences among these three programs are in bulk editing, geo-targeting, and minimum bidding.

Differences in Bulk Editing: Uploading Spreadsheets Versus the AdWords Editor

For large accounts, launching and managing PPC campaigns can require time-consuming and tedious work in spreadsheets, choosing hold terms, writing ad copy, and managing URIs and bids. Traditionally, advertisers made bulk edits to large accounts by uploading revised spreadsheets that contained campaign changes. Currently, Google AdWords offers a larger suite of PPC management tools than the other programs. One very valuable tool is the AdWords Editor, which is used to make bulk changes to a campaign. Bulk changes are typically made for several purposes: to tag tracking URIs, to change ad text, and to modify bids. The ability to bulk-edit a campaign provides useful shortcuts that can save you valuable time.

The AdWords Editor is a desktop tool that can replace spreadsheet uploads. You can download the AdWords Editor from the Tools section within AdWords. The Editor tool allows you to make offline changes to your campaign and then post those changes online to your AdWords account. Use it to change multiple keywords, ads, and bids at once or to create new campaigns, ad groups, or keywords.

The AdWords Editor allows you to make changes to accounts by cutting and pasting from a comma-separated value (CSV) file. You can export the whole account, select campaigns, select ad groups, or select smaller sections that you are currently viewing.

One drawback to the AdWords Editor is that it imports ad groups, keywords, and ads separately, but it groups them together when it exports the campaign file. You have to take the time to paste each element into the Editor rather than uploading an entire spreadsheet at once.

Another limitation of the AdWords Editor is that it does not allow bulk campaign additions.

> Advertisers seeking to add campaigns in bulk might look into the AdWords API. Google charges by the transaction for use of its API, however. Microsoft adCenter and YSM also offer APIs for custom applications and both are free of charge. However, as of this writing, Microsoft hasn't released its API to all advertisers.

A big benefit of the AdWords Editor is the advanced search features that it offers. Advanced searches allow advertisers to make bulk edits without dealing with a spreadsheet download. You can not only search through elements of your account, but also import past performance data and use it to search through your campaign. The AdWords Editor is a powerful tool that makes large accounts far more manageable.

In more traditional fashion, YSM offers spreadsheet uploads for bulk editing. However, YSM limits the upload capability for spreadsheets only to select campaigns that meet certain criteria of age and ad spend.

> *Ad spend* is short for *advertising spend*. It might also be called *click spend*. In PPC, it is the amount of money spent to generate clicks. Do not confuse it with the amount budgeted for clicks. Sometimes in PPC, ROI is replaced by *return on advertising spend* (ROAS). This term shows that the calculated return does not include other expenditures, such as operational costs.

For example, you cannot create a new YSM account and import a campaign. As a result, advertisers can't export a spreadsheet from an AdWords account and upload it to a YSM account to quickly start a new campaign. On the other hand, Microsoft adCenter offers a campaign import for new accounts. After campaigns are in place, however, you can make bulk edits only at the ad group level.

Some advertisers prefer the simplicity of spreadsheet uploads for making bulk changes. They favor Yahoo!'s method over the AdWords Editor. Opinions may change as Google expands the functionality of the AdWords Editor.

Differences in Geotargeting

In YSM, advertisers can target users nationally, by states and territories, or by predefined designated marketing areas (DMAs). Rather than following borders, these regions segment populations in a way that makes more sense for businesses.

In Microsoft adCenter, advertisers can target by country, region, or "city." This city targeting is available for a select list of locations, but includes entire metropolitan areas. It is similar to targeting a DMA in YSM or AdWords. Google AdWords offers targeting by DMA, by radius around a point, or by defining a closed area on a map. AdWords offers the most flexible targeting options. Advertisers who want to target very specific areas will find themselves overdistributed in YSM. That is, they show ads to visitors located outside the range of their business. In adCenter, a locally targeted campaign would not bring much traffic anyway, unless it was covering a very large area.

AdWords is much more flexible in its geotargeting options because it gets enough traffic to make narrowly targeted campaigns viable. You should not think that narrow targeting is a silver bullet for reducing competition, however. Local ads compete equally with national ads on Google AdWords, and perhaps in some cases get a small boost in Quality Score.

AdWords Quality Scores

AdWords uses "Quality Scores" to determine where an ad will rank. The higher your Quality Score is, the higher your ads will rank. AdWords also has Quality Scores to determine distribution on the content network and to calculate the minimum bid required to compete in an auction on the search network. The search network and the content network comprise the Google network. In some cases, data used in Quality Scores is pulled only from Google and not the Google network. According to Google, this is how Quality Scores are used (*https://adwords.google.com/support/bin/answer. py?answer=10215*).

Google calculates a keyword's minimum bid using:

- The keyword's CTR on Google; the CTR on the Google Network isn't considered
- The relevance of the keyword to its ad group
- The quality of your landing page
- Other relevance factors

To calculate a keyword-targeted ad's position on a search result page Google uses:

- The matched keyword's CTR on Google; the CTR on the Google Network is not considered
- The relevance of the keyword and ad to the search query
- Other relevance factors

To calculate a keyword-targeted ad's eligibility to appear on a particular content site, as well as the ad's position on that site, Google uses:

- The ad's past performance on this and similar sites
- The quality of your landing page
- Other relevance factors

Therefore, targeting your ad locally will not avoid your national competitors, but it will remove your ads from locations that you do not serve. The value in local targeting comes from filtering out unqualified clicks.

Differences in Minimum Bids and Quality Scoring

In Microsoft adCenter, the minimum bid is $0.05, as of this writing. In YSM, the minimum bid is $0.10. In Google AdWords, the minimum bid is variable and can rise to a very high level. These high minimum bids in Google come from the manner in which Google determines click cost. The bid is a function of competitive bids, of the ad copy, and of the site's relevance and quality to the search terms. Thus, low-quality or low-relevance sites may have to pay very high costs per click even when there is little competition. The high minimum bids for some terms in Google have had a negative impact on affiliate advertisers, made-for-AdSense sites, single-page sites, bridge sites, and others.

 A bridge or doorway site is usually a single-page site. It offers little content of its own, and the sole reason for its existence is to be a gateway to the real site being marketed. Bridge sites began to spring up because they provided a way for a company to have multiple PPC listings for a set of terms.

Because minimum bids can vary widely, counting the number of advertisers bidding on a keyword will not necessarily provide a gauge of the level of competition. The existence of fewer advertisers might mean that a keyword tends to require high minimum bids and is therefore still competitive.

For the content network, Quality Scores determine the minimum CPC required to compete in an auction for specific sites. It is important to have highly themed keywords and ad text. For the search network, Google bases minimum bids on keyword-ad text relevance and landing page quality. For an outline of a high-quality landing page, visit Google's help center at *https://adwords.google.com/select/siteguidelines.html*. We discuss landing pages in more detail later in this chapter.

After making changes to ad text and landing pages, advertisers might still find that their minimum bids are too high. Some keywords do not perform well across campaigns for PPC. Google uses this information to estimate minimum bids. Non-commercial general queries might not get low enough minimum bids to make them perform well in an AdWords campaign.

Differences in minimum bids affect the profitability of Google AdWords compared to Microsoft adCenter and YSM. Keywords that might be too general to bid on in Google AdWords might still be feasible for YSM and adCenter because of lower minimum bids. AdWords' minimum bids can also raise the costs of highly specific terms that have little competition. In adCenter and YSM, you might not bid on very specific keyword phrases because they won't receive enough traffic to make it worth your time. In AdWords, you might not bid on the terms because they cost too much.

Summary of the Differences Among AdWords, adCenter, and YSM

As a more evolved system, Google AdWords sets the standard for other PPC programs. AdWords offers a larger set of management tools and has targeting options that are more refined. Anyone who is able to optimize an AdWords campaign effectively ought to be able to manage a Microsoft adCenter or Yahoo! campaign as well. The rest of this chapter will focus on PPC optimization geared largely toward Google AdWords.

Goal Setting, Measurement, Analytics Support, and Closing the Loop

Creating an optimized campaign starts by setting appropriate goals. Before setting up ad groups and bidding on keywords, an advertiser needs to understand ROI, come up with a plan for converting visitors, and set a budget. Setting boundaries for spending and creating a plan for making the greatest use of your budget will save you headaches later.

Calculating Return on Investment

Advertisers who use PPC need to understand the concept of ROAS or ROI. In contrast to more traditional forms of marketing, PPC provides metrics for tracking campaign performance to a high level of detail. Setting goals and assigning a value to those goals allows you to track costs and values. The equation for ROI is as follows:

$$ROI = [(value - cost) / cost] * 100\%$$

To achieve a positive ROI, you must pick reasonable goals, assign values to those goals, and create a system for achieving those goals.

Goals and Values

It is very easy to generate a large number of impressions and clicks without seeing any results. To avoid this, first define the actions that you want your visitors to take on your site. Typical business goals include:

* Branding or driving awareness of the site or product
* Driving online transactions
* Building relationships

Tasks associated with those goals might be subscribing to a newsletter or RSS feed, placing an order or requesting a quote, or completing a contact form. Then you need to quantify the value of each of these "conversion" types. AdWords offers separate conversion-tracking scripts for several types of goals, such as a purchase/sale, lead, signup, page view, and other goals. These roughly correspond to visitors at different stages of the buying cycle, and they deserve different values.

 AdWords allows advertisers to set static or dynamic conversion values in conversion tracking scripts. You can then retrieve revenue information about your conversions by running a report in the AdWords interface that opts to include value information for conversion columns.

Tracking and Metrics

You should track the success of all PPC elements through website analytics and conversion tracking. Google offers a free analytics program called Google Analytics. With it you can track multiple campaigns and get separate data for organic and paid listings. Whatever tracking program you use, you have to be careful to keep track of performance metrics correctly.

The first step in optimizing a PPC campaign is to use appropriate metrics. Profitable campaigns with equally valued conversions might be optimized to:

- Reduce the CPC given the same (or greater) click volume and conversion rates.
- Increase the CTR given the same (or a greater) number of impressions and the same (or better) conversion rates.
- Increase conversion rates given the same (or a greater) number of clicks.
- Reduce the cost per conversion given the same (or a greater) number of conversions.
- Increase profits in general by varying multiple metrics. Increasing profits might mean improving one metric at the expense of another controlling metric. For example, you might reduce the CPC and it might also reduce the click volume, but overall the result should be increased profits.

Notice that conversion metrics are included in all of the methods for optimizing a campaign. Tracking conversions is challenging. Uncertainty in conversion tracking and values makes it difficult to optimize a campaign, apart from diagnosing obvious problems with the setup of the campaign. If you do not track the sources of conversions in your site, your optimization methods will be approximate, less competitive, and less remunerative.

Closing the Loop

Closing the loop refers to making use of different stages of the sales cycle to produce a lead or sale, or to develop a relationship with a visitor that might lead to sales in the future. The buying cycle has three stages: (1) forming a perception, (2) researching, and (3) buying. With a good sales team and customer relationship management, much of the process of closing the loop occurs offline. The effort, however, begins online with effective targeting. Campaigns with a high ROI are effective in closing the loop.

The first steps in closing the loop are as follows:

1. Properly target the campaigns.
2. Create ad text that qualifies visitors.
3. Send visitors to the most relevant landing page or to a custom landing page.

Targeting and qualifying visitors

Visitors from PPC ads signal their interest through the queries they use, the sites they visit, the language they employ (e.g., French, German, or Chinese), and the location from which they search. PPC gives advertisers unique opportunities to target a range of visitors with specialized ads and landing pages to close the loop more effectively. Major PPC ad programs allow advertisers to reduce wasted clicks by "targeting" specific user interests and "excluding" disinterested individuals. This refined targeting further increases the potential efficiency of a campaign.

Qualifying visitors who are late in the sales cycle

PPC also provides a unique opportunity to help target visitors who are already at the buying stage. Specific search terms such as model numbers or keywords that have the word *buy* or *sale*, for example, indicate that a visitor is ready to make a purchase.

Relevant landing pages

Using appropriate conversion goals for different visitors helps advertisers close the loop, improving customer acquisition rates. A single landing page may offer multiple conversion opportunities. Alternatively, you can create separate landing pages that are specialized to each type of conversion. The keywords themselves and your initial performance should determine your strategy, although it might take some experimentation.

Your success depends on matching visitor expectations. If they are ready to buy, don't show them a landing page with a free white paper. If visitors are still forming an opinion of your products or services, don't show them a "Buy now" button. PPC is great for direct marketing because visitors reveal information about their interests. Take advantage of the information provided in their keywords.

Closing the loop offline

After making a sale, try to develop a continuing relationship. Offer surveys to your customers, ask permission to inform them of future deals and specials, and notify them about updates and related products. By keeping customers engaged longer, making repeat sales, and creating positive buzz for your company, you increase the value of online conversions. You can then afford to be more competitive with your PPC bidding.

Using Metrics to Set a Budget

To confidently set a budget and start a campaign, you will need to estimate some initial costs and determine a baseline for gauging the success of your start-up campaign. You will also need to define a conversion, determine an average value for a conversion, and establish an average conversion rate.

Estimating Conversion Rates

It takes experience to estimate conversion rates. A site that generates high-value leads might have a conversion rate of around 2%. An e-commerce site will have a higher conversion rate, maybe 6% to 8% depending on the bid terms. A site that makes a free offer will probably have double-digit conversion rates, perhaps around 15%.

For example, let's say your site sells widgets, a classic example of a fake product. On average, the sale of a widget is worth $20 to you. After researching your competition, coming up with a healthy keyword list, and designing a few custom landing pages, you figure a conversion rate of about 6% (see the previous sidebar, "Estimating Conversion Rates"). To break even, you will need to target a cost per conversion of $20, but in your plan you would like it to be less than this so that you will have a positive ROI. You know that you want to generate at least 100 sales per month. So, you will need to generate at least 1,667 clicks per month:

100 conversions * (100 clicks / 6% conversions) = 1,667 clicks

And you will want to keep your budget under $2,000 to gain a positive ROI:

$20 / conversion * 100 conversions = $2,000

To keep the budget under $2,000 you will need an average CPC lower than $1.20:

$2,000 / 1,667 clicks = $1.20

So, you will adjust your campaign to receive 1,667 clicks at a CPC of less than $1.20. When you get started, you may find that this is not possible, so you will redo your calculations. You can use Google's Traffic Estimator (*https://adwords.google.com/select/TrafficEstimatorSandbox*) to see whether these numbers are in the ballpark.

Do not be discouraged if estimates from Google do not align with your expectations. The Traffic Estimator is not precise. It does not include the content network, and it is not good with medium- to low-traffic keywords.

You don't have to do a calculation such as this to get your campaign going. Just knowing the average cost per conversion that you want to aim for to generate a positive ROI puts you ahead of the game.

Return on Investment and Profit

Optimizing a campaign to increase your ROI is a good move, but do not forget the bottom line, which is profit. Some small PPC programs boast a high ROI, but your program will not be an unqualified success if it generates only a few sales per month. Although volume is important, the real bottom-line measurement is profit. You might set bids low to achieve a lower cost per conversion and watch your ROI skyrocket, but this could cause profits to drop. Google allows advertisers to specify the value of conversions in their tracking code. For some keywords, it is worth the time to determine how profits change with ad position and to determine the optimal position for your ad given a specific bid landscape. This is better than targeting a specific cost per conversion that generates a positive ROI. The approximation of ROI is more convenient because markets, ad positions, and query variations under which ads appear are volatile.

Pay-per-Click Return on Investment and Goals Summary

As we mentioned before, the first step in PPC optimization is to choose your goals and come up with a plan for getting visitors to respond accordingly. To maximize ROI, translate each unique goal into a measurable action that a visitor to your site can accomplish. Those actions should be assigned values. The budget of your campaign should be based on the projected value and cost of the goals you define.

Continuing to improve your ability to "close the loop" helps increase the value of online actions and makes your campaign more competitive. This relationship building occurs mainly offline, but properly developing your site and planning a PPC campaign can simplify those efforts.

All of this planning happens before logging on to Google AdWords and looking at your campaigns. The next few sections of this chapter focus on how to optimize the elements of a PPC campaign.

Keyword Discovery, Selection, and Analysis

We'll start with an overview of the types of keywords you will need to consider. See Table 3-1 for a summary of AdWords' keyword matching options.

Table 3-1. AdWords' keyword matching options

Match type	Description	Syntax	Possible matched queries
Broad	Matches queries with the same words, in any order, and possibly with other words. Also might show for singular/plural variations, synonyms, and related terms.	`brown shirts`	`brown shirts`, `shirts brown`, `cool brown shirts`, `brown polo shirts`, `brown shirts cheap`, `brown shirt`
Phrase	Matches queries with the same words in the exact order and possibly other terms before or after (but not in between).	`"brown shirts"`	`brown shirts`, `cool brown shirts`, `brown shirts cheap`

Table 3-1. *AdWords' keyword matching options (continued)*

Match type	Description	Syntax	Possible matched queries
Exact	Matches queries that contain the same words in the exact order without any other words.	[brown shirts]	brown shirts
Negative	Excludes queries that contain the matched term. Can be used with broad, exact, and phrase match.	-brown	Doesn't match any query that contains the word *brown*.

Keyword Research

Keyword research is a lengthy topic in itself. What follows is a brief overview of keyword research and four steps by which an advertiser should proceed.

Step 1: Look through your site and identify major themes

Generate a long list of different root terms. A common mistake is to leave out large portions of your site and to focus only on the main product or service that you offer. Typically, this will lead you to the most competitive terms that you could bid on, and it will not always be profitable for you to bid for top positions for these terms. Many companies are willing to lose money to rank at the top of Google for their primary product or service. If your goal is to make profits, you will need to be more strategic, more thorough, and more creative with your keyword list.

Step 2: Research the competition for your root terms

Evaluating your competition will give you an idea of how much effort it will take to compete. Look at the ad text and landing pages of your competitors. If they are highly specialized to the bid term, you have found a competitive term and should expect to have to match the efforts of your competitors. Some advertisers have employed competitive measures such as the keyword effectiveness index (KEI) to gauge competition. The KEI is the ratio of search traffic to the number of competing websites that appear for a specific term. This is not useful for Google AdWords due to minimum bids. If a keyword does not display many ads (or, more accurately to KEI, if it doesn't have a lot of organic listings), it does not necessarily mean that there is low competition, because the term might require a high minimum bid.

Step 3: Use a keyword research tool to generate variations from your list of root terms

KeywordDiscovery and Wordtracker are two popular research tools that offer free trials. You might also use a thesaurus. KeywordDiscovery and Wordtracker give relative traffic estimates for keywords. These tools don't get enough data to predict traffic on Google. Matching is too complex to calculate how much traffic a broad-matched keyword might see. Traffic estimates from keyword tools are used to calculate how much more traffic you might expect from one keyword relative to another keyword.

If you come up with a keyword variation that shows zero occurrences in the database of a keyword tool, you should still bid on it. Google gets far more traffic than these tools can account for, and if you sense that a term seems like it will get traffic, it actually may.

To generate negative keywords, you should use variations that pop up in a keyword brainstorming tool. Google's Keyword Tool is more useful for this. It is located at *https://adwords.google.com/select/KeywordToolExternal*.

Using Google's Keyword Tool to generate keyword lists from a URI or a list of keywords will show you some of the terms that Google considers to be related to your site. If you see keywords that are not related, add them as negative keywords even if you do not see how the terms you are bidding on might expand to match them. Google's broad match can branch out quite a bit. Generate a healthy list of negative keywords and continue to add to it as your campaign continues.

If you use Google Analytics, manually tag your URIs and leave off the utm_term parameter, instead of using Google's auto-tagging feature. If you do this, reports in Analytics will show the search queries that generated clicks rather than the matched terms that generated clicks. Alternatively, Google offers Search Query Performance reports. These will give an incomplete list of queries that generated clicks for your ads.

Step 4: Choose the right keyword set

Use keyword research tools, a thesaurus, and search queries to generate more root terms that are unique. Search terms that are harder to find will have less competition. AdWords' tool and Wordtracker's Keyword Universe can help you find new terms to target. Refer to Chapter 1 for more details on Wordtracker. Perform searches to find other keywords that competing sites target in their HTML titles and body text. This technique may uncover new terms. Staying on top of industry news and events can help you find new keywords to target. You should continually try to think of new root terms to add to your campaigns.

In the course of your keyword research, you will probably find terms that you are not sure you want to bid on or that you want to block with negative keywords. Instead of doing nothing with these keywords, you should bid on them using a lower maximum CPC than you used for more successful terms. If you do not bid on such a keyword directly and if you do not block it, another broad-matched keyword will probably display ads for it. The performance of the broad-matched keyword might be made worse by the borderline keyword. You can always decide to block borderline keywords later.

Keyword research is one of the more creative aspects of PPC. Typically, you will find that only a small group of terms generates most of the traffic on a site as well as most of the conversions. But discovering those lesser-known terms can benefit your site by providing less expensive clicks.

The Right Keywords and the Myth of the Long Tail

The keywords that perform best in PPC advertising are unique commercial keywords with high search demand. A unique keyword is one that does not contain a popular root term. These unique keywords have less competition than more general terms. They have a high value. Competition for these keywords will be lower because broad-matched terms will not usually show ads for them.

Sometimes when reading about PPC you will encounter the term *long tail*. Although a few keywords may get a large number of searches, many other keywords get only a few searches each, yet may add up to a significant number of searches. These are called long tail keywords and some have high conversion rates. However, long tail keyword phrases are less useful for PPC and more useful for search engine optimization (SEO) because of broad matching in PPC. You don't need to bid on every keyword variation that you can think of in your PPC campaign. AdWords will automatically show your ads for popular variations of your terms that fit your ads and targeting. Terms without a search history will not show ads because they have "low search volume." Bidding on them makes your campaign bulkier and more difficult to manage.

Target part and model numbers

You will, however, want to bid on long tail terms such as locations, part numbers, and model numbers. Typically, model numbers are unique keywords that will not be covered by a broad match. Terms with locations properly narrow the targeting of your keywords (e.g., "small business new york"). You will also want to expand from one- or two-keyword phrases. However, adding filler words to three- or four-keyword phrases to generate a new, low-traffic term is unnecessary.

Broad matches versus direct bidding

You should not rely too heavily on broad matching. Broad matching will usually build from a root term, but it can also use synonyms and terms that are more general than your current keyword phrases. Bidding directly on a keyword phrase improves the chances that your ads will show for that term. For example, if you were bidding on the term *small business idea*, it will probably expand to show for a term such as *best small business idea* (these keyword terms are in italics instead of in quotes because quoted terms are phrase-matched in AdWords; this section discusses only broad match). If you are bidding on *small business*, it too might show ads for *small business idea* or for *best small business idea*. You probably would not want to take the chance that your ad would not show, and you would at least bid on *small business* and *small business idea*.

You want to bid on different keyword variations if you think broad matching will not cover them or if you think they will have different conversion rates or CTRs. If the terms have different conversion rates or CTRs, you will want to set different bids.

This can mean using overlapping matching for the same term. For example, if you were bidding on the term *small business*, you could reasonably expect that *small business* and variations of that term would perform differently. You might bid on [small business] and "small business," as well as on the broad-matched variation. The more restrictive match type for a specific query will always show the ad. Bidding on both the exact match and phrase match variations will allow you to track the performance of each variation separately and to set bids separately.

Avoid adding duplicate keywords to your AdWords campaign because they will compete against each other, and the term with the higher CPC will show ads. In addition, duplicate keywords make tracking the success of keywords more difficult. The Find Duplicate Keywords link under the Tools menu in AdWords Editor helps you find duplicate keywords in your campaign (see Figure 3-3).

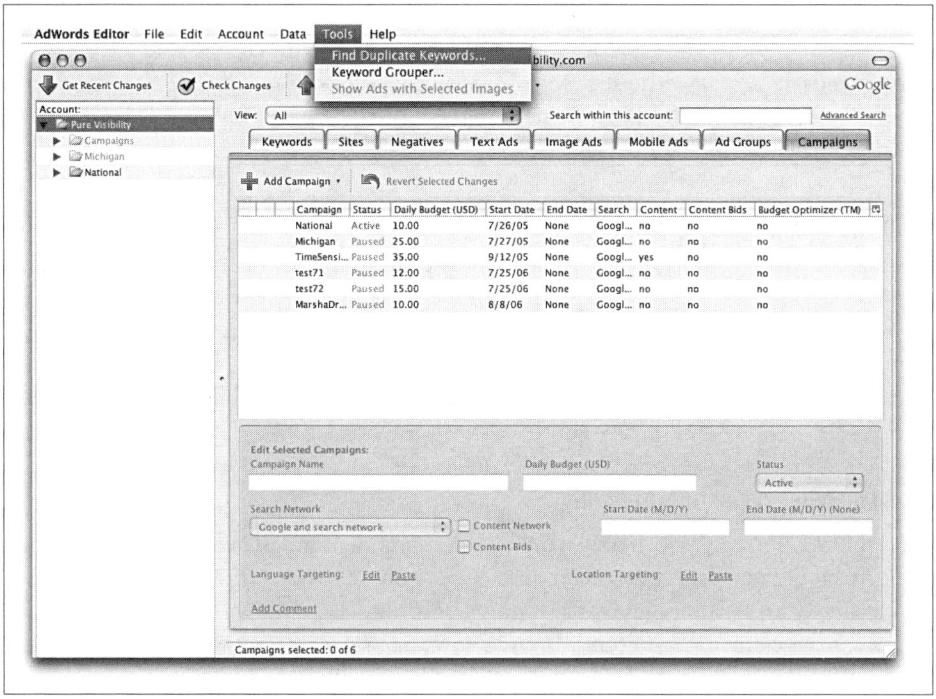

Figure 3-3. AdWords Editor's Find Duplicate Keywords tool

When searching for duplicates, you will want to find keywords, in any word order, that have the same match type. Whether or not you want to look in the same campaign or across all campaigns will depend on your account setup. Duplicate keywords that are targeted to different geographical regions are not a problem. Once you complete your search, you can select duplicate terms, delete them, and post the changes to your account (see Figure 3-4).

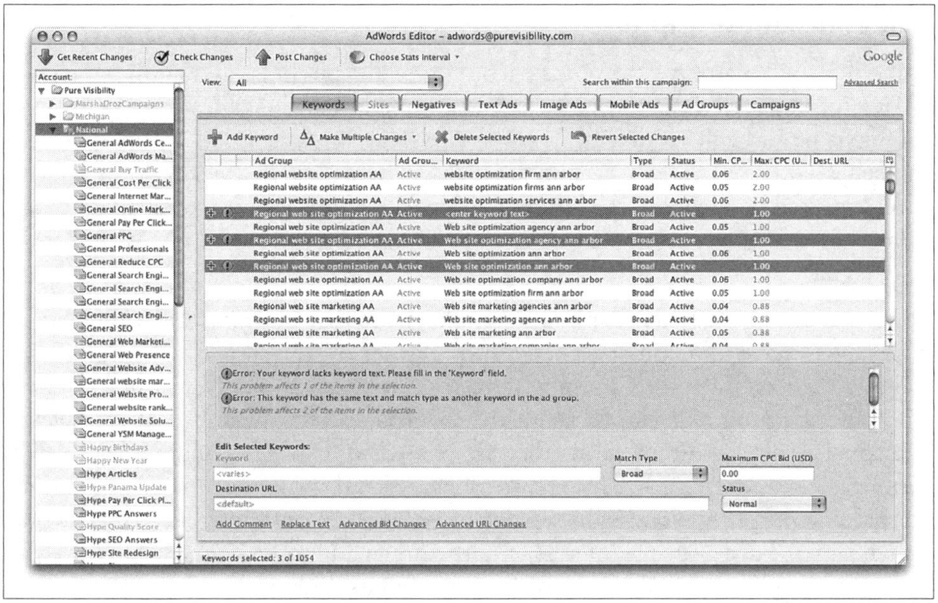

Figure 3-4. Selecting and deleting duplicate keywords

Keyword phrases that are more general in nature typically determine the success level of a PPC campaign. "Tricks" such as bidding on model numbers or very specific product terms are no longer secrets. Unique terms with high search demand and low minimum bids are so difficult to find that you will probably get more benefit by just using a large keyword list, setting smart goals, and making smart bids.

Organizing and Optimizing Ad Groups

Once you have generated your list of keywords, the next step is to organize them into groups. An *ad group* is a set of related keywords and keyword phrases. Grouping ads together helps organize what can be a lengthy list of keywords and phrases into groups or sets of related ads for easier management.

A focused, themed ad group has many advantages. Perhaps most important is that it enables you to write very specific ads for well-focused ad groups. All of the keywords in an ad group can have the same ad copy. The performance of each keyphrase affects the quality and determines the CPC for others in the group. Therefore, the ability to judge the right level of grouping is a useful skill. Many writers on PPC strategy emphasize grouping and regrouping keywords and keyphrases as the main optimization strategy. We think that grouping should be one component of optimization, not the entire focus.

Guidelines for Grouping

You will want to group your terms according to theme, bids, and common words. During the keyword discovery phase, some groupings may become apparent but others might be difficult to determine. One easy way to develop ad groups is to ask yourself what types of ads you can write that will best describe the keywords in question. A general guideline for ad groups is *smaller groups are better*. A unique keyword should be placed in its own separate ad group so that you can write a well-targeted ad.

Ad groups can be themed according to root keywords, by meaning, or by the phrases that they all have in common. They can be further organized according to bidding and landing page themes. Grouping terms that perform similarly will make setting bids easier because bids can be set at the ad group level rather than at the level of individual terms. Grouping terms that are related to a specific landing page makes performance easier to track. This allows for aggregated tracking at the ad group level. For bidding purposes, you might separate general terms with low bids, or keywords for which you have a special interest, into their own ad groups. This makes it easy to see report data in the AdWords interface and to adjust bids at the ad group level.

Example Themed Ad Groups

A *themed ad group* is a set of ads that target a specific group of keywords. The campaign can be broken down or "themed" into discrete keyphrase groups. AdWords Editor offers a Keyword Grouper in the Tools section on the main menu bar (see Figure 3-5). It shows how you might divide ad groups according to common keywords and makes the divisions for you automatically.

The following is a sample keyword list for a site for Dog Day Care:

```
dog day care
doggy day care
puppy daycare
canine boarding
dog boarding
dog kennel
puppy kenneling
dog grooming
dog training
puppy training
dog obedience training
canine behavioral work
puppy grooming
```

If you were to put these keywords into AdWords in one ad group and set the maximum CPC at $1.00, you could have poor results, for a couple of reasons. First, you would be forced to write an ad that encompasses all of these keywords. If the ad did not directly relate to each keyword, your Quality Score would be lowered. This would give your ads a lower rank.

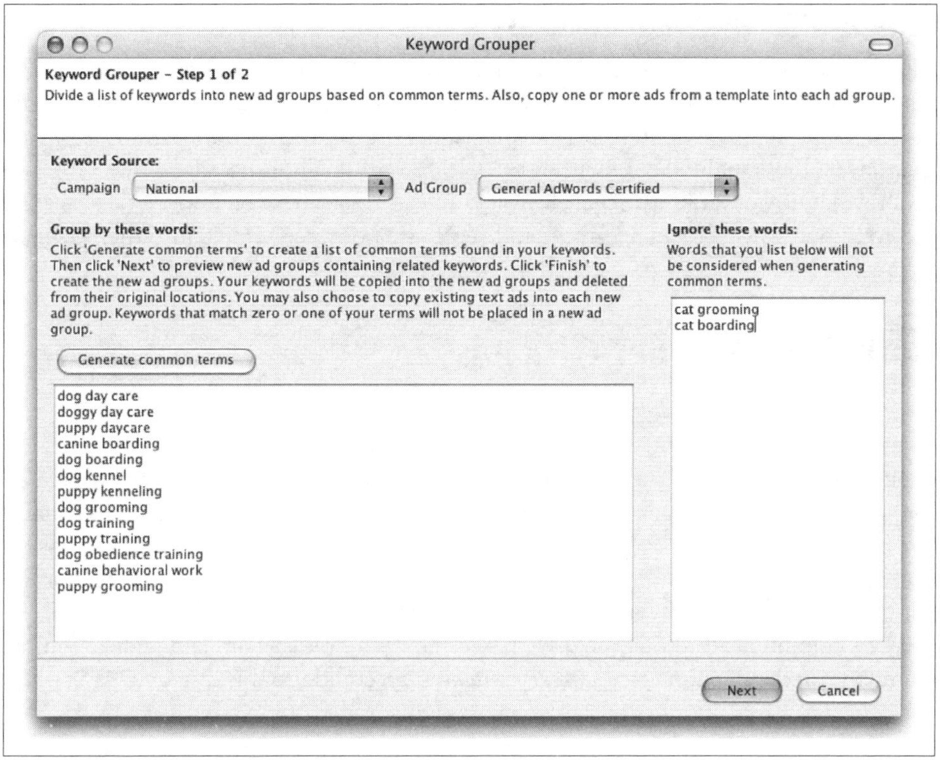

Figure 3-5. AdWords Editor's Keyword Grouper

Second, setting an ad group bid is not a good strategy when you have many different unrelated keywords. In this case, the only bid strategy that is cost-effective is to set individual bids on the keyword level. Setting bids on the keyword level can be easy when you have only a few keywords, as in the preceding example. If you have a much larger list of keywords, however, setting and maintaining individual bids could be very time-consuming. A better strategy is to put keywords into smaller themed groups, such as these:

Day care
   Dog day care, doggy day care, puppy daycare

Boarding
   Canine boarding, dog boarding

Kennels
   Dog kennel, puppy kenneling

Training
   Dog training, puppy training, dog obedience training, canine behavioral work

Grooming
   Dog grooming, puppy grooming

Optimizing Ad Groups After Launch

After you have launched your campaign and have some statistical information about your keywords and ads, you can start to optimize your ad groups. Because Google uses Quality Scores to determine ad placements, grouping is important. Keywords that have a low Quality Score within Google can cause all of the ads in that group to be shown at lower rankings regardless of your bids. So, it can be important to review the components within an ad group and segregate poor performers into their own ad groups.

Optimizing Pay-per-Click Ads

A PPC ad is made up of five parts: the title, two description lines, a display URI, and a destination URI. The title introduces the ad and captures the attention of a search engine user. It repeats keywords and is as specific as possible to the user's query. Use the description lines to communicate the benefit and tell the visitor what to do and what to expect once the site has been reached (i.e., a call to action). Typically, ads do not waste characters on company names, unless branding is an important goal for the company or unless the key terms are trademark terms. Instead, the display URI can be used to communicate the company's name. For example, a company called Sample Company on the domain *www.samplecompany.com* could use this display URI:

    SampleCompany.com

It could also put in other relevant parts of the URI that fit. For example, if Sample Company was bidding on "sample product" and its destination URI was *http://www.samplecompany.com/sampleproduct/*, its display URI could look like this:

    www.SampleCompany.com/SampleProduct/

Capitalize the first letters of the company name in the display URI. Keywords in landing page destination URIs add even more emphasis. Just make sure they will fit in the space allotted.

Ads shouldn't be repetitive and make unverified superlative claims. The description lines should state a benefit that is informational, unique, and easy to read. A good ad will incorporate many of the keywords from its ad group. Recognizing keywords in the ad increases the likelihood that a user will click on the ad. Search engine users typically skim ads, so you should try to be concise, and use short, suitable, action-oriented words. For example, if Sample Company was selling a product that takes a long time to manufacture and get out the door, and it focuses on a fast turnaround, it might be tempted to write a description line that reads as follows:

    Fast Turnaround Sample Products.

But a better description line would be:

    Get Sample Products in Two Days.

This description states a benefit ("two-day delivery"), is less generic, and has a call to action, while not being too pushy ("Get"). The description could have a more specific call to action. If a company is trying to generate leads, the landing page should have a contact form and a phone number. The phone number can be put directly into the ad. Note, however, that Microsoft adCenter doesn't allow this. In that case, Sample Company might use this call to action:

```
Call 800-555-5555 for a Free Quote.
```

The description should use action phrases such as "buy now," "learn more," "get info," "compare prices," and so on. It should also try to give visitors a reason to perform the action immediately. Our final ad for Sample Company might look like this:

```
Custom Sample Products
Get Sample Products in Two Days.
Call 800-555-5555 for a Free Quote.
SampleCompany.com/SampleProduct/
```

Poorly written ads often suffer from overly generic text. They lack stated benefits, have no call to action, and use language that does not click with search engine users. Ads that are not well coordinated don't send visitors to the most relevant landing page. Our Custom Sample Products ad might sound generic because of the nature of the example, but it exhibits the following useful features:

States a benefit
Get your products in only two days.

Has a call to action
Call the 800 number to get a quote.

Gives a reason to request a quote
It's free!

Uses a relevant landing page
It uses a page about "sample products."

Tempts search engine users
It promises to be fast and inexpensive, which everybody likes.

The Custom Sample Products ad managed to repeat the user's query a few times. This might be overdoing it. An advertiser using this ad might test other titles that use variations on the keyword sample products. Testing and measuring ad performance helps to further optimize PPC campaigns.

Measuring Ad Performance

The convention for measuring an ad's success is to use CTR. Although CTR may not be the best metric for maximizing profits, it is the easiest one to use. Ad text can influence conversion rates. Sometimes advertisers purposely reduce their CTR by using ad text that filters out unqualified clicks and improves conversion rates. For example, an ad might list starting prices if a lot of potential PPC visitors are looking for low-priced products and if the advertiser's products are expensive. To take into account varying conversion rates, advertisers might use the following profit-per-impression equation to help decide which ads are performing best:

Profit per impression = [(value / conversion) * conversion rate * CTR] – (CPC * CTR)

This works only if the value per conversion is constant or can be averaged for all types of conversions. However, because most advertisers use CTR to optimize ads and because it is a good approximate measure for ad performance, that's what we will discuss here.

Optimizing Ad Copy

Tests to get the best ad copy can be broken down into two phases: first, identifying the variation in the ad copy that you want to measure, and second, identifying the tools you'll use to measure which variation works better.

Advertisers should then test these multiple ads to fine-tune campaigns and find out what works.

Creating ad copy variation

Ad copy is better or worse relative to other ads. Basically, any measurement is made relative to another ad that is used with the same keyphrases and, if possible, the same landing page.

To measure these differences you have to vary the ad copy systematically. The different strategies could fill a chapter on their own, but optimizing ad copy uses subtle changes in the fundamentals of PPC ad copy writing described earlier in this chapter, in "Optimizing Pay-per-Click Ads." These changes include:

Incorporating a different call to action
> For example, instead of "Request a Quote," you might try "Request More Info" or "Download Our White Paper." One action might result in greater acquisition rates than another.

Listing various benefits
> You might try out different deals—"free shipping" or "10% off orders over $100"—and see which works best for your ads. It's easy to make generic ads that don't list benefits. These ads don't perform as well. If the ad describes a service, at least highlight a particular aspect of the service that might appeal to or qualify a visitor—"Made in the USA" or "Serving Southeast Michigan" are examples.

Changing emphasis
> By rearranging the title and description lines, the copy of your ad can appeal to different aspects of the sale. For example, if your site offers free shipping, you might want to highlight that in the title line rather than in the second description line. This will attract greater attention and increase CTRs.

Wording, punctuation, and capitalization

AdWords allows you to use one exclamation mark in your ad. You can also capitalize the first letter of each word in your ad description. For example, instead of writing:

"Free trial for first-time buyers."

you might try:

"Free Trial for First-Time Buyers!"

or:

"First-time buyers get a Free trial."

Testing ads the easy way: AdWords optimized ad serving

Advertisers should test multiple ads to fine-tune campaigns and find out what is effective. For this purpose, AdWords offers optimized ad serving. This means advertisers can circulate multiple ads at once and Google will automatically start to circulate "better-performing" ads more frequently. In this approach, AdWords optimizes performance automatically, based on a performance algorithm developed by Google.

The problem with optimized ad serving is that it is not sufficiently sensitive to random variation. In other words, one ad can often get ahead completely by chance. Such an ad will appear more frequently than the others and this can skew performance data. It is possible to have ads with identical ad copy circulating at different rates because one was "outperforming" the other!

In general, avoid circulating better-performing ads more frequently, especially in the middle of an experiment. To optimize your ad group, you want to decide which ad has the better CTR as soon as possible and circulate that ad 100% of the time.

Testing ads the hard way: Confidence interval testing

When testing ads, it is important to:

1. Have a controlled experiment where ads circulate "at the same time." By "at the same time," we mean they are rotated evenly throughout the day. Choose the Rotate ad-serving feature rather than the Optimize feature in AdWords.

2. Make sure ads circulate at a similar average position. Average positions can vary because competition and bidding vary. Broad-matched terms in particular might show ads for queries that have different levels of competition.

3. Have enough data to make a judgment with high statistical certainty. This is huge!

Point 3 requires a bit of math. This can look a little daunting, but once you understand the goal, it becomes a matter of plugging in the right numbers. You are trying to figure out whether one ad is performing better than another, or whether it's just too close to call. It is impossible to be 100% certain that one ad is better than another.

The best you can do is say that you are 99% or 95% confident that one ad is actually performing better than the other one.

Clicks on PPC ads can be treated as a binomial distribution (even though in the strictest sense they are not because a single impression in AdWords can generate multiple clicks). Each ad has a separate distribution, and you can specify a confidence interval for the difference in each distribution. For the confidence interval that you specify, you can calculate a margin of error for the mean proportion of each distribution (the mean proportion is the ad's CTR). If the margin of error shows that the difference between the proportions is either less than or greater than zero, you can be confident, up to the interval you specified, that there is a difference in the average CTRs of each ad. Given two ads being tested, here is the math.

For a $(1 - \alpha)100\%$ confidence interval for $(p_1 - p_2)$:

$$(p_1 - p_2) \pm Z_{\alpha/2}\sqrt{p_1 q_1/n_1 + p_2 q_2/n_2}$$

For the purposes of ad testing:

I = impressions
CTR = click-through rate
C = clicks

And:

$p_1 = CTR_1$
$p_2 = CTR_2$
$q_1 = 1 - CTR_1$
$q_2 = 1 - CTR_2$
$n_1 = I_1 = C_1 / CTR_1$
$n_2 = I_2 = C_2 / CTR_2$
$Z_{\alpha/2}$ = the z-value corresponding to an area $\alpha/2$ in the tail of a standard normal distribution

For 99% confidence:

$Z_{\alpha/2} = 2.58$

For 95% confidence:

$Z_{\alpha/2} = 1.96$

The final equation for ad testing is:

$$(CTR_1 - CTR_2) \pm Z_{\alpha/2}\sqrt{CTR_1^2(1 - CTR_1)/C_1 + CTR_2^2(1 - CTR_2)/C_2}$$

This formula applies for a large sample where the number of clicks on each ad is greater than 5. If the interval contains 0, you cannot be confident that the CTRs of the ads are not equal.

As an example, say you had two ads that have been circulating for a while with different titles and you want to know whether you can be 99% confident that the ads are performing differently. Both ads are showing in about the same average position, optimized ad serving is turned off, and they have been circulating at the same time. You get the following data.

For the first ad:

$C_1 = 60$ (the ad received 60 clicks)
$CTR_1 = .030$ (the CTR was 3%)

For the second ad:

$C_2 = 40$ (the ad received 40 clicks)
$CTR_2 = .020$ (the CTR was 2%)

You calculate the confidence interval using these numbers:

$$(0.03 - 0.02) \pm 2.58\sqrt{0.03^2(1 - 0.03)/60 + 0.02^2(1 - 0.02)/40}$$
$$= 0.010 \pm 0.013 = (0.023, -0.003)$$

Because the confidence interval goes from positive to negative, it contains zero. Therefore, you cannot be 99% certain that these ads do not have the same CTR.

You want to know whether you can be 95% certain, so you put in 1.96 for the z-factor:

$$(0.03 - 0.02) \pm 1.96\sqrt{0.03^2(1 - 0.03)/60 + 0.02^2(1 - 0.02)/40}$$
$$= 0.010 \pm 0.0097 = (0.0197, 0.0003)$$

Because the confidence interval is always positive, you can be 95% certain that these ads have different CTRs. You should delete the second ad and go with the first.

If you are testing ads with identical ad text and want to optimize for conversion rates, you can use this same equation. You would substitute conversion rates for CTRs and conversions for clicks.

Both 95% and 99% certainty are good rules of thumb. When circulating identical ads in AdWords, it would be unusual to get CTRs between these intervals after 30 or 40 clicks on each ad, but you might see 80% to 85%.

Beware of unreliable testing results on the Web. They are everywhere! Another myth about PPC is that you should never stop testing your ads. If you find ad text that works, and you find that the changes you make keep having a negative effect on performance, you should stop testing. Run the ad that works by itself.

Dynamic Keyword Insertion in Ads

Dynamic keyword insertion (DKI) gets a section of its own because all the major PPC programs offer some variation of it, and because it is popular to use in large campaigns.

Besides loading ad text with keywords, you can use DKI for tracking URIs and for generating dynamic landing pages. DKI automatically inserts a matched term into the text of an ad or into a destination URI. If the matched term does not fit in the space allotted, AdWords will substitute a default term that you specify. For example, if you are bidding on "buying blue widgets" and a bunch of terms related to "blue widgets" in the same ad group, you might put this in the title of your ad:

```
{keyword:blue widget sale}
```

If someone searches "buying blue widgets" or a matched variation of "buying blue widgets," your title will appear as follows:

```
buying blue widgets
```

If you wrote your title as:

```
buy {keyword:blue widgets} now
```

and someone searched "buying blue widgets," your title would appear as:

```
buy blue widgets now
```

because "buying blue widgets" does not fit in the space allowed for the title, and it's a good thing because that title doesn't make sense. Other variations of the DKI syntax that vary in capitalization include:

Keyword
Capitalizes the first word and leaves all other terms in lowercase (e.g., `Sample term`)

KeyWord
Capitalizes the first letter of each word (e.g., `Sample Term`)

KEYWord
Puts the first word in uppercase and capitalizes the first letter of all other words (e.g., `SAMPLE Term`)

KEYWORD
Puts the whole phrase in uppercase (e.g., `SAMPLE TERM`)

If you do not use these properly, editors will reject your ad (especially the last variation). You can also put the keyword into the destination URI. For example:

```
http://www.example.com/?{keyword}
```

AdWords automatically escapes spaces in the matched term with "%20." You might use keywords in the destination URL for tracking or to insert the matched term into a title on your landing page. A large site might use it to initiate a site search to find the most relevant products or content.

For tracking purposes, you can also use this syntax in your destination URI:

```
source={ifsearch:GoogleAdWordsSearch}{ifcontent:
GoogleAdWordsContent}
```

This tracks whether a click came from the search network or from a content network. You might use a third-party tracking program and change the settings to recognize the source of clicks.

Pay-per-Click Ad Optimization Summary

To optimize PPC campaigns with major ad groups, you should test multiple ads to find the text and landing pages that work best for a group of keywords. Write ads specific to your keywords. Write unique ads that initiate action by highlighting benefits. Consider DKI to repeat keywords in the ad text for ads that circulate for a large number of related phrases that contain variable keywords. You can also use DKI for tracking or creating dynamic landing pages. Ads should work together with keywords and landing pages. They should all reinforce one another.

Optimizing Landing Pages

Landing pages are custom-designed to convert visitors. AdWords evaluates them to determine minimum bids. Low-quality landing pages can indicate a low-quality site. Some advertisers have claimed that they saw their minimum bids decrease after moving their landing pages into a well-established site. Landing pages do not determine ad rank.

Overall, Google's move to set minimum bids using landing page quality had wide-ranging effects, including affiliate advertisers, made-for-AdSense sites, single-page sites, and bridge sites. They've had an impact on other advertisers as well, particularly on those bidding on very specific or very general keywords. Minimum bids also affected those sites with designs that are not visible to search engine spiders—for example, Flash designs. The landing page quality score from Google made it impossible for these types of advertisers to be profitable because the level of the minimum bids required is now higher.

Landing Pages for AdWords

AdWords provides general guidelines for creating a high-quality landing page, at *https://adwords.google.com/select/siteguidelines.html*.

You should provide substantial and unique content directly related to a visitor's original query. In other words:

- Use a content-rich landing page. Do more than simply display other ads or lead visitors directly to a contact or sign-up form.

- Be original. Do not simply mirror the content and appearance of another site.

- When asking for personal information, provide a privacy policy.

- Link to other pages in your site that explain more about your business and its products and services.

- Use some basic SEO principles to make your site visible to search engine spiders and to help spiders see that your pages are relevant to the keywords. In particular, put keywords and related variations into HTML titles and the landing page copy. Also consider building links to the page with keywords in the text of the links.

AdWords provides a keyword tool that will generate a list of terms from a URI that you supply. You can use this tool to see whether the AdWords spider will deem your landing page relevant to your keywords. AdWords will also show a Quality Score column for your keywords. To find it, go to the ad group view, click "Customize columns," and select Show Quality Score (see Figure 3-6). Consider placing keywords with low Quality Scores into separate ad groups along with more specific ad text and a specialized landing page. If a new keyword has a poor Quality Score but is otherwise closely related to keywords in your ad group that have great Quality Scores, you might wait to see whether CTRs on the new keyword raise its score.

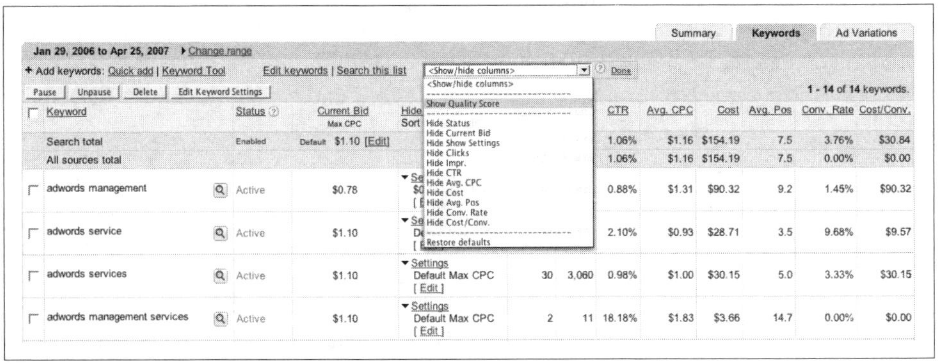

Figure 3-6. The Quality Score column in AdWords

Landing Pages for Visitors

Landing pages are supposed to be goal-oriented and focused on the visitor's original query. It often makes sense to pick out pages that are already in a website (e.g., in a large shopping site). You will usually want to make custom pages specifically for PPC and test out variations of those pages. See Figure 3-7 for a sample landing page.

A good landing page has titles with keywords that focus the page on a particular theme.

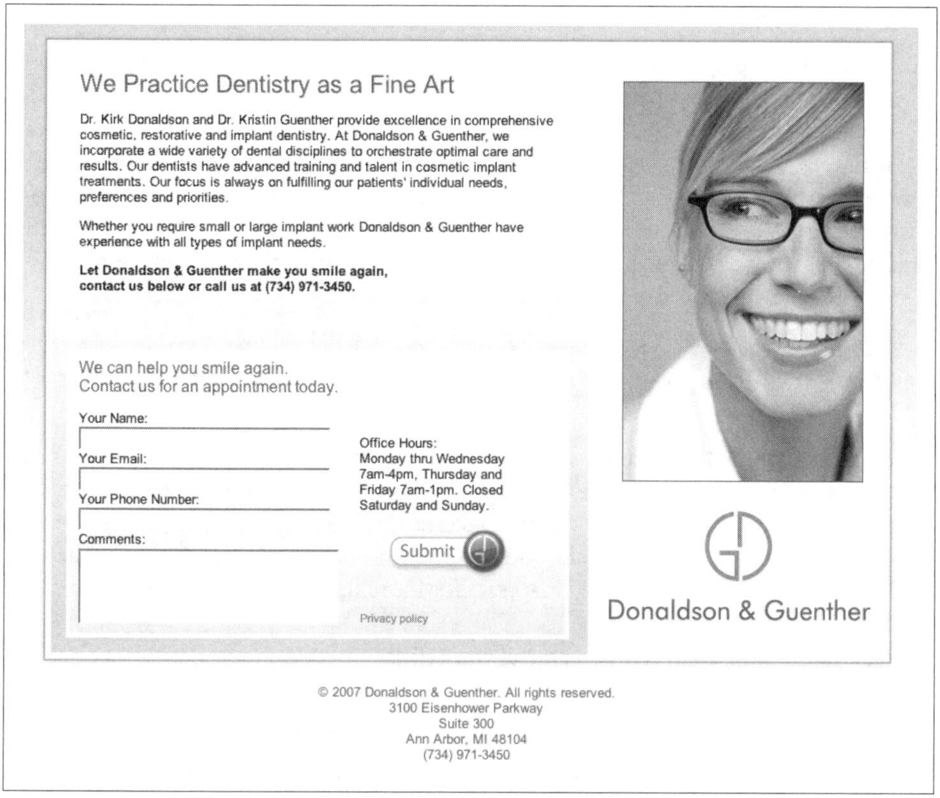

We Practice Dentistry as a Fine Art

Dr. Kirk Donaldson and Dr. Kristin Guenther provide excellence in comprehensive cosmetic, restorative and implant dentistry. At Donaldson & Guenther, we incorporate a wide variety of dental disciplines to orchestrate optimal care and results. Our dentists have advanced training and talent in cosmetic implant treatments. Our focus is always on fulfilling our patients' individual needs, preferences and priorities.

Whether you require small or large implant work Donaldson & Guenther have experience with all types of implant needs.

Let Donaldson & Guenther make you smile again, contact us below or call us at (734) 971-3450.

We can help you smile again.
Contact us for an appointment today.

Your Name:

Your Email:

Office Hours:
Monday thru Wednesday
7am-4pm, Thursday and
Friday 7am-1pm. Closed
Saturday and Sunday.

Your Phone Number:

Comments:

Submit

Privacy policy

Donaldson & Guenther

© 2007 Donaldson & Guenther. All rights reserved.
3100 Eisenhower Parkway
Suite 300
Ann Arbor, MI 48104
(734) 971-3450

Figure 3-7. A sample PPC landing page

Break out sections of the landing page with different titles. Use a similar strategy for ad titles. Keep the language simple and easy to scan, and highlight benefits of your product or service.

Complete conversions with clear calls to action

Examples of good calls to action include a well-labeled button, a link that addresses the user's needs, or a contact form right on the landing page. You don't have to shout at the visitor. In fact, putting in flashing links, obtrusive pop ups, or other distracting images or text that does not fit the site's design may cause a visitor to reject the offer. People tend to filter out and ignore such annoying advertising.

Always include a company phone number on your landing pages. Consider adding help links if the conversion process is complicated. If your site is trying to generate form leads, request only the most necessary information in your form fields.

Use persuasive copy

Don't be afraid to use long copy. Longer copy can result in better-qualified leads. Simply putting a contact form on a page with a paragraph of copy might lead to a lot of time-consuming contacts from visitors who are looking for information which could have been included in your site or from visitors who are not really interested in your products or services. If a visitor is interested, she will want her questions answered. She will take the time to find the information. If your copy is lengthy, include in it multiple points where a visitor can decide whether to execute a conversion without having to skim the rest of the page.

Keep your content easy to scan. Break it up into clearly labeled sections. Include bullet points, use bold type, and make sure the fonts you use are large enough to be easily read.

Highlight the points that differentiate you from your competitors. If appropriate, include positive testimonials, reviews, and case studies that show the superiority of your product or service. Address visitor concerns and try to get feedback from the visitors who do contact you. If certain issues come up often, you might address them in the landing page on your site. See Chapter 5 for more tips on writing persuasive copy.

Support the ad claims that triggered the visitor's click

Landing pages should be directly relevant to the text of an ad. They work together with ads to generate conversions. The landing page might also have a URI that is short and that includes keywords so that it fits in an ad's "display URL" field.

Include multiple conversion points for different stages of the buying cycle

In addition to a buy button or a quote request, landing pages can have a newsletter sign-up, a free white paper, a catalog request, a sign-up to become a member of a company's forum, or some other device designed to keep the conversation going with visitors. Some visitors are not ready to make a purchase or aren't quite sure your company is right for them, but they are willing to give you their email address. Including a secondary call to action keeps the dialog going.

Display large images of products or services

Exhibiting a large, detailed image of your product is the easiest way to communicate what you are selling. Images that follow a certain theme can also quickly establish context.

Forgo navigation menus

You want to keep visitors on your landing page as long as possible. That is where the most relevant content is for their query. If they click on your ad and see other navigation links, they might click away, get lost in other parts of your site, and leave.

Yet, you should still include footer links to your home page, your privacy policy, and other relevant pages in your site. These are for visitors who read through your landing page content and haven't found what they were looking for.

Check out the landing pages of your competitors. If a competitor has been advertising on Google for a long time, their landing pages are probably working well for them. You do not need to duplicate their efforts, but you should note what strategies they employ and attempt to provide something better for your landing pages.

Testing Landing Pages

Test landing pages to improve conversion rates. This brings up another testing issue: conversion rates are not the same as acquisition rates.

One kind of landing page might have a lower conversion rate, but its customer acquisition rate might be equal to or greater than a landing page with a higher conversion rate because it generates leads that are of a higher quality. The assumption behind conversion rate optimization (CRO) is that conversion rates and acquisition rates are proportional at a constant value across landing pages. If you get lost in conversion statistics, you might forget this fact and design a page that is not specific enough about your business to result in sales.

Titles, images, and copy might all be tested with different versions of landing pages. An easy way to perform A/B split testing (i.e., testing one variation against another) using one landing page is to use a tool such as Google's Website Optimizer (*http:// www.google.com/websiteoptimizer*). The Website Optimizer randomizes titles, images, and copy within the template of the landing page. This tool provides a quick overview of the combinations that have the highest conversion rates. In addition to landing page A/B testing, you can circulate a couple of ads with the same ad text but with different destination URIs. Then you can compare conversion rates directly. If your site does not receive a large number of conversions, you do not want to test a lot of landing page variations all at once. It will take too long to get enough data to see what works. Unless the pages perform very differently, you should expect somewhere around 40 conversions on each landing page before you can make a good statistical judgment.

You also can test different conversion strategies. For example, you could test a landing page that focuses on acquiring more information through a white paper rather than a page that focuses on requesting a quote. This test may require different ad text which will increase the complexity of your testing because it affects both CTRs and conversion rates. In addition, both types of conversions will have different values, one of which might not be well defined. A white paper request would most likely require a longer sales cycle. To properly track the success of these types of ads, you will need to track leads over a long period, and then compare the costs of the two types of ads with the sales that resulted.

Testing ads is not easy; testing landing pages is even more challenging. Keep in mind that landing page experiments usually take more time. Sometimes, though, if you get lucky, you will find a little change that makes a significant impact on conversion rates.

Optimizing Bids

PPC programs use an auction that is like a second-price sealed bidding system with private values. This means you do not know how much your competitors are bidding. Everyone has different bids for each keyword. Typically, people overbid in second-price auctions with private values. The larger the number of competing bidders and the more uncertain the value of what is being bid on, the more extreme the overbidding gets. A PPC auction is a little more complicated than a second-price auction because multiple positions are being bid on simultaneously and Quality Score factors affect rankings. The lesson from this is *if you don't want to lose money, you need to figure out the value that keywords have for you.* You do this, of course, by tracking conversions and determining a value per conversion.

AdWords offers a variety of bidding options as well as "dayparting" options; that is, adjusting bids according to the time of day. Because the special bidding options of AdWords, preferred bids, and budget-optimized bids do not maximize profits or target a specific cost per conversion, they typically are less effective than setting maximum bidding limits.

We will not consider preferred and budget optimized bids further.

Penalties for New Accounts

New accounts do not have a history. Account history is important because Google uses historical CTRs to calculate Quality Scores. For new accounts, Google uses aggregated Quality Scores from historical data, and these scores tend to be low. For competitive keywords, very high initial bids are required to get a high position. Many advertisers will overbid at the start to quickly establish a better Quality Score. Because AdWords normalizes CTRs by position to calculate Quality Scores, overbidding *should not* be necessary. In theory, your ad should get the same Quality Score if it is located at the top of the search engine results and gets a high CTR, as it will if it is located at the bottom of the search engine results and therefore gets a high CTR for that position.

Overbidding works, however. Keywords with a high minimum CPC may require an overbid at the start. Minimum required bids will usually decrease as keywords establish good CTRs, and you may be able to make up for the high bids later with a lower-target cost per conversion.

Another way to start a new account without having to immediately face high prices is by building up slowly. To establish a high average CTR for your account, start a few ad groups with well-targeted keywords that have lower competition. Establishing a great history from the start should enable you to pay less when you bid on new keywords with high competition. Newly added keywords will then benefit from the established Quality Scores that your account has already gained. For keywords with lower competition you will probably be able to afford higher positions. Keep track of what you have to pay to get a certain average position. After so many impressions (maybe about a thousand for a keyword or a group of related keywords), you might see a jump in position for the same bid. This jump can be rather dramatic for keywords based on your own trademark because CTRs will be very high for these terms. If you see the jump, you will know that AdWords has updated the Quality Score for some of your keywords.

Initial Bid Strategies

If you want to be very cautious, "shade" your initial bids. That is, purposely bid lower than your estimated target. On the other hand, if you want to be aggressive, you should overbid for a short period to quickly establish a high CTR. This will work even though these values are supposed to be normalized when calculating Quality Scores and this shouldn't provide any benefit to your account. If you'd rather be middle of the road, you should build up your account from a set of strong keywords and work from an initial budget calculation such as the one in "Differences in Minimum Bids and Quality Scoring," described earlier in this chapter. Using the numbers from "Closing the Loop," also earlier in this chapter, with a conversion rate of 6% and a value per conversion of $20, you will break even with a CPC of $1.20:

($20 / conversion * 6 conversions) / 100 clicks = $1.20 / click

The dominant strategy in a second-price sealed auction is to set your maximum CPC to $1.20. However, in PPC, you are not bidding for one item. Your ad may show in a range of positions. Assuming that your conversion rates do not depend on position (a reasonable assumption), you will want to show your ad in lower positions if it brings roughly the same amount of traffic, because it will be cheaper. So, your decision about where to rank is more complicated and depends on the bids of your competitors. However, if you set your maximum CPC at $1.20 and your conversion rate turns out to be 6% or higher, you will make a profit.

Bid Gaps

Bid gaps refer to large differences in bids between the keywords showing ads at two positions. The concept came from Overture's (now YSM's) straight bidding system where bid gaps were plainly visible to advertisers. In a straight bidding system you can see your competitor's bids. For example, in the old Overture system you could have seen a bid for the number one position at $2 while the bid for the number two position was at $0.10. The advertiser in the number one position would pay $0.11 per click even though their bid was at $2. An advertiser entering this auction would most likely figure that ranking number one was not as profitable as ranking number two.

They might "bid-jam" the number one position by posting a bid of $1.99 and pay only $0.11 per click. The number one slot would then have to pay $2 per click and the number two slot would pay $0.11 per click (see Figure 3-8).

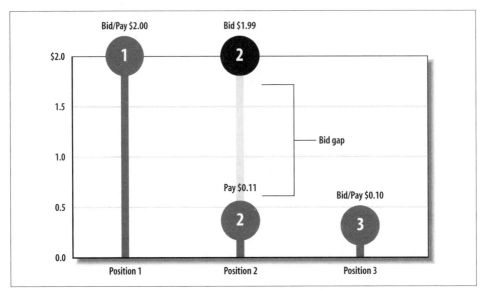

Figure 3-8. Bid gaps in an old-style Overture auction

You would have to watch out because new advertisers entering the auction would do the same thing and eventually the bids would even out. Automated bidding tools became a useful way to monitor positions and bids and to force competitors to bid the most money possible for their clicks. The bid-gap concept shows how pricing can vary a lot between positions, how setting your bids higher than what you actually value a keyword at can cause competitors to pay more, and how newly entering advertisers can raise costs.

No major PPC program employs a straight bidding system anymore. The concept of bid gaps still exists but it is not as visible. Instead of a gap in bids, there might be a gap in ad rank. This gap is a combination of Quality Scores and bids. In theory, an advertiser could still bluff about the value of a click to bid-jam a competitor. In practice, you do not know competitors' bids or their Quality Scores.

 You should be suspicious of alternative bidding methods produced by PPC programs such as AdWords. These systems know where Quality Scores and bids are set, so they could come out with tools that automatically bid-jam competitors. Although this would benefit you and raise greater revenue for the PPC program, it is unfair to advertisers who use traditional bidding methods.

One way to try to identify gaps is by comparing your average CPC to your bid. If your average position is three at a bid of $5 per click and you are paying only $2 per click, you are located in a gap. Bidding higher than $5 might raise your average CPC by a large amount for a proportionally lower increase in conversions.

Bidding is extremely difficult in an AdWords-style auction. At any moment you do not know what the bid landscape looks like. You can run reports on historical data to try to guess the bid landscape, but obviously these results will be imprecise and not entirely predictive of future performance. The best you can do is to monitor how costs and conversions vary by average position. For example, you calculate that your average value is $20 per conversion for a particular keyword. You run reports and find that when ads show in position two for that keyword you pay on average $1 per click. When it shows in position three for that keyword, you pay on average $0.20 per click. Your CTR is 2% at position two and 1.8% at position three, and your conversion rates are identical at 5%. You calculate which position is more profitable:

Profit / impression = [(value / conversion) * conversion rate * CTR] – [CPC * CTR]

For position two:

($20 / conversion) * (5 conversions / 100 clicks) * (2 clicks / 100 impressions) – ($1 / click) * (2 clicks / 100 impressions) = $0 / impression

For position three:

($20 / conversion) * (5 conversions / 100 clicks) * (1.8 clicks / 100 impressions) – ($0.20 / click) * (1.8 clicks / 100 impressions) = $0.0144 / impression

It is more profitable to be at position three.

Results such as these do not occur very often:

- You must vary your bids a lot to get precise average positions such as these.
- You must gather a great deal of data with ads in these positions to make accurate calculations.
- You must compare performance at different times.
- You must know the average value of a conversion.

In addition, after you make your calculations, the bid landscape may change entirely, or your broad-matched keywords might start to show for a wider range of queries!

The concept of bid gaps has limited use in modern PPC bidding systems, but it illustrates how your bids affect competitors' prices and how the prices for ad positions can vary widely. For adjusting bids in the current bidding systems, the next best thing is to target an average cost per conversion and try to identify positions that bring in a lot of conversions at a low cost per conversion.

Adjusting Bids

To ensure that your account is profitable, track conversions to a profitable cost per conversion. If you cannot track all conversions (e.g., phone calls), you should still track other types, such as form leads. Then estimate the average number of phone calls you get for each form lead. It can be as high as 50/50. By tracking form leads, you will be able to see which keywords probably do not generate any conversions.

Tracking Phone Call Conversions

Several technologies are available for tracking phone call conversions. At the simplest level, you can assign unique phone numbers for your marketing campaigns and your website so that all calls to the unique numbers can be traced back to the campaigns. More sophisticated tools not only track calls from different campaigns, but also can track by keywords and search engines (e.g., *http://www.clickpath.com*). In addition, these tools provide the capability to record phone calls and measure actual conversions. These tools are very powerful, and they remain surprisingly expensive. We hope that less costly "offline conversion tracking" systems will become available in the future.

Identify keywords with underperforming conversions and do something to improve their performance. For example, you might (1) delete the keyword, (2) lower the price of the bids, (3) bid on something more specific, (4) write better ad text, or use another method. But you must identify poor performers and do something about them. If you do so, you are ahead of the game.

Make sure you are not classifying a keyword as a poor performer too soon. If you are meticulous, you might go back to the confidence interval equation from "Optimizing Ad Copy," earlier in this chapter. For the keyword in question, take its average CPC and determine what conversion rate you would need for it to meet your target cost per conversion. Then use the confidence interval equation to see whether you can be 95% certain that this keyword has a different conversion rate from your target conversion rate. The upcoming sidebar, "Determining Whether a Keyword Meets a Target Cost per Conversion," shows a sample calculation.

The less time-consuming method is to glance at the keyword, see that its cost per conversion is a little high, and try some optimization methods to remedy this. If you spend too much time analyzing keywords, you will lose money because your time is valuable.

You should identify strong performers and monitor for poorly performing campaigns, ad groups, or keywords. If a keyword has an exceptionally low cost per conversion, try raising your bid to see whether you can increase profitability. When browsing through your account, take advantage of its hierarchy. First, check for campaigns that are performing poorly. Then, look for the poorly performing ad groups. Finally, search further into the ad groups to see whether any keywords are doing badly.

Determining Whether a Keyword Meets a Target Cost per Conversion

Assume a target cost per conversion of $20.

The keyword in question has an average CPC of $0.40:

($0.40 / click) * (1 conversion / $20) = .02 conversions / click

The keyword would need a 2% conversion rate to meet the target, which we will call CR_2.

The keyword has already generated 30 conversions at a conversion rate of 1.5%.

The equation is:

$$(CR_1 - CR_2) \pm Z_{\alpha/2}\sqrt{CR_1^2(1 - CR_1)/C_1 + CR_2^2(1 - CR_2)/C_2}$$

where C = conversions and CR = conversion rate.

Because you are highly confident of the 2% conversion rate, you can plug in a very high number for C_2. You can approximate:

$$CR_2^2(1 - CR_2)/C_2 = 0$$

The new equation is:

$$(CR_1 - CR_2) \pm Z_{\alpha/2}\sqrt{CR_1^2(1 - CR_1)/C_1}$$

For this example:

$$(0.015 - 0.02) \pm 1.96\sqrt{0.015^2(1 - 0.015)/30} = (0,0.01)$$

It is close because the interval contains zero. You would probably figure that the keyword is not within the 95% confidence interval so that it does indeed have a conversion rate that is lower than the necessary target. You would do something to lower the cost per conversion of this keyword, such as lowering its bid.

Keywords in an ad group can have separate, keyword-level bids. If a separate bid isn't set, the keyword uses the ad group bid in auction. If you set only ad-group-level bids all the time, you might be reducing the ranking of more specific, high-converting terms because a very general term is performing below par. It is usually necessary to set keyword-level bids to improve campaign performance.

Some keywords do not get a lot of traffic, so it is difficult to tell whether they are performing well. If you are bidding on a low-traffic keyword, group it with similar higher-traffic keywords for bidding and monitoring. Such judgment calls are best made by humans rather than by automated tools because we are easily able to group similar keywords and set reasonable bids.

Automated Bidding

Manual bidding can get cumbersome, especially for professional PPC managers who handle multiple accounts. Automated bid tools may save time in setting bids and may improve account performance. BidRank and Atlas Search are bid management tools that are popular but pricey. They typically can manage bids in multiple programs all at once and can target a specific ROI or cost per conversion.

The Big Picture

Advertisers who fail at PPC are often misbidding. They might be:

- Blindly bidding for position, holding on to number one no matter what
- Targeting keywords that reach beyond the subject matter of their site
- Wasting their budget to show at high positions and then dropping out of auctions early in the day when they could receive more clicks and conversions by lowering their bids and spreading out their budget
- Focusing only on less relevant terms that appeal to them despite poor performance, such as competitors' trademarks
- Pushing to increase traffic without paying attention to costs
- Setting poor goals

Branding

Notice that in this section we did not talk about advertisers whose goal is branding. Branding is a tricky PPC goal that can easily lead to overspending. People ask: "Why isn't my site ranked at the top for [insert popular industry term here]?" The short answer is that all competitors using PPC really, *really* want to rank at the top for their popular industry term. This desire for position inflates bids and makes it more difficult to reap a profit. A little bit of restraint can save you money.

Bid Optimization in Action: The E-Grooming Book Example

Judy runs a site selling an e-book about dog care based on her experience raising show dogs. The e-book costs $30 and there are no costs associated with distributing it—basically, anyone who wants to read the book buys it with a credit card and downloads it from her website. To simplify the example, assume that Judy has no overhead costs and the only costs come from advertising, so in this case, ROAS and ROI are equal.[1] So, if it costs Judy $30 per conversion, she breaks even. Each penny less than $30 per conversion is profit.

---

[1] In this example, Judy has two rich uncles, one of whom gives her credit card service free of overhead and another who provides her with free web hosting. Judy's uncles make this example simpler, so we're delighted that she has them.

Judy sets up an AdWords account with bids running at the ad group level. She runs one national campaign with two ad groups. After about a month the campaign is profitable, running at $18.33/conversion with a conversion rate of 3% and an average CPC of $0.55, but Judy has read this chapter and knows that conversion rates could be as high as 6%, so she believes that she has room to adjust bids to increase profits.

Judy's campaign has two ad groups: "grooming" and "care." The grooming ad group has 20 conversions, a 2% conversion rate, and an average cost per conversion of $35. The care ad group has 30 conversions, a 6% conversion rate, and an average cost per conversion of $10. The grooming ad group is not profitable so far. Even though the account as a whole is profitable, it could be more profitable by lowering bids on the grooming ad group. Judy sees that the ad group bid is at $0.86 and the average CPC is at $0.70. She assumes that the actual conversion rate of the ad group was 2% and uses that to figure an average CPC required to get below her breakeven point. Because Judy wants at least a $5 profit per book sale, she targets $25/conversion for her ad group to make sure that it is profitable.

Judy uses the conversion calculation and determines that she'll need an average CPC of $0.50 to reach this target:

($25 / conversion * 2 conversions) / 100 clicks = $0.50 / click

Judy can be absolutely sure that she'll reach this average CPC by bidding $0.50 at the ad group level, so she changes the ad group to that level and then waits another month to see how the group performs at the new level.

After a month, Judy returns to the ad group and sees that it's now at least profitable, but she wants more traffic from the group, so she decides that she's ready to control the ad group's performance at the keyword level. Judy has not gotten much data for this ad group, so she decides to group keywords according to how similar she thinks they are to develop a bidding strategy. Her list looks like this:

```
dog grooming
dog grooming book
dog grooming books
dog grooming supply
dog grooming supplies
dog grooming ebook
dog grooming ebooks
dog grooming e book
dog grooming e books
dog grooming tip
dog grooming tips
dog grooming product
dog grooming products
dog grooming kit
dog grooming kits
dog grooming accessory
dog grooming accessories
```

Judy knows that her strategy should assume that more relevant keywords are going to have higher conversion rates and she wants them to be seen more often. Based on that strategy, keywords for books would have the highest conversion rates and would get the highest bids. Keywords for supplies, on the other hand, are less important. Someone interested in supplies might be interested in a book about grooming, but he is less likely to buy a book on dog care than on subjects such as clippers and combs. Judy decides dog grooming is specific enough to deserve its own category, with a lower bid than book terms but perhaps a bid which is still of value. Keyword phrases for "tips" are unique and probably low in traffic, but Judy thinks they are associated with people searching for information, so she associates them with books. So, for bidding purposes, Judy considers the words related in this way:

```
dog grooming

dog grooming book
dog grooming books
dog grooming ebook
dog grooming ebooks
dog grooming e book
dog grooming e books
dog grooming tip
dog grooming tips

dog grooming supply
dog grooming supplies
dog grooming product
dog grooming products
dog grooming kit
dog grooming kits
dog grooming accessory
dog grooming accessories
```

Judy now decides to optimize her care ad group, which has an average cost per conversion of $10. Looking at the care ad group, Judy sees that the average CPC is $0.60. She generated 30 conversions from 500 clicks, a conversion rate of 6%. From these numbers, Judy calculates that she made $600 in profit.

(30 conversions * $30 / conversion) − (500 clicks * $0.60 / click) = $600

At a CPC of $0.60, her ad's average position is 3.2. She's making a profit, but raising bids might increase her profit.

Raising bids will get her a higher position and a greater number of clicks. If, for example, she raises her bids and her average cost-per-click figure *is* $0.80, she'll only need 100 more clicks—a total of 600 clicks—to get the same profit.

$600 / [($30 / conversion) * (6 conversions / 100 clicks) − $0.80 / click)] = 600 clicks

If the account gets her more than 600 clicks at an average CPC of $0.80, she'll get a greater profit than when her average cost per click was $0.60. This assumes that the conversion rate isn't affected by the increase in position, a reasonable assumption. To optimize the care ad group, Judy raises bids and waits a month, seeing what the increase in position does for her sales.

Other Pay-per-Click Issues

There are a number of other things you'll definitely want to get right.

The Content Network

The content network refers to ads placed next to relevant content in regular websites that opt to show ads. Google determines when to show an ad by the bidded keywords and the ad text. Landing pages, performance history on similar sites, and keyword and ad text relevance influence the ranking of your ads on the content network. Early on in Google's history, advertisers discovered that the best way to lose large amounts of money without any results was to run a campaign that was opted into the content network. Google and its search network have much higher conversion rates on average, so the quality of a click is higher on these networks. Campaigns are opted into the content network by default. It is worth considering whether to leave.

"Domain ads" are included in the content network, which may convert poorly. Domain ads show on parked domains that sometimes show up in Google's search results.

Because the content network developed a poor reputation, Google has made efforts to clean it up by:

- Allowing advertisers to set separate content bids
- Allowing advertisers to specify negative sites
- Offering placement performance reports
- Employing smart pricing
- Using filters and offline analysis to detect invalid clicks

Smart pricing automatically reduces the amount that an advertiser pays for a click if Google determines that the click has a low value. Advertisers that venture into the content network should either set separate content bids or create a separate campaign targeted only to the content network. Creating a separate campaign can increase management time quite a bit. However, it allows you to see cost and conversion information easily in the AdWords interface without having to run a lot of reports. It also allows you to test different themes in your ad groups and to set negative keywords without having to worry about their effect on Google and the search network.

It is possible that some ad groups that do well in the content network won't do well on Google and the search network. Always treat data from each separately when running ads in the content network and search network. This is especially important when testing ads and landing pages. If you lump data together, ads that are performing better than others on the search network may look like they are performing worse. CTRs and conversion rates in the content network depend heavily on what sites an ad shows on and where it shows. This can be variable across ads.

Rearranging ad groups, adding negative keywords, and adding negative sites can improve performance on the content network. You can find sites that do not convert well by running a placement performance report. To exclude these sites go to the Tools section and click on Site Exclusion in the AdWords interface (see Figure 3-9).

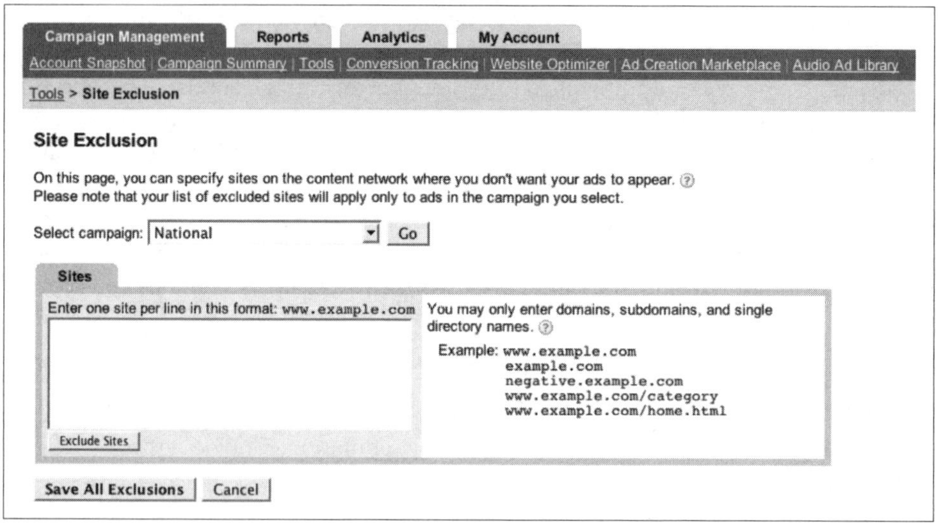

Figure 3-9. The AdWords Site Exclusion tool

In the Tools section, you can also find a link to add negative keywords to your campaign (see Figure 3-10). Negative keywords should identify themes that are not relevant to your ad groups. For example, if you sell parts for cars, but not for trucks, you would add *truck* and *trucks* to the list of negative keywords. Distribution on the content network is affected by how well your ad groups are themed. Overdistribution is, however, an issue for ad groups that are very tightly themed. You can tell when ads are being overdistributed by the number of impressions they receive. If your ad group for "Product X Model 555" gets a thousand times more impressions than your ad group for "General Product X Terms," it is likely that your ads for model 555 are being overdistributed. How changes to your account will affect results on the content network is a little more of a guessing game. Advertisers should be more cautious when using the content network. It is a good idea to ensure that Google and the search network are performing well before taking on the content network.

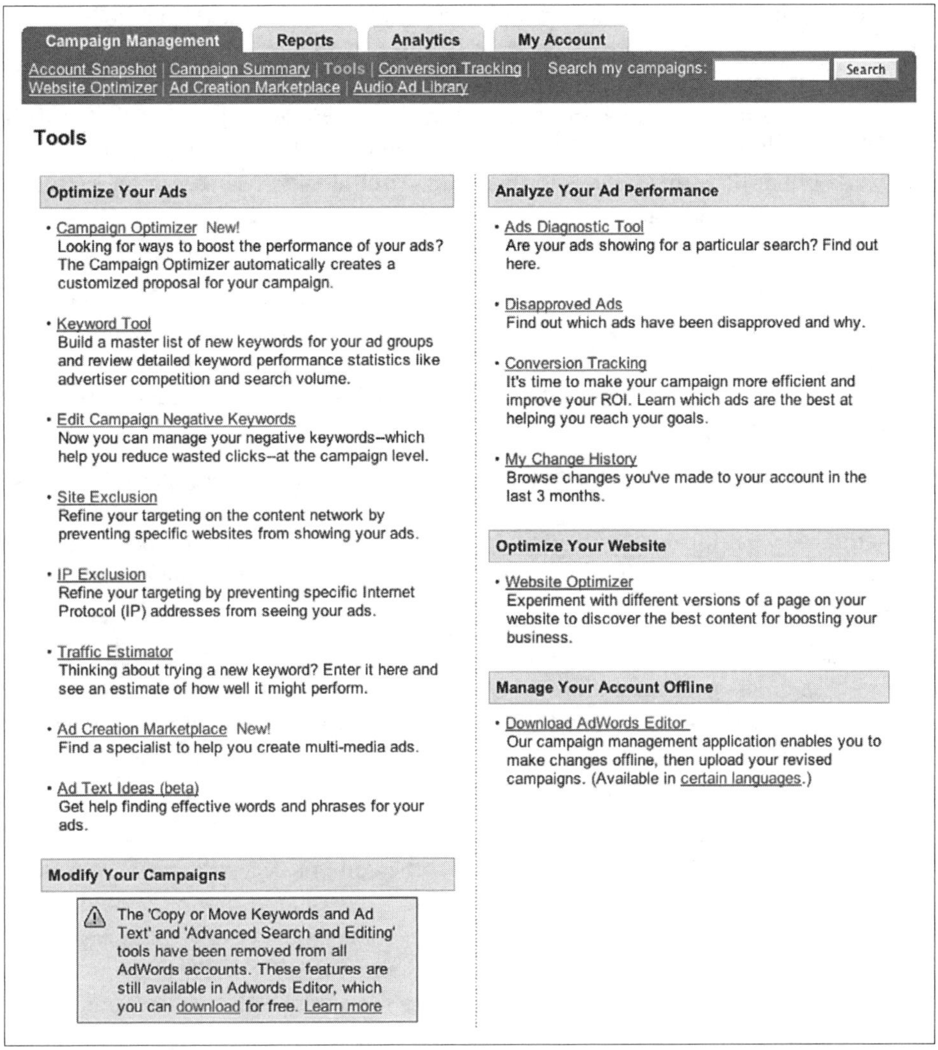

Figure 3-10. Link to edit negative keywords in AdWords

Click Fraud

Click fraud occurs when an ad is clicked on by a person or automated program for the purpose of generating ad revenue or inflating costs for advertisers. Site owners who sign up for AdSense show AdWords ads on their sites and get revenue when an ad is clicked on. Site owners might click on their own ads or use automated bots to get their ads clicked on. This type of fraud shows up in the content network. You can combat it by tracking performance and excluding sites that perform poorly.

For very expensive keywords, advertisers might also click on their competitors' ads to deplete their competitors' budgets faster. Advertisers with a high maximum CPC compared to their overall budget might track clicks by IP addresses. Google Analytics does not provide this information about site visitors, so advertisers who want to track IPs should use a different statistics program or should check the logfiles of their site. AdWords offers IP address exclusion so that search engine users with an excluded address will not see your ads.

Click fraud is a major problem when it does not affect competing advertisers equally. It reduces the value of a click and forces advertisers to bid lower on keywords to stay profitable. Sophisticated attempts at fraud will spread costs over a large number of advertisers so that it is not easily detected. Major PPC programs have systems to filter out fraudulent clicks, but a certain degree of click fraud is inherent in the PPC method of advertising.

To help combat click fraud, AdWords provides invalid clicks reporting. Invalid clicks include accidental clicks as well as fraudulent clicks. Most of these clicks are filtered out before they get into the AdWords system. You can also contact Google about a suspected case of click fraud at *https://adwords.google.com/support/bin/request. py?clickquality=1*.

Repeat clicks are not necessarily considered click fraud. Advertisers are charged for repeat clicks unless they are excessive. Clicks from visitors who are shopping around will get separately billed to the advertiser. In AdWords, a single impression might legitimately generate multiple clicks for a CTR over 100%. A cached page in a visitor's browser registers only one impression, so a search engine user going back and forth between ads might click multiple times with only one impression.

Advertisers should also track performance on the content network. AdWords offers placement performance reports for this purpose. At a minimum, you should establish a target cost per conversion and restrain bids and budgets to constrain your ad spending. Spending time and money tracking IP addresses is a waste for most advertisers, but it might be worthwhile for those who have very high bids on competitive terms.

Trademark Issues

Three major questions arise regarding trademarks.

How do I stop advertisers from bidding on my trademark?

Microsoft adCenter and YSM don't allow advertisers to bid on competitor trademarks. An advertiser can bid on trademarks if she is a reseller, if she is providing noncompetitive information, or if she is otherwise using the term generically. If you find advertisers bidding on your trademark, you can contact the program in question.

For Yahoo!, you email *trademarkconcern-ysm@yahoo-inc.com* with the following information:

- The search term which, when entered, caused the advertiser's listing to appear
- The trademark on which your claim is based
- The registration number, if you own a current registration for the trademark on the Principal Register in the U.S. Patent and Trademark Office
- A description of this evidence, if you have evidence of any consumer confusion resulting from the advertiser's bid on the search term
- The status of your communications with the advertiser if you have contacted the advertiser about your concerns

You can find information about filing a trademark concern with Microsoft by going to *http://support.msn.com* and clicking the Trademark link under Standard Services.

AdWords allows advertisers to bid on competitor trademarks, but you can stop advertisers from using your trademark in ad text. To do this, you fill out the AdWords complaint form at *https://services.google.com/inquiry/aw_tmcomplaint*.

Can I bid on competitor trademarks?

You cannot bid on competitor trademarks in YSM or Microsoft adCenter. You can always bid on trademarks in AdWords, but you are not allowed to use a trademark in ad text if the trademark owner has filed an approved complaint, unless you are using the term generically.

Should I bid on my own trademark or company name?

Unless you picked a poor company name, you will want to bid on it if you do not have high, natural, non-PPC rankings for the term. If someone is searching for your company directly, you want to help her find you. Besides hearing about you offline, a search engine user might query your company's name on a return visit after shopping around and then decide to do business with you. You do not want to miss these visitors. If you have a very general name it might not be practical to bid on it.

If you are already ranked well organically for your company name, you might still bid on your trademark if one of the following is true:

- Other competing companies are bidding on it in AdWords.
- Affiliates get a share of sales by bidding on it in AdWords.
- You can use landing pages that convert better than the highest organic search result.
- Your organic listing is not a strong one and competing companies are listed just below your site.

If it looks like other companies might be stealing clicks from your company or if others might potentially be cutting into your profits, you will probably want to bid on your trademark. CTRs are usually high for these terms, and you will have a low CPC. If you are not sure it is worth it, you can always try it for a month and compare the number of conversions that your site has generated for trademarked terms compared to previous months.

A common situation in which you would want to bid on your trademark is when visitors query your company name along with the services you offer. For instance, say your query is "Some Company widget-making services." The "widget-making services" portion of the query will trigger broad-matched ads from competitors. Someone who originally was going to use "Some Company" might suddenly discover that there are cheaper widget makers because she explored competing ads.

If your company name was "Some Company" and *somecompany.com* was your website, here are some of the terms you would want to bid on if you decided to bid on your trademark:

- some company
- somecompany
- somecompany.com
- some company.com
- www.somecompany.com
- some company {location of a branch or office}
- some company {services/products you provide}
- somecompany {location of a branch or office}
- somecompany {services/products you provide}
- {any misspellings}

Summary

PPC programs are constantly changing. The auction method of buying advertisement spots is here to stay. Over time, tracking and reporting have become more sophisticated, and as a result, so have optimization methods. Advertisers should expect optimization tools and data to continue to develop, making it easier to achieve PPC success.

Optimizing a PPC campaign is a matter of improving visitor targeting, keeping all of the elements—keywords, ads, and landing pages—closely related, and adjusting bids to meet profit goals. This small list has big implications. To conclude this chapter, here is a bulleted summary of popular optimization techniques:

- Choose appropriate profit-driven goals.
- Target campaigns and keywords to the right audience:
  - Use location targeting to separate regions that convert better than others or to exclude regions that do not generate conversions.
  - Use language targeting to find the correct audience and to generate conversions.
  - Add negative keywords to prevent irrelevant queries from triggering ads.
  - Exclude visitor IP addresses that are a source of click fraud. Set separate content bids or create separate campaigns for the content network so that performance can be monitored separately.
  - Exclude poorly performing sites on the content network.
  - Set bids so that ads are running all day according to your budget. Raise the budget if your account is profitable and shuts off before the day is over.
  - Identify times and days when your conversion rates are higher. Use this day-parting to set bids lower at times when conversion rates are lower.
- Set up ad groups with closely related, tightly themed keywords:
  - Rearrange ad groups so that they are more tightly themed.
  - Put keywords with low CTRs into separate ad groups with more specific ads.
  - Delete duplicate keywords.
  - Restrict matching on poorly performing keywords (i.e., from "broad" to "phrase" to "exact").
  - Delete poorly performing keywords and add more specific keywords.
- Write ads that feature your keywords and the interests of potential visitors:
  - Repeat user queries in ad text.
  - Highlight benefits and use a call to action in ad text.
  - Circulate multiple ads, find the best-performing ad, delete the others, and build on what worked.
  - Write ad text that qualifies visitors to reduce wasted clicks.
  - Use the diagnostic and preview tools of the ad delivery system to make sure key queries are triggering the right ads.
- Create goal-driven landing pages with clear calls to action that directly target your keywords and the interests of potential visitors:
  - Create specialized landing pages.
  - Send visitors to the most relevant landing page.
  - Use the AdWords keyword tool to make sure Google generates a relevant keyword list from your landing page URIs.

- — Lower minimum bids by improving the quality of landing pages.
- — Repeat visitor queries on landing page headlines.
- — Write persuasive landing page copy.
- — Make executing a conversion easy for interested visitors.
- Set bids to meet realistic profit-driven goals:
  - — Track conversions!
  - — Lower bids on poorly performing keywords.
  - — Raise bids on keywords that perform well.
- Continue to monitor and optimize your site and your ad campaigns based on performance:
  - — Improve the design of your site so that it is user-friendly and visible to search engine spiders.
  - — Continue searching for new keywords.
  - — Continue tracking queries that generate clicks.
  - — Refine your advertising goals according to the feedback you get from PPC data as your account acquires a history.

PPC Case Study: BodyGlove.com

In this chapter, we'll show you how to put into action the pay-per-click (PPC) optimization techniques that you learned in Chapter 3 and the conversion boosting techniques you'll learn in Chapter 5, as well as how to use metrics to guide optimization efforts, which we'll cover in Chapter 10. This chapter features a case study that shows how to maximize your PPC advertising budget.

Body Glove PPC Optimization

Body Glove International provides high-quality protective products for people and objects alike. In 2001, the Body Glove Mobile Accessories Group at Fellowes, Inc., developed protective cases for cell phones, laptops, and other handheld electronic devices. In 2007, Body Glove's goal was to develop brand recognition and presence in this very competitive market through a combination of different types of advertising, including a PPC campaign. The primary goal of the campaign was to generate high visibility while minimizing cost per conversion.

We were responsible for creating the campaign and then improving it as a way to conduct an initial market assessment and identify the key ways in which it could be improved for the final quarter of 2007.

Market Analysis

The market for cell phone cases is extremely competitive. As accessories, the products are fairly inexpensive to make and are used as promotional vehicles or branding tools. Competitors include cell phone case companies as well as cell phone manufacturers, such as Motorola and Nokia, and even cell phone service providers such as Verizon and AT&T (see Figure 4-1, which shows a typical search engine result from 2007 for cell phone covers).

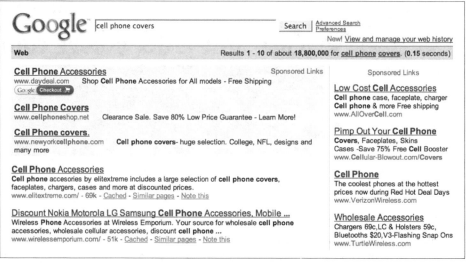

Figure 4-1. A typical search result for the phrase "cell phone covers"

Our first goal was to identify the projected traffic and costs for cell phone cases. We created a list of candidate keyphrases and then broke them into three categories based on their relative price:

- Low cost per click (CPC): $0.25–$0.75
- Medium CPC: $0.76–$1.50
- High CPC: $1.51–$2.50

We used the list of candidate keyphrases to create two scenarios (see Figure 4-2). The first assumed a 3% conversion rate for any given click and the second assumed 5%, both typical for e-commerce sites. We then used a combination of tools, including Wordtracker, KeywordDiscovery, and Google's Traffic Estimator tool, to identify the expected traffic and costs per conversion in the current market for each scenario.

Scenario 1: 3% conversion Rate

Summary	Est Monthly Clicks	Avg. CPC	Total Cost	Est. Conversions	Cost per conversion
Low	309	$0.55	$172.89	9	$18.64
Medium	3201	$1.71	$5,989.10	96	$62.36
High	2623	$2.25	$5,741.43	79	$72.97
Totals	6133	$1.94	$11,903.41	184	$64.69

Scenario 2: 5% conversion Rate

Summary	Est Monthly Clicks	Avg. CPC	Total Cost	Est. Conversions	Cost per conversion
Low	309	$0.55	$ 172.89	15	$11.18
Medium	3201	$1.71	$ 5,989.10	160	$37.42
High	2623	$2.25	$ 5,741.43	131	$43.78
Totals	6133	$1.94	$11,903.41	307	$38.81

Figure 4-2. Keyphrase scenarios

Research confirmed our suspicions that this market was enormously competitive. In fact, the average price across all the keyphrases that we examined showed that the competition was willing to spend as much as $2.25 per click! At the conversion rates in scenarios 1 and 2, the average cost per conversion or sale is $64.69 or $38.81, more than the value of the product, which averages around $30. Typically, we'd like to see the cost per conversion at about 10% of the gross value. In this case, the cost per click is around 10%. At our estimated conversion rates, it appears that the cost per conversion exceeds the cost of the product! Advertising for cell phone cases is either a loss leader or a marketing exercise. If this campaign were run in isolation, it would not pay for itself through the sale of the item because the costs are simply too high. Service providers and phone resellers can afford to have a loss leader to promote phone covers, however, if they are making lots of money off service plans, warranties, and high-end phones.

Based on these findings, we developed two key goals for Body Glove Mobile Accessories:

Phase one goal

> To increase the conversion rate of paid search visitors by improving the usability and effectiveness of their website

Phase two goal

> To make cost per conversion less than or equal to the total value of the product

Armed with these specific goals we created the campaign.

Campaign Creation and Kickoff

We performed traditional keyphrase research, relying on the use of Body Glove's brand name and the names of key cell phone brands for our root keyphrases. We focused on keyphrases and bids that were in the $0.75 to $1.25 range to keep costs down.

Initial ad copy was diverse and included a number of different experiments. Because few people considered surfing in the context of cell phones, we wanted to try to differentiate "cell phone cases" through that term as well as some others that were specific to the brand name, such as use of the word *glove*. Figure 4-3 shows four examples of starting ads that we used as a baseline for the project.

Our primary concern at the beginning of the project was the ability of the Body Glove site to convert. Although the design of the site was arresting, with handsome shots of Body Glove products (see Figure 4-4), the actual purchase pages lacked prominent calls to action that were going to help conversions (see Figure 4-5).

Figure 4-3. Four baseline ads for variations on "cell phone cases"

Body Glove agreed with our assessment but wanted to begin immediately to learn about the market interest and potential traffic. We agreed that the pages would be incrementally improved in conjunction with the ad copy and keyphrases as the campaign progressed.

With our long-term plans for incremental improvement in place, we initiated the campaign.

Figure 4-5 shows the original product page. Note the call to action, which is simply an invitation to enter a zip or postal code. After the code is entered, the retailer results would show up and the "buy now" call to action would appear as a text hyperlink. Not only was this call to action fairly small, but it was also below the fold on most computer screens.

Initial Outcome and Improvements

As expected, initial conversion rates were fairly low and costs per conversion were fairly high because of the extremely competitive market and the first iteration of the product pages. From August until mid-October, we incrementally tweaked bids and some ad copy to improve click-through rates (CTRs) and CPC. The average CPC steadily improved, while the average ad position slowly improved from about 2 to 1.8 as our quality scores improved. Figure 4-6 shows the improvement in average CPC from September 2007 through January 2008, as the holiday season progressed.

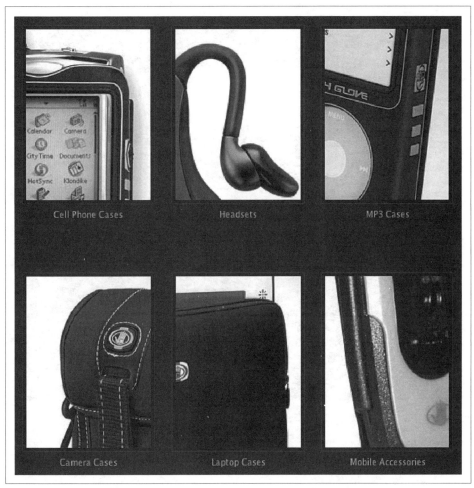

Figure 4-4. Body Glove category page

We were particularly pleased with the steadily decreasing CPC during the very competitive and busy Christmas season in December, when traffic and spending from competitors increased dramatically.

Dramatic Results

On November 1, 2007, the Body Glove Mobile Accessories Group implemented our design recommendations on their product pages, as shown in Figure 4-7.

Now the call to action is above the fold; it is also clearly marked by a blue gradient button with BUY NOW in a large font. The name of the brick-and-mortar dealer is still visible as well. This was a critical requirement of the marketing goals for Body Glove.

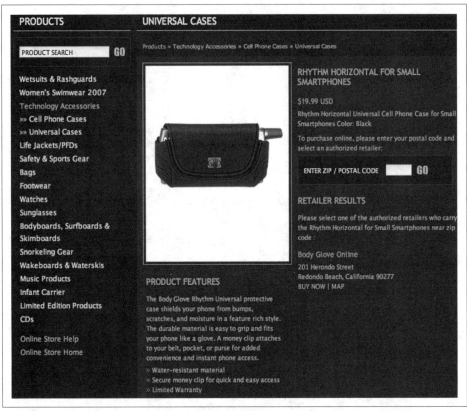

Figure 4-5. The original product page

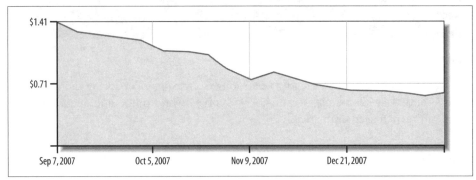

Figure 4-6. Average CPC, by month

Figure 4-7. The improved product page

The results were immediate and dramatic. The following week's conversion rates increased by 100%, and between November 2 and December 20, 2007, the conversion increased *600%* from 0.34% to nearly 2.4%. The majority of these changes came from improvements in the landing pages and the boost from the Christmas shopping season. The only major change made to the PPC campaign at this time was a general decrease in the use of underperforming keyphrases around November 9. Figure 4-8 shows the dramatic increase in conversion rate.

Note that the increased conversion rate stayed relatively steady after the holiday season, indicating that the landing and product pages continued to be effective in slower market periods.

Between December 1 and December 20, we also dramatically reduced the number of keyphrases on which we were bidding. We focused on the most visible and highest-quality terms, which created high CTRs from qualified visitors to take advantage of the new landing and product pages. In particular, we found unique keyphrases that were relatively low cost and not very competitive, based on their bids and number of clicks. This allowed us to enjoy high CTRs and conversion rates even after the holiday season.

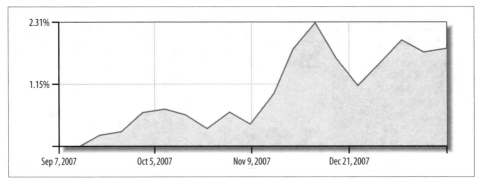

Figure 4-8. Conversion rates for Body Glove cell phone cases, by month

Overall, during the months of November and December the Body Glove cell phone case campaign enjoyed a conversion rate of 1.67% at a cost per conversion of about $39.63. This was slightly higher than the average price of a cell phone case, but with improved landing pages, the conversion rate and the cost per conversion should continue to improve dramatically.

Summary

Accessory product markets are incredibly competitive. Body Glove's combination of brand recognition and quality gave the company advantages that many companies don't enjoy. Body Glove was, however, still competing against companies that see cell phone accessories as promotional tools first and actual products second. Through a careful PPC campaign and incremental improvements to Body Glove's website product pages, Body Glove's accessory conversions showed excellent progress. This effort demonstrated the importance of steady, incremental improvement and the use of metrics to improve on previous findings. We expect some exciting years ahead for Body Glove in the online marketing space.

Conversion Rate Optimization

Conversion rate optimization (CRO) is the art and science of persuading your site visitors to take actions that benefit you, by making a purchase, offering a donation, or committing to some positive future action.

CRO uses a wide variety of techniques, including persuasive copywriting and credibility-based web design, to convert prospects into buyers. By planning, designing, and optimizing your website to persuade, you can ensure that it will act as a more efficient sales tool. You can compare a conversion-optimized website to a successful (but commission- and salary-free) digital salesperson who works for you 24/7, 365 days a year, qualifying leads, building rapport, and even closing sales.

The Benefits of CRO

The importance of CRO becomes clear in light of the poor performance of unoptimized e-commerce websites with average conversion rates of between 2.5% and 3.1%.[1,2] Although "your mileage may vary," you can expect that high-quality optimization will increase conversion rates by 50% to 200% or even more. For example, in Chapter 4 we discuss a case in which the increase was more than 600%.

With margins falling and advertising costs rising, a high-performing website has become essential for online success. CRO helps you to meet the following business goals:

- An increase in sales, revenues, and profits
- The generation of more leads for your sales team

---

[1] Fireclick. January 19, 2008. "Conversion Rate: Global." Fireclick Index, *http://index.fireclick.com* (accessed January 19, 2008).

[2] Shop.org. September 18, 2007. "The State of Retailing Online 2007." National Retail Federation, *http://www.nrf.com/modules.php?name=News&op=viewlive&sp_id=365* (accessed February 15, 2008). The shopping cart abandonment rate peaked at 53% in 2003. The conversion rate for e-commerce sites peaked in 2002 at 3.2%. In the 2007 report, e-commerce conversion was 3.1%.

- Boosting "opt-ins" to build your email list
- Reduction of customer acquisition costs
- More page views for advertising
- Engagement of more users
- A permanent improvement to conversion rates

CRO uses proven persuasive techniques to encourage site visitors to act because they have experienced your polished site design, compelling copy, unique selling proposition (USP), and irresistible calls to action. With increased sales, more leads, and higher engagement, what's not to like about CRO? Yet despite these advantages, we've found that CRO is usually the last step taken in optimizing websites.

Most website owners focus on getting more traffic to boost online sales. But paying to advertise an underperforming website is throwing good money after bad. CRO, on the other hand, makes your website work harder for you by producing more sales *now* from your existing website traffic. Its goal is to make every site visit count. However, to maximize your success you need to focus on conversion quality for the life of your site. The savviest optimizers don't stop after their initial success. They continuously tweak their sites to maximize their return on investment (ROI).

Best Practices for CRO

What follows are the best-practice principles behind CRO. It might seem at first like an extremely broad, almost intangible idea. However, you can achieve conversion by following very specific steps using tools you already have at your disposal. CRO uses what you already know about your customers and their psychology to your advantage by using language, imagery, and a level of engagement that will make your site stand out among those of your competitors.

First, we'll explore how the principle of *source credibility* can make your site appear more trustworthy. Next, we'll discuss the psychology of persuasion, including:

- The six primary psychological persuaders
- Maximizing conversions with personas

Then we'll highlight the top 10 factors that you can use to maximize your site's conversion rate, including:

- Credibility-based design
- Easy navigation
- Logo credibility
- Memorable slogans
- Benefit-oriented headlines
- Best content placement

- Calls to action
- Benefit-oriented content
- Using "hero shots"
- Interactivity and engagement

You'll learn how to stage your CRO campaign through the discovery, planning, and optimization phases. Finally, we'll show these techniques in action by analyzing two examples of best conversion practices.

Source Credibility: Designing Gut Reactions

Source credibility theory helps to explain the visceral reaction that users have to your site. People tend to believe messages from sources that appear to be credible. So, if users perceive your website to be credible and authoritative, your messages will be more persuasive. A credibility-based visual design and logo help to convey your company's credibility traits, such as "expert" and "trustworthy."

But what makes a site credible? Research shows that credible sites have a number of specific characteristics. For example, they have a professional look and feel that instills confidence in their visitors.[3] They have well-structured content with intuitive navigation that enables visitors to find what they are looking for quickly and easily. They use layouts optimized for how visitors view and absorb information on the Web. These websites start with a USP that codifies and clarifies exactly what makes them a better choice than the competition.

Believable websites that download quickly and are responsive to queries have higher conversion rates.[4] They communicate with visitors in customer-focused language. They use *trigger words* designed to click with users. They provide engaging benefit-oriented content that focuses on visitor needs and goals. Credible sites are successful because they solve problems and answer questions with content tailored to their target market and even adapted to the different personalities or *personas* of their target customers. In short, they are persuasive.

The Psychology of Persuasion

Nobody likes to be coerced or manipulated. To be persuaded, however, is OK. The persuasive techniques that you'll learn in this section will make a favorable response to your requests more likely. In fact, many of the conversion best practices found on the

[3] Robins, D., and J. Holmes. 2008. "Aesthetics and credibility in web site design." *Information Processing and Management* 44 (1): 386–399. Preconscious judgments of aesthetics influence perceived credibility of websites. *Voilà!* Instant credibility.

[4] Akamai. 2007. "Boosting Online Commerce Profitability with Akamai." *http://www.akamai.com* (accessed February 15, 2008). Akamai estimated a 9% to 15% improvement in conversion rate after a website is "Akamaized."

Web are based on these psychological principles. For example, testimonials and awards use *social proof* to invoke the wisdom of the crowd, free white papers exchanged for contact information use *reciprocity*, and uniformed people showing wares and services are presumed to be *authoritative*. Airlines and hotels use *scarcity* when they say that only *x* number of tickets or rooms are left at a given price. All of these techniques are used on the Web to increase desire and to influence people to buy now.

The six persuaders

Persuasive techniques *influence* people to comply with requests. Although there are thousands of techniques that you can use to get people to convert, most of them fall into six basic categories, according to Robert Cialdini's *Influence: Science and Practice* (Allyn & Bacon). These six persuaders are *reciprocation, consistency, social proof, liking, authority,* and *scarcity*. Skilled salespeople use these techniques in conjunction with social norms to induce a sense of urgency in customers, and to avoid a loss of face or loss of opportunity.

Reciprocation: Repaying an obligation. Humans feel obligated to repay a gift from others. Reciprocation is a social norm that obligates the recipient to repay a favor in the future. This ensures continuing relationships which sociologists say is beneficial to society.

On the Web, you can use reciprocity and rewards to increase the likelihood that customers will provide you with their contact information. You can use free online tools and multimedia downloads to induce the recipient to give her contact information. You can also request contact information from your customers before the fact, in exchange for content. Site owners often trade a free white paper for an email address, for example. Reciprocation in the form of asking for contact information after the fact has been shown to be more effective in getting detailed contact information than reward (asking for contact information before the fact).[5]

Consistency and commitment: Little yeses. One key to getting people to convert is our human need for consistency. Once we commit to something, we want our future actions to appear consistent with that decision. That small initial commitment makes us more likely to agree to larger requests that are similar.

On the Web and with your sales force, be sure to get prospects to commit with "little yeses" to move the buying process along toward the big "Yes!" For example, asking a prospect whether she agrees that saving money, time, or effort is a good idea will yield an easy yes. If you follow up with a question about her problem and then offer the same type of savings through your solution, you are more likely to get a positive response.

---

[5] Gamberini, L. et al. 2007. "Embedded Persuasive Strategies to Obtain Visitors' Data: Comparing Reward and Reciprocity in an Amateur, Knowledge-Based Website," in *Persuasive 2007* (Stanford University, CA: April 26–27), 194.

Social proof: A bestseller! Humans often decide what is correct by observing what other people think is correct. This "social evidence" can stimulate compliance with a request. Telling a person that many other people have made the same choice encourages your prospect to comply. The principle of social proof works best under conditions of uncertainty and similarity.

You can use social proof to your advantage to raise perceived credibility on the Web. Impressive client lists, third-party seals of authority, and Amazon's "Customers Who Bought This Item Also Bought…" are forms of social proof. Glowing testimonials can have the same effect. In fact, customer endorsements from peers have a significant positive effect on trust, as well as on attitudes and willingness to buy.[6] Remember to back up your claims so that there is no backlash.

Another behavior influenced by social proof is the fear factor about buying online. After hearing stories of hackers and identity theft in the news media, many buyers who are not tech-savvy are apprehensive about buying online. As a result, online retailers must build confidence and trust with visitors by decreasing perceived risk and uncertainty.

The more confident we are in our decisions, the more likely we are to buy. Trust, information quality, familiarity, and reputation have strong effects that support our intention to buy. Increase perceived credibility by deploying third-party *e-seals* of approval such as those from the Better Business Bureau, eTrust, and HACKER SAFE. You may get a higher conversion rate with a trust graphic,[7] but we encourage you to experiment and test different e-seals. Naturally, all third-party seals must be used strictly in accordance with the rules and regulations of the awarding organizations.

Liking: Friends selling bonds. Most people tend to say yes to people they know or like. We are more likely to convert when a product or service is associated with physically attractive people, positive circumstances or attributes, and/or people who are similar to us. Additionally, a recommendation from a friend or someone we know has much more weight than a cold call from a stranger.

The wording that you use on your website can significantly affect your conversion rates. Sophisticated marketers create personas, or personality archetypes, that help to customize different paths for different types of customers. Each path has copy that is tailored for that persona's level of education, different personality characteristics, and needs. By populating your paths with friendly, tailored, benefit-oriented copy, you can kick-start the liking process. You'll learn more about personas later in this chapter.

---

[6] Lim, K. et al. 2006. "Do I Trust You Online, and If So, Will I Buy? An Empirical Study of Two Trust-Building Strategies." *Journal of Management Information Systems* 23 (2): 233–266. Although rewards received more replies, reciprocation got more detailed responses.

[7] McAfee. 2008. "HACKER SAFE certified sites prevent over 99.9% of hacker crime." *http://www.scanalert.com/ site/en/certification/marketing/* (accessed February 18, 2008). McAfee claims an average increase in conversion rate of 14% among 150 million unique visitors who see the HACKER SAFE mark. Your mileage may vary.

Authority: Dutiful deference. Systemic societal pressures have instilled deference to authority in most humans. We tend to obey people who appear authoritative, especially those with impressive titles and the trappings of what people in the culture consider signs of success.

To enhance the authority effect on credibility, you can emphasize the titles and education of your staff on your website. Be sure to mention any books, studies, and articles that your staff has published. Including images of people in suits or uniforms where appropriate will add gravitas to the authority of your website.

Scarcity: Exclusive limited numeric offer! When an opportunity appears to be less available, people assign it a higher value. We are more likely to desire a scarce opportunity when it has recently become scarce or when we have to compete for it. We also hate to lose established freedoms. This is called *psychological reactance*.

You can use perceived scarcity to sell more products and services on the Web. By limiting the number of products or services that you sell, you can evoke the scarcity principle. For example, when travelers go to Orbitz.com to buy airline tickets, they are often told that there are only X available seats left at that price (see Figure 5-1).

Figure 5-1. Orbitz.com using scarcity to sell airline tickets

Similarly, Amazon.com shows the number of books left before a new order must be placed, citing attendant delays if you don't act now. Amazon also calculates the time you have left to make your purchase to receive it by a certain date.

Building trust to close the sale

Successful sites build trust and confidence in their visitors and make clear to the visitor how he can take action that will lead to a sale. At each decision point, successful sites reassure visitors with information designed to keep buying momentum high and uncertainty low.

Ease of use is most important in building trust in the information gathering stage. *Structural assurance* becomes more important in the evaluation and purchasing stages.

Maximizing Conversion with Personas

The most successful websites are the ones built with input from marketers who understand *who* their customers are and *what* unique personality traits their customers have. They understand *which* common needs and goals their customers possess and the psychology of *why* they buy. Personas, the composite personality archetypes of your customers, help you target different personality types to maximize conversion rates. You can discover the personas of your customers by conducting user interviews, by observing focus groups, and by analyzing search behavior.

Personality types influence the ways in which people make decisions and the questions they ask. Psychologists have identified four main personality types: Jung called them Intuitor, Sensor, Thinker, and Feeler. The Eisenberg brothers, coauthors of *Call to Action: Secret Formulas to Improve Online Results* (Thomas Nelson), call them Competitive, Spontaneous, Methodical, and Humanistic.

Each of your visitors perceives value in a different way. Here is a summary of each dominant personality type:[a]

- Competitive: Their questions focus on the *what*. They want control and they value competence. They can put off immediate gratification for future gain. They want rational options and challenges.

- Spontaneous: Their questions focus on *why* and sometimes *when*. They are impulsive and fast-paced. They want to address their own immediate needs.

- Methodical: Their questions focus on *how*. They are detail-oriented and organized. They want facts and hard data to make decisions.

- Humanistic: Their questions focus on *who*. They tend to be altruistic and can sublimate their own needs for others. They want testimonials, the big picture, and incentives.

Websites that use personas (e.g., "business" or "consumer" at IBM.com) direct consumers to different paths based on their particular interests or goals. To maximize conversion rates, you can tailor your copy to the personality type of the person you are targeting. You can adapt your website paths and sales techniques to a person's particular level of education and desires by using "trigger words" and content styles that feel familiar to your target audience.

---

[a] Eisenberg, B. et al. 2006. *Persuasive Online Copywriting—How to Take Your Words to the Bank*. New York: Future Now, 60–64. *http://www.futurenowinc.com* (accessed February 15, 2008). This is an updated PDF of the original 2002 book from Wizard Academy Press.

Assurance includes credibility boosters such as a privacy policy link under an email form, or a VeriSign or HACKER SAFE certification where a customer will enter a credit card number.[8]

---

[8] Chau, P. et al. 2007. "Examining customers' trust in online vendors and their dropout decisions: An empirical study." *Electronic Commerce Research and Applications* 6 (2): 171–182.

Top 10 Factors to Maximize Conversion Rates

There are more than a thousand ways to optimize your website to maximize conversion rates.[9] What follows are the 10 most important factors that you can use to boost conversions with your website.

Factor #1: Use a Credibility-Based Professional Design

Your site has just a moment to be trusted, or busted.[10] A professionally designed site makes the type of first impression (fast, mistake-free, attractive, and credible) that prevents scaring away more business than you get. Amazingly, trust is built on the "thin slice" of a first impression, as Malcolm Gladwell, author of the bestseller *Blink* (Little, Brown and Company), has found. What goes into credibility-based design? Your site needs to be:

Fast

> Your site will be judged in the blink of an eye, so it must become visible very quickly. Site owners often make the mistake of using heavy graphical elements that slow their sites down. Many visitors leave before these elements have even loaded. Page display times greater than four seconds put you at a credibility disadvantage.

Mistake-free

> This goes beyond spellchecking. Your site must be free of style errors, coding errors, design errors, factual errors, grammatical errors, redundancies, and incomplete content. Such errors significantly reduce perceived quality, harm credibility, and derail intent to purchase.[11] In fact, the *perception* of flaws in a site affects perceived quality by more than twice as much as do actual flaws. Thus, small errors can become magnified in your visitors' eyes. This is one of the two most important factors cited as making the best first impression. The other factor is attractiveness.

Attractive

> Studies have found that attractiveness is the single most important factor in increasing credibility. Testing the same content with high and low aesthetic treatments, one study found that a higher aesthetic treatment increased perceived credibility.[12] When a company has invested in professional website and logo design, consumers infer that the firm can be trusted.[13]

---

[9] Eisenberg, B. February 21, 2003. "How to Decrease Sales by 90 Percent." ClickZ, *http://www.clickz.com/showPage.html?page=1588161* (accessed June 5, 2008.) Found over 1,100 factors that affect conversion rates.

[10] Lindgaard, G. et al. 2006. "Attention web designers: You have 50 milliseconds to make a good first impression!" *Behavior and Information Technology* 25 (2):115–126. See also the introduction to Part II.

[11] Everard, A., and D. Galletta. Winter 2005–2006. "How Presentation Flaws Affect Perceived Site Quality, Trust, and Intention to Purchase from an Online Store." *Journal of Management Information Systems* 22 (3): 55–95.

[12] Robins and Holmes. "Aesthetics and credibility in web site design," 397.

[13] Schlosser, A. et al. 2006. "Converting Web Site Visitors into Buyers: How Web Site Investment Increases Consumer Trusting Beliefs and Online Purchase Intentions." *Journal of Marketing* 70 (2): 133–148. Site investment equals trust in a firm's abilities.

Sites that are credible convert visitors into buyers. This is the bottom line of commercial website design. Mistake-free, attractive pages and logos are the keys to increasing credibility. And you've seen that speed is important if you are going to deliver that necessary experience to your visitors. All of this is available with professional website design, because true professional website design is credibility-based design.

Factor #2: Make Website Navigation Easy

Users frequently criticize difficult navigation in website usability surveys. If visitors can't find what they're looking for, they will bail out of your website and look elsewhere. Your site design should allow your visitors to get where they want to go quickly and easily with a minimum number of clicks. Avoid using your internal company jargon, which visitors may not understand. Feature a consistent integrated navigation design using popular conventions. Write compelling, benefit-oriented link text to encourage visitors to click to your products or services. Longer link text has been shown to convert better than shorter link text. We'll explore optimum link length later in this chapter.

To help orient visitors, use site maps and a logical hierarchy that is not too deep. Users prefer tabbed navigation to other forms of web navigation.[14] They also prefer that vertical navigation, if used, appear on the left because that is where most users look first.

Factor #3: Optimize the Credibility of Your Logo

Your logo is often the first impression that your visitors have of your company. Does your logo present your company as expert and trustworthy? How do you know? It helps to have an extensive background and training in commercial art and psychology. But barring that, you may find the following introduction helpful.

Dr. William Haig, coauthor of *The Power of Logos* (John Wiley and Sons), provides a framework for designers to create credibility-based logo designs.[15] These "source credibility" logos have been shown to increase conversion rates by up to a factor of four.

> A logo which contained the credibility traits of a website company induced 2x to 4x more clickthroughs than logos which did not have the same credibility traits and were thus considered non-credible.[16]

---

[14]Burrell, A., and A. Sodan. "Web Interface Navigation Design: Which Style of Navigation-Link Menus Do Users Prefer?" in *ICDEW 2006* (Atlanta: April 3–7, 2006), 10 pages.

[15]Haig, W., and L. Harper. 1997. *The Power of Logos: How to Create Effective Company Logos.* New York: John Wiley. Haig coined the term "credibility-based logo design" in his master's thesis at the University of Hawaii, "Credibility Compared to Likeability: A Study of Company Logos," in 1979. His *Logos* book expanding on his thesis followed.

[16]Haig, W.L. 2006. "How and Why Credibility-Based Company Logos are Effective in Marketing Communication in Persuading Customers to Take Action: A Multiple Case Study Toward a Better Understanding of Creativity in Branding." Ph.D. dissertation, Southern Cross University, Lismore, Australia.

The psychology behind credibility-based logos is to encourage the acceptance of messages that motivate consumers to take action. Logos lend credibility to the company's main message. So, if the source of a message is perceived to be credible and trustworthy (partly as a result of your logo design), the messages your company transmits will be more influential. In persuasive communication theory this is called *source credibility*.

The key to Haig's theory is to translate nonverbal communication into design forms that convey the specific credibility traits of the company in a logo. Haig found that a successful logo must:

- *Be credibility-based.* It must incorporate attributes—such as competent, knowledgeable, trustworthy, cutting-edge, conservative, dynamic, exciting, traditional, forward-thinking, and innovation—that are specific to the company.
- *Symbolize* the company's core competency.
- *Be designed to communicate* that the company is trustworthy.
- *Be planned* in content and in design form.
- *Use a symbol* over, or next to, or to the left of the company name.
- *Be prominent in application* and be frequently and consistently used.
- Have a graphical symbol and name that *work together.*

Your logo is a graphical icon that symbolizes the credibility of your business. Effective logos are designed for immediate recognition. As described in Alina Wheeler's *Designing Brand Identity: A Complete Guide to Creating, Building, and Maintaining Strong Brands* (John Wiley and Sons), they inspire trust, admiration, and loyalty, and imply superiority. Make sure your logo is professionally designed to symbolize your company's unique credibility traits.

Haig said this about credibility and conversion:

> Only 1–5 visitors out of 100 follow the links on a website to the "purchase" page. My work shows that over 90 percent do not even get to the "follow the link" stage. Only about 8 to 10 percent do at "first glance" within the first few seconds. My work shows that a credibility-based logo design can increase the "first glance rate" by up to 4 times. This means that a "credibility-based logo" and a "credibility-based home page" with consistent credibility traits expressed through design will more than double the visitors to the "purchase" page. That is big bucks baby!

To view some examples of credibility-based logo designs, see Haig's website at *http://www.powerlogos.com.*

Factor #4: Write a Memorable Slogan

A tagline or a brief branding slogan should be placed near your logo. *Slogan* is derived from the Gaelic word *sluagh-ghairm* which means battle cry. Your slogan should be a memorable phrase, a battle cry that sums up your company's benefits and image.[17] Your tagline should be an abbreviated version of your USP that links the slogan to your brand.

Some memorable taglines include:

- "A diamond is forever." (DeBeers, 1948)
- "When it absolutely, positively has to be there overnight." (FedEx, 1982)
- "Got milk?" (California Milk Processing Board, 1993)

Your slogan, your logo, and your brand name are three key elements that identify your brand. Together they create *brand equity*, which differentiates how consumers respond to your marketing efforts. A higher differential increases what consumers know about your brand, allowing you to charge a premium for your offerings.

Brand names are rarely changed, whereas logos and taglines often change over time as your company evolves. Ideally, taglines should be designed for future expansion. Good slogans:

- Communicate the *biggest benefit* that your product provides
- Are simple yet *memorable*
- Use *active voice*, with the adverb near the verb for more impact
- *Differentiate* your brand
- *Link* your slogan to your brand name
- Are designed for *future expansion*
- *Embrace ambiguity* (puns and other wordplay, for example, are inexact but memorable)
- *Prime* your desired attributes
- Jump-start recall with *jingles*

Larger companies often hire brand management firms to create their taglines, their USPs, and their logos, spending millions in the process. You don't need to spend millions to come up with an effective tagline; you've got this book. Later in this chapter we'll show you how to create a compelling USP.

---

[17]Kohli, C., L. Leuthesser, and R. Suri. 2007. "Got slogan? Guidelines for creating effective slogans." *Business Horizons* 50 (5): 415–422.

Factor #5: Use Benefit-Oriented Headlines

Your initial headline contains the first words that your visitors will read on your site. So, to improve conversion rates, grab their attention. Use headlines that clearly state the most important benefits that your product or service offers. For example, emphasize saving money, time, and energy. Think search engine optimization (SEO) when writing your headlines by including the keywords that you want to target. Finally, design your headlines for scanning by placing your most important keywords up front.[18] Note how this *feature-laden* headline:

Use half the watts with low-voltage fluorescent light bulbs!

can become the following *benefit-oriented* headline:

Energy-efficient fluorescent light bulbs save you money!

The use of passive voice permits the placement of keywords early in headlines. Used in body copy, however, passive voice creates impersonal and potentially confusing language. Headlines that ask visitors to *act* can boost click-through rates (CTRs). Combining these headlines with free offers increases conversion rates even more.

Optimum link length

Headlines are often used as link text. Longer link text, on the order of 7 to 12 words, has been shown to have higher success rates than shorter link text (see Figure 5-2).[19]

Success here is defined as the likelihood of a link bringing the user closer to where she wants to go. Longer link text is more likely to contain the right trigger words that the user seeks. The more likely that a trigger word is present, the higher the scent of a link.

Factor #6: Give Important Content the Best Placement

The position of components on your web pages can make a significant difference in your website conversions and site flow-through. Users look first at the top-left corner of your web page and scan to the right and then to the left in an F-shaped pattern.[20] They end up in the center of your page where the most important content should reside.[21] They focus less on the right side of web pages, or to areas that look like ads. Because most people focus first on the left side of the screen, navigation works well on the left side for left-to-right readers. The right side of the screen works well for testimonials, calls to action, and sign-up forms. As with all best practices, be sure to experiment to maximize conversion rates for your situation (see Chapter 10).

[18]Nielsen, J. September 6, 1998. "Microcontent: How to Write Headlines, Page Titles, and Subject Lines." *Alertbox, http://www.useit.com/alertbox/980906.html* (accessed February 18, 2008).

[19]Spool, J. et al. 2004. "Designing for the Scent of Information." User Interface Engineering, *http://www.uie.com* (accessed March 30, 2008). Figure 5-2 reproduced by permission.

[20]Nielsen, J. April 17, 2006. "F-Shaped Pattern For Reading Web Content." Alertbox, *http://www.useit.com/ alertbox/reading_pattern.html* (accessed February 17, 2008).

[21]MarketingSherpa. 2004. *Landing Page Handbook* 1. Warren, RI: MarketingSherpa, 91.

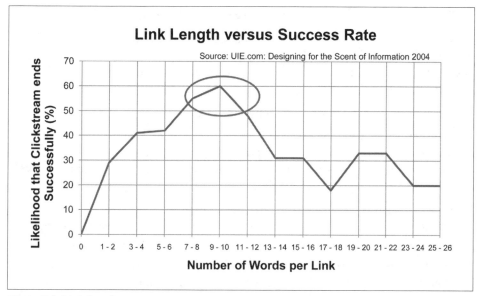

Figure 5-2. Link length versus success rate

To boost click-through and conversion rates, place your most important links, forms, and calls to action in the first screen (i.e., above the fold). In an eye-tracking study of web pages, 76.5% of the users clicked on links above the fold, whereas the rest clicked on links below the fold.[22]

To maximize conversion rates on landing pages, repeat the search terms that brought users to your page in the first screen. Think of your visitors as grazing *informavores* with very short attention spans.[23] They look for morsels of useful information to devour. Break up your copy with compelling subheadlines to make your content easy to digest.

Factor #7: Include Appealing Offers and Calls to Action

Your offer is a *call to action*. You are asking your visitors to act: to purchase, sign up, or opt in. Well-drafted calls to action motivate users to move further into the sales process.[24] For example, this:

SUBMIT NOW

becomes this:

Click here to download your free white paper

---

[22]Weinreich, H. et al. 2006. *"Off the Beaten Tracks: Exploring Three Aspects of Web Navigation."* In *WWW 2006* (Edinburgh, Scotland: May 23–26, 2006), 133–142.

[23]Pirolli, P. 2007. *Information Foraging Theory: Adaptive Interaction with Information.* New York: Oxford University Press. A theoretical but fundamentally important book for web designers.

[24]Eisenberg, B. et al. 2006. *Call to Action: Secret Formulas to Improve Online Results* (Nashville, TN: Thomas Nelson), 144.

Factor #8: Deploy Persuasive, Benefit-Oriented Content

Write persuasive, compelling copy with benefits that appeal to the needs of your customers. Whether you are showing the benefits of your service or offering product descriptions on your e-commerce website, your content must convey benefits that capture your visitors' attention.

For example, avoid feature-oriented copy such as this:

> **5.7 liter hemi 4 valve engine.** The Tundra engine incorporates a number of innovative, high-tech features that boost horsepower and fuel efficiency. It provides high compression ratios, hemispherical cylinder heads, and four valves per cylinder to improve combustion.

Instead, use personas to create targeted, benefit-oriented copy (see the "Maximizing Conversion with Personas" sidebar, earlier in this chapter). The following copy assumes that a prospect is looking for power and status in a vehicle:

> **5.7 Liter Hemi V8 provides maximum horsepower for towing heavy loads.** The tough Tundra truck boasts a high-tech 5.7 liter V8 engine with plenty of power to tow the heaviest of payloads. You'll turn heads towing your boat to the beach, while saving money with our innovative fuel-efficient design.

Do I want more power? Yes! Do I want to turn heads? Yes! Sign me up for one of those bad boys.

Benefit Bullets and Value Hierarchies

The *benefit bullet* format presents the benefits of your product in the order of its *value hierarchy* to your target market. In other words, list the strongest benefits of your product first, and its weakest benefit last. For example, with the new Tundra truck you can:

- Tow heavy loads (powerful 5.7 liter V8 engine)
- Arrive in style (new streamlined design)
- Save money (fuel-efficient engine with four valves per cylinder)

Avoid features. Think benefits. Features appeal to the intellect, benefits appeal to emotions. Without an emotional buy-in, customers won't click.

Factor #9: Use Illustrative Product and Service Images—The "Hero Shot"

The images that you display on your web pages can significantly improve your conversion rates. If you sell products, including images of those products is an obvious choice.

If you sell a service, you can add an image that represents the benefit and value of your service (see Figure 5-3).

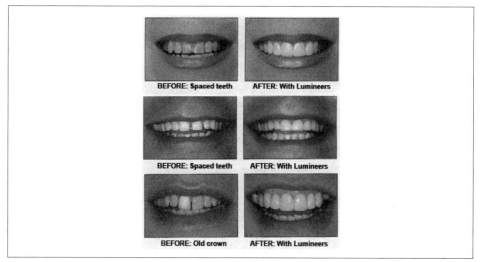

Figure 5-3. Before and after shots for a cosmetic dentistry site

Use the source credibility effect by showing attractive people in uniforms who are administering your offerings and services or answering the phone. Place a picture of your staff on your "About Us" page to improve your credibility and trust by showing that your staff is real.

Follow these best practices for product images:

- Use *one high-quality image* that represents your product or service. If you sell a product, use a photo of the product.

- *Don't use clip art* or stock photos that are not relevant to the product.

- Position your descriptive text to the *right* of your product images. It is uncomfortable for your visitors to read text that is to the left of the product image. Note that most catalogs have the product on the left and the descriptive text on the right.[25]

- For multiple images displayed on one page, *place your most important products in the center or on the left* of the page. Studies have shown that people look at the thumbnails on the right last.[26]

- *Make your product images clickable.* People enjoy clicking on images to view larger, more detailed versions of your "hero shot" (i.e., a picture of your product or service). You can also consider using a pop-up window that offers a larger, more detailed image with additional text describing the product.

[25]MarketingSherpa. 2005. *Landing Page Handbook* 1. Warren, RI: MarketingSherpa, 51.
[26]Ibid., 49.

- Add a *descriptive caption* under the image. Studies show that your headline and caption are the two content items on your web pages that are read the most.[27] Captions and part numbers also make good SEO copy (see Figure 5-4).

20 oz. LAVA® Lamp with Logo

The essential design element in any Google cube, there's just something we love about Lava Lamps. Maybe because they ooze gooey coolness. This 14.3" tall model features a brushed chrome base and endless waves of color. Choose one or buy all four of the Google colors in red, blue, green and yellow. Google logo on the base. LAVA® and the LAVA® motion lamp trademarks are owned by Haggerty Enterprises, Inc.

#GO42029

Price: $23.50

Click on Color   Color: Red

Quantity: 1

🔍 more views   Add To Cart   check stock

Figure 5-4. Google lava lamp

Factor #10: Use Interactive Elements to Engage Users

Immediately interest and engage your site visitors with interactive website components. These elements invite your visitors to focus their attention on your message. They include audio, video, and web-based devices such as Flash movies and interactive customer support tools such as LivePerson.

Interactivity in various forms, such as forums, a feedback form, and search tools, have been shown to boost website usability[28] and user satisfaction.[29] You can use these technologies to engage your website visitors in real time and get them to take actions that lead to more conversions.

For example, adding a *video or Flash movie* to your website that illustrates the benefits of your product or service will improve conversions (see Figure 5-5).

[27]Ibid., 51.

[28]Teo, H.H. et al. 2003. "An empirical study of the effects of interactivity on web user attitude." *International Journal of Human-Computer Studies 58* (3): 281–305.

[29]Lowry, P. et al. 2006. "A Theoretical Model and Empirical Results Linking Website Interactivity and Usability Satisfaction." In *HICSS 2006* (January 4–7, 2006), 9 pages.

Figure 5-5. Toyota Highlander Hybrid Flash movie

If you add the LivePerson customer support tool to your website and train your customer support staff to use it effectively, you can increase your conversions by up to 500% and reduce the length of your sales cycle by 48%, according to LivePerson (see Figure 5-6).[30]

Figure 5-6. LivePerson symbol

Adding a *video spokesperson* increased the conversion rate of DiscoveryStore.com by 78% (see Figure 5-7 for an example).[31]

Remember, it's not simply the presence of an interactive feature that is important, but rather how well you use it. The speed and content quality of the chat message are higher predictors of interactivity than the mere presence of a chat function.[32]

Staging Your CRO Campaign

The next discussion is divided into three sections: *discovery*, *planning*, and *optimization*. While these include important techniques for CRO, they're not the only techniques.

---

[30]LivePerson. 2007. "Hoover's increases conversion rates and average order values with LivePerson's proactive chat." LivePerson, *http://www.liveperson.com/customers/hoovers/results.asp* (accessed February 17, 2008).

[31]MarketingSherpa. July 19, 2005. "Video Spokesmodel Lifts Ecommerce Conversions 78%: A/B Test Results." MarketingSherpa, *https://www.marketingsherpa.com/barrier.html?ident=24086* (accessed February 17, 2008).

[32]Song, J., and G. Zinkhan. 2008. "Exploring the Determinants of Perceived Web Site Interactivity." *Journal of Marketing* 72 (2).

Figure 5-7. Example from MyWeddingFavors.com of a video spokesperson

You will want to implement these along with the other methods described elsewhere in this book, including website testing, search-friendly site development, and high-performance web design.

Discovery

As you learned earlier in this chapter, in "The Benefits of CRO," most websites convert at only a fraction of their true potential: 3.1%, according to a Shop.org study (*http://www.shop.org/soro*). The reason for this startling statistic is that most websites have not been planned with the conversion needs of target visitors in mind.

This process involves *discovering* who your target visitors are so that you can understand their specific needs, goals, psychology, and hot buttons. By discovering their unique needs, you can write content to address those needs and answer their questions so that they convert.

Discovering personas

Using discovery questions enables you to identify who your prospective customers are. The following questions will help you discover how to use your website to persuade customers to buy from you or to become a lead for your sales team.

Demographics. What kinds of people buy from your website? Are they male or female? What is their age? What is their occupation? What is their income and education, and how do these factors play an important role in their buying decision?

Psychographics. Different personality types respond differently to who, what, where, why, and when. Knowing this information allows you to build personas to tailor content to each personality type.

Geographic region. Where is your target market located? Do you sell globally, nationally, or just to the locals in your hometown? If you cater to a local market, can you provide your customers with a map and directions to your office or retail store?

Customer pain points and goals. What is the main problem that your typical prospect wants to fix? What is the *most important factor* to the prospect who is considering buying your offerings?

Value proposition. Why would a prospect favor your business over all other competitors? What makes your company unique? For example, if you are a pizza company and you offer "Delivery in 30 minutes or it's free," tell the world! This information allows you to position your business as the best choice with a strong value proposition and guarantee.

Benefit hierarchy. What benefits are important to your target prospect? Construct a list of these benefits in order, beginning with the most important. Knowing this information allows you to write content that speaks to the heart of your website visitors, and helps to move them past their emotional tipping point.

Key frustrations and objections. What are the biggest frustrations and objections that your prospects have when conducting business with companies in your industry? Do your customers hate to pay shipping and handling fees? Do they feel that your products cost too much? Do they have specific questions that you can answer on your website? This information allows you to create content that reduces your prospects' reluctance to buy. To address their objections, provide answers to their most pressing questions and rebuttals to their objections to buying. You can also reduce key frustrations and objections by offering free shipping, low prices, satisfaction guarantees, toll-free phone numbers, FAQs, or easy financing. Plus, you can provide trust-builders such as privacy policies and security seals.

Buying criteria. What specific factors do your prospects look for when making decisions to buy your products or services? Knowing this information allows you to write content that positions you as the expert in the industry who helps customers make good decisions.

Risk reversal. How can you lower or even eliminate the risk in buying your product or service? How can you encourage your clients to trust you? Risk-reversal techniques create offers that many customers can't refuse. Examples include 100% satisfaction guarantees, free return shipping, free trials, and unconditional money-back guarantees.

Keyword phrases. What keyword phrases does your target market use in search engines such as Google, Yahoo!, and MSN Search to find your product or service? Incorporate these search terms into your web pages to mirror their queries and optimize your site for search engines.

The Unique Selling Proposition (USP)

The competition on the Web is fierce. You need to differentiate yourself from your competitors and position your company as the best choice in the market. What makes your company unique?

Having a compelling USP will dramatically improve the positioning and marketability of your company and its products. It accomplishes three things for you:

- It clearly sets you apart from your competition, positioning you as the best choice for your customers' *unique* needs.
- It persuades others to *exchange money* for your product or service.
- It is *a proposal* or offer that you make for acceptance.

Your USP is the force that drives your business to succeed. You also can use it as a branding tool and a selling tool. In addition, your widely deployed USP allows you to build a lasting reputation while you're making sales. The ultimate goal of your USP and marketing is to have people say, "Oh yes, I've heard of you. You're the company that...", and continue by requesting more information or by purchasing your product.

Your USP communicates the very essence of what you are offering. It needs to be so compelling and so benefit-oriented that it can be used as a headline all by itself to sell your product or service. Because you want to optimize your website and all of your marketing materials, create your USP before you create content and advertisements.

The following seven-step process shows you how to construct a USP for your business.

Step 1: Use your biggest benefits. Clearly describe the three biggest benefits of owning your product or service. You have to explain to your prospects exactly how your product will benefit them. What are the three biggest benefits that you offer? For example:

- Faster delivery
- Lower cost
- Higher quality

Step 2: Be unique. Essentially, your USP separates you from the competition, sets up buying criteria that illustrates your company as the most logical choice, and makes your product or service the "must have" item.

You can state your USP in your product description, in your offer, or in your guarantee, but it should always create desire and urgency:

> **Product**: "The Fluke VR1710 Voltage Quality Recorder Is an Easy-to-Use Instrument That Will Help You Instantly Detect Power Quality Problems."
> **Offer**: "Order the New Fluke VR1710 Voltage Quality Recorder to Quickly Detect Power Quality Problems."
> **Guarantee**: "The New Fluke VR1710 Voltage Quality Recorder Will Help You Quickly Detect Power Quality Problems, Guaranteed."

Winning USP Examples

Federal Express (FedEx) nearly equals the U.S. Post Office in the overnight package shipping market with the following USP:

"Federal Express: When it absolutely, positively has to be there overnight."

This USP allowed FedEx to quickly gain market share in the express delivery market, increasing its sales and profits.

In today's competitive market, your business cannot thrive if you are using copycat marketing. Your small business absolutely, positively has to have a USP that cuts through the clutter. Your USP must position you not as the best choice, but as the *only* choice.

Building your USP is worth the effort because of the added advantage you'll have in the market. Using a powerful USP will make your job of marketing and selling much easier.

The following are two powerful USPs that alleviate the "pain" experienced by consumers in their industries.

Example #1—The food industry:

- Pain: The kids are hungry, but Mom and Dad are too tired to cook!
- USP: "You get fresh, hot pizza delivered to your door in 30 minutes or less—or it's free." (Domino's Pizza original USP)

Example #2—The cold medicine industry:

- Pain: You are sick, feel terrible, and can't sleep.
- USP: "The nighttime, sniffling, sneezing, coughing, aching, fever, best-sleep-you-ever-got-with-a-cold medicine." (NyQuil)

Step 3: Solve an industry "pain point" or "performance gap." Identify which needs are going unfulfilled in your industry or in your local market. The need or gap that exists between the current situation and the desired objective is sometimes termed a *performance gap*. Many businesses succeed by basing their USP on industry performance gaps.

Learn about the most frustrating things your customer experiences when working with you or your industry in general. Use your USP to alleviate that pain and make sure that you deliver on your promises.

Step 4: Be specific and offer proof. Consumers are generally skeptical of advertising claims. Alleviate their skepticism by being specific and, where possible, offering proof. For example, "You'll lose 10 pounds in 60 days or your money back!"

Step 5: Condense your USP into one clear and concise sentence. The most powerful USPs are so well written that you would not change or even move a single word. After you have composed your USP, your advertising and marketing copy will practically write itself.

Step 6: Integrate your USP into your website and all marketing materials. Besides your website, you should include variations of your USP in *all* of your marketing materials, including:

- Advertising and sales copy headlines
- Business cards, brochures, flyers, and signs
- Your "elevator pitch," phone, and sales scripts
- Letterhead, letters, postcards, and calendars

Your slogan can be an abbreviated version of your USP, or the whole phrase.

Step 7: Deliver on your USP's promise. Be bold when developing your USP, but be careful to ensure that you can deliver. Your USP should have promises and guarantees that capture your audience's attention and compel them to respond. In the beginning, it was a challenge for FedEx to absolutely, positively deliver overnight, but the company subsequently developed the system that allowed it to consistently deliver on the promise.

Planning

Now that you know what the profiles of your visitors look like and what information they need to make a buying decision on your website, the next step is *planning* your website. Planning includes the following steps:

1. Creating the redesign plan
2. Planning your website design and color scheme

Step 1: Create the redesign plan: planning your site architecture

Site planning includes specifying which web pages are needed and how they are organized. It also establishes the paths that your visitors will take through your website. One way to start this is to jot down a site map containing a line-item list of web pages that your website will contain.

For a website that sells expensive business solutions or enterprise software, your site map might look like this:

- Home Page
- About Us
  — Company history
  — Management staff
  — Employment opportunities

- Contact Us
- Solutions for IT Professionals
  — Network management solutions
  — Enterprise information system (EIS)
  — Electronic data interchange (EDI)
- Solutions for Financial Officers
  — General ledger software
  — Fixed assets software
- Solutions for Marketing and Sales Departments
  — How marketing can boost leads
    - Marketing Tool 1
    - Marketing Tool 2
    - Marketing Tool 3
    - Marketing Tool 4
  — How the sales force can increase sales
    - Sales Tool 1
    - Sales Tool 2
    - Sales Tool 3
    - Sales Tool 4
- Lead Generator: White Paper
- Lead Generator: Webinar

Map out every page of your web site with these things in mind:

- Which visitor profiles are likely to visit each web page?
- Which specific keywords might they use at the search engines to get there?
- What sorts of questions does the prospect who has landed on that page need to have answered?
- What specific strategy will the web page take to answer these questions?
- What actions might each profile take next?

Step 2: Plan your website design and color scheme

The colors that you use for your website will influence your visitors. Your color scheme will cause your visitors to react to your website either positively or negatively. Picking the wrong colors can sound a red-alert alarm in your visitors' psyches and send them scurrying for cover. This results in high bail-out rates and plummeting conversion rates.

Identifying your customers' personalities and personas will allow you to pick the colors that they prefer. For example, IBM knows its customers are buyers of serious computer hardware, software, and high-end consulting services. It chose the more serious blue and black color scheme to communicate more credibility and trust, and uses this color scheme and style in its website design to unify all of its marketing materials (see Figure 5-8).

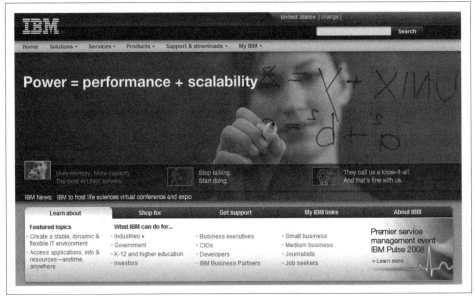

Figure 5-8. IBM.com home page

PartyCity.com knows its customers are party animals. Its customers want to ensure that their parties are bright, cheery, and fun, so PartyCity chose to use bright and fun colors such as red, green, bright blue, and even pink! (See Figure 5-9.)

Once you've tailored the colors to the psychological moods of your target audience, the end result will transform your website into a powerful tool to appeal to and draw your prospects in like a magnet.

Optimization

After discovery and planning, the *optimization* phase is where you create a site plan that is complete with information architecture and personas. In this phase, you'll create web template mockups to finalize effective layouts. You'll write targeted persuasive copy, headlines, and offers. You'll put your USP into action with a winning slogan and initial body copy. Finally, you'll optimize your conversion paths and progressively improve conversion rates by testing different alternatives.

Figure 5-9. PartyCity.com home page

Optimize with persuasive copywriting

Persuasive copywriting is the key to website success. Your words must inform, *excite*, and persuade your visitors to take action. To persuade, your words must be relevant to your visitors' needs. To achieve relevance, you must orient your content to the users' point of view and give them what they want.

Be brief. Be bold and inject personality into your prose. Stand out from the crowd by surprising them with unexpected words, ideas, and an ironclad guarantee. Be relevant. Make your offer irresistible.

Your customers are busy, and your copy must grab their attention quickly, as people spend only a fraction of a second evaluating your pages. Turbo-charge your words to make them sparkle and persuade.

Effective copy has a number of unique characteristics:

- It appeals to the *value hierarchies* of your customers.
- It includes *benefit-oriented* headlines and content.
- It contains primary and secondary *calls to action*.
- It uses effective and accepted *writing techniques*.
- It incorporates the *six persuaders*.

Appeal to the value hierarchies of your customers. Psychologists use *value hierarchies* to help them understand what is important to individuals.[33] Value hierarchies *frame* the most important value that your company's product or service offers to customers. By focusing on *what matters most* to your customers, you'll keep your content *relevant.*

Create benefit-oriented content. Benefit-oriented content directly addresses the value hierarchies of customers by showing *how* your products and services will fulfill your prospects' needs. Your copy should emphasize, amplify, and illuminate the benefits of your products and services. Saturate your copy with benefits and avoid feature-oriented copy.

There are some exceptions. The type of copy that you use in your site depends on your target market. In the computer parts industry, for example, features and specifications are frequently more important than value-oriented copy. Most OEMs and retailers offer their value-oriented content as the default view, with tabs or links to detailed lists of features and specifications. Often, a particular new feature will dominate the marketing for a particular product. As a rule, follow the standards and expectations of your industry and market.

Write engaging headlines and copy. Your headlines need to appear to be relevant to your visitors to catch their attention. Enticing headlines will lure more people to your site because they also appear off-site in RSS feeds and resultant news stories.

Make your headlines short, punchy summaries of the important topic that follows. Omit articles and quantifiers (*a, an, and, the*) and use subject/noun/verb combinations in newspaper style.

Here are some tips for writing engaging headlines that convert:

- *Include keyword phrases* in the headline when optimizing for search engines or bidding in a pay-per-click (PPC) campaign. This can help you rank higher in the search engines and shows visitors from your PPC campaign that the web page is relevant.

- *Highlight the benefits* with effective headlines that explicitly tell your visitors the benefits of your website, product, or service. For example, FabricWorkroom.com's headline summarizes its products and benefits: "Shop FabricWorkroom.com for Custom Home Decor and Designer Fabrics at Discount Prices."

- *Front-load keywords* in headlines for better keyword prominence and scanning. In general, active voice is strongest for ad copy. For SEO purposes, however, passive voice can help to front-load headlines with keywords.[34] Users often scan only the first two words in headlines, subheads, summaries, captions, links, and bulleted lists, so make the first two words count.

---

[33]Mentzer, J. et al. 1997. "Application of the means-end value hierarchy model to understanding logistics service value." *International Journal of Physical Distribution & Logistics Management* 27 (9/10): 630–643.

[34]Nielsen, J. October 22, 2007. "Passive Voice Is Redeemed for Web Headings." *Alertbox, http://www.useit. com/alertbox/passive-voice.html* (accessed February 17, 2008).

- *Use action-oriented copy* to tell visitors what they should do on your web page. For example, if you are offering a white paper for download on your landing page, tell your visitors to download the white paper in your headline. Simple, yes, but effective.

- *Arouse curiosity* so that your visitors are compelled to read further. Your headlines should leave your readers asking "How?" as their curiosity gets the better of them. For example: "How to Increase Your Landing Page Conversion Rates by 50% to 200%."

- *State only the facts* in your headline. Often, this is the best approach to take. For example, here is a headline for a Fluke Instruments product: "The Fluke VR1710 Voltage Quality Recorder Offers an Easy-to-Use Solution for Detecting Power Quality Problems."

- *Use an editorial style* to write ads that don't sound like ads. Writing headlines (and content) in an editorial style (similar to a newspaper story) can be the best way to capture the attention of your visitors and keep them reading. For example: "New VoIP Service Saves Homeowners Hundreds of Dollars in Phone Charges per Year."

- *Use subheadlines* directly underneath your headline to provide an additional place to improve conversions by adding and amplifying benefits to your web pages. Subheads are also a great place to include keywords for SEO. Jakob Nielsen recommends that headline writers "reduce duplication of salient keywords" in subheadlines and decks to increase the number of keywords that users scan.[35] Because users often read only the first couple of words in each text element, the use of different keywords in subheads and decks improves relevance and potential search engine rankings.

- *Test and retest* because headlines account for such a significant opportunity for increasing your conversion rate. Use A/B split-testing or multivariate software to test multiple headlines to find the one that improves your conversion rate the most.

Here are some tips for writing engaging copy:

Start (and end) each paragraph with a bang
> The first and last sentences of your paragraphs should pop. Pack your paragraphs with benefits to arouse your readers' interest and compel them to take action on your web pages. Design your copy so that readers can scan it quickly.

Include calls to action when writing links, buttons, and offers
> Your calls to action are the offers that you use to compel your visitors to take a desired action on your website. These actions can be to purchase a product or service, to sign up and become a lead for your sales team, or to "opt in" with an email address to learn more about a product so that you can market to them.

[35]Ibid.

Use action words and expressions in your hyperlinks

This causes visitors to click. Examples of action words and expressions are "Buy now for a 15% discount," "Discover…," "Learn how to…," "Click here to…," "Sign up for…," and "Search."

Use primary responses and secondary or back-up responses

The primary response to a website that you want is usually to purchase your product or become a lead. But for every one person who responds this way, there are usually 10 others who *almost* bought or *almost* clicked but never connected.

Develop ways to move these almost-buyers or almost-leads closer to a sale with backup responses

Perhaps your visitor is not ready to buy just now but would like to know about your future monthly specials. All he has to do is sign up for your free newsletter, or a similar backup response that you offer him.

Test descriptive text in your buttons

This will increase your conversions. Instead of using the standard "Submit" wording on buttons, use more descriptive text such as "Download now" to increase conversion rates. Button text is a good candidate for A/B split-testing.

Adopt a writing style. Your writing style affects your conversion rates. Be consistent throughout your online writing to build customer confidence and reduce customers' perceived risk of buying from your company. Use the personas you have developed to target your writing toward your audience.

Pain versus gain

People are more likely to avoid loss than they are to accept gains.[36] People don't like to lose their freedoms, and will fight to retain them.[37] You can either approach your copy from a positive, benefit-oriented perspective, or show your visitors what they'll lose if they don't go with your company.

Past, present, or future tense

Present tense talks about what is happening now. Present tense is more immediate and engaging—for example, "I am optimizing." Past tense ("I have optimized") and future tense ("I will optimize") are less engaging.

You, me, and them

Put yourself in your users' shoes and talk directly to them about how your products and services can help them make their lives better. First person is from the perspective of the writer: "I am optimizing." Second person takes the perspective of the reader: "You are optimizing." A second person pronoun directly addresses *your* readers and is the most engaging.

---

[36]Fiske, S. 1980. "Attention and weight in person perception: The impact of negative and extreme behavior." *Journal of Personality and Social Psychology* 38 (6): 889–906.

[37]Cialdini. *Influence: Science and Practice*, 215.

Be consistent

Build trust by being consistent and reliable in your communications with prospects. Avoid changing voice, tense, or pronouns in the middle of your pages. It confuses the reader.

Effective writing techniques. You can use a number of proven copywriting techniques to spice up your site. Use poetic meter, vary word choice and sentence length, appeal to emotions, and surprise your readers with sparkling verse and unexpected words. Of course, the effectiveness of these techniques will depend on your audience; again, use your personas to tailor copy.

Use verbs and active voice

Strong verbs have more impact than adverbs and adjectives. Sprinkle your prose with powerful verbs to give your words momentum and verve. Use active voice ("He optimized the copy") for copy, rather than passive voice ("The copy was optimized"). Passive voice is less engaging and more confusing to your reader. However, as discussed earlier, for shorter headlines, subheads, and bullet points, passive voice can be useful in some cases.

Tug emotions through effective mental imaging

Paint a picture of how your customers will benefit from your offerings. Effective writers don't describe what their characters look like, they describe key specifics about what the characters do, see, and hear. Our minds fill in the rest of the picture.

Write for scanning

People don't *read* very much online. They skim and scan, foraging for useful information.[38] To make your content easy to scan, break your copy into discrete, subject-size chunks. Use short, punchy paragraphs to make your points with:

- Half the word count
- Meaningful headlines and subheads
- Highlighted keywords
- Bulleted lists
- One idea per paragraph

Emphasize the highlights

Emphasize the most important sections of your copy, using bold and italics to highlight important phrases. Emphasis helps your readers pick up the gist of your page as they scan. You should arrange your highlighted phrases so that readers skimming them will understand your story in brief.

[38]Nielsen, J. May 6, 2008. "How Little Do Users Read?" Alertbox, *http://www.useit.com/alertbox/percent-text-read.html* (accessed June 7, 2008).

Avoid jargon and hype

Using insider jargon erects a barrier to reader flow. Avoid hype when describing your offerings—your visitors are highly skilled at detecting it. Instead, use clear, specific wording and make claims you can back up.

Use testimonials

Testimonials lend your offerings credibility through social proof. Learning what other people think of your book (Amazon), product, or service lends credibility to your company statements.

Don't be a wimp

Don't go halfway and say this *could*, *should*, *may*, or *might* happen. Be positive! Say that this will *absolutely* happen when visitors give you their credit card. Visitors need to be confident in their decisions and need to perceive that buying is a low-risk operation.

Offer a guarantee

Customers want to reduce the risk of their investments. One way to remove an objection is to offer an iron-clad money-back guarantee. By reducing their risk, you increase confidence, which makes it more likely that your visitors will buy.

Ask for the order

Asking your prospective customers to place an order is an obvious point, but you'd be surprised how often this is omitted.

Use graphics to enhance the sales experience

Finally, adding high-quality graphics that depict the actual product or service can enhance your conversion rates. Avoid generic graphics such as clip art or stock images that are unrelated to your offerings. Actual high-quality product shots are best.

You can use the six persuaders you read about earlier in combination with these writing techniques to create powerful prose that elicits action from your visitors.

Put it on paper and build graphical mockups

As Kelly Goto and Emily Cotler describe in their book *Web Redesign 2.0: Workflow That Works* (Peachpit Press), by creating wireframes and paper prototypes, you can make changes quickly without tying up your design team. You can use Fireworks for rapid prototyping, or Dreamweaver, which offers more functionality. In general, Adobe Creative Suite (Photoshop, Illustrator, etc.) is effective for mocking up prototypes and wireframe models.

Wireframe web templates and mockups to finalize "look and feel." Create mockups of optimized templates that follow popular website conventions, such as top navigation. Put important content above the fold, the logo and tagline on the top left, and contact information in the top right. (For more details, check out Jakob Nielson and Marie Tahir's *Homepage Usability: 50 Websites Deconstructed* [New Riders].) This wireframe layout shows what elements will appear where on your pages (see Figure 5-10).

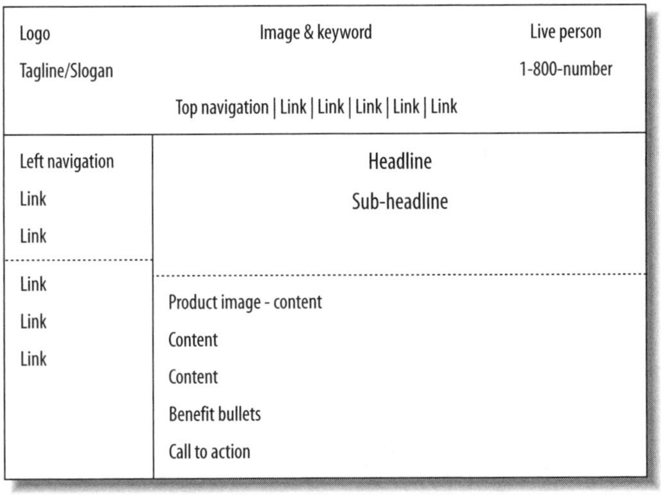

Logo	Image & keyword	Live person
Tagline/Slogan		1-800-number
	Top navigation | Link | Link | Link | Link | Link	

Left navigation	Headline
Link	Sub-headline
Link	
Link	Product image - content
Link	Content
Link	Content
	Benefit bullets
	Call to action

Figure 5-10. Wireframe layout

There are several types of web pages to optimize: home, lead generation, direct sales, and e-commerce product and category pages. Overall, you can apply the same principles described earlier to each page type.

MyWeddingFavors.com is an example of a well-optimized home page that includes most of the conversion builders we've discussed (see Figure 5-11).

MyWeddingFavors.com uses:

- Professional design and colors optimized for its target market
- Intuitive navigation
- Logo and USP in the top-left corner
- Contact information and Live Chat in the upper-right corner
- Testimonials/credibility builders such as third-party HACKER SAFE logos
- "Hero shots" of top products or services above the fold
- Calls to action

One addition would improve the MyWeddingFavors.com home page: a privacy policy displayed directly below the signup form.

Taking a different approach are sales teams for companies that sell complex or expensive products or services, such as legal services, business software, dental services, or advertising, which mainly use lead generation. Lead generation pages get website visitors to accept a free offer (such as free information or a white paper) and to fill out a form with their contact information. The form generates the lead that the sales team can then use to cultivate a relationship and close a sale.

Figure 5-11. Conversion elements integrated into the MyWeddingFavors.com home page

Advertising in these lucrative and competitive markets can be expensive. Therefore, your lead generation page must be optimized to maximize conversions (leads) to generate an ROI for your advertising budget. For example, advertising on Google AdWords for the hyper-competitive keywords *human resources software* can cost upward of $10 *per click*! Some conversion builders to include on your lead generation pages are:

- Professional design and colors optimized for your target market
- No navigation to keep visitors on the page instead of clicking away
- Logo and USP in the top-left corner
- Contact information in the upper-right corner
- Benefit-oriented headline optimized with keywords used in Google AdWords ad
- Benefit-oriented copy with benefit bullets
- Testimonials and credibility builders

- Privacy policy (ideally placed under the signup form)
- Hero shots of the product or service above the fold
- A compelling offer (such as a free white paper or consultation)
- A lead generation form

A software provider with a website called UltimateSoftware.com uses the lead generation page shown in Figure 5-12, which includes most of these conversion builders.

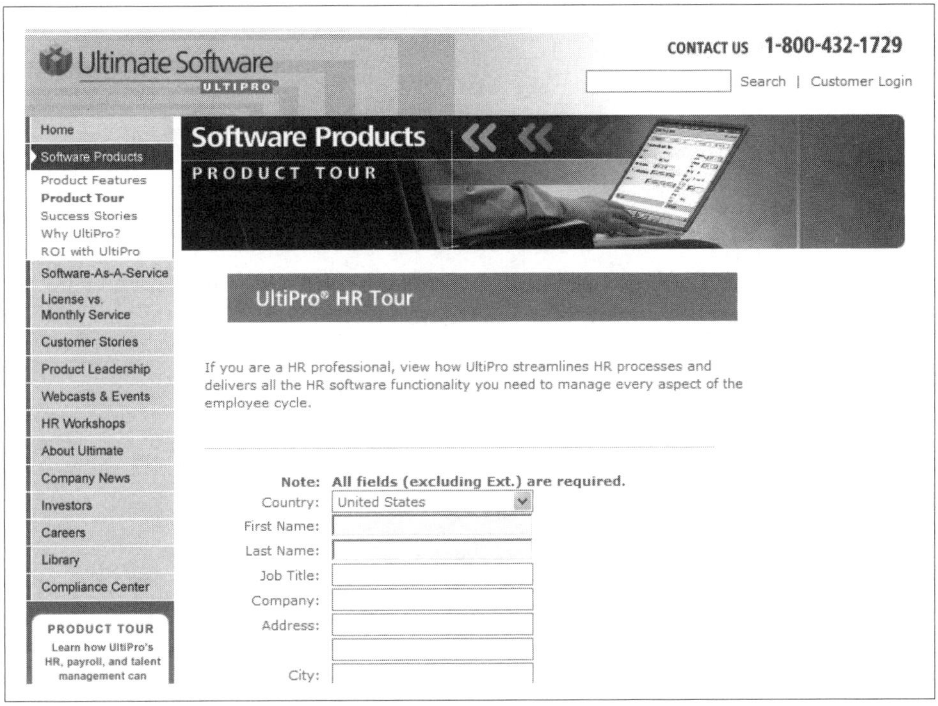

Figure 5-12. Ultimate Software's lead generation page

Optimize your conversion paths to get the click

Optimizing the steps that visitors take on their way to conversion can yield significant improvements in your website's conversion rates (see Chapter 4 for an example). A *conversion path* or *conversion funnel* is a path that a visitor takes from entering your website to the point where the visitor becomes a conversion in the form of a sale or lead (see Figure 5-13).

How efficient is your website at getting visitors to click from your home page to the most important interior page or pages? Are your most popular products (or services) featured prominently on your home page with persuasive headlines, descriptive copy, and enticing product images? Optimize your website's conversion paths and increase your sales.

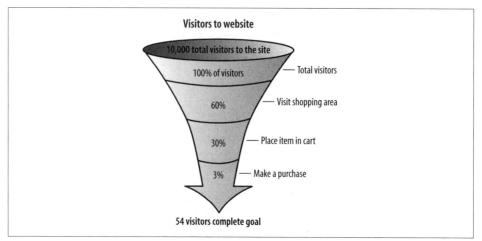

Figure 5-13. Conversion funnel

Google Analytics provides Funnel and Navigation Reports, which help you simplify the checkout process of your website (see Figure 5-14).

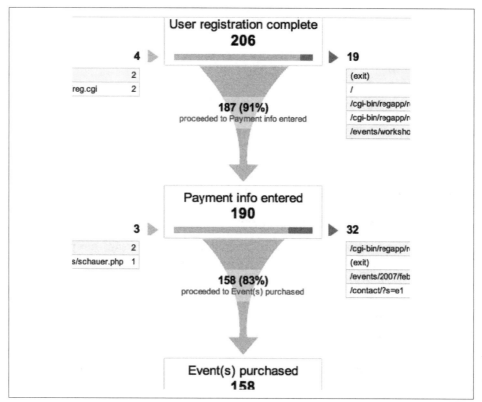

Figure 5-14. Google Analytics' Funnel and Navigation Report

This report shows how many of your website visitors enter the conversion funnel and how many actually make it to the end. This report also shows where your visitors go if they drop out of the process. This can help you identify and correct obstacles to conversion.

For more details on optimizing your site with web metrics, including Google Website Optimizer, see Chapter 10.

Test Everything

Successful sites test everything to maximize ROI. They test alternative headlines, call-to-action text, body copy, images, page component layout and design, text color, link text, and landing pages. They use tools to compare those alternatives, such as Google's Website Optimizer to conduct multivariate tests and A/B split-testing to find out which combinations work best to maximize conversion rates. One company selling an expensive product enjoyed a tenfold increase in its CTR by changing the text in a button from "Buy Online" to "Price and Buy."[39] It pays to test.

You can read about these testing methods and tools in Chapter 10.

Summary

CRO turns your website into a veritable persuasion machine. Sites that are conversion-optimized squeeze more leads, sales, and opt-ins from their visitors. CRO uses benefit-oriented persuasive copywriting and credibility-based web design to *influence* visitors to accept your message and comply with your requests. Benefit-oriented copy appeals to your visitors' emotions and meets their needs, which increases their desire. By combining desire, confidence, and trust-building elements such as testimonials, credibility-based professional design, and third-party badges, you will convert more of your prospects into buyers.

This chapter detailed some of the best practices that improve conversion rates. You also learned how to write persuasive copy, what the six persuaders are, and what our automatic response is to source credibility. You can maximize your conversion rate by testing different elements against one another with specialized tools. The most important factors for high conversion rates are:

- Credibility-based professional design optimized for your target market
- Credibility-based logo and memorable USP/slogan in the top-left corner
- Intuitive navigation
- Contact information, form, and/or Live Chat in the upper-right corner

---

[39]Weischedel, B., and E. Huizingh. 2006. "Website Optimization with Web Metrics: A Case Study." In *ICEC 2006* (Fredericton, New Brunswick, Canada: August 14–16, 2006), 463–470.

- The use of personas with tailored copy and trigger words for each customer personality type
- Persuasive, benefit-oriented copy and headlines (reflect keywords in PPC ads)
- Fast response times for browsers and queries
- Clear primary and secondary calls to action
- Useful engagement devices
- Illustrative product or service images—"hero shots" above the fold
- Testimonials, credibility builders (e-seals), and risk reversers (100% guarantee)
- No presentation flaws
- Privacy policy (ideally placed under the input form)
- Testing, tracking, and design iteration

Web Performance Optimization

Web performance optimization streamlines your content and tunes your server to deliver web pages faster. In the following chapters, you'll learn how to optimize your web pages and multimedia, shrink your Cascading Style Sheet (CSS) and HTML file sizes, and reduce server requests with sprites and suturing. You'll learn how to squeeze your Ajax code and make it more robust. You'll explore advanced techniques such as improving parallel downloads, caching, HTTP compression, and URL rewriting.

Finally, in Chapter 10 you'll read about best-practice metrics and tools to measure and optimize your search engine marketing (SEM) campaigns and improve website performance. First, let's explore the user psychology of delay, and trends in web page growth.

The Psychology of Website Performance

Previous research has shown that user frustration increases when page load times exceed 8 to 10 seconds without feedback.[1,2] Newer evidence shows that broadband users are less tolerant of web page delays than narrowband users. A JupiterResearch survey found that 33% of broadband shoppers are unwilling to wait more than four seconds for a web page to load, whereas 43% of narrowband users will not wait more than six seconds.[3]

---

[1] Bouch, A. et al. 2000. "Quality is in the Eye of the Beholder: Meeting Users' Requirements for Internet Quality of Service." In *CHI 2000* (The Hague, The Netherlands: April 1–6, 2000), 297–304.

[2] In my own book, *Speed Up Your Site: Web Site Optimization* (New Riders), I determined an average of 8.6 seconds for tolerable wait time.

[3] Akamai. June 2006. "Retail Web Site Performance: Consumer Reaction to a Poor Online Shopping Experience." Akamai Technologies, *http://www.akamai.com* (accessed February 10, 2008). This is a JupiterResearch abandonment survey commissioned by Akamai.

The Effects of Slow Download Times

Even small changes in response times can have significant effects. Google found that moving from a 10-result page loading in 0.4 seconds to a 30-result page loading in 0.9 seconds decreased traffic and ad revenues by 20%.[4] When the home page of Google Maps was reduced from 100 KB to 70–80 KB, traffic went up 10% in the first week and an additional 25% in the following three weeks.[5] Tests at Amazon revealed similar results: every 100 ms increase in load time of Amazon.com decreased sales by 1%.[6]

Overall, slow web pages lower perceived credibility and quality. Keeping your page load times below tolerable attention thresholds will help to lower user frustration,[7] create higher conversion rates,[8] and promote deeper flow states.

Speed and Flow

Speed is the second most important factor, after site attractiveness, to increasing flow in users (see Figure II-1).[9] People who are more engaged while browsing your site will learn faster and show an improved attitude and behavior toward your site.

To increase perceived speed, strive to display your initial useful content in less than one or two seconds by layering and streamlining your content. Once total load time exceeds six to eight seconds, provide linear feedback to extend the tolerable wait time by lowering stress levels and allowing users to plan ahead.[10] See Chapter 7 for techniques on using CSS to streamline your content to display faster.

[4] Linden, G. November 6, 2006. "Marissa Mayer at Web 2.0." Geeking with Greg, *http://glinden.blogspot.com/2006/11/marissa-mayer-at-web-20.html* (accessed February 8, 2008).

[5] Farber, D. November 9, 2006. "Google's Marissa Mayer: Speed Wins." CNET Between the Lines, *http://blogs.zdnet.com/BTL/?p=3925* (accessed February 10, 2008).

[6] Kohavi, R., and R. Longbotham. 2007. "Online Experiments: Lessons Learned." *Computer* 40 (9): 103–105. The Amazon statistic was taken from a presentation by Greg Linden at Stanford: *http://home.blarg.net/~glinden/StanfordDataMining.2006-11-29.ppt.*

[7] Ceaparu, I. et al. 2004. "Determining Causes and Severity of End-User Frustration." *International Journal of Human-Computer Interaction* 17 (3): 333–356. Slow websites inhibit users from reaching their goals, causing frustration.

[8] Akamai. 2007. "Boosting Online Commerce Profitability with Akamai." Akamai Technologies, *http://www.akamai.com* (accessed February 10, 2008). Based on the finding that 30% to 50% of transactions above the four-second threshold bail out, Akamai estimated that by reducing the percentage of transactions above this threshold from 40% to 10%, conversion rates will improve by 9% to 15%.

[9] Skadberg, Y., and J. Kimmel. 2004. "Visitors' flow experience while browsing a Web site: its measurement, contributing factors and consequences." *Computers in Human Behavior* 20 (3): 403–422. Flow is an optimal experience where users are fully engaged in an activity.

[10]Nah, F. 2004. "A study on tolerable waiting time: how long are Web users willing to wait?" *Behaviour & Information Technology* 23 (3): 153–163.

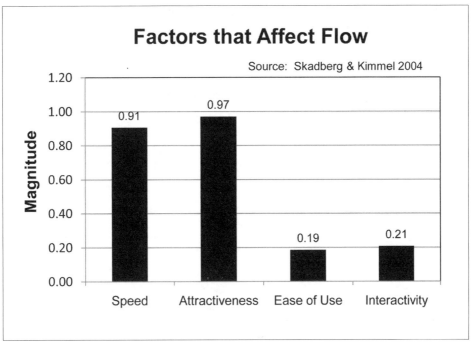

Figure II-1. Factors that affect flow in websites

Fast First Impressions

People make snap decisions about the aesthetic value and thus the credibility of your pages. In as little as 1/20th of a second, users form a first impression of your page that does not change significantly over time.[11] Confirming these results, Noam Tractinsky and others found that the average attractiveness ratings of web pages after being exposed for only half a second were consistent with the ratings after 10 seconds.[12]

Clearly you only have a very short time to make a good first impression on the Web.

Growth of the Average Web Page

The average home page has grown in size and complexity over the years. From 2003 to 2008, the size of the average web page grew more than 3.3 times from 93.7 KB to more

---

[11]Lindgaard, G. et al. 2006. "Attention web designers: You have 50 milliseconds to make a good first impression!" *Behaviour and Information Technology* 25 (2): 115-126.

[12]Tractinsky, N. et al. 2006. "Evaluating the consistency of immediate aesthetic perceptions of web pages," *International Journal of Human-Computer Studies* 64 (11): 1071-1083.

than 312 KB (see Figure II-2). During the same five-year period, the number of objects (separate files, such as images, CSS, and JavaScript) in the average web page nearly doubled from 25.7 to 49.9 objects per page.[13,14]

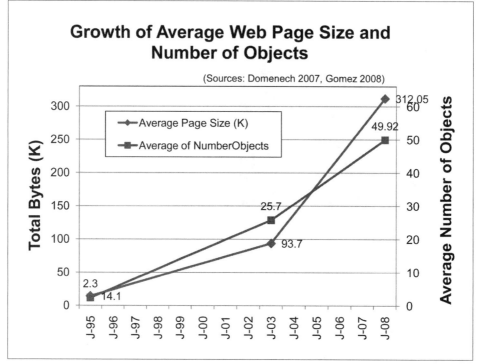

Figure II-2. Growth of web page size and objects over time

Object Overhead Dominates Web Page Delay

In the Web's early days, when there were few objects per page, total page size dominated web page response times. With the growth of the number of objects per page, however, the latency due to *object overhead*, not the objects themselves, now dominates most web page delays (see Figure II-3).[15]

For four or more external objects per page, the overhead of *description time* (DT in the graph, caused by the dependency between objects) for objects plus *waiting time* (WT in the graph, caused by limited parallelism) for threads makes up more than

[13]Domenech, J. et al. 2007. "A user-focused evaluation of web prefetching algorithms." *Computer Communications* 30 (10): 2213–2224.

[14]Flinn, D., and B. Betcher. "Re: latest top 1000 website data?" Email to author, January 8, 2008. Gomez, Inc. provided the top 1000 web page data from June 2006 to January 2008 (available at *http://www. websiteoptimization.com/secrets/performance/survey.zip*).

[15]Yuan, J. et al. 2005. "A More Precise Model for Web Retrieval." In *WWW 2005* (Chiba, Japan: May 10–14, 2005), 926–927. Figure used by permission.

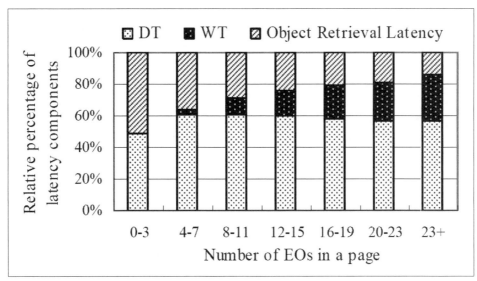

Figure II-3. Relative distribution of latency components showing that object overhead dominates web page latency

50% of web page delay. As the number of objects increases, the delay from downloading the actual objects pales in comparison, with only 20% or less due to object size as the number of objects per page exceeds 20.

Because of this object overhead, *improving parallelism* is a more effective way to optimize throughput than Content Delivery Networks (CDNs), DNS caching, or persistent connections.[16] Persistent and pipelined connections are more effective on connections faster than 200 Kbps. Therefore, narrowband users suffer the most from the inexorable increase in web objects.[17] You'll learn how to improve parallelism in Chapter 9.

Response Time Guidelines

From 2003 to 2008, web page size has more than tripled and the number of external objects has nearly doubled. So, over time narrowband users (56K and ISDN) have experienced slower response times. Broadband users, however, have experienced somewhat faster response times. For broadband users, the average download time of the Keynote Business 40 Internet Performance Index (KB40) has decreased from 2.8 to 2.3 seconds from February 2006 to February 2008 (see Figure II-4).[18]

---

[16]Bent, L., and G. Voelker. 2002. "Whole Page Performance." In *WCW 2002* (Boulder, CO: August 14–16, 2002), 8.

[17]Hall, J. et al. 2003. "The Effect of Early Packet Loss on Web Page Download Times." In *PAM 2003* (La Jolla, CA: April 6–8, 2003).

[18]Berkowitz, D., and A. Gonzalez. "Andy: Keynote data for your use." Email to author (February 8, 2008). Keynote Systems, Inc. provided the graph of the KB40 response time from February 2006 to February 2008.

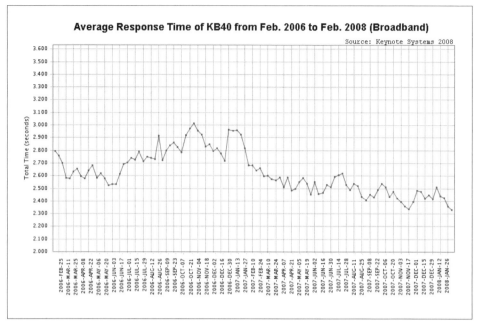

Figure II-4. Average KB40 website performance over broadband from February 2006 to February 2008 (Source: Keynote Systems, Inc.)

So, the increase in the average speed of broadband is faster than the increase in the size and complexity of the average web page. That is one reason why broadband users expect faster response times, yet narrowband users experience slower response times. Keynote recommends the following response times for different connection speeds:[19]

- Two to three seconds for business/high-end home speeds
- Three to five seconds for entry-level DSL
- 20 to 30 seconds for dial-up users (implies a total page size of 100 KB at 20 seconds)

So, the old 8- to 10-second rule has diverged. With the response time trend shown in Figure II-4, we recommend three- to four-second total load times for broadband users. Given the growth in average page size shown in Figure II-2, we recommend keeping your HTML code under 40–60 KB (which will load in less than 8 to 12 seconds), and page graphics under 40–60 KB (another 8 to 12 seconds of progressive load) for dial-up users. This equates to an absolute limit for dial-up of 120 KB.

Note that there are some exceptions. These recommendations apply to landing pages, home pages, and pages where the user is likely to navigate quickly. For pages where the user expects to linger, such as a white paper, breaking up the page can be annoying and can make printing and searching more difficult.

[19]Rushlo, B. "web performance download time guidelines?" Email to author, February 21, 2008. Keynote response time guidelines.

Summary and Next Steps

With the spread of broadband, high-speed users are no longer willing to wait 8 to 10 seconds for a page to load. Today you have three to four seconds to respond, or you risk abandonment. Although broadband users have seen faster load times, narrow-band users have been left behind. With the average web page sporting more than 50 external objects, object overhead now dominates most web page delays. Minimizing HTTP requests while still retaining attractiveness has become the most important skill set for web performance optimizers.

In the following chapters, you'll learn how to optimize your content by reducing file sizes, using CSS, and applying advanced server- and client-side techniques.

Web Page Optimization

Web page optimization streamlines your content to maximize display speed. Fast display speed is the key to success with your website. It increases profits, decreases costs, and improves customer satisfaction (not to mention search engine rankings, accessibility, and maintainability).

Streamlining transforms your pages to display navigable content faster, and to defer or delay off-site content. In this chapter, you'll learn how to reduce HTTP requests, convert to semantic markup to more easily style with Cascading Style Sheets (CSS), optimize graphics and multimedia, and defer or delay the loading of off-site content.

To maximize web page display speed, you can employ the following 10 techniques:

- Minimize HTTP requests.
- Resize and optimize images.
- Optimize multimedia.
- Convert JavaScript behavior to CSS.
- Use server-side sniffing.
- Optimize JavaScript for execution speed and file size.
- Convert table layout to CSS layout.
- Replace inline style with CSS rules.
- Minimize initial display time.
- Load JavaScript wisely.

Using the best practices in this chapter, you'll transform your HTML and multimedia to give your site more hurtle and less turtle. First, let's explore some common web page problems and trends that confront web performance engineers.

Common Web Page Problems

The size and complexity of the markup that you use in your web pages determine, for the most part, their initial display speed. Pages that are large and complex, especially those with nested tables and mispositioned CSS and JavaScript files, delay the time it takes for useful content to display. Sleek and streamlined pages *feel* faster because of quicker feedback through progressive display. The idea is to streamline your markup using standards-based techniques and let your code get out of the way of your content.

CSS and JavaScript File Placement

Positioning CSS in the top (head) and JavaScript at the bottom (body) of your HTML enables progressive rendering. Mispositioned CSS or JavaScript can delay the rendering of content in browsers. See the upcoming section "Put CSS at the top, JavaScript at the bottom" for more details.

As Steve Souders describes in his book *High Performance Web Sites* (O'Reilly), 80% of web page response time is in the content. Most of this time is spent dealing with the objects that make up a web page. As the number of objects per page increases beyond four, *object overhead* dominates total web page delay.

As you learned in the introduction to Part II, most popular web pages go well past this threshold, averaging more than 50 objects per page and more than 300 KB in total file size. Improperly coded, Ajax-enhanced pages can slow down interactivity, even after the page has loaded.

Clearly, there is room for improvement in the performance of the average website.

Oust Oodles of Objects

With the advent of Ajax, DHTML, and Web 2.0 mashups, some web pages have turned from simple HTML documents into full-blown interactive applications. With this increased complexity comes a cost: larger web pages. The number of external objects has grown accordingly as web pages have become more complex. Each additional object adds one more HTTP request and more uncertain delay.

Each object adds latency to your load time, increasing it an average of 0.25 seconds per object on dial-up and 40 ms on cable.[1] Overseas users suffer the most from object overage because long-distance connections require more *hops* and present more opportunities for data loss.

---

[1] Chung, S. 2007. "The investigation and classifying the web traffic delay & Solution plans presentation." In *ICACT2007* 2 (February 12–14, 2007): 1158–1161.

Untangle Tables

Tables are a poor substitute for CSS layout. Despite the widespread adoption of CSS, 62.6% of web pages still use tables for layout.[2] The average table depth has decreased by half since 2006, from nearly 3 to about 1.5.[3] Complex nested tables can cause rendering delays with browsers because tangled tables must be parsed and rendered before your content displays.

Some database-driven sites create table-based content modules that are assembled on the fly into table-based templates. All of these nested tables will bog down browsers and overwhelm your content-to-code ratio. This reduces the potential search engine rankings of your web pages.

You can reduce the depth of nested tables by styling, labeling, and positioning content areas with CSS and using simpler skeleton tables for layout. You can then target content within labeled container cells with compound selectors such as:

```
td#main p{}
```

Or, you can use CSS entirely to position, style, and target content like this:

```
div#main ul{}
```

See "Step 7: Convert Table Layout to CSS Layout," later in this chapter, for some tips on creating and debugging CSS layouts, and Chapter 7 for tips on CSS drop-down menu creation. Teaching all the intricacies of CSS layout is beyond the scope of this book; we encourage you to refer to some of the excellent books on the subject, including *CSS Mastery* by Andy Budd (friends of ED), and *CSS Web Site Design* by Eric Meyer (Peachpit Press).

Optimize Overweight Graphics

The average web page has more than 54% of its page weight in graphics.[4] In fact, more than 60% of the pixels above the fold are used by graphics on the average web page.[5]

---

[2] In a July 2007 random survey of 500 pages indexed by Binghamton University's Ryan Levering for this book, 62.6% of pages used the table tag and 85.1% used the div tag. Tables nested to an average maximum depth of 1.47, with an average number of 12.57 table tags per page. The average maximum HTML depth was 15.35, demonstrating how divs have replaced table nesting. The data for this web survey is available at *http://www.websiteoptimization.com/secrets/web-page/survey.xls*.

[3] Levering, R., and M. Cutler. 2006. "The Portrait of a Common HTML Web Page." In *DocEng '06* (Amsterdam, The Netherlands: October 10–13, 2006), 200. Tables nested to an average maximum depth of 2.95.

[4] According to Levering's 2007 survey, the average total image size was 118,683 bytes. The average total page size was 218,937 bytes, and 266,070 uncompressed. Thus, images make up at least 54.2% of the average web page.

[5] Levering and Cutler. "The Portrait of a Common HTML Web Page," 200. More than 60% of the area above the fold is used for graphics in the average web page.

Unfortunately, many of the graphics on the Web are fat and unoptimized. As digital camera resolution has increased, the file size of digital originals has ballooned, and some online graphics exceed 1 MB. Trying to view such bloated graphics on a dial-up connection is like trying to get a camel to pass through the eye of a needle.

The cost of banner advertising

Most popular media and blog sites use image-heavy advertising to generate revenue, at a cost of about one-sixth more objects and one-third more latency.[6] A survey of the top 1,300 Alexa sites (*http://www.alexa.com*) found that 56% of these web pages contained ads or some form of "extraneous content."[7] Blocking ads reduced the number of objects and bytes by 25% to 30%, resulting in a proportional reduction in latency.

We've analyzed web pages with 300 KB to 500 KB of banner ads. Without ad size policies in place, the total impact of advertising can become even more significant. If you use graphical ads, set file size criteria for the banner ads of your advertisers, criteria that are appropriate to banner dimensions.

The growth in the number and size of advertisements has caused significant delays for users. However, displaying ads also incurs the overhead of remote network hosting (in most cases) and additional logic to deliver ads to the screen (usually done with JavaScript). Remote JavaScript is the most inefficient ad delivery method, yet it is in widespread use because of its convenience. In "Step 1: Minimize HTTP Requests," we'll show how server-side includes can deliver ads to save HTTP requests. In "Step 10: Load JavaScript Wisely," you'll learn how to make JavaScript load asynchronously.

The Growth of Multimedia

The popularity of Flash and the likes of YouTube, Yahoo! Video, and MySpace have increased the use of multimedia on the Web. As broadband penetration has increased, videos have grown in size, bit rate, and duration (see Figure 6-1).

In 1997, 90% of online videos were less than 45 seconds in length (see Figure 6-1).[8] In 2005, the median video was about 120 seconds long.[9] By 2007, the median video was 192.6 seconds in duration.[10] The median bit rate of web videos grew from 200

---

[6] Krishnamurthy, B., and C. Wills. 2006. "Cat and Mouse: Content Delivery Tradeoffs in Web Access." In *WWW 2006* (Edinburgh, Scotland: May 23–26, 2006), 337–346.

[7] Ibid., 346.

[8] Acharya, S., and B. Smith. 1998. "An Experiment to Characterize Videos Stored On the Web." In *MMCN 1998* (San Jose, CA: January 1998), 166–178.

[9] Li, M. et al. 2005. "Characteristics of Streaming Media Stored on the Web." *ACM Transactions on Internet Technology* 5 (4): 601–626.

[10] Gill, P. et al. 2007. "YouTube Traffic Characterization: A View From the Edge." In *IMC 2007* (San Diego: October 24–26, 2007), 15–28. About 24% of videos are interrupted because of poor performance or poor content quality.

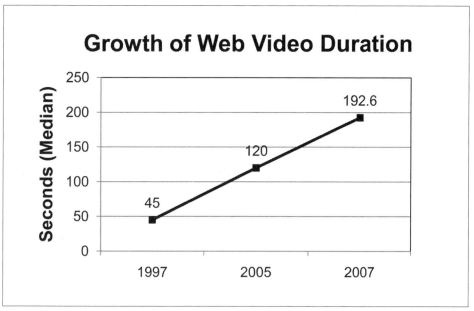

Figure 6-1. Growth in the duration of web videos

Kbps in 2005 to 328 Kbps on YouTube in 2007. So, by late 2007, the median video weighed in at more than 63 MB in file size.

The majority of multimedia traffic comes from files that are larger than 1 MB, but most requests come from files smaller than 1 MB. More than 87% of all streaming media is abandoned by users in the first 10 seconds, however, wasting up to 20% of server bandwidth.[11] Although only 3% of server responses are for videos, they account for 98.6% of the bytes transferred.[12] So, although videos account for a small percentage of requests, they make up the majority of the traffic on the Web.

Overall, for videos longer than 30 seconds, about 13% of home and 40% of business users experience quality degradation with their streaming media, caused by rebuffering, stream switching, and video cancellation. For sessions longer than 300 seconds, the results are even worse. In "Step 3: Optimize Multimedia," you will learn how to combat the growth of multimedia with specialized tools and techniques.

[11]Guo, L. et al. 2005. "Analysis of Multimedia Workloads with Implications for Internet Streaming." In *WWW 2005* (Chiba, Japan: May 10–14, 2005), 519–528.
[12]Gill, P. et al. "YouTube Traffic Characterization," 20.

How to Optimize Your Web Page Speed

To optimize your web page speed, start by stripping out all inline style. Pare down your markup to pure HTML structure. Next, look at your page to see whether any elements can be created by more efficient means. You can often morph HTML structural elements with CSS to replicate table-based elements more efficiently.

What Are CSS Sprites?

Originally used by 2D video game programmers to save resources, sprites have been adapted for the Web using CSS. A CSS sprite is a grid of images merged into one composite image. This sprite is then set as a CSS background image for multiple classes, and individual cells are displayed using background positioning for each class. CSS sprites save HTTP requests, but you must use them with caution to ensure accessibility. See Chapter 7 for an analysis of sprites used by AOL.com.

After your code has been stripped of style and refactored, convert that embedded style into rule-based CSS. To enable progressive display, position CSS files in the head and JavaScript files at the end of your body code. Minimize the number of HTTP requests by combining files, and by converting graphical text to CSS text. Use CSS spacing, CSS sprites, image maps, and background colors to save requests. Optimize any remaining images and multimedia to the lowest acceptable quality and frame rates. Enable caching for persistent objects and distribute them over different servers to minimize latency. Finally, use HTTP compression to shave an average of 75% off XHTML, CSS, and JavaScript file sizes. You'll learn how to configure your server for caching and HTTP compression in Chapter 9.

Switch to Semantic Markup

The foundation of these techniques is a switch to web standards (XHTML 1.0 and CSS2 or 3). By converting old-style nonsemantic markup into semantic markup, you can more easily target noncontiguous elements with *descendant selectors*.

Artificial XHTML structure can crop up in web pages created manually and with some WYSIWYG programs. This "fake structure" uses the font tag or CSS to artificially simulate structural markup, such as <h1>, <dl>, or <ul>.[13] One problem with fake structure is that it cannot be easily targeted with type or descendant selectors that are designed to point to structural elements.

---

[13]Levering's 2007 survey concluded that 32.8% used the font tag and only 58.5% used the h1 tag.

High Performance Web Site Tips

The following tips are derived from the book *High Performance Web Sites* (O'Reilly) by Steve Souders:

- Make fewer HTTP requests to reduce object overhead.
- Use a content delivery network.
- Add an `Expires` header.
- Gzip/compress text components.
- Put stylesheets at the top in the head.
- Put scripts at the bottom of the body.
- Avoid CSS expressions which are CPU-intensive and can be evaluated frequently.
- Make JavaScript and CSS files external.
- Reduce Domain Name System (DNS) lookups to reduce the overhead of DNS delay by splitting lookups between two to four unique hostnames.
- Minify JavaScript.
- Avoid redirects which slow performance. It's better to CNAME or alias.
- Remove duplicate scripts to eliminate extra HTTP requests in Internet Explorer.
- Configure `ETags` for sites hosted on multiple servers. `FileETag none` in Apache removes `Etags` to avoid improper cache validation.
- Make Ajax cacheable and small to avoid unnecessary HTTP requests.

In addition, proper structural markup conveys helpful information to whoever is maintaining the site with headings, paragraphs, and list items. Semantic markup can save countless hours of work in site redesigns. Search engines look for structural markup to see what information is most important. Accessibility and cross-platform access through mobile devices is enhanced when you use structural markup. Screen readers key off structural waypoints and users tab through a page based on semantically meaningful markup. For all these reasons, you should avoid fake structure like the plague.

So, for example, this (adapted from a real web page):

```
<p style="color:red"><strong>Fake descriptive term</strong><br>
   <font size="2" color="black">Description of first term here, no
structure to target!</font><br>
<strong>Fake descriptive term 2</strong><br>
   <font size="2" color="black">Description of second term here, no
structure to target</font></p>...
```

becomes this, by abstracting the inline styles to a matching structural element:

```
<style type="text/css">
<!--
dl dt{font-weight:bold;color:red;}
dl dd{font-size:0.9em;color:#000;}
--></style></head><body>
```

```
<dl>
    <dt>Descriptive term 1</dt>
    <dd>Description 1 here, no problem targeting</dd>
    <dt>Descriptive term 2</dt>
    <dd>Description 2 here, styled by a single CSS rule </dd>
</dl>
```

Notice how clean the structural HTML code is when compared to the unstructured example.

The last code sample is easier to target with CSS using simple descendant selectors (dl dt and dl dd). The first nonsemantic sample forces the use of embedded styles. For more information about web standards, see *http://www.webstandards.org* and *http://www.w3.org*.

Use container cells for descendant selectors

If you plan your web page to use container divs from the start—#masthead, #content, #navigation, and #footer can be your major container divs—you can avoid the need to embed classes within structural elements. You can then target enclosed content with descendant selectors. For example, the following navigation menu can be targeted through the surrounding nav element:

```
<style type="text/css">
<!--
#nav ul, #nav ul li {list-style:none;}
#nav ul li {font-weight:bold;}
--></style>
```

Here's the HTML markup:

```
<div id="nav">
    <ul>
        <li>Burma</li>
        <li>Shave</li>
    </ul>
</div>
```

Now you can declare these styles for *all* of your navigation, content, and other areas without the need to embed classes within HTML elements. The idea is to strip your HTML down to its structure, group the content within labeled divs, and target this structure with CSS selectors, descendant or otherwise.

If all browsers were as well behaved as Opera, Firefox, and Safari, you could use "grouping" elements such as body and html to avoid embedding classes within container divs. Instead, we recommend using labeled container divs such as #nav, #content, and #footer. Use CSS IDs for these main container divs that are used only once per page and then use CSS classes for most everything else. Keep in mind that CSS IDs have stronger specificity than CSS classes.

Now that you've learned how to overcome common web page problems, and the fundamentals behind those techniques, let's explore the top 10 steps you can use to speed optimize your web pages.

Step 1: Minimize HTTP Requests

Each unique object in a web page requires a round trip to the server, that is, an HTTP request and a reply. Each object introduces indeterminate delays. As you learned in the introduction to Part II, when the number of objects is greater than four, object overhead dominates page download times.

By minimizing the number of objects in your web pages, you can minimize the number of HTTP requests that are required to render your page and thus reduce object overhead. By requiring fewer HTTP requests, you'll speed up load times and make them more consistent.

The key to minimizing HTTP requests is to combine files and convert graphics-based techniques to CSS. You can convert graphical text to CSS text; combine external images, scripts, and CSS files; and eliminate frames and JavaScript includes. Convert spacer cells into CSS margins, and replace JavaScript behavior with CSS :hover techniques. Combine multiple decorative images into one CSS sprite.

Image Replacement Schemes

Image replacement schemes work by substituting static or dynamic images for text, usually headers. These replacement techniques include sIFR3 (*http://novemberborn.net/sifr3*), swfIR (swf Image Replacement, *http://www.swfir.com/*), and Stewart Rosenberger's Dynamic Text Replacement scheme (*http://www.stewartspeak.com/projects/dtr/*). Note that using CSS to hide and show images actually doesn't work well in screen readers. JavaScript is more appropriate for the job.

Convert graphical text to styled text

Graphical text is often used for headers or menu items to achieve a certain look. As yet, search engines can't read text embedded in graphics. Rasterized text also introduces unnecessary HTTP requests. You can instead use CSS to style headers, or use an image replacement scheme (see the "Image Replacement Schemes" sidebar, previously). By converting to CSS text, you lose some control but gain in speed, potential search engine rankings, and accessibility.

So this:

```
<div align="center">
<img src="graphictext.gif" width="115" height="24" alt="graphic text example">
</div>
```

Graphic Text

becomes this:

```
<style type="text/css">
<!--
h1 {font:bold 18px palatino,times,serif;color:#03c;text-align:center;}
-->
</style></head><body>
<h1>CSS Text</h1>
```

CSS Text

Use text overlays. One variation on this theme is to separate graphical text from background images. To achieve high-quality text in a JPEG you need to increase the quality of the entire image so that it is higher than it needs to be, or use regional compression. In some cases, it may be more efficient to remove the text from the JPEG and overlay the text as either CSS text or, as a last resort, a transparent GIF or PNG with the text embedded in the image. With a graphical text overlay you trade an additional HTTP request for a smaller background image. A CSS text overlay avoids this trade-off.

Convert spacer cells to CSS margins or padding

A common practice is to use spacer cells with a single-pixel GIF that is stretched to enforce the spacing distance. Here is an example from Nasa.gov:

```
<!-- Empty spacer row -->
<table><tr>
<td colspan="2" width="223"><img border="0" alt="" height="10" width="223" src="/
images/common/spacer.gif"></td>
</tr>
```

Even rocket scientists can use some help with their HTML. A better way would be to use CSS to add spacing between cells:

```
<style type="text/css"><!--
.vmargin {margin-top:10px;} --></style></head><body>
<table><tr>
<td colspan="2" width="223" class="vmargin">Content goes here</td>
</tr>
```

Even better is to use relative "em" spacing to allow for changes in font size made by the user and div elements:

```
<style type="text/css"><!--
.vmargin {margin-top:1em;} --></style></head><body>
<div class="vmargin">Content goes here</div>
```

Combine remaining images and map or sprite

You can reduce the number of HTTP requests that your pages require by combining adjacent images into one composite image and mapping any links using an *image map*. Instead of multiple HTTP requests, this technique requires only one (see Figure 6-2). So, this:

```
<div align="center">
<h4 align="center">Two Images = Two HTTP Requests</h4>
<p><img src="1.gif" alt="first image"> <img src="2.gif" alt="second image"></p>
</div>
```

becomes this, by combining the images into one composite image and using a client-side usemap:

```
<div align="center">
<h4 align="center">One Combined Image = One HTTP Request</h4>
<map name="map1">
<area href="#1" alt="1" title="1" shape="rect" coords="0,0,100,100">
<area href="#2" alt="2" title="2" shape="rect" coords="100,0,210,100"></map>
<img src="combined.gif" width="210" height="100" alt="combined image client-side
imagemap" usemap="#map1" border="0">
</div>
```

Figure 6-2. A tale of two images = two requests

This HTML creates a client-side image map with two target areas that correspond to the "1" and "2" squares in the composite image. For the rect(angle) shape, coordinates are measured from the top-left corner of the image to the bottom right, so 0,0,100,100 defines an area starting in the upper-left corner (0,0), down to X = 100 pixels to the right, and Y = 100 pixels down (100,100).

We'll explore the use of CSS sprites to consolidate decorative images in Chapter 7.

Combine and optimize CSS and JavaScript files

Many developers create separate stylesheets and import them into their pages as needed. There are two problems with this approach: (1) it requires additional HTTP requests, and (2) you can encounter the same-domain connection limit. Combining files in the head of your HTML documents can avoid these problems. Browsers must load and parse external CSS files referenced within the head of your HTML before they parse the body content. By minimizing the HTTP request load, you can maximize the initial display speed of your content. So, this:

```
<link rel="stylesheet" type="text/css" href="/css/fonts.css" />
<link rel="stylesheet" type="text/css" href="/css/nav.css" />
<script src="/js/functions.js" type="text/javascript"></script>
<script src="/js/validation.js" type="text/javascript"></script>
```

becomes this, by combining the CSS files into one file and the JavaScript files into one file:

```
<link rel="stylesheet" type="text/css" href="/css/combined.css" />
<script src="/js/combined.js" type="text/javascript"></script>
```

Suture CSS or JavaScript files. A similar approach to saving HTTP requests is to automatically combine external CSS or JavaScript files by *suturing* them together on the server. You can combine stylesheets or JavaScript files on demand to create one master file. Done properly, these combined files can also be cached.

Here is how this digital surgery would work for CSS. You need to tell the server two things: first, to parse CSS files for PHP commands, and second, to send the correct MIME type. Add the following lines to your *httpd.conf* file for Apache:

```
AddHandler application/x-httpd-php .css
header('Content-type: text/css');
```

Next, you can merge your CSS files together with PHP inside the CSS file, like this:

```
<?php
  include("layout.css");
  include("navigation.css");
  include("advanced.css");
?>
```

To deliver files based on browser environment variables (e.g., to simulate an @import to filter out older browsers), you could use software such as phpsniff, available at *http://sourceforge.net/projects/phpsniff/*.

Cache dynamic files. As specified earlier, the dynamic CSS file will not cache properly. If you add the following headers to the top of your PHP file after the content type, they will cache for three hours (adjust 10,800 seconds as necessary):

```
header('Cache-control: must-revalidate');
header('Expires: ' . gmdate('D, d M Y H:i:s', time() + 10800) . ' GMT');
```

Put CSS at the top, JavaScript at the bottom. Steve Souders found that moving stylesheets to the top in your head element makes pages load faster by allowing them to load progressively. With scripts, the opposite is true. If possible, move external JavaScript files to the bottom of your pages, or delay or defer the loading of JavaScript files in the head. Progressive rendering is blocked for all content that is placed after scripts in your HTML.

We'll explore CSS optimization in more detail in Chapter 7. In Chapter 8, we'll touch on JavaScript optimization. Chapter 9 shows how to delay the loading of scripts, even when they are referenced in the head of your HTML documents.

Eliminate (i)frames and JavaScript includes

More than 52% of web pages use frames, the vast majority of which are iframes used to display advertising.[14] Frames, iframes, and JavaScript includes can be especially

---

[14] Levering's 2007 survey found that most frames are iframes (found in 51.2% of web pages), whereas only 0.8% are frames. Note that some dynamically created frames were not counted in this survey, so these figures will be higher.

harmful to web performance because they introduce extra HTTP requests and can include entire web pages within other web pages.

For advertising, you can eliminate the extra HTTP requests required by the preceding methods by using a server-side include-based ad delivery system such as 24/7 Real Media's Open AdStream (*http://www.247realmedia.com*). Here is some sample code from Internet.com that can be added to a web page to include a banner ad:

```
<!--#include virtual="/banners/adstream_sx.ads/_PAGE_@750x100-1"-->
```

This technique uses server-side includes (SSIs) to include the banner ad directly into the page, saving an HTTP request. The inserted code looks like this:

```
<div id="topvisibility"><table ALIGN="CENTER">
<tr>
<td align="center">
<A HREF="http://itmanagement.earthweb.com/RealMedia/ads/click_lx.cgi/intm/it/www.
datamation.com/datbus/article/3739896i/1286136569/468x60-1/OasDefault/SSO_BluRay_
GEMS_1d/bluray2_750x100.jpg/34376565343564363437666663326530" target="_top"><IMG
SRC="http://itmanagement.earthweb.com/RealMedia/ads/Creatives/OasDefault/SSO_BluRay_
GEMS_1d/bluray2_750x100.jpg" ALT="" BORDER="0"></A><img src="http://itmanagement.
earthweb.com/RealMedia/ads/adstream_lx.cgi/intm/it/www.datamation.com/datbus/article/
3739896i/1286136569/468x60-1/OasDefault/SSO_BluRay_GEMS_1d/bluray2_750x100.jpg/
34376565343564363437666663326530?_RM_EMPTY_" Width="1" Height="1" Border="0"></td>
</tr>
</table>
</div>
```

The resultant ad displays as shown in Figure 6-3, saving an HTTP request.

Figure 6-3. SSI inserted banner ad (750×100 pixels)

The editors at Internet.com noticed an increase in speed after switching from JavaScript-based ad serving to SSI-based ad serving. Again, the idea is to shunt work to the server in exchange for less work for the browser.

Step 2: Resize and Optimize Images

More megapixels! That is what digital camera manufacturers are hawking these days. As a consequence of this pixel pushing, photographs destined for the Web have become larger in size and higher in resolution. We see sites with full-size unoptimized or partially optimized JPEGs resized into small thumbnails with height and width dimensions. These files can be more than 1 MB in size and yet occupy only 100×100 pixels in screen real estate. One megabyte is around a hundred times larger than these files need to be.

A better way is to crop and resize your images to the final dimensions that you want them to assume on your page. Then optimize them in a good-quality graphics program such as Photoshop or Fireworks. You can achieve higher compression ratios using specialized graphics tools from companies such as BoxTop Software (*http://www.boxtopsoft.com*), VIMAS Technologies (*http://www.vimas.com*), xat (*http://www.xat.com*), and Pegasus Imaging (*http://www.pegasusimaging.com*). The idea is to reduce the image to the lowest acceptable quality and resolution for the Web (72 dpi).

 JPEG Wizard from Pegasus Imaging is one of the few graphics optimization programs that can recompress JPEGs without the generation loss introduced in a decompress-compress cycle. It does this by working within the JPEG Discrete Cosine Transform space to avoid the decompress step.

You can often switch formats to save even more bytes. For example, you can often substitute PNG-8s used with or without dithering for JPEGs or GIFs at smaller file sizes. Figure 6-4 shows the effect that file format and quality have on file size.

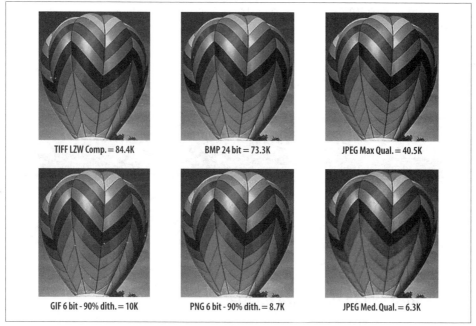

Figure 6-4. Image file size versus format

TIFFs, BMPs, and maximum-quality JPEGs are unsuitable for the Web (see the first row of Figure 6-4, all greater than 40 KB saved from original in Photoshop). Switching to a different format can make a significant difference in file size. The PNG in Figure 6-4 is 13% smaller than the GIF at equivalent settings. Although this smooth-toned balloon is an extreme example, for most flat-color images PNGs are 10% to 30% smaller than GIFs due to PNG's superior compression algorithm.

Here is a summary of the techniques you can use to fully optimize your images, available from *http://www.websiteoptimization.com/speed/tweak/graphic-optimization/*:

- *Plan ahead* to maximize file size savings (e.g., simplify background images).
- *Contextually crop* to show only the most relevant parts of the image.
- *Resize images* to the exact pixel dimensions that you want for each web location.
- *Combine images* to save HTTP requests, and optionally create a usemap or CSS sprite.
- *Blur backgrounds for JPEGs*. Experiment with "surface blur" settings to see which ones give a clean yet simplified appearance.
- *Use CSS borders or backgrounds* instead of embedding borders in images. Don't leave blank background borders of one color to achieve layout goals. Instead, use a tightly cropped image combined with a coded background color.
- *Replace GIFs and JPEGs with PNG images* where appropriate; dither where necessary.
- *Specify image size* in HTML with width and height attributes.
- *Use Smart Sharpen* in Photoshop CS2 or later to make your images pop.
- *Overlay text with CSS* or a transparent GIF or PNG instead of embedding text in JPEGs to allow higher compression.
- *Minimize noise* in all images before optimizing. Typical savings are 20% to 30% off the file size. We recommend Noise Ninja (*http://www.picturecode.com/*) and Neat Image (*http://www.neatimage.com/*) to reduce noise.
- *Minimize dithering* for GIFs and PNGs.
- *Minimize bit depth* for GIFs and PNGs.
- *Use weighted optimization* (regional compression) using alpha masks to optimize backgrounds more than foregrounds.
- *Use "lossy" compression* for smaller GIFs and PNGs (where available).
- *Reduce or eliminate drop shadows* in layered images. Adjust layers in Photoshop to reduce the width and depth of drop shadows to make images more compressible.

Step 3: Optimize Multimedia

As you learned in "The Growth of Multimedia," earlier in this chapter, multimedia makes up only a small portion of server requests but accounts for the majority of traffic on the Internet. So, the optimization of streaming media—and movies in particular—has become more important in maximizing web page speed and reducing bandwidth bills.

Behind the scenes, multimedia authors create a *reference movie* that points to different sizes of movies. The reference movie gets the speed of the user's connection from the QuickTime Control Panel to select the right movie. Users usually don't know to set this parameter, however, and the bandwidth of the user is generally not tested. Thus, broadband users typically see tiny, low-quality movies. Thankfully, in the newer version of the QuickTime Control Panel, there is a new default setting of "automatic"; although this is helpful for those who don't know to set their speed, you should change your connection speed setting to match your connection type, that is, modem, DSL, cable, and so on.

Optimizing videos for the Web

Movies optimized for the Web should be short in duration, small in dimension, and optimized with the appropriate *codec*. We have seen videos 10 to 30 minutes long automatically loaded and playing into home pages, some 50 MB to 175 MB in file size. Although this may grab the attention of high-bandwidth users, it is better to respect your visitors' bandwidth and provide a static placeholder image and a play button.

Take a look at the Apple.com website for an example of a best practice regarding showcasing video to a potentially wide-range audience (*http://www.apple.com/trailers/*). Apple takes the approach of allowing users to choose different size movies to better match their bandwidth abilities. Sizes from "small" (320×240 pixels) to "HD" (1,920×1,080 pixels) can be viewed. Overall, this was a lot of up-front work for Apple; it had to compress one movie many different times, into many different sizes. However, the extra work pays off with satisfied site visitors who are able to find content that meets their needs and the amount of bandwidth available to them.

Video frame rates and dimensions. Higher frame rates (frames per second, or fps) increase the fluid motion of the picture. However, each frame rate has 50% more data per frame than the next lower frame rate, for the same file size. To sacrifice some fluidity for greater usability by more viewers, you can reduce the frame rate to as little as 8 fps. However, frame rates lower than 12 fps to 15 fps have been shown to reduce users' perception of video quality.[15]

The minimum dimensions should be 320×240 pixels. Anything smaller has little impact and will be harder to view. For users on a fast connection, you can offer a 640×480 pixel video. To maintain quality, increase the data rate in proportion to the image size using the following formula (especially with H.264):

Data rate =(frames per second * movie width * movie height) / 30,000

[15]Gulliver, S., and G. Ghinea. 2006. "Defining User Perception of Distributed Multimedia Quality." *ACM Transactions on Multimedia Computing, Communications and Applications* 2 (4): 241–257.

This translates to:

$$DR = (FPS * W * H) / 30{,}000$$

Remember that doubling image size (320×240 to 640×480) requires a 4× (not 2×) increase in data rate. For example, a 320×240 movie with 15 fps needs to be compressed to about 38.4 KB of data per second, whereas a 640×480 movie at the same frame rate needs to be compressed to about 153.6 KB of data per second to maintain quality. We'll talk more about compression next.

Video production tips: Minimize noise and movement. To create highly optimized videos you must start with the original, high-quality video files.

You can think of video creation as a war against unnecessary digital noise in your content. The more noise in your video, the less it can be compressed, and the larger the final result. The less movement there is, the lower the noise; and the less fine detail in the background, the smaller the video. Here are some tips on creating high-quality videos that optimize well:

- Minimize camera motion with a tripod if possible.
- Minimize subject motion.
- Use a lot of light.
- Use a simple background or blur the background (avoid background movement).
- Avoid camera pans and zooms.
- Use professional equipment.
- Use a digital format.
- If a tripod is not an option, use a *gyroscopic stabilizer* (*http://www.ken-lab.com*) or an image-stabilized lens.

Editing your video. After you've captured your video with minimum noise, it's time to edit out unnecessary frames and test for playback. Break up longer videos into smaller segments that are a few minutes long at most. Edit out the parts of the movie that aren't essential to your message. Here are some additional tips:

- Reduce dimensions to web standards.
- Use the minimum frame rate for smooth playback.
- Crop fuzzy edges.
- Reduce video noise (with filters).
- Adjust contrast.
- Adjust gamma level (for cross-platform viewing).
- Restore black and white.
- Deinterlace.
- Choose the best codec for the job that you are trying to accomplish.

For example, if you are compressing video for the Web, choose a web codec such as H.264 or WMV. If you are simply archiving your video for later use, try the Photo-JPEG codec. There are about 30 different codecs, and they each have a different use. Where you plan to deliver your video should determine the codec that you select. H.264 is one of the best for web and small device playback, such as a video phone, so we'll focus on that here.

Compressing videos for the Web. Now that you've got your video prepared and adjusted, you can compress it. People are more accepting of *temporal compression* (over time) than *spatial compression* (frame per frame). You must compress the size of your video so that it can be successfully streamed or downloaded to your target audience. This process is called *encoding* in the industry, and it is full of hard, interdependent decisions:

Streaming media format
QuickTime versus RealMedia versus Windows Media

Supported playback platforms
Windows versus Mac or both

Delivery method
True real-time streaming versus HTTP streaming

Overall data rate
Compression versus quality versus bandwidth required

Audio quality
Mono versus stereo; CD quality, cassette tape quality, or cell phone quality

Codec
H.264 versus Sorenson versus WMV (the current leaders)

You'll need to make some decisions to give the best compromise between quality and size. QuickTime Pro provides a fast and convenient way to create optimized videos. For more control, you can use Autodesk's Cleaner (*http://www.autodesk.com*). Sorenson Video 3 Pro (*http://www.sorensonmedia.com*) can sometimes make videos smaller than H.264 at similar quality. Finally, Telestream's Episode Pro (*http://www.telestream.net/*) offers maximum control over video compression with the ability to compress to H.264, Flash, iPod, and other formats (see Figure 6-5). It is an excellent application and can batch-compress into all the popular formats and workstreams.

Figure 6-6 shows the settings we used to optimize a test video in QuickTime Pro.

The unoptimized 30-second video was 6.8 MB and the optimized version was 816 KB at 360×240 and 544 KB at 234×156 pixels in dimension. Because H.264 is what we recommend as the best codec, we will expand on its specifics.

Figure 6-7 shows the standard video compression dialog for QuickTime Pro. You can see that we have chosen H.264 as our compression type. It's helpful for you to understand this dialog's three main sections: Motion, Data Rate, and Compressor.

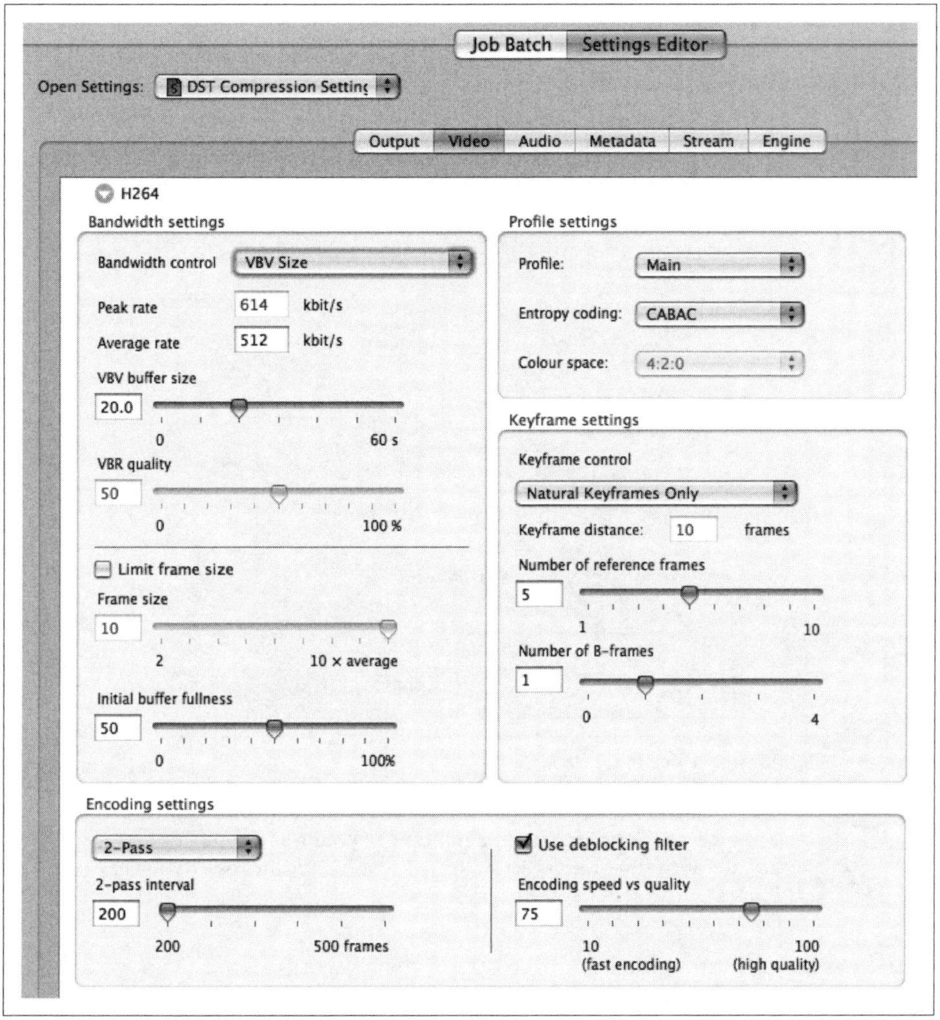

Figure 6-5. Episode Pro optimizing a video

The Motion section is where you can choose the frame rate (in fps) and the key frames. If you are planning to compress your video, you might want to choose something other than Current in the Frame Rate box because Current does not remove any frames. A good starting point is 15 fps; this alone results in a 50% reduction in size for video that is 30 fps (or, more accurately, 29.97 fps).

Also in the Motion section is a Key Frames area. A key frame is a frame of uncompressed data from which the frames in between the key frames key off. So, if you set the key frames to 15 (and your frame rate is 15 fps), you will be creating an uncompressed frame every second.

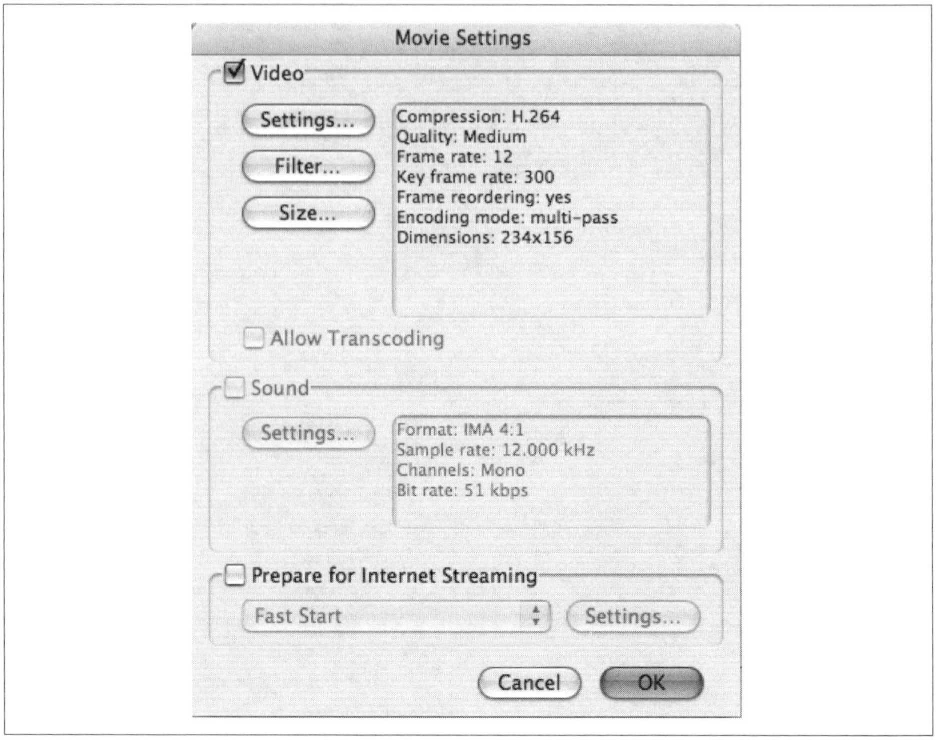

Figure 6-6. Optimizing a video in QuickTime Pro

> Always set your key frames to a multiple of your frame rate! For example, if your frame rate is set at 15 fps, you will want to set your key frames to 15, 30, 45, 60, 90, and so on.

H.264 has a great automatic key frame option that is worth trying. Also, you should make sure the Frame Reordering box is checked (unless you are using a real-time encoder for a live broadcast).

Next is the Compressor section, where you'll find three options: Quality, Encoding, and Temporal. However, note that you don't see the Temporal option in Figure 6-7 because it's a hidden option that we will explain how to find shortly.

The Quality area is where you can control the look of individual frames. Set it to Medium and compress, and then see how large your movie is. You will be surprised how good a Medium setting can look. For Encoding, always click the "Best quality (Multi-pass)" radio button. Yes, it takes twice as long, but your movie can be half as small in file size.

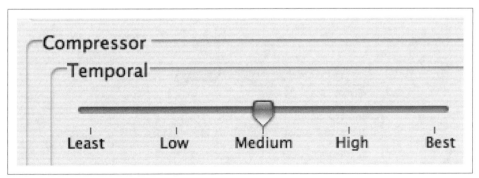

Figure 6-7. QuickTime Pro standard video compression settings

Now, here is how to show the hidden Temporal slider. Put your cursor over the Quality slider and press the Option key (on a Mac) or the Alt key (on Windows). Notice that when you press the Option key the slider changes to read Temporal (see Figure 6-8). This means you can separate the spatial (frame-per-frame look) from the temporal (smoothness of playback or quality of delta frames).

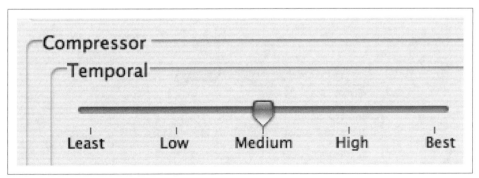

Figure 6-8. Temporal compression slider

The last section of the dialog is the Data Rate section. We recommend that you click the Automatic radio button for your first try, but if you want to try to make your movie smaller you can lower the data rate. Use Table 6-1 for reference.

Table 6-1. Video resolution and frame rate guidelines

Use scenario	Resolution and frame rate	Example data rates
Mobile content	176 × 144, 10–15 fps	50–60 Kbps
Internet/standard definition	640 × 480, 24 fps	1–2 Mbps
High definition	1280 × 720, 24 fps	5–6 Mbps
Full high definition	1,920 × 1,080, 24 fps	7–8 Mbps

Closing credits. Creating optimized videos for the Web requires a number of coordinated steps.

First, create a clean, noise-free video with the minimum possible number of zooms, pans, and background detail and movement. Then prepare your video for compression by cropping fuzzy edges, adjusting contrast and gamma, and deleting any unnecessary frames. Finally, compress your video with a high-quality compressor such as Episode Pro. Use the data-rate formula (FPS * W * H)/30,000 as a starting point, and always use a two-pass variable bit rate (VBR) and a multiple of 10 times your fps for your key frames.

Flash optimization tips

Some typical problems we see with Flash are unoptimized images and too many frames instead of tweened symbols. A *tween* is the calculation of all the changes between frames, which is more efficient than having a lot of frames instead (see Figure 6-9). You can significantly reduce the file size of Flash movies by optimizing your images in Photoshop, not in Flash. Reduce the number of frames, minimize the number of fonts, and tween between symbols.

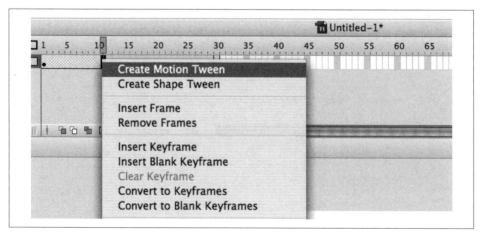

Figure 6-9. Creating a Flash motion tween

Step 4: Convert JavaScript Behavior to CSS

Embedded JavaScript is widely used on the Web, with 84.8% of pages using some JavaScript.

JavaScript is used for form validation, menus and rollovers, browser sniffing, statistics, and more complex Ajax applications. You can accomplish a number of these techniques with more efficient methods, however.

You can use CSS to control drop-down menus and rollovers with the :hover pseudoclass (for more details, see Eric Meyer's *More Eric Meyer on CSS* [New Riders].) Chapter 7 shows a drop-down menu conversion example that saved 46.4% off HTML file size by switching from JavaScript to CSS :hover to control the menu behavior. Typically, you'll save 40% to 60% off HTML and JavaScript file sizes by converting to CSS :hover techniques, with a slight increase in CSS file size (which cache reliably). Now that Internet Explorer 7 and later support the :hover pseudoclass on the necessary elements, the :hover behavior hack that is in widespread use should eventually fall out of favor.[16] You can analyze server-side logfiles instead of using client-side statistics. Browser sniffing in particular can be done more efficiently with a tool such as BrowserHawk (discussed next).

Step 5: Use Server-Side Sniffing

Browser sniffing is one area where JavaScript is in widespread use. To minimize the JavaScript overhead that your users must download, you can substitute server-side or PHP and JSP sniffing instead. BrowserHawk from cyScape (*http://www.cyscape.com*) uses server-side browser sniffing or hybrid sniffing to detect a wide variety of parameters, including Flash, screen size, connection speed, cookies, and browser and software versions (see Figure 6-10).

Sniffing with BrowserHawk

Here is some sample code that shows how BrowserHawk is enabled in a page and some sniffed parameters:

```
<%
// First import the com.cyscape.browserhawk namespace
%>
<%@ page import = "com.cyscape.browserhawk.*" %>

<%
// Now we get an immutable (unchangeable) instance of the browser object which
// represents the "basic" properties this browser supports.
%>
```

---

[16]The :hover behavior hack is a JScript behavior used to add the :hover pseudoclass to elements other than the anchor element in Internet Explorer 5 through 7, which do not properly support the :hover pseudoclass on all elements.

Figure 6-10. The BrowserHawk home page, which sniffs your browser environment variables

```
<% BrowserInfo browser = BrowserHawk.getBrowserInfo(request); %>

<%
// At this point, our browser object contains all the basic browser capability
// information for the current visitor. Next, display this information to the screen
%>

Your browser is: <%= browser.getBrowser() %> <%= browser.getFullversion() %><P>

Your platform is: <%= browser.getPlatform() %><P>
Browser major version: <%= browser.getMajorver() %><P>
Browser minor version: <%= browser.getMinorver() %><P>
Container* browser: <%= browser.getContainerBrowser() %><P>
Container version: <%= browser.getContainerVersion() %><P>
Container full version: <%= browser.getContainerFullversion() %><P>
Supports AJAX? <%= browser.getXMLHttpRequest() %><P>
Supports ActiveX controls? <%= browser.getActiveXControls() %><P>
Browser data file version: <%= browser.getBDDVersion() %>, dated: <%= browser.
getBDDDate() %><P>
BrowserHawk version in use: <%= BrowserHawk.getVersion() %><P>
```

For extended properties that can change with each session, you use the following code:

```
<%
    // First we create the ExtendedOptions object.  This object is used to
    // set various preferences and options, such as selecting which
    // extended properties we want tested and related testing parameters.
    ExtendedOptions options = new ExtendedOptions( );

    // Now we tell BrowserHawk which tests we want it to perform on the
    // browser. If there are other settings you want to check as well, you can
    // just add them to this list.   See the ExtendedOptions class in the
    // BrowserHawk documentation for more information.
%>
options.addProperties("PersistentCookies, SessionCookies, JavaScriptEnabled, Width,
Height, WidthAvail, HeightAvail, Plugin_Flash, Broadband");

Session cookies enabled? <%= extBrowser.getSessionCookies( ) %><p>
Persistent cookies enabled? <%= extBrowser.getPersistentCookies( ) %><p>
JavaScript enabled? <%= extBrowser.getJavaScriptEnabled( ) %><p>
Screen resolution: <%= extBrowser.getWidth( ) %> x <%= extBrowser.getHeight( ) %><p>
Available browser window size: <%= extBrowser.getWidthAvail( ) %> x <%= extBrowser.
getHeightAvail( ) %><p>
Flash plug-in version installed: <%= extBrowser.getPluginFlash( ) %><p>
Broadband connection? <%= extBrowser.getBroadband( ) %><p>
```

You can also cache these results and get more granular data on the connection speed of the user, version numbers, and capabilities. Once you have sniffed the user's browser, you can deliver conditional content based on these variables.

XSSI browser sniffing

Using conditional server-side includes (XSSIs), you can create environment variables that closely mimic JavaScript-based sniffing. For example, this common JavaScript filter:

```
IS_IE = (document.all) ? true : false;
IS_MAC = (navigator.appVersion.indexOf(" Mac") != -1);
IS_OPERA = (navigator.userAgent.indexOf(" Opera") != -1);
IS_OPERAMAC = IS_OPERA && IS_MAC;
```

becomes this XSSI equivalent:

```
<!--#if expr="$(HTTP_USER_AGENT) = /MSIE [4-9]//" -->
    <!--#set var="isIE" value="true" -->
<!--#endif -->
<!--#if expr="$(HTTP_USER_AGENT) = /Mac/" -->
    <!--#set var="isMAC " value="true" -->
<!--#endif -->
<!--#if expr="$(HTTP_USER_AGENT) = /Opera/" -->
    <!--#set var="isOPERA" value="true" -->
<!--#endif -->
<!--#if expr="(${isOPERA} && ${isMAC})/" -->
    <!--#set var="isOPERAMAC" value="true" -->
<!--#endif -->
```

Now you can use these XSSI variables to conditionally include code within your XSSI includes without the need for JavaScript:

```
<!--#if expr="${isIE}" -->
    ie.js
<!--#elif expr="${isOPERAMAC}" -->
    operamac.js
<!--#elif expr="${isOPERA}" -->
    opera.js
...
<!--#endif -->
```

It is faster to set environment variables at the server by configuring your *httpd.conf* file using BrowserMatchNoCase. For example:

```
BrowserMatchNoCase "MSIE [4-9]" isIE
BrowserMatchNoCase Mac isMAC
BrowserMatchNoCase Opera isOPERA
```

Step 6: Optimize JavaScript for Execution Speed and File Size

After replacing as much JavaScript as possible with CSS and server-side techniques, optimize any remaining JavaScript to minimize file size. You can use abbreviated object, variable, and function names to shave bytes. You can automate the process by using a tool such as w3compiler to automatically abbreviate and whitespace-optimize your scripts.

Beyond minifying JavaScript, you can often *refactor* or rewrite procedures with less code to accomplish the same thing (see *http://www.refactoring.com*). Remember to measure first, then optimize. You can use a JavaScript profiler to locate performance bottlenecks. Mozilla's Venkman JavaScript Debugger (*http://www.mozilla.org/projects/venkman/*) can profile JavaScript code.

Loop optimizations such as unwinding can also help you to gain some cycles to increase your JavaScript execution speed. Often, built-in functions perform faster than hand-crafted code. For advice on increasing execution speed and minifying JavaScript, read Chapter 8. Finally, combine and compress external JavaScript files to save HTTP requests and bandwidth where possible.

Step 7: Convert Table Layout to CSS Layout

Using CSS to lay out your page can save you a significant amount of markup, typically 25% to 50%.[17] First look at the layout to see whether you can substitute CSS lists and positioned divs to simulate the effects that are typically done with tables.

---

[17]According to Jeffrey Zeldman's *Designing with Web Standards* (New Riders), converting to CSS layout typically saves from 25% to 50% off XHTML file size, and a net savings overall. We've found similar results in our conversions.

Next, strip down the content to structural markup and build it back up again using CSS style and positioning. Then test the new layout with different browsers. We recommend using BrowserCam (*http://www.browsercam.com*) to quickly test your new CSS layout on different browsers (see Figure 6-11).

Figure 6-11. BrowserCam.com renders web pages on different browsers

CSS page layout

You can use CSS to position your entire layout or to format smaller sections of your web pages. We often see tables used to format pages when CSS could have been used more efficiently. You can create multicolumn layouts using CSS floats and margins applied to divs (*http://alistapart.com/topics/code/css/*). You can make complex hierarchical menus by using lists controlled by CSS, not lists controlled by JavaScript as is usually the case, as described in *More Eric Meyer on CSS*. You can create simple rollover effects using CSS, with and without graphics. For examples of CSS rollover effects and menu conversion, see Chapter 7.

Step 8: Replace Inline Style with CSS Rules

Replacing table layout with CSS layout certainly saves you bandwidth and reduces maintenance headaches. Stripping down your markup to bare structure and replacing any inline style with CSS rules will help fully optimize your HTML.

Inline style includes the deprecated font tag, inline style blocks, and nonbreaking spaces. Inline style such as:

```
<p style="font-size:12px;color:black;">Hardcoded text here.</p>
<p style="font-size:12px;color:black;">Inline style redux</p>
```

bulks up your code and makes it harder to make style changes. It is more efficient to abstract multiple duplicate styles into CSS rules, like so:

```
<style type="text/css">
p{font-size:12px;color:#000;}
</style></head></body>
<p>Unencumbered text here</p>
<p>Free and easy</p>
```

Replacing inline style, font tags, and nonbreaking spacing with CSS rules can reduce your HTML footprint significantly (by 15% to 20% or more), depending on the amount of embedded style. The key to this type of code cleanup is to plan ahead for targeting content elements with CSS using the CSS architecture you'll read about in Chapter 7.

CSS architecture uses structural HTML markup (p, ul, dt, etc.) and labeled containers (#main, #nav, #footer) that allow simple type and descendant selectors to target noncontiguous content. Once your CSS architecture is in place, targeting similar content is only a matter of creating targeted CSS rules using selectors to style the same type of elements and declarations to apply your styles. You'll learn more about optimizing your HTML with CSS, as well as shrinking your style sheets, in Chapter 7.

Step 9: Minimize Initial Display Time

You can improve the perceived speed of your web page by loading something useful fast.

For example, the Weather Underground home page displays the weather search form quickly in the top-left corner of the screen (see Figure 6-12). Unlike other weather sites that require different elements to load first, Weather Underground gives priority to the most important part of the page first so that you can find the forecast for your area fast.

You can ensure that your useful content (i.e., content that users can navigate with) loads quickly by layering your tables or divs.

Figure 6-12. Weather Underground loads useful content first

Multimedia can also benefit from fast start techniques. Flash presentations can load a separate file quickly while others stream in the background. Movies can load a static placeholder image or preview to show something quickly to help engage the user. QuickTime Pro lets you set up a movie to start playing from a web server before the movie has completely downloaded. This is called a "Fast Start" movie (see Figure 6-13).

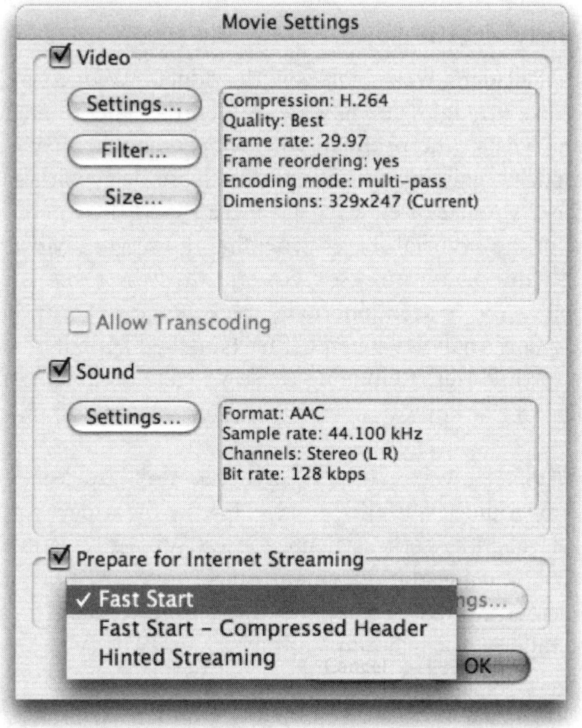

Figure 6-13. QuickTime Pro Fast Start movie

Web page optimization is not only about raw speed, but also about managing your users' experience.

Step 10: Load JavaScript Wisely

External scripts referenced in the head of your pages are especially harmful because they delay the display of your body content. Delays before your body content displays make it more likely that users will bail out. Human-computer interaction (HCI) research has shown that delays before viewing pages are less frustrating than delays after a page has loaded.[18]

Post-loading delays are a common problem with Ajax-enabled pages. When it is poorly written, Ajax can make things especially difficult on narrowband users. Even with HTTP compression, the latency due to grabbing all those separate files can cause indeterminate delays. Ajax also introduces polling with the XMLHttpRequest object (XHR). XHR-based communication has efficiency issues that we'll address in Chapter 8.

The perils of third-party widgets

Webmasters are outsourcing web services with widgets. Widgets are third-party gizmos that embed everything from Google AdWords, Flickr images, and Twitter tweets to iTunes playlists. The problem with widgets is that they can delay the display of your web pages by many seconds and increase delay variability. Widgets are typically used with a snippet of external JavaScript, and their performance relies on the response time of the external server providing the service. Most web service providers lack the extreme data-farm resources and thus the responsiveness of a company such as Google. We've seen external survey widgets, Technorati blog tracking code, and even Google Analytics when it first launched actually hang browsers and cause web pages to time out. Removing these widgets or moving these third-party tags to the end of your markup can help to minimize customer impact.

Give your widgets a WEDJE. However, there is a better way. By using Widget Enabled DOM JavaScript Embedding (WEDJE), you can rewrite the widget embed code to effectively make your JavaScript work asynchronously. WEDJE creates a cross-platform, cross-browser defer by using the document object model (DOM) to append a div, create a script element, and then append the script element to the div, all with JavaScript. An example of the technique follows:

```
<script type="text/javascript">      // create div below
(function(){document.write('<div id="wedje_div_example">Loading widget...<\/div>');
s=document.createElement('script'); // create script element
s.type="text/javascript";            // assign script to script element
s.src="http://www.example.com/scripts/widget.js";
                                     // assign script s to div element
setTimeout("document.getElementById('wedje_div_example').appendChild(s)",1);})()
</script>
```

[18]Dellaert, B., and B. Kahn. 1999. "How Tolerable is Delay? Consumers' Evaluations of Internet Web Sites after Waiting." *Journal of Interactive Marketing* 13 (1): 41–54.

When these elements are linked together in this way, browsers appear to decouple the loading and execution of the attached JavaScript, making widget execution asynchronous! Here is the matching external JavaScript file, *widget.js*, which grabs the `div` we created earlier and loads an image:

```
document.getElementById('wedje_div_example').innerHTML+='<img src="http://www.
example.com/images/example.gif" width="60" height="60" />';
```

Another option is to use iframes to load ads, but iframes can ruin the context-sensing abilities of contextual ads and so you must use them carefully. For more details on WEDJE, see Mike Davidson's blog post on the subject at *http://www.mikeindustries.com/blog/archive/2007/06/widget-deployment-with-wedje*. (Note that this technique has some strange Internet Explorer 6-related issues, but you can filter with conditional comments to use on only Internet Explorer 7 and later.)

Chapter 9 has more coding details on delaying the loading of external scripts.

Summary

Web page optimization streamlines your pages to download and display faster. As your website performance improves, your bailout rates and bandwidth bills will go down while your conversion rates and profits will rise. In this chapter, you learned how to minimize HTTP requests, optimize graphics and multimedia, substitute server-side for client-side sniffing, and load JavaScript wisely.

To reduce the overhead of multiple objects that causes the majority of web page delay, minimize the number of objects referenced within your web pages. Also, put all of your images, still and motion, on a strict file size diet. Minimize the size of the head of your HTML, and layer your markup to display useful content quickly and maximize your potential search engine rankings. Finally, move your CSS to the top and your scripts to the bottom of your pages to enable progressive display.

CHAPTER 7

CSS Optimization

Cascading Style Sheet (CSS) optimization transforms your HTML by abstracting inline style and behavior into minimal stylesheets. Whereas CSS makes a site easier to maintain, CSS optimization makes it load faster and makes it more search engine-friendly.

In this chapter, you'll learn how to shrink your stylesheets and HTML at the same time. CSS-specific techniques include (1) grouping declarations and selectors, (2) merging common styles into shared classes, (3) inheritance, (4) abbreviating with shorthand properties, and (5) abbreviating class and ID names. HTML-oriented techniques include replacing JavaScript behavior with CSS, designing markup for descendant selectors, and CSS layout. By combining these techniques, you can reduce HTML and CSS file sizes by up to 50%, according to Jeffrey Zeldman's *Designing with Web Standards* (Peachpit Press). When you plan your site in this way, you are giving it what we call *CSS architecture*.

Build on a CSS Architecture

Good CSS architecture involves planning from the very beginning for CSS layout, style, and behavior. This way you can avoid most of the limitations and browser quirks that creep into an unorganized CSS layout.

To create a solid CSS architecture, use the following techniques:

- Use a reset stylesheet to equalize rendering behavior.
- Plan for descendant selectors by using labeled container cells for main page sections (masthead, navigation, content, footer, and side columns).
- Position external CSS files in the head element to enable progressive rendering.

The preceding chapter dealt with planning for descendant selectors and positioning CSS files. We will expand on reset stylesheets next. The general idea is to use appropriate structural markup so that you can apply the most prevalent CSS rules to those elements. Then you can use classes for *exceptions*, minimizing the need to litter your markup with classes. This technique optimizes your CSS and markup at the same time.

Anatomy of a CSS Rule

A CSS rule consists of the following components: a *selector* and a *declaration block* of one or more declarations each followed by a semicolon. A declaration consists of a property name and a corresponding value separated by a colon, demonstrated as follows.

```
                                          Declaration
                                              |
          CSS RULE                    ┌───────┴───────┐
                          Selector { property : value ; }
```

The selector specifies what HTML elements are targeted. Selectors use simple *type* (p, h1, ul), *descendant* (ul, li, or .nav a), or more complex patterns to target elements:

```
.nav > div a:hover
```

or:

```
a[href$=".rss"]:not[class="grouped"]
```

The declaration block specifies the properties of the target elements and their values. Declarations come in longhand and some come in shorthand varieties. For example:

```
margin:  2em 2em 2em 2em;
```

or, in shorthand notation:

```
margin: 2em;
```

You'll learn how to combine selectors and shorthand declarations in powerful ways later in this chapter.

Use a Reset Stylesheet

One solution to overly specific CSS selectors and cross-browser compatibility is to use a reset stylesheet. Advocated by Eric Meyer and Yahoo!, reset stylesheets set up a known set of default style rules to equalize browser rendering behavior. An example from Eric Meyer follows:

```
html, body, div, span, applet, object, iframe,
h1, h2, h3, h4, h5, h6, p, blockquote, pre,
a, abbr, acronym, address, big, cite, code,
del, dfn, em, font, img, ins, kbd, q, s, samp,
small, strike, strong, sub, sup, tt, var,
b, u, i, center,
dl, dt, dd, ol, ul, li,
fieldset, form, label, legend,
table, caption, tbody, tfoot, thead, tr, th, td {
    margin: 0;
    padding: 0;
    border: 0;
    outline: 0;
    font-size: 100%;
    vertical-align: baseline;
```

```
        background: transparent;
    }
    body {
        line-height: 1;
    }
    ol, ul {
        list-style: none;
    }
    blockquote, q {
        quotes: none;
    }
    blockquote:before, blockquote:after,
    q:before, q:after {
        content: '';
        content: none;
    }

    /* remember to define focus styles! */
    :focus {
        outline: 0;
    }

    /* remember to highlight inserts somehow! */
    ins {
        text-decoration: none;
    }
    del {
        text-decoration: line-through;
    }

    /* tables still need 'cellspacing="0"' in the markup */
    table {
        border-collapse: collapse;
        border-spacing: 0;
    }
```

This reset stylesheet zeros out margins, padding, borders, and outlines for all type selectors (this is more efficient than the universal selector * because of CPU overhead), as well equalizing font size to 100%, setting vertical-align to baseline to equalize browser differences, and so on:

```
    margin: 0;
    padding: 0;
    border: 0;
    outline: 0;
    font-size: 100%;
    vertical-align: baseline;
    background: transparent;
```

Note that this reset stylesheet is intentionally left generic. You should customize it to match your preferences with text, background, and link colors.

By resetting visiting browsers to default behavior, you can be more confident in styling your markup and omitting default values. This technique helps to eliminate the majority of browser differences that plague developers when debugging CSS. For some examples of reset stylesheets, visit *http://developer.yahoo.com/yui/reset/* and *http://meyerweb.com/eric/tools/css/reset/*.

Browser Support for CSS

The majority of browsers today support the CSS techniques detailed in this chapter. CSS2 browsers include Internet Explorer 7 and later (with some exceptions for Internet Explorer 6, namely the universal selector, *), Firefox 2 and later, Safari 3 and later, Konqueror 3.5.7 and later, and Opera 9.5b and later, which support CSS shorthand, multiple classes, and grouping. The CSS3 attribute selector matching techniques detailed in this chapter are supported by the aforementioned browsers. For details on browser support for CSS2 and CSS3 see *http://www.quirksmode.org/css/contents.html*.

Top 10 Tips for Optimizing CSS

The following 10 best practices are designed to speed-optimize your CSS, and your HTML markup:

1. Replace inline style with type selectors to target multiple instances of identical elements.
2. Use descendant selectors to avoid inline classes.
3. Group selectors with common declarations.
4. Group declarations with common selectors.
5. Combine common styles into shared classes.
6. Use inheritance to eliminate duplicate declarations.
7. Use CSS shorthand to abbreviate rules and colors.
8. Abbreviate long class and ID names.
9. Use CSS2 and CSS3.*x* techniques.
10. Replace JavaScript behavior with CSS techniques.

In addition, you can eliminate extraneous whitespace by removing tabs, comments, and returns.

Tip #1: Replace Inline Style with Type Selectors

This section starts with simple type selectors to streamline markup, and then it moves through grouping, inheritance, and CSS shorthand, and finally to some applied techniques to replace JavaScript behavior.

Web pages that use inline style pepper HTML code with unnecessary font and style tags. This effectively hardcodes the presentation directly within the HTML. Unless the style is used only once, it is more efficient to create a CSS rule and target all elements of a certain kind with type selectors (i.e., p, ul, h2, etc.). For example, this:

```
<h2 style="font-size:1.2em;color:red;">Little red Corvette</h2>
<h2 style="font-size:1.2em;color:red;">Baby you're much too fast to embed</h2>
<h2 style="font-size:1.2em;color:red;">Little red Corvette</h2>
<h2 style="font-size:1.2em;color:red;">You need a love that's gonna last</h2>
```

becomes this, by abstracting the inline style to a block style:

```
<style type="text/css"><!--
    #main h2{font-size:1.2em;color:red;}
--></style>
```

The corresponding HTML cleans up to this:

```
<div id="main">
    <h2>Little red Corvette</h2>
    <h2>Baby you're much too fast</h2>
    <h2>Little red Corvette</h2>
    <h2>You need a love that's gonna last</h2>
</div>
```

Note how clean the code becomes after you remove the inline styles. This CSS technique also helps search engine optimization (SEO) by boosting keyword density and prominence.

Tip #2: Use Descendant Selectors

Descendant selectors (sometimes called contextual selectors) target elements that are contained within other elements using the inherent structure of your markup. Labeling your container cells (e.g., <div id="footer">) allows you to target content that is enclosed within elements without the need for inline classes. Here is a minimalist example:

```
<style type="text/css"><!--
    div.warning p{color:red;} /* descendant selector */
--></style></head><body>

<div class="warning">
  <p>Warning! Meltdown is imminent.</p>
</div>
```

The descendant selector in the preceding code (div.warning p) targets the paragraph element that is contained within the <div> element. Rather than explicitly embedding classes into each element that you want to target, it is more efficient to use a descendant selector to target descendants of elements, labeled or otherwise.

The child selector, >, allows finer-grained targeting and does not target all descendants, just the most immediate children. For unordered lists, the W3C recommends using child selectors to style nested lists, not descendant selectors. Keep in mind that Internet Explorer 5.5 and 6 do not support the child selector, but Internet Explorer 7 and later do.

```
ul > li{font-weight:bold;}
```

Tip #3: Group Selectors with Common Declarations

CSS allows you to group multiple selectors that share the same declaration. This optimization technique allows you to apply the same style to multiple selectors, separated by commas, to save space.

So, instead of this:

```
.sitehead {
    font-weight: normal; font-size: 12px; color: #0b2475; font-family: arial,
helvetica, sans-serif;
}
.sitenav {
    font-weight: normal; font-size: 12px; color: #0b2475; font-family: arial,
helvetica, sans-serif;
}
```

do this, by grouping multiple selectors with common declarations:

```
.sitehead, .sitenav {
    font-weight: normal; font-size: 12px; color: #0b2475; font-family: arial,
helvetica, sans-serif;
}
```

Even better, use the font shorthand property (more on this shortly):

```
.sitehead, .sitenav {
    font: 12px arial,helvetica,sans-serif;color:#0b2475;
}
```

Tip #4: Group Declarations with Common Selectors

CSS allows you to group multiple declarations that share the same selector into one rule set, separated by semicolons. This technique allows you to apply multiple declarations to one selector to save space.

So, this:

```
body {font-size: 1em;}
body {font-family: arial, helvetica, geneva, sans-serif;}
body {color:#000000;}
body {background:#ffffff;}
```

becomes this, by grouping multiple declarations that share the same selector:

```
body {
```

```
        font-size: 1em;
        font-family: arial, helvetica, geneva, sans-serif;
        color: #000000;
        background: #ffffff;
    }
```

Even better, use shorthand properties to abbreviate this rule even further, like this:

```
body{font:1em arial,helvetica,sans-serif;color:#000;background:#fff;}
```

Note that you need only one or two font faces and a default for the generic font family. We omitted the third geneva font face here.

Also, by combining the grouping of selectors that share the same declaration and declarations that share the same selector, you can apply multiple declarations to multiple selectors. This technique allows you to create compact yet powerful CSS rules.

So, this:

```
#nav {font-size:1em;}
#nav {color:#000;background:transparent;}
#nav ul {font-size:1em;}
#nav ul li {font-size:1em;}
```

becomes this:

```
#nav, #nav ul, #nav ul li {font-size:1em; color:#000;background:transparent;}
```

Tip #5: Combine Common Styles into Shared Classes

One technique that you can use when optimizing CSS is to merge common declarations into separate classes. Not unlike "orthogonalizing" a database into normal forms by eliminating redundant fields, this technique modularizes CSS. The feature that makes this possible is the ability to assign *multiple classes to one element* which the aforementioned CSS2-compliant browsers support.

For example:

```
<div class="nav align">...</div>
```

This ability to reference multiple classes gives authors new options when styling their content. For elements that share the same styles (e.g., text-align:center) you can group these shared styles into one shared class.

So, this:

```
<style type="text/css">
    .nav{color:red; text-align:center;}
    .main{color:#000; text-align:center;}
    .footer{color:#00f; text-align:center;}
</style></head><body>

<div class="nav">...</div>
<div class="main">...</div>
<div class="footer">...</div>
```

becomes this, after grouping the common center style into one shared class:

```
<style type="text/css">
    .nav{color:red;}
    .main{color:#000;}
    .footer{color:#00f;}
    .align{text-align:center;}
</style></head><body>

<div class="nav align">...</div>
<div class="main align">...</div>
<div class="footer align">...</div>
```

The fourth `.align` class merges the common style (in this case, the `text-align:center` declaration) into a class now shared by three elements. The additional class saves space by eliminating redundant common declarations (which can bulk up larger stylesheets). In effect, you are normalizing your CSS.

Tip #6: Use Inheritance to Eliminate Duplicate Declarations

You can use inheritance to flow property values down the document tree and eliminate duplicate declarations. An element inherits the properties of its parent element unless otherwise specified. So, this overdeclared example:

```
<style type="text/css">
    body{font:1em arial,helvetica,sans-serif;}
    p.normal1em{font:1em arial,helvetica,sans-serif;} /* extra declaration */
    div {font:1em arial,helvetica,sans-serif;}        /* another one */
    #content em{color:red;} /* em for emphasis color */
    #content em.ed {color:#00331a;}
</style></head><body>

<div id="content">
    <p class="normal1em">Normal text here, brute forced from the p rule.
    <em class="ed">Editors note: Note that inherited CSS can provide
    this approach more efficiently.</em></p>
</div> </body>
```

becomes this, by moving the common font declaration up into the body rule and eliminating the p rule and div rules which are implied by inheritance:

```
<style type="text/css">
<!--
    body{font:1em arial,helvetica,sans-serif;}
    #content em{color:red;} /* em for emphasis color */
    #content em.ed {color:#00331a;}
--></style></head><body>

<div id="content">
    <p>Normal text here, inherited from the body rule.
    <em class="ed">Editors note: Note the inherited style
    that CSS provides with this approach...</em></p>
</div> </body>
```

The child div and paragraph elements now inherit the same font size and family from the body rule. The idea is to simplify your style to remove redundant declarations. If you see the same terms repeated in your properties or class names, this is usually an area where you can squeeze some more bytes out of your CSS and markup.

 It is a best practice to use functional class names that describe the purpose of the class rather than embed values within names (e.g., .default versus .bluetext1). After all, designs can change, but the function of the class will not. A .bluetext{color:red;} or .marg3em{margin:2em;} would not make sense after a redesign.

Tip #7: Use CSS Shorthand

Some CSS properties and colors can be written in longhand or shorthand notation. Longhand CSS explicitly spells out every related property in great detail. Shorthand properties use the shorthand built into CSS for popular properties, including font, border, and margin. Shorthand hex colors abbreviate longhand #rrggbb triplets to #rgb shorthand.

Using shorthand colors

You can specify color values in CSS in three ways: by name, with RGB values, or as hexadecimal numbers. The most efficient way to set colors is to use hex or, in some rare cases, short color names. Longhand hex colors are specified as three red, green, and blue triplets, like this:

```
p { color: #fdca30; }
```

You can abbreviate colors that have an identical value for each pair, that is, #rrggbb;, with only one value per pair, so this:

```
p { color: #ffcc00; }
```

becomes this, using shorthand hex notation:

```
p {color: #fc0;}
```

Named colors can ease maintenance, but they are generally longer than their shorthand hex equivalents (other than red and tan).

Shorthand properties

CSS shorthand properties allow you to consolidate several related properties into one abbreviated property declaration. For example, you can combine font-size and font-family into a single font rule.

Shorthand properties in CSS2 succinctly specify property declarations according to built-in rules (replication, inheritance) and defaults (none, normal). The list of shorthand properties is as follows:

```
font:      <font-style> <font-variant> <font-weight> <font-size> / <line-height>
<font-family>
border:    <border-width> <border-style> <color> transparent
    border-color: top right bottom left  (uses replication)
    border-style: top right bottom left  (uses replication)
    border-top: <border-top-width> <border-style> <color>
        (top/right/bottom/left)
    border-width: top right bottom left  (uses replication)
background: <background-color> <background-image> <background-repeat>
    <background-attachment> <background-position>
list-style: <list-style-type> <list-style-position> <list-style-image>
margin:    <margin-width> top right bottom left  (uses replication)
outline:   <outline-color> <outline-style> <outline-width>
padding:   <padding-width> top right bottom left (uses replication)
```

Property value replication. For CSS properties that can specify values for four sides of a box (border, border-color, margin, padding, outline, etc.), you can use replication to save space. Here is how replication works. If there is one value, it applies to all sides. Two values apply to the top/bottom, and right/left sides. Three values apply to top, right/left, and bottom. For example:

```
body { margin: 2em; }            /* all margins set to 2em */
body { margin: 1em 2em; }        /* top & bottom = 1em, right & left = 2em */
body { margin: 1em 2em 3em; }    /* top=1em, right & left=2em, bottom=3em */
body { margin: 1em 2em 3em 4em; } /* top = 1em, right=2em, bottom=3em,left=4em */
body { margin: top right bottom left;} /* full syntax */
```

The margin shorthand property. The margin shorthand property sets the margin for all four sides of a box using one, two, three, or four widths in one abbreviated property. margin takes the place of the margin-top, margin-right, margin-bottom, and margin-left properties. The syntax of the margin shorthand property is as follows:

```
margin: <margin-width>{1,4} | inherit
```

or:

```
margin: <margin-width> top right bottom left
```

where the margin-width value can be a length (px, em, etc.), a percentage, or auto. Here is a minimal example:

```
div { margin: 1em; }
```

This CSS rule sets the margin around all divs to 1 em space. You can set all sides of a box to one width and zero out the widths of one or more sides like this:

```
div { margin: 1em; }
div { margin-bottom: 0; }
```

The padding shorthand property works exactly like the margin shorthand property discussed earlier. For more information, visit the W3C's box model page at *http://www.w3.org/TR/REC-CSS2/box.html.*

The border shorthand property. The border shorthand property sets the same width, style, color, and image for all four borders of a box. Unlike the padding and margin shorthand properties, the border property cannot set different values for the different sides of a border. The syntax of the border shorthand is as follows:

```
border: <border-width> <border-style> <color> transparent inherit
```

For example, the following CSS rule:

```
div { border: solid red; }
```

sets a medium (the default initial value) red border for all sides of the div. This is equivalent to:

```
div {
  border-top: solid red;
  border-right: solid red;
  border-bottom: solid red;
  border-left: solid red;
}
```

You can set the border style for all four sides of a box, and then set one or two sides to save space. For example:

```
#nav div {
  border: 1px solid #fc0;
  border-right: 1px solid #c30;
  border-bottom: 1px solid #c30;
}
```

You can also do this in another way by using defaults:

```
#nav div {
  border-width: 1px; /* defaults to solid */
  border-color: #fc0 #c30 #c30 #fc0;
}
```

Plus, you can zero out a border on one or more sides by specifying a zero width. For example:

```
p {
  border: 1px double red;
  border-width: 1px 0 0 1px;
}
```

Note that if you omit a property, the border shorthand uses the initial value of the property. So, if a color is specified and you use border:solid;, the browser will use the default medium solid border, with a color specified in the color property.

The font shorthand property. The font property is a shorthand property for setting the font-style, font-variant, font-weight, font-size, line-height, and font-family properties, all in one abbreviated notation. You should set font-stretch and font-size-adjust with their individual properties. The syntax of the font: shorthand property is as follows:

```
font: <font-style> <font-variant> <font-weight> <font-size> / <line-height> <font-
family>
```

The `font-size` and `font-family` are required properties, whereas the other properties will revert to their defaults if they are missing. Here is a minimalist example:

```
p { font: 0.9em serif; }
```

This CSS rule sets all paragraph text to 90% of the current font size with the default serif font family. A more complete example utilizing the entire font property follows:

```
p { font: italic small-caps bold 0.9em/110% "new century schoolbook", serif; }
```

To abbreviate a longhand declaration:

```
.errormsg {
    font-size: 12px; color: #ff0000; font-family: arial, helvetica, sans-serif;
font-weight: bold;
}
```

do this, using the shorthand `font:` notation:

```
.errormsg {
    font:bold 12px arial,helvetica,sans-serif;color:#f00;
}
```

Note that you can change the order in which some properties appear. Most browsers will allow this. However, to avoid any problems with current or future browsers that may be stricter in their interpretation, it is a best practice to supply the properties in the order that the W3C lists them in the specification. For more information on the font shorthand, see *http://www.w3.org/TR/REC-CSS2/fonts.html#font-shorthand* and *http://www.w3.org/TR/css3-fonts/#font-shorthand*.

The background shorthand property. The background property is a shorthand property that sets the background properties of an element as a color, an image, or, as a fall-back, both. The background property sets the following properties: background-color, background-image, background-repeat, background-attachment, and background-position, in one shorthand notation. The syntax for the background property is as follows:

```
background: <background-color> <background-image> <background-repeat> <background-
attachment> <background-position> inherit
```

Here is a minimalist example:

```
body {background: gray;}
```

This CSS rule sets the background-color of the body element to gray. It is better to use the body rather than the html element here, which targets the entire HTML document. This shorthand rule is equivalent to:

```
body {
    background-color: gray;
    background-position: 0% 0%;
    background-size: 30% 30%;
```

```
        background-repeat: repeat;
        background-attachment: scroll;
        background-image: none;
    }
```

A more complete example of a background shows the entire rule:

```
div { background: gray url(steel.png) repeat fixed 50%; }
```

This shorthand rule is equivalent to:

```
div {
    background-color: gray;
    background-image: url(steel.png)
    background-repeat: repeat;
    background-attachment: fixed;
    background-position: 50% 50%;
}
```

For more information on background shorthand, see *http://www.w3.org/TR/CSS21/ colors.html* and *http://www.w3.org/TR/css3-background/*.

The list-style shorthand property. The list-style property sets list-style-type, list-style-position, and list-style-image in one abbreviated notation. The syntax is as follows:

```
list-style: <list-style-type> <list-style-position> <list-style-image> inherit
```

For example, this:

```
ul { list-style: none; }
```

sets all unordered lists to not display a list-item marker. The following example sets all ordered lists to uppercase Roman numerals:

```
ol { list-style: upper-roman inside; }
```

A final example illustrates the entire shorthand rule. Note that specifying a list-style-type of disc is a fallback for when the image is not available.

```
ul { list-style: url("http://example.com/bullet.png") disc outside; }
```

The preceding code is shorthand for the following:

```
ul {
    list-style-image: url("http://example.com/bullet.png");
    list-style-marker: disc;
    list-style-position: outside;
}
```

Note that the "outside" property is the default, and is optional in the preceding shorthand version. For more information, see *http://www.w3.org/TR/CSS21/generate. html#propdef-list-style-position* and *http://www.w3.org/TR/css3-lists/*.

The outline shorthand property. The outline property sets the outline-color, outline-style, and outline-width in one shorthand notation. Outlines differ from borders in that they take up no space, and they can be nonrectangular. The syntax of the outline property is as follows:

```
outline: <outline-color> <outline-style> <outline-width> inherit
```

The outline style and width accept the same values as their border counterparts. The outline-color property accepts all color values and also invert. invert performs a color inversion of the pixels on the screen to ensure visibility of the outline. An outline is the same width on all sides, unlike a border property.

For example:

```
button { outline: thick solid; }
```

This rule draws a thick solid outline around all buttons to highlight them. You can show which element has focus by using the outline property. Because they overlay the element and do not take up additional space, turning outlines on and off should not cause your web pages to reflow.

For example, you can use the focus and active pseudoclasses to set outlines according to the state of a button:

```
button:focus  { outline: thick solid black; }
button:active { outline: thick solid red; }
```

These CSS rules draw a thick black line around a button when it has focus, and a thick red line around a button when it is active. Note that Internet Explorer 5 through 7 do not support the outline property, but Internet Explorer 8b1 does. For more information, visit *http://www.w3.org/TR/css3-ui/#outline1* and *http://www.w3.org/TR/CSS21/ui.html#outline-focus*.

Tip #8: Abbreviate Long Class and ID Names

Verbosity is a virtue in some programming circles, but not when you craft CSS. Long class names may be more easily understood by subsequent designers, but your users must download those extra bytes (at least the first time they load the CSS file). So, this:

```
#content .textadvertisingrectangle{text-align:center;}
```

becomes this, after some class name abbreviation:

```
#content .textadbox{text-align:center;}
```

At the extreme end, you could "pull a Yahoo!" by using one- or two-letter class names, like this:

```
#c .ta{text-align:center;}
```

Be sure to watch out for namespace collisions when you do this for more complex applications with layered stylesheets.

Abbreviating class and ID names to one or two characters is an extreme technique, and you should use it only after your website design is set in stone. As most sites are not static, reserve this technique only for exceptional situations. Yahoo! uses this technique, as well as URI rewriting, to squeeze every byte possible out of its home page, because it has the busiest page on the Web.

Using semantically meaningful names

Whenever possible, use class and ID names that are semantically meaningful and search-friendly. For example:

```
<style type="text/css">
<!--
    .box {border:1px solid #000;}
    .bio h2, .bio h3 {color: #c00;background:#0cc;}
    .testimonial h2, .testimonial h3 {color: #0c0; background:#c0c;}
--></style></head><body>

<div class="box bio">
    <h2>Our Staff Bios</h2>
    <div>
        <h3>Barack Obama</h3>
        <p>Senator Obama ran for president in 2008...</p>
        <h3>Albert Gore</h3>
        <p>Vice President Gore raised awareness of global warming ...</p>
    </div>
</div>
<div class="box testimonial">...</div>
```

This way, you need to change only the class name in the div, which uses multiple classes, to achieve a different look. The bio class would have one look and the testimonial class would have another.

Comments in CSS

You can manually or automatically remove comments from your CSS files. Another strategy is to use PHP comments in your CSS. Once parsed, these comments will automatically disappear. First, you need to tell your server to parse your CSS files for PHP by adding the following lines to your *httpd.conf* or *.htaccess* file:

```
AddHandler application/x-httpd-php .css
php_value default_mimetype "text/css"
```

Next, include one- or multiline comments within your CSS file:

```
<?php
// this comment will disappear, a one-liner
?>
```

For multiline comments:

```
<?php
/* multiline comment here, allows longer
```

```
    comments, that also don't appear in your CSS
*/
?>
```

Again, you trade some server processing power for size.

Tip #9: Use CSS2 and CSS3.x Techniques

Attribute selectors were introduced in CSS2, and the modern browsers listed at the beginning of this chapter, with the exception of Internet Explorer 6, support them. Internet Explorer 7 and later support attribute selectors, which allow authors to target elements with attributes that match certain characteristics. In CSS2.1, these selectors can match attribute characteristics in four ways:

[att]
> Match when the element has the att attribute.

[att=val]
> Match when the element's att attribute value is exactly val.

[att~=val]
> Match when the element's att attribute value is a space-separated list of words, one of which is exactly val. The value may not have spaces.

[att|=val]
> Match when the element's att attribute value is a hyphen-separated list of words, beginning with val.

You can match elements that have an attribute, or that have a certain attribute value. For example, the following rule:

```
div ul *[href] {color:red;}
```

looks for any element with an href attribute set, inside a ul, inside a div, and sets the color to red. You could use this to select elements inside a navigation bar, for example.

CSS3 adds substring matching to attribute selectors. Substring matching allows you to look for subsets of strings used in attribute values. Here is the syntax of CSS3 attribute selectors:

[att^=val]
> Matches elements with the att attribute whose value begins with val

[att$=val]
> Matches elements with the att attribute whose value ends with val

[att*=val]
> Matches elements with the att attribute whose value contains at least one instance of the substring val

The most powerful selector here is the * selector, which looks for substrings anywhere in the attribute value:

```
<style type="text/css">
    a[href*="/services"] {color:green;} </style></head><body>
<p><a href="http://www.example.com/services/invisalign/">Invisalign</a></p>
```

You can look for strings at the beginning or end of attribute values. For example, to highlight all PDF files, you'd do the following:

```
a[href$=".pdf"] {background: url(pdflink.gif) no-repeat right top:padding-right:
10px;}
```

To highlight all external links, you can look for any anchor that begins with http:, like so:

```
a[href^="http:"] {background:url(externallink.gif) no-repeat right top;padding-right:
10px;}
```

This rule flags all absolute URIs with a background graphic that displays an external link image. It also flags internal links that are absolute, so you'll need to filter all absolute links from your own site like this:

```
a[href^="http://www.example.com"], a[href^="http://example.com"] {background-image:
none;padding-right:0;}
```

Tip #10: Replace JavaScript Behavior with CSS Techniques

JavaScript is commonly used for rollovers and drop-down menus. However, in many cases you can substitute CSS :hover effects for JavaScript rollovers. Here is a real-world example that uses graphics rollovers for a left navigation bar (see Figure 7-1) that also uses graphical text (complete with underlines):

```
<img src="images/nav/nonav_top.gif"><br>
<a href="/tourism/" onMouseOver="act('tourism')" onMouseOut="inact('tourism')">
<img src="images/nav/tourism_off.gif" alt="Tourism" name="tourism" border="0"></a>
<br>
<a href="/trade/" target="_blank" onMouseOver="act('trade')"
onMouseOut="inact('trade')">
<img src="images/nav/trade_off.gif" alt="Trade" name="trade" border="0"></a><br>
```

Figure 7-1. How not to do a menu

This menu has three things wrong with it:

- JavaScript is used for the rollovers.
- Graphics are used for the text.
- There is no structure to target.

Here is what we'd recommend doing to convert this menu to CSS lists:

- Use CSS instead of JavaScript.
- Use text for the graphical text.
- Use lists for the tables.

With all CSS conversion projects, first strip the HTML markup down to a bare structure:

```
<ul>
<li><a href="/tourism/">Travel &amp; Tourism</a></li>
<li><a href="/trade/">Trade</a></li>
...
</ul>
```

Then target your unordered list items with the following descendant selectors:

```
<style type="text/css">
    ul {list-style:none;}
    ul li a:hover{text-decoration:underline;}
</style>
```

Now you've substituted CSS behavior (:hover) for JavaScript behavior, greatly simplifying the code. We'll explore how to style a similar menu later in this chapter.

One of the best uses of CSS is to save round trips to the server. As you learned in the introduction to Part II, web page latency is dominated by object overhead. You can minimize that overhead by using CSS in creative ways to save HTTP requests by substituting CSS-styled elements and hover effects for images and JavaScript.

CSS buttons

You can simulate graphical buttons with links and CSS and style input elements for forms to make them stand out to improve conversion rates. The speed benefit of using CSS to create buttons is that you save an HTTP request for each unique button. You can achieve this effect by changing the `display` property of an anchor to block, and setting the width and height as well as styling the background and border of the button (see Figure 7-2):

```
a {
    display: block;
    width: 7em; /* needed for ie5x win */
    padding: 0.2em;
    line-height: 1.3em;
    background: #faa;
    border: 1px solid #000;
    color: #000;
    text-decoration: none;
    text-align:center;
}
```

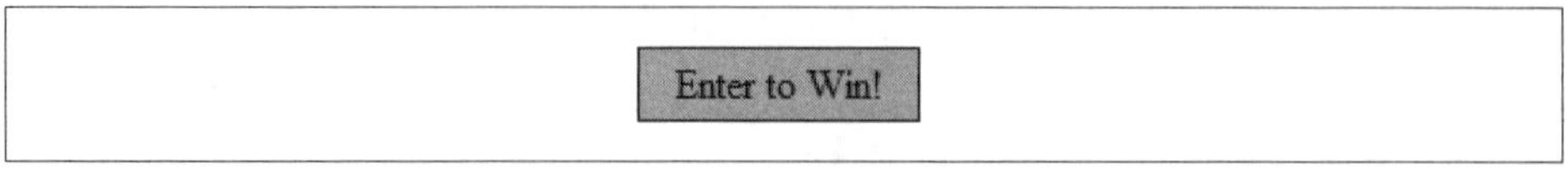

Figure 7-2. A text-based button

The width is set for the Windows version of Internet Explorer 5, without which only the link text would become active. We use line-height instead of height to avoid having to vertically center the text manually. Make sure the button is wide enough to contain the text without wrapping at reasonable font sizes.

CSS rollovers

Next, you can easily add a rollover effect by setting the background and text color with the :hover pseudoclass (see Figure 7-3):

```
a:hover {
    background:#633;
    color:#fff;
}
```

Figure 7-3. Adding rollover effects

Many CSS techniques are based on the :hover pseudoclass, including rollovers, drop-down menus including nested menus, and remote rollovers where one hotspot controls another.

Mono-image menu rollovers

You can use CSS to create simple rollover effects. But for more complex rollovers the classic method is to use two images for each button: one for the "on" state and one for the "off" state. The problem with this method is that it doubles the necessary HTTP requests and can cause flickering problems when the "off" image is not preloaded. A better way is to combine the on and off state images into one mini sprite and switch the background position on rollover (see Figure 7-4):

```
a:link, a:visited {
    display: block;
    width: 127px;
    height:25px;
    line-height: 25px;
    color: #000;
    text-decoration: none;
    background: #fc0 url(image-rolloverdual.png) no-repeat left top;
    text-indent: 25px;
}
```

```
a:hover {
    /* background: #c00; */
    background-position: right top;
    color: #fff;
}
```

Figure 7-4. Mini CSS sprite for menu rollover

The background in the off state (:link) positions the background image to the left and top, showing the off state portion of the image. On rollover (:hover), the background position is shifted to the right, displaying the "on" portion of the background image. The width value effectively clips the image to show only the portion of the image that you want to display. Note that the next section shows a more complex CSS sprite example.

You may want to zero out margin and padding values to eliminate rendering differences between browsers thusly:

```
a {
    margin:0;
    padding:0;
}
```

This will zero out all the margins and padding for *all* links, however. It is better to be specific in your selectors to avoid coding extra CSS:

```
#nav ul li a {
    margin:0;
    padding:0;
    ....
}
```

See the "Use a Reset Stylesheet" section, earlier in this chapter, for more ideas along these lines.

Very old browsers (older than version 5) may not work with some of these positioning techniques. To hide your CSS from older browsers, the @import method is the easiest to implement. For example:

```
<link rel="stylesheet" type="text/css" href="basic.css" />
<style type="text/css"> @import "modern.css"; </style>
```

You can also use this technique to highlight visited links. For extra credit, create the preceding effect entirely with CSS.

CSS sprites

CSS sprites expand this approach to group multiple images into one composite image and display them using CSS background positioning. Some of the busiest sites on the Internet use CSS sprites to improve response times. Both AOL.com and Yahoo.com use sprites extensively to save numerous HTTP requests for their intricate interfaces.

AOL.com CSS sprites. AOL.com uses CSS sprites on its home page to improve performance. AOL uses a CSS sprite for the icons in its main directory navigation bar (Autos, Finance, Food, etc.) on the left side of its home page (see Figure 7-5).

Figure 7-5. The AOL.com home page uses CSS sprites

Its main CSS file sets up the directory navigation bar list:

```
<link rel="stylesheet" type="text/css" href="http://www.aolcdn.com/_media/aolp_v23.1/
main.css" />

#sm_col .dir ul li a, #sm_col .nav2 li a, #sm_col .nav3 li a {
    line-height:1.2em;
    padding:.28em 0 .28em 2.3em;
    border-bottom:1px solid #fff;
    overflow:hidden;
```

```
}
#sm_col .dir ul li a, #aiw, #sm_col .nav2 li a, #sm_col .nav3 li a {
    display:block;
    width:10.28em;
}
...
#sm_col ul.serv li a:hover, #sm_col .nav2 li a:hover, #sm_col .nav3 li a:hover,
.eight .dir ul li a:hover {
    background-color:#fff;
}
```

This CSS sets the styles for the height of the directory menu, padding (with plenty of room for the background icon—2.3 em—on the left), and a white border on the bottom, and hides any overflow. AOL displays the anchor as a block to make it clickable and set the width to 10.28 em and the rollover color to white. Note that AOL could use background instead of background-color to save six bytes.

Then AOL sets the background of each directory class (as well as some other IDs) to dir_sprite.png (see Figure 7-6):

```
.d1, .d2, .d3, .d4, .d5, .d6, .d7, .d8, .d9, .d10, .d11, .d12, .d13, .d14, .d15,
.d16, .d17, .d18, .d19, .d20, .d21,.d22, .d23, .d24, .d25, .d26, .d27, .d28, .d29,
.d30, .d31, #aim_sprTbEdt, #games_sprTbEdt, #sports_sprTbEdt, #weather_sprTbEdt,
#radio_sprTbEdt, #horoscopes_sprTbEdt, #video_sprTbEdt {
    background:transparent url("dir_sprite.png") no-repeat 4px 0;
}
```

Figure 7-6. AOL menu sprite, dir_sprite.png (truncated)

This rule assigns the background image of the directory sprite to these classes and IDs. For the subsequent directory menu items, it is just a matter of shifting the background image up 36 or 38 pixels to show each subsequent icon.

```
.d2 {
    background-position:4px -36px;
}
.d3 {
    background-position:4px -74px;
}
.d4 {
    background-position:4px -112px;
}
```

So, when you assign the class .d2 for finance, it shifts the background up 36 pixels, showing the Finance icon (clipping within the dimensions of the list item with overflow:hidden). The assignment of the sprite as a background to multiple classes, and the shifting of background-position for each class, is the essence of CSS sprites. The HTML code looks like this for the directory:

```
<div id="cols">
<div id="sm_col">
...
<a name="dir"><h6>Directory</h6></a><div class="dir">
<ul id="om_dir_col1_" class="serv c">
<li><a id="d1" class="d1" href="http://autos.aol.com/?ncid=AOLCOMMautoNAVIdira0001">
Autos</a></li>
<li><a id="d2" class="d2" href="http://money.aol.com">Finance</a></li>
<li><a id="d3" class="d31" href="http://food.aol.com">Food</a></li>
<li><a id="d4" class="d3" href="http://games.aol.com">Games</a></li>
<li><a id="d5" class="d4" href="http://body.aol.com">Health & Diet</a></li>...</ul>
```

Yahoo.com CSS sprites. AOL uses classes and IDs to label its menu items. Yahoo!, on the other hand, uses inline styles to embed the positioning of its sprite directly into the list items (see Figure 7-7). AOL's version uses slightly more code, but the code is more flexible.

To maximize accessibility and usability, it is best to use CSS sprites for icons associated with links, or for decorative effects. AOL found that using CSS sprites for every graphic caused accessibility and usability problems for browsers in High Contrast Mode on Windows machines with images turned off. For more information on CSS sprites, see *http://www.websiteoptimization.com/speed/tweak/css-sprites/* and *http://www.alistapart.com/articles/sprites/*.

List-based menus

For drop-down menus, you can substitute lists for tables and CSS for JavaScript to save a significant amount of HTML markup and JavaScript code. Here is an example from CableOrganizer.com (see Figure 7-8).

Figure 7-7. The Yahoo! home page uses CSS sprites

Figure 7-8. CableOrganizer.com CSS menus

CableOrganizer reduced its HTML file by 46.4% (from 97 KB to 52 KB) by recoding its page using CSS techniques. Here is the original JavaScript-powered XHTML markup for its main menu on the left:

```
<div id="categories" class="left-nav">
    <ul>
        <li><a href="http://cableorganizer.com/surface-raceways/" title="Wire Raceway,
Wire Duct, Conduit" id="menu1Link" onmouseover="ypSlideOutMenu.showMenu('menu1');"
onmouseout="ypSlideOutMenu.hideMenu('menu1')">Raceway, Duct &amp; Conduit </a> </li>
        <li><a href="http://cableorganizer.com/cord-covers/" title="Electrical Cord
Cover" id="menu2Link" onmouseover="ypSlideOutMenu.showMenu('menu2');"
onmouseout="ypSlideOutMenu.hideMenu('menu2')">Cord Covers</a> </li>
```

The JavaScript file (*menus.js*) is 6.12 KB. The entire *menus.js* file was eliminated using CSS :hover to re-create the drop-down behavior. Here is the HTML markup for the same menu using CSS for behavior:

```
<div id="cat">
<ul>
<li><a href="/surface-raceways/"><span>Raceway, Duct, Conduit</span></a>
<div class="sub">
<ul>
<li><a href="/surface-raceways/">Raceways: HOME</a></li>
<li><a href="/cable-raceway/">Cable Raceway</a></li>
...</ul></div></li>
<li><a href="/cord-covers/">Cord Covers</a><div class="sub"><ul><li>...
```

In the CSS, CableOrganizer set the left-column categories to float left with a width of 153 pixels:

```
#mainwrap table tr td#lcol #cat,#cat{float:left;position:relative;overflow:
visible;top:0;left:0;width:153px;margin:0;padding:0;}
```

CableOrganizer positioned the submenus with a left margin of 155 px to offset the menus to the right (note that relative measurements would scale better):

```
#cat ul div.sub{position:absolute;top:-3px;margin:0 0 0 155px;padding:0;clear:
both;width:105%;height:505%;}
```

Next, CableOrganizer hid the submenus by setting the visibility to none:

```
#cat ul li div.sub,#cat ul ul,#cat li:hover ul{display:none;}
```

Then it is just a matter of setting the visibility of the submenus on :hover like so:

```
body #cat #mainwrap li a:hover div.sub,body #cat li:hover div.sub,body #cat li:hover
ul,body #cat li:hover li:hover ul{display:block;}
```

This disjointed rollover is accomplished by including the .sub (menu) div within the li. So, the li a:hover div.sub{display:block;} (and display:none) turns the submenu on and off.

Conditional Comments to Avoid CSS Hacks

The tricky part of CSS is allowing for different browsers. Using Internet Explorer's proprietary conditional comments is one solution. Other browsers ignore these comments and only Internet Explorer 5 and later interpret them. Conditional comments also validate. For example, to remedy the lack of :hover support for list items in Internet Explorer 6, CableOrganizer included the behavior fix only for Internet Explorer 6 with conditional comments, like this:

```
<!--[if IE 6]><link rel="stylesheet" href="http://css.cableorganizer.com/
ie6home.php" type="text/css" /><style type="text/css">body {behavior:url(http://
css.cableorganizer.com/csshover.htc);}</style><![endif]-->
```

The Internet Explorer behavior file from Peter Nederlof (the whatever:hover) uses JScript to attach the :hover event to any element (see *http://www.xs4all.nl/~peterned/csshover.html*).

Auto-expanding menus. You've no doubt seen the body ID/class method used to highlight the current menu item (*http://www.websiteoptimization.com/speed/tweak/current/*). You can also use a similar method to expand the menu of the current section upon entry into the page. Wendy Peck created such a menu for a client (see Figure 7-9).

Figure 7-9. Automatically expanding menus

The initial products page demonstrates all the menus deployed using the following CSS:

```
<style type="text/css">
.one, .two, .three, .four, .five, .six {
    display: list-item;
}
</style>
```

Each menu is labeled with a number and is displayed with `display:list-item;`. Click on any menu and the CSS deploys that menu (see Figure 7-10).

Figure 7-10. Menus expanded with CSS

The submenus default to hidden, and we auto-deploy the submenu of the page you are on with a simple declaration of visibility. Let's look at how this is done. First, we set up our menus:

```
<div id="left">
 <h3>PRODUCTS: Programs</h3>
    <ul class="leftmenu">
        <li><a href="#">Strategic Business and Design</a></li>
    </ul>
    <ul class="sub one">
        <li> <a href="#">Organizational Future by Design</a>&trade;</li>
        <li> <a href="#">Strategic Planning For Action&trade;</a></li>
        <li> <a href="#">Mergers and Reorganizations</a></li>
    </ul>
```

```
<ul class="leftmenu">
    <li><a href="#">Executive Leadership </a></li>
</ul>
    <ul class="sub three">...
```

Next, we set up our menus with standard CSS markup, and hide all of the submenus:

```
<style type="text/css">
.sub a:link {
    color: #666;
    text-decoration: none;
}
.sub a:visited {
    color: #666;
    text-decoration: none;
}
.sub a:hover {
    color: #000;
    text-decoration: none;
    border-bottom:1px solid #ff3;
}
.sub {
    display: none;
}
</style>
```

Note that you can further optimize these styles using grouping, like so:

```
<style type="text/css">
.sub a:link, .sub a:visited {
    color:#666;
}

.sub a:hover {
    color:#000;
    border-bottom:1px solid #ff3;
}

.sub a:link, .sub a:visited, .sub a:hover {
    text-decoration:none;
}

.sub {
    display:none;
}
</style>
```

Then, to display the appropriate submenu, we use a second class (one, two, three, four...; ideally these would be class names related to the topic of the page instead in case the order changes) to set the display property of the menu. So, when you click on the Executive Leadership menu and go to the Executive Leadership page, we include this brief CSS snippet in the page (to make it easier for the client to understand and change):

```
<style type="text/css">
.three {
    display: list-item;
}
</style>
```

This technique uses multiple classes to control the display of submenus. The sub class is common to all submenus, and the classes one, two, three, and so on give a label to each menu to turn them on selectively. You could also use the body ID/class method to automatically display the menus, but we chose to simplify the CSS to make it easier for the client to understand and edit.

The body ID/class method. To accomplish the same effect with the body ID/class method, you would first label each page with a class in the body tag:

```
<body class="executive">
```

Then you'd use a compound descendant selector to display the appropriate menu, like this:

```
.strategic .one, .executive .three, .sales .five... {display:list-item;}
```

Summary

You should not use CSS optimization in isolation. To fully optimize your CSS, you need to transform your HTML markup. Replace table-based artificial structure and inline redundant styles with standards-based semantic markup using CSS rules that act on similar elements via external stylesheets. You can shrink your CSS by grouping selectors and declarations, using shorthand properties and colors, and by combining common declarations into shared classes. What is even more effective is to transform your markup by using CSS to style lists and layout and replace JavaScript behavior.

By architecting for CSS design from the start with labeled container divs, you can use descendant selectors to target your content, without the need for embedding classes within elements. The new attribute selectors offer more granular control without the need for inline classes for some techniques.

To recap, here are some techniques that you can use to optimize your CSS and HTML pages:

- Use a reset stylesheet.
- Plan for descendant selectors by using labeled container cells.
- Position external CSS files in the head.
- Replace inline styles with type selectors.
- Group selectors with common declarations.
- Group declarations with common selectors.

- Combine common styles into shared classes where appropriate (assign multiple classes for individual elements).
- Use inheritance to eliminate duplicate declarations.
- Use shorthand properties and colors.
- Abbreviate long class and ID names.
- Use CSS sprites to save HTTP requests where appropriate.
- Replace JavaScript behavior with CSS :hover techniques.
- Use CSS buttons, not graphics.
- Use list-based menus, not graphics or JavaScript.
- Use the body ID/class method to highlight and deploy menus for the current page.
- Use external stylesheets instead of inline styles and style blocks.
- Use CSS2 and CSS3.x techniques.
  — Use attribute selectors to avoid extra classes and IDs.
  — Highlight different types of links and objects with attribute selectors (PDF, external).

CHAPTER 8
Ajax Optimization

First described by Jesse James Garrett,[1] Asynchronous JavaScript and XML (Ajax) is a new way to boost the interactivity of websites.

Ajax[2] is a cross-platform set of technologies that allows developers to create web pages that behave more interactively, like applications. It uses a combination of Cascading Style Sheets (CSS), XHTML, JavaScript, and some textual data—usually XML or JavaScript Object Notation (JSON)—to exchange data asynchronously. This allows sectional page updates in response to user input, reducing server transfers (and resultant wait times) to a minimum. Properly coded, Ajax pages replace the old full-page paint, decide, click, and wait approach with streamlined partial page redraws, thereby boosting response times, interactivity, and usability.

> The communications pattern now known as Ajax was developed before 2005. Web developers using DHTML, iframes, image-cookie communication systems, Java applets, and Flash had experimented with richer communication forms that resulted in a more desktop-like experience. Until it had the new moniker "Ajax," however, the partial-page update pattern wasn't commonly utilized by web developers. Maybe the time wasn't right. Maybe large-scale examples were missing or maybe the terms *Rich Internet Applications* (RIAs), *remote scripting*, and *inner browsing design* failed to capture the imagination of the browsing public.

Ultimately, the goal of Ajax is to increase conversion rates through a faster, more user-friendly web experience. Unfortunately, unoptimized Ajax can cause performance lags, the appearance of application fragility, and user confusion. It can even

---

[1] Garrett, J. February 18, 2005. "Ajax: A New Approach to Web Applications." Adaptive Path, *http://www.adaptivepath.com/publications/essays/archives/000385.php* (accessed April 15, 2008).

[2] Ajax was a mythological Greek hero who played an important role in Homer's *Iliad*. He is described as the strongest of all the Achaeans. Although not the origin of this technology's name, it is certainly a suitable lineage for the power the technology provides.

harm your search engine rankings. The purpose of this chapter is to help you avoid these possible pitfalls and reap the rewards of Ajax.

We recommend the following best practices for optimizing the performance, stability, and usability of Ajax applications:

- Applying Ajax appropriately to a problem
- Using a well-constructed and supported Ajax library
- Minimizing your JavaScript code footprint
- Reducing HTTP request requirements
- Choosing the correct data format for transmission
- Ensuring that network availability and performance concerns are addressed
- Employing a JavaScript cache
- Carefully polling for user input
- Providing a fallback mechanism for search engines and accessibility when JavaScript is turned off
- Saving state with the fragment identifier

Common Problems with Ajax

Before we explain the best practices that you can use to optimize your Ajax, let's look at some common problems that Ajax-based websites face. We have encountered the following issues when analyzing and optimizing Ajax for clients:

- Mandatory JavaScript-style architecture effects
  — Accessibility problems
  — Search engine optimization (SEO) problems caused by lack of indexing by non-JavaScript-aware spiders coupled with one-page architecture issues
- Perception of browser and code errors by users
- Network effects
  — Lags in response time when the user expects immediacy
  — Timeouts and retries because of intermittent network issues
  — Lack of appropriate network and server error handling
  — Dependency and data ordering problems
- One-page architecture effects
  — Breaking the Back button and bookmarking
  — Difficulty with standard web analytics systems
  — Indexability of deep content by search robots

Ajax: New and Improved JavaScript Communications

What Garrett described was a modified web communication pattern that was gaining great popularity. This was demonstrated by Google services such as Gmail, Google Suggest, and Google Maps. No longer would a user click and wait for a full-page refresh. Instead, JavaScript would be used to make communication requests behind the scenes and to asynchronously update portions of the page.

Figure 8-1 shows that individual requests are spawned behind the scenes and parts of the page are updated. Here's how it works. Ajax applications insert an Ajax engine between the server and the user. The Ajax engine updates the page in response to user requests, with and without data from the server. For example, consider the type-ahead functionality provided by Google Suggest (*http://www.google.com/webhp?complete=1*). As the keystrokes are entered, we see in the network trace that requests are made on the partial queries to update the suggestion list below. You can see in the final packet what appears to be a JavaScript function call containing the terms and number of results that show in the drop-down list (see Figure 8-2).

This ability to quickly and dynamically filter such a large data set is powerful. Because the data packets returned are quite small, it keeps things snappy unless you are unlucky and encounter some network hiccups along the way.

In this chapter, we show that when misused, Ajax can be dangerous. Increased speed at the expense of application robustness or search engine rankings is not a trade-off that developers should accept. First let's start with the most dangerous question of all: is Ajax even necessary for our website?

Proper Application of Ajax

As with many web technologies, there is an initial hype phase followed by a pragmatic phase. Presently, Ajax is still in the tail end of the hype phase. Adventurous web developers are ready to apply Ajax to just about any problem that they encounter, seeking the possibility of a rich and speedy desktop-like experience with little consideration for the appropriateness of the pattern.

For an example of the possibility for over-Ajaxifying something, consider the idea of adding Ajax to a simple contact form. You might imagine having some basic fields to collect name, address, city, state, zip code, and so on. Now, in adding Ajax to everything, you might consider making an asynchronous request to the server with an Ajax call to validate the fields as the user fills them out. For information such as "name," this clearly would be pointless. You might simply be checking whether the user has put anything in the field. Standard client-side JavaScript can easily handle such data validation.

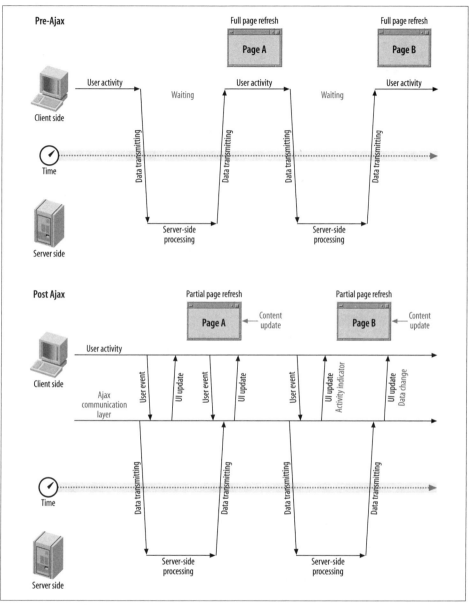

Figure 8-1. Asynchronous Ajax versus the traditional web communications model

But don't immediately jump to the conclusion that Ajax is inappropriate for use with form validation. When used with other fields it might make perfect sense. For example, consider validating the zip code field. You could provide basic client-side JavaScript code that checks whether numbers are entered. It is not rational, however, to go to the server to ensure that numbers were entered. Rather, send the value and see

Figure 8-2. Google suggestions courtesy of Ajax requests

whether the entered zip code is actually valid. You could even populate related fields such as city and state based on the entered zip code. Or if these fields are already entered, you could check to see whether they match the zip code provided (see Figure 8-3).

Without Ajax, this idea could not have been carried out unless one of the following occurred:

- A full-page server-post round-trip sequence was used; that would be annoying to the user.

- All of the zip code data was downloaded for local client use, which certainly isn't necessary.

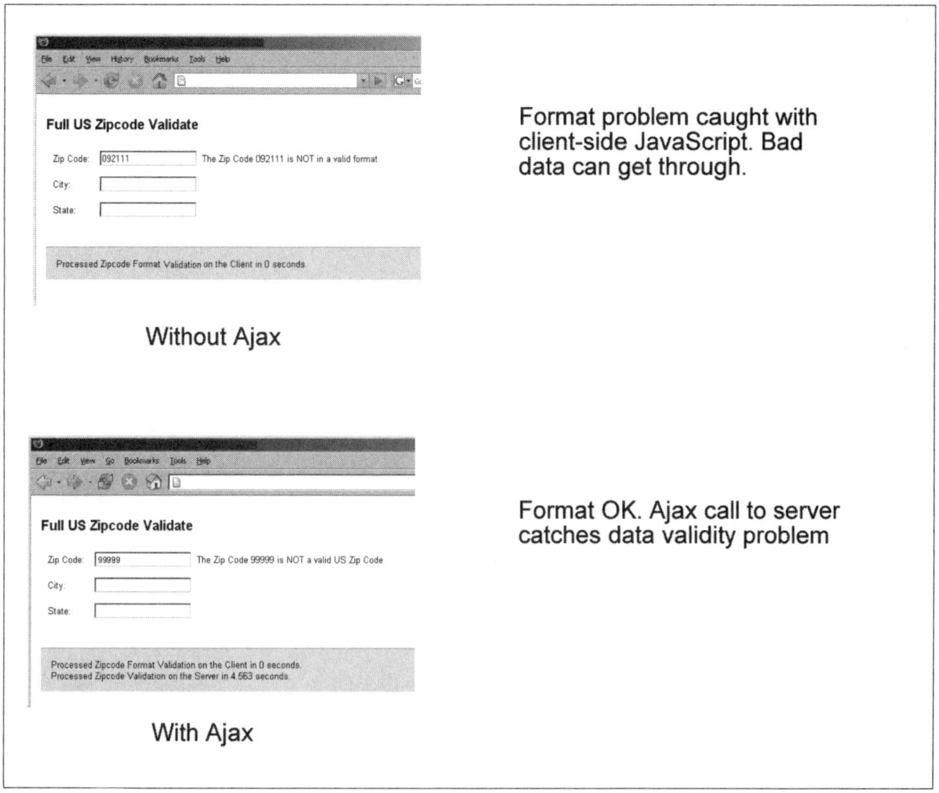

Figure 8-3. Ajax is good for some things, but not everything

Another common misuse is submitting all form data via Ajax. Sometimes it is the right thing to do—for example, if the form is only a small part of the page or the results of the form repaint parts of the current page. If the form submission repaints the entire page, however, it makes more sense to stick to basics and perform a normal CGI submit. Otherwise, unnecessary JavaScript must be written, the user must deal with potential Back button problems, and the page will not behave as the user expects it to.

Later we will discuss the Back button and other Ajax architectural effects in more detail, in the "Understanding the Ajax Architecture Effect" section of this chapter.

Like other technologies, Ajax has its trade-offs. Even though the requests are smaller, going to the network can be dangerous and certainly takes more time than doing things client-side.

It is best to use Ajax only when needed, and then to do so optimally.

Rolling Your Own Ajax Solution

When you implement your first Ajax solution, you'll discover that the improved communication power of the Ajax pattern is caused primarily by the XMLHttpRequest object commonly referred to in a shorthand form as XHR. The XHR object is natively supported in browsers such as Firefox, Opera, and Safari, and was initially supported as an ActiveX control under Internet Explorer 6.*x* and earlier. In IE 7.*x*, XHRs are natively supported, although you can always fall back to the ActiveX version if necessary. Given the variations in implementation, it is best to abstract the creation of an XHR. The most basic Ajax request that you would make will likely employ a simple wrapper function such as this, ordered in preference for native and more modern implementations first:

```
function createXHR( )
{
    try { return new XMLHttpRequest( ); } catch(e) {}
    try { return new ActiveXObject("Msxml2.XMLHTTP.6.0"); } catch (e) {}
    try { return new ActiveXObject("Msxml2.XMLHTTP.3.0"); } catch (e) {}
    try { return new ActiveXObject("Msxml2.XMLHTTP"); } catch (e) {}
    try { return new ActiveXObject("Microsoft.XMLHTTP"); } catch (e) {}
    return null; // no XHR support
}
```

Now you can just create an XHR with a simple call:

```
var xhr = createXHR( );
```

Once you've created the XHR, use the XHR object's open( ) method to begin forming the request that you are interested in, specifying the HTTP method, URI, and a Boolean value that indicates whether the request is to be synchronous or asynchronous. In this case, true means that you want it to be asynchronous or have a non-blocking behavior, which is the default for the object:

```
xhr.open("GET","helloworld.php",true);
```

Synchronous Versus Asynchronous Communication

Although most requests should be made asynchronously so that the user can continue working without the browser locking up as it is waiting for a response, do not assume that synchronous data transfer is always an inappropriate choice. The reality is that some requests must, in fact, be made synchronously because of dependency concerns.

Once the request has been initialized, assign a callback function to the onreadystatechange event handler. This function will be invoked as data is returned from the server.

```
xhr.onreadystatechange = function( ){responseCallback(xhr);};
```

Finally, send the request on its way....

```
xhr.send( );
```

Later, your function would be invoked as data is provided, moving through readyState values of 2, 3, and finally reaching 4 when the request is finished. Next you would look at the HTTP status code to see whether everything arrived OK and then start to consume your data. We will show this in the callback function shortly.

An Illustrative Example

As shown in the following function, first pull out the XML document object model (DOM) tree from the responseXML property of the passed XHR object. Then use DOM methods to pull out the portion of the packet in which you are interested. Next decide how you want to insert the response into the page. In this case, for brevity, just directly insert it with the innerHTML property. Even so, the DOM code is a bit nasty for a "Hello World" example.

```
function responseCallback(xhr)
{
  if (xhr.readyState == 4  && xhr.status == 200)
    {
      var xmlResponse = xhr.responseXML;

      var responseString = xmlResponse.getElementsByTagName("message")[0].firstChild.
nodeValue;

      var output = document.getElementById("output");
      output.innerHTML = responseString;
    }
}
```

Here is the complete example:

```
<!DOCTYPE html PUBLIC "-//W3C//DTD XHTML 1.0 Transitional//EN" "http://www.w3.org/TR/
xhtml1/DTD/xhtml1-transitional.dtd">
<html xmlns="http://www.w3.org/1999/xhtml">
<head>
<meta http-equiv="Content-Type" content="text/html; charset=iso-8859-1" />
<title>Ajax Hello World</title>
<script type="text/javascript">
function createXHR()
{
   try { return new XMLHttpRequest(); } catch(e) {}
   try { return new ActiveXObject("Msxml2.XMLHTTP.6.0"); } catch (e) {}
   try { return new ActiveXObject("Msxml2.XMLHTTP.3.0"); } catch (e) {}
   try { return new ActiveXObject("Msxml2.XMLHTTP"); } catch (e) {}
   try { return new ActiveXObject("Microsoft.XMLHTTP"); } catch (e) {}
   return null;
}

function sendRequest()
{
    var xhr = createXHR();

    if (xhr)
```

```
            {
              xhr.open("GET","sayhello.php",true);
              xhr.onreadystatechange = function(){responseCallback(xhr);};
              xhr.send();
            }
}

function responseCallback(xhr)
{
   if (xhr.readyState == 4  && xhr.status == 200)
      {
        var parsedResponse = xhr.responseXML;

        var responseString = parsedResponse.getElementsByTagName("message")[0].
firstChild.nodeValue;

        var output = document.getElementById("output");
        output.innerHTML = responseString;
      }
}

window.onload = function ()
{
 document.getElementById("button1").onclick = sendRequest;
};

</script>
</head>
<body>
<form action="#">
 <input type="button" value="Say it!" id="button1" />
</form>

<br /><br />
<div id="output"> </div>

</body>
</html>
```

The server-side code that is called is quite simple. It generates a response packet containing a message that says "Hello World" to the user with a time and IP address of access information:

```
<?php
header("Cache-Control: no-cache");
header("Pragma: no-cache");
header("Content-Type: text/xml");

$str =  "Hello World to user from " . $_SERVER['REMOTE_ADDR'] . " at ". date("h:i:s A");

print "<?xml version='1.0' encoding='UTF-8'?>";
print "<message>$str</message>";
?>
```

Note the use of the cache control headers. We will discuss this later when we attempt to make Ajax applications and caches play nicely together.

You can see the example of the data that is returned in Figure 8-4.

 If you run this example locally, you may run into problems. Security restrictions will force you to run it off a server and not on your desktop.

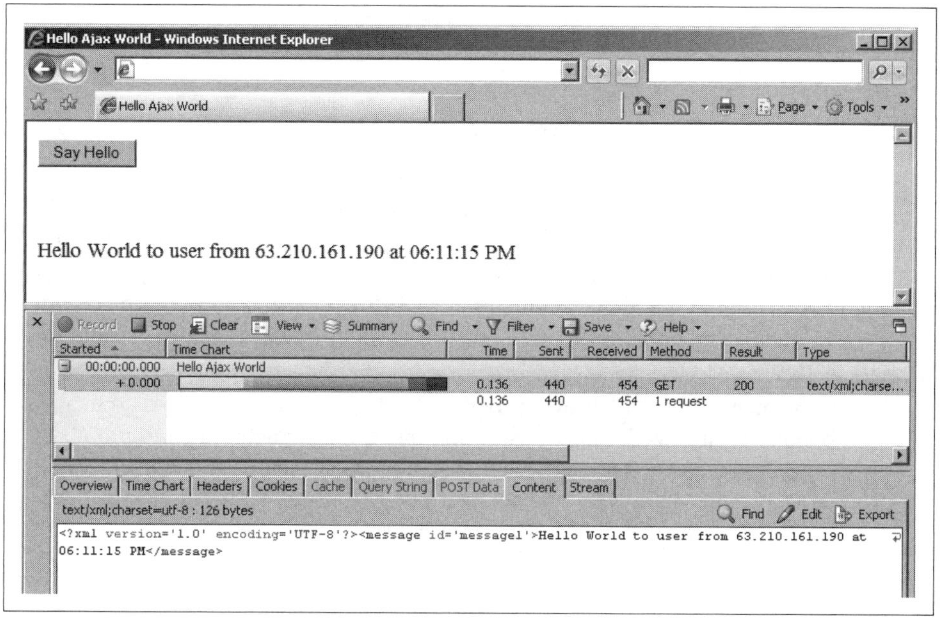

![Screenshot of "Hello Ajax World" in Windows Internet Explorer showing a "Say Hello" button and the text "Hello World to user from 63.210.161.190 at 06:11:15 PM", with a network trace panel below showing the XML response.]

Figure 8-4. "Hello World," Ajax version

Prelude to Ajax optimizations

The goal is not to teach Ajax here. Rather, the "Hello World" example illustrates a number of important optimization ideas.

First, you might ask, why did we write our own wrapper facility? Aren't there Ajax libraries out there that we can use? The answer is a resounding "yes." Second, it looks as though to do anything complicated you are going to write a lot of DOM code. That is certainly true and you are going to want to employ techniques to make DOM coding easier and the code footprint smaller. You might even want to avoid DOM coding entirely.

Third, using XML as a data format for the response packet seemed kind of pointless here. All we did was to pull out some text to shove it onto the screen. There must be an easier way to do that.

Finally, even in this simple example we are being quite naive with regard to all the things that might go wrong. Is it possible that the XHR object doesn't get created? Is it possible that the request never returns? Can requests that return properly have errors within them? Could the data be corrupted or even compromised upon delivery? The answer to all these questions is "yes."

Bad things can and do happen to good Ajax applications. You very likely won't even realize that something has happened unless you have some instrumentation code in place. Ajax optimization shouldn't focus only on making things fast. The user won't care how fast things run if your code unexpectedly breaks.

HTTP Analysis Tools

To understand Ajax properly and debug any problems that you may encounter, you have to be very network-aware. It is certainly a good idea to be armed with an HTTP analysis tool such as the one used in Figure 8-4. HTTP analysis tools come in two types. First, you can use an HTTP proxy to intercept, monitor, or even change requests from your browser. Windows users commonly use Fiddler (*http://www.fiddlertool.com*). Charles (*http://www.charlesproxy.com*) is one of many popular proxies available for other platforms.

Second, you might consider a browser toolbar. Firebug (*http://www.getfirebug.com*) is a very popular toolbar with Firefox users. Internet Explorer users often use toolbars such as Nikhil's Web Development Helper (*http://projects.nikhilk.net/Projects/WebDevHelper.aspx*) or any one of the numerous commercial HTTP monitoring programs available today, such as HttpWatch (*http://www.httpwatch.com*).

Relying on Ajax Libraries

An optimal Ajax application should not only be fast for users to use, but also be fast for developers to build. There are a number of open source JavaScript libraries that you might turn to, such as Prototype (*http://www.prototypejs.org*), jQuery (*http://www.jquery.com*), and the Yahoo! User Interface Library (YUI; *http://developer.yahoo.com/yui/*). They make Ajax programming easier and faster. As an example, take a look at a library rewrite of our "Hello World" example. It is much smaller.

```
<!DOCTYPE html PUBLIC "-//W3C//DTD XHTML 1.0 Transitional//EN" "http://www.w3.org/TR/
xhtml1/DTD/xhtml1-transitional.dtd">
<html xmlns="http://www.w3.org/1999/xhtml">
<head>
<meta http-equiv="Content-Type" content="text/html; charset=UTF-8" />
<title>Prototype Hello Ajax World</title>
<script type="text/javascript" src=" prototype.js"></script>
<script type="text/javascript">
function sendRequest()
```

```
{
  new Ajax.Request("sayhello.php",{method:"get",onSuccess: responseCallback});
}

function responseCallback(response)
{
  var responseString = response.responseXML.getElementsByTagName('message')[0].
firstChild.nodeValue;
    $("output").update(responseString);
}

Event.observe( window, "load", function() { Event.observe("button1", "click",
sendRequest);} );
</script>
</head>
<body>
<form action="#">
 <input  type="button" value="Say it!" id="button1"  />
</form>

<br /><br />
<div id="output"> </div>

</body>
</html>
```

Here we show the jQuery version, which is even terser:

```
<!DOCTYPE html PUBLIC "-//W3C//DTD XHTML 1.0 Transitional//EN" "http://www.w3.org/TR/
xhtml1/DTD/xhtml1-transitional.dtd">
<html xmlns="http://www.w3.org/1999/xhtml">
<head>
<meta http-equiv="Content-Type" content="text/html; charset=UTF-8" />
<title>JQuery Hello Ajax World</title>

<script type="text/javascript" src="jquery.js"></script>
<script type="text/javascript">

function responseCallback(responseXML)
{
    var msg = responseXML.getElementsByTagName('message')[0].firstChild.nodeValue;
    $('#output').html(msg);
}

$(document).ready(function(){
   $('#button1').click(function(){$.get("sayhello.php", responseCallback);});
 });


//-->
</script>
</head>
<body>
<form action="#">
```

```
<input  type="button" value="Say it!" id="button1"  />
</form>

<br /><br />
<div id="output"> </div>

</body>
</html>
```

If we desired, we could make the jQuery JavaScript code quite small by chaining even further, as shown here:

```
$(document).ready(function( ){$('#button1').click(function( ){$.get("sayhello.php",
function(responseXML){$('#output').html(responseXML.
getElementsByTagName('message')[0].firstChild.nodeValue;)};);});});
```

This shows how quickly you can start to optimize your code size with jQuery. Of course, you have to also factor in the library footprint.

Finally, the YUI version is shown next. It is probably the most straightforward of the bunch coding-wise, but the inclusion of multiple script files requires more HTTP requests. To be fair, however, Yahoo! provides a special minified, gzipped, and cached version of its library online in case you want to take advantage of all of its optimization work. Yahoo! will also serve the files from its server closest to the user for optimal response time. The minified and gzipped version of Yahoo!'s Ajax library is 73.2% smaller than the unoptimized version.[3]

```
<!DOCTYPE html PUBLIC "-//W3C//DTD XHTML 1.0 Transitional//EN" "http://www.w3.org/TR/
xhtml1/DTD/xhtml1-transitional.dtd">
<html xmlns="http://www.w3.org/1999/xhtml">
<head>
<meta http-equiv="Content-Type" content="text/html; charset=UTF-8" />
<title>YUI Hello Ajax World</title>
<script src="http://yui.yahooapis.com/2.3.0/build/yahoo/yahoo-min.js" type="text/
javascript"></script>
<script src="http://yui.yahooapis.com/2.3.0/build/event/event-min.js" type="text/
javascript"></script>
<script src="http://yui.yahooapis.com/2.3.0/build/connection/connection-min.js"
type="text/javascript"></script>
<script type="text/javascript">

function sendRequest( )
{
  YAHOO.util.Connect.asyncRequest('GET', "sayhello.php", { success:responseCallback
}, null);
}

function responseCallback(response)
```

---

[3] Yahoo!'s YUI Ajax library was 143.4 KB unoptimized versus 38.46 KB after minimization, or about 73.2% smaller overall. For the individual files, *yahoo.js* was 28.5 KB originally versus 5.86 KB minified, *event.js* was 79 KB unoptimized versus 17 KB minified, and *connection.js* was 35.9 KB unoptimized versus 13.6 KB optimized. These numbers were for version 2.3.0 of YUI.

```
{
   var msg = response.responseXML.getElementsByTagName("message")[0].firstChild.
nodeValue;
   document.getElementById("responseOutput").innerHTML = msg;
}

YAHOO.util.Event.addListener('button1','click', sendRequest );

//-->
</script>
</head>
<body>
<form action="#">
 <input  type="button" value="Say it!" id="button1"  />
</form>

<br /><br />
<div id="output"> </div>

</body>
</html>
```

Evaluating an Ajax Library

You would expect that employing a library would abstract basic functionality. But what about more advanced functionality? Table 8-1 shows you what to look for when evaluating an Ajax library.

Table 8-1. Characteristics of Ajax libraries

Library feature	Description
Ajax communications	Good libraries should address network problems such as timeouts, retries, and error issues. They should also provide helpful functions to sequence requests and address caching concerns. Advanced libraries may add support for history management, offline storage, and persistence.
DOM utilities	Most popular Ajax-oriented JavaScript libraries provide methods to make working with DOM elements easier. For example, the $( ) function is commonly implemented by such systems as a greatly enhanced form of document.getElementById( ).
Event management	A significant headache for Ajax developers is addressing cross-browser event concerns. Because of poor management of events and more time spent on a single page, Ajax applications that do not manage events properly may leak memory. Older versions of Internet Explorer are particularly prone to this.
Utility functions	Ajax libraries should provide functions to address the serialization of user-entered form data. Other data format encoding and decoding functions, such as dealing with JSON data packets, are also typically included.
UI widgets	Higher-level libraries that go beyond core communications may provide widgets that encapsulate both higher-level UI and tie in with lower-level Ajax and DOM facilities. User interface elements such as auto-suggest menus and data grids that tie to remote resources are some of the more sought-after "Ajaxified" interface widgets.
Visual effects	Users expect not only improved communications, but also richer interfaces in Ajax applications. Many libraries provide basic animation and visual effects. Be careful, however. Don't be seduced by transitions and visual effects that may be more DHTML glitz than Ajax plumbing.

Using an existing library is certainly an optimal practice, but proceed with caution. Ajax is still in a nascent state and so are some of the libraries. Many of the popular libraries provide only the most basic form of network timeouts and error checking. Only a few libraries include performance enhancements such as response caches or request bundling. Most of the libraries optimize their JavaScript file size. This is fortunate because they can get quite large.

JavaScript Optimization

Given the intrinsic (and often prolific) use of JavaScript in Ajax, you should concentrate on improving your use of JavaScript to reduce your download footprint.

Many of the popular library authors understand the JavaScript bloat problem. They provide their code in a standard, fully commented and maintainable version as well as in a "minified" version. You should be familiar with "minification" and how it works. Also be aware of the potential problems that you may encounter if you are to fully optimize your Ajax application. It is likely that there will be code outside your library that will need to be compressed as well.

First, we should note that many of the techniques for JavaScript optimization are similar to those used for markup and CSS, as discussed in Chapters 6 and 7. We'll breeze through those, but even as we do, keep in mind that you must apply all JavaScript optimizations more carefully. If you apply them improperly, they may break the page!

Remove JavaScript Comments

You can safely remove all JavaScript comments indicated by // or /* */. They offer no value to the typical end-user and just increase file size. You do need to be aware that script-masking comments such as this:

```
<script type="text/javascript">
<!-
  alert("code here");
//-->
</script>
```

might be useful to preserve in the case of non-JavaScript-aware bots or old browsers. It is probably best to include scripts outside the document, however, as it is easier to make them XHTML-compliant.

Conditional comments

You also need to be aware of the conditional commenting system of Internet Explorer often used with script includes or CSS. For example, a conditional comment-aware browser will read the following statement and will then include the *patch.js* file if it is an older Explorer version but not a newer version:

```
<!--[if lt IE 7]><script src="patch.js" type="text/javascript"></script><![endif]-->
```

Browsers that do not understand such a comment extension will, of course, safely ignore the statement. During your XHTML optimization you should not remove such conditional comments, because you may otherwise inadvertently break your JavaScript. Fortunately, advanced page optimization tools are aware of this detail, although many simpler ones are not.

Reduce Whitespace Carefully

JavaScript is fairly whitespace-agnostic and you can easily reduce the whitespace between operators. For example, instead of writing this:

```
var str = "JavaScript is "   +
          x   +
          " times more fun than HTML ";
```

you can write this:

```
var str="JavaScript is "+x+" times more fun than HTML";
```

Be cautious when condensing, however. JavaScript treats line breaks as implicit semicolons. If you do not terminate lines with semicolons, you may find that whitespace reduction can cause problems. For example, the following legal JavaScript uses implied semicolons:

```
x=x+1
y=y+1
```

A simple whitespace remover tool might produce this:

```
x=x+1y=y+1
```

This code would obviously throw an error. If you add in the needed semicolons, the code will work:

```
x=x+1;y=y+1;
```

Do note that if you add characters to make the code legal, you may gain little in terms of byte savings, although you will make your script look "visually" more compressed.

Use JavaScript Shorthand

You can employ a number of shorthand JavaScript statements to tighten up your code. You can use numerous abbreviated assignments to shave a few bytes.

For example, this:

```
x=x+1;
y=y*10;
```

can become this:

```
x++;
y*=10;
```

You may also find that you can reduce simple if statements using a ternary operator, so this:

```
var big;
if (x > 10) {
  big = true;
}
else {
  big = false;
}
```

can become this:

```
var big = (x > 10) ? true : false;
```

If you rely on some of the weak typing characteristics of JavaScript, this can also achieve more concise code. For example, you could reduce the preceding code fragment to this:

```
var big  = (x > 10);
```

Also, instead of this:

```
if (likeJavaScript == true)
   { /* something */ }
```

you could write this:

```
if (likeJavaScript)
   { /* something */ }
```

Use String Constant Macros

If you find yourself repeating portions of strings or whole strings over and over again, you will find that a simple string macro using a global variable remapping can shave off a number of bytes. For example, if you have a number of alert( ) invocations in your program, like this:

```
alert("An error has occurred");
```

you could set a global variable, like this:

```
msg="An error has occurred";
```

to serve as a string constant and then replace the repeated strings in the various alert( ) calls as follows:

```
alert(msg);
```

You can even use this macro expansion idea for partial strings. For example, use the earlier string constant that we set and modify it:

```
alert(msg+": email address is required");
```

There is one caution with this technique. You need to make sure that you use the string often enough so that the macro makes sense and that the macro identifier is short enough to provide an overall savings.

Avoid Optional Constructs and Kill Dead Code Fast

In many situations, you can remove code and syntax constructs without harming the code. For example, given blocks for `if` statements and various loops that contain a single statement, you can remove the braces, so this:

```
if (likeJavaScript)
  {
    alert("It's great!");
  }
```

becomes this:

```
if (likeJavaScript)
  alert("It's great");
```

You also may see that some statements, such as `var`, are not always needed. In Java-Script, variables spring into existence in the global space upon first use, so if you are using globals—which you shouldn't be, because they are a bad practice that increases the chances for variable namespace collisions from other included scripts—you can omit the `var` statement. When you do, this:

```
var global;
global = "domination";
```

would become simply this:

```
global = "domination";
```

As another byte-shaving example, you also can remove a `return` statement with no argument just before the end of a function. So, this:

```
function doWork()
  {
   /* complex code */
   return;
  }
```

becomes this:

```
function doWork()
  {
    /* complex code */
  }
```

You can employ other byte-shaving tricks to tune code, but generally you should let a tool such as w3compiler (*http://www.w3compiler.com*) do that for you.

Shorten User-Defined Variables and Function Names

For good readability, any script should use variables such as `numRequests` instead of `n`. For download speed, however, the lengthy variable names are a liability. Here again, writing your source code in a readable fashion and then using a tool to prepare it for delivery is valuable. Remapping all user-defined variable and function names to short one- and two-letter identifiers can produce significant savings.

Some optimization programs allow you to control the remapping process with an abbreviation list. Be careful, though, if you expect some functions to be called by other scripts such as API calls. You may not want to remap these names because this can cause syntax errors.

Remap Built-in Objects

The bulkiness of JavaScript code, beyond long user variable names, comes from the use of built-in objects such as `Window`, `Document`, `Navigator`, and so on. For example, given code such as this:

```
alert(window.navigator.appName);
alert(window.navigator.appVersion);
alert(window.navigator.userAgent);
```

you could rewrite it as this:

```
w=window;n=w.navigator;a=alert;
a(n.appName);
a(n.appVersion);
a(n.userAgent);
```

Commonly, we see people perform remaps of frequently used methods such as `document.getElementById( )` like this:

```
function $(x){return document.getElementById(x)}
```

Given the chance for name collision, if you decide to employ such a technique, we would suggest a slight variation, such as this:

```
function $id(x){return document.getElementById(x)};
function $name(x){return document.getElementsByName(x)}
function $tag(x){return document.getElementsByTagName(x)}
```

and so on.

Object and method remapping is quite valuable when the remapped items are used repeatedly, which they generally are. Note, however, that if the window or navigator object were used only once, these substitutions would actually make the code bigger. Be careful if you are optimizing by hand. Fortunately, many JavaScript code optimizers will automatically take this into account.

This warning brings up a related issue regarding the performance of scripts with remapped objects: in addition to the benefit of size reduction, such remappings may actually improve script execution times because the objects are copied higher up JavaScript's resolution chain. Although this technique does improve both download and execution performance, it does so at the expense of local browser memory usage.

Name Collision Alert

One major problem with shorthand JavaScript coding practices is variable namespace pollution. When scripts are included in a web page they all use the same variable namespace. So, if more than one library has a function called init( ), one will be overwritten. To avoid this, you can employ prefixing in your definitions, like so:

```
function MyLibNamePrefix_init() { }
```

Or better yet, you might create an object wrapper such as this:

```
var MyLibName = {
    init : function ();
}
```

You'll note, though, that both of these techniques fly in the face of the name reduction tip discussed earlier, because now you will have to reference either `MyLibNamePrefix_init( )` or `MyLibName.init( )` to invoke your hopefully protected code. You should be especially concerned with minimalist naming of functions such as $( ) because many libraries and code examples on the Web co-opt this popular identifier.

Inline Localized Functions

In the original example, we associated a callback function with the onreadystatechange. Because it is so small, we may as well inline it as an anonymous function, like so:

```
if (xhr)
  {
    xhr.open("GET","sayhello.php",true);
    xhr.onreadystatechange = function(){if (xhr.readyState == 4  && xhr.status ==
200)
    {
    var parsedResponse = xhr.responseXML;

    var responseString = parsedResponse.getElementsByTagName("message")[0].
firstChild.nodeValue;

    var output = document.getElementById("output");
    output.innerHTML = responseString;
    }};

    xhr.send( );
    }
```

Assume Default Values

Very often in coding, we are explicit in what we write so that later on we don't have to remember as much. As an example, in method calls some parameters can often be omitted because defaults will be provided. Consider the use in Ajax of the open( ) method. You must specify the method and URI, but you do not have to pass in the final Boolean value of true to achieve the default asynchronous nature of an Ajax request. So, this:

```
xhr.open("GET","sayhello.php",true);
```

becomes this:

```
xhr.open("GET","sayhello.php");
```

And thus, we kiss five more bytes goodbye.

Every Byte Counts

Taken individually, none of the byte-shaving techniques described so far is going to provide spectacular savings. When you put them together, however, you can routinely see a 20% to 40% reduction in code size. The size of this reduction depends on how readable you made the code when adding comments, whitespace, and the descriptive identifier names. As an example, consider our original "Hello World" listing, which weighs in at 1,499 bytes. Certainly, it is not in need of major optimization. It lacks comments and other things that we might see in a more production-oriented situation, but we can still see some reduction. If we crunch down the script portion of the page, as shown next, we reduce the overall file size to 1,043 bytes, which is more than a 30% savings:

```
<!DOCTYPE html PUBLIC "-//W3C//DTD XHTML 1.0 Transitional//EN" "http://www.w3.org/TR/
xhtml1/DTD/xhtml1-transitional.dtd">
<html xmlns="http://www.w3.org/1999/xhtml">
<head>
<meta http-equiv="Content-Type" content="text/html; charset=iso-8859-1" />
<title>Ajax Hello World</title>
<script type="text/javascript">
d=document;M="Msxml2.XMLHTTP";function c(){try{return new XMLHttpRequest(
)}catch(e){}try{A=ActiveXObject;return new A(M+".6.0")}catch(e){}try {return new
A(M+".3.0")}catch(e){}try {return new A(M)}catch(e){}try {return new A("Microsoft.
XMLHTTP")}catch(e){}}function s(){var x=c();if(x){x.open("GET","sayhello.php");
x.onreadystatechange=function(){if(x.readyState==4&&x.status==200)
d.getElementById("output").innerHTML=x.responseXML.
getElementsByTagName("message")[0].firstChild.nodeValue};x.send();}}
window.onload=function(){d.getElementById("button1").onclick=s}
</script>
</head>
<body>
<form action="#">
 <input type="button" value="Say it!" id="button1" />
</form>
```

```
<br /><br />
<div id="output"> </div>

</body>
</html>
```

Applying many of the ideas in Chapter 6 for markup optimization, we can reduce this further to 1,023 bytes, which makes it nearly 32% smaller than the original:

```
<!DOCTYPE html PUBLIC "-//W3C//DTD XHTML 1.0 Transitional//EN" "http://www.w3.org/TR/
xhtml1/DTD/xhtml1-transitional.dtd"><html xmlns="http://www.w3.org/1999/xhtml"><head>
<meta http-equiv="Content-Type" content="text/html; charset=iso-8859-1" /><title>Ajax
Hello World</title><script type="text/javascript">d=document;M="Msxml2.
XMLHTTP";function c(){try{return new XMLHttpRequest(
)}catch(e){}try{A=ActiveXObject;return new A(M+".6.0")}catch(e){}try {return new
A(M+".3.0")}catch(e){}try {return new A(M)}catch(e){}try {return new A("Microsoft.
XMLHTTP")}catch(e){}}function s(){var x=c();if(x){x.open("GET","sayhello.php");x.
onreadystatechange=function(){if(x.readyState==4&&x.status==200)d.
getElementById("output").innerHTML=x.responseXML.getElementsByTagName("message")[0].
firstChild.nodeValue;x.send();}}window.onload=function(){d.
getElementById("button1").onclick=s}</script></head><body><form action="#"><input
type="button" value="Say it!" id="button1" /></form><br /><br /><div id="output">
 </div></body></html>
```

Finally, if we apply an optimization to the ID values that represent the touch points between the markup and script, renaming the button from button1 to b and the output div ID to simply o, we can chop a few more bytes off and reach an even smaller size of 1,001 bytes (making it more than 33% smaller):

```
<!DOCTYPE html PUBLIC "-//W3C//DTD XHTML 1.0 Transitional//EN" "http://www.w3.org/TR/
xhtml1/DTD/xhtml1-transitional.dtd"><html xmlns="http://www.w3.org/1999/xhtml"><head>
<meta http-equiv="Content-Type" content="text/html; charset=iso-8859-1" /><title>Ajax
Hello World</title><script type="text/javascript">d=document;M="Msxml2.
XMLHTTP";function c(){try{return new XMLHttpRequest(
)}catch(e){}try{A=ActiveXObject;return new A(M+".6.0")}catch(e){}try {return new
A(M+".3.0")}catch(e){}try {return new A(M)}catch(e){}try {return new A("Microsoft.
XMLHTTP")}catch(e){}}function s(){var x=c();if(x){x.open("GET","sayhello.php");x.
onreadystatechange=function(){if(x.readyState==4&&x.status==200)d.
getElementById("o").innerHTML=x.responseXML.getElementsByTagName("message")[0].
firstChild.nodeValue;x.send();}}window.onload=function(){d.getElementById("b").
onclick=s}</script></head><body><form action="#"><input type="button" value="Say it!"
id="b" /></form><br /><br /><div id="o"> </div></body></html>
```

We can go even further if we can jettison some of the bulky DOM code that clutters up our callback function.

Bundle Your Scripts

JavaScript developers commonly break out their JavaScript into separate *.js* files and then include them in the document, like so:

```
<script src="text/javascript" src="global.js"></script>
<script src="text/javascript" src="navigation.js"></script>
<script src="text/javascript" src="popup.js"></script>
<script src="text/javascript" src="lightbox.js"></script>
```

Employ Compression Tools Safety

Many tools exist for optimizing JavaScript. Unfortunately, many of them mangle the code during this process.

The dynamic nature of JavaScript makes it difficult to safely rename and remap user- and browser-defined variables, functions, and objects. For example, you know that you want to go from `veryLongDescriptiveName` to `v`. But what happens when you have a statement such as `alert(eval("very"+"longDescriptiveName"))`? Was the compressor smart enough to go inside the string and deal with it, and even so, should it? The dynamic nature of JavaScript makes static analysis tricky. You have to either be very conservative in choosing which variables to remap (i.e., locals), or run the risk of changing the meaning of the code. The danger of breaking code during minification is especially ominous when there are interdependencies between scripts in different windows and frames. Minification can be risky if you use tricky code with `eval()` and `with()` or if you aggressively overwrite and extend built-in JavaScript constructs.

Many of the tools based on the Rhino JavaScript engine do a good job of compressing safely, such as the YUI Compressor (*http://www.julienlecomte.net/yuicompressor/*) and Dojo ShrinkSafe (*http://www.dojotoolkit.com/docs/shrinksafe*). Some open source tools such as Dean Edwards' Packer (*http://dean.edwards.name/packer/*) as well as commercial tools such as w3compiler (*http://w3compiler.com*) have more aggressive optimization features. The most powerful tools will leverage the interdependencies between web technologies and allow for very granular tuning, but you need to understand how to use them or you may break your code.

Given that all the code tends to be included in all pages and that all included Java-Script shares the same variable namespace, there is little reason for this separation other than perhaps organizational convenience. Instead of using separate files, consider making one bundled and minified *.js* file that contains all of the files. This may not seem like a significant change, but it can have a great effect. As we will discuss shortly, browsers employ a two-connection limit to a website.[4] So, in the preceding example, only *global.js* and *navigation.js* will be fetched at once. The *popup.js* file won't be fetched until one of these files loads. Bundling them into one file eliminates this problem.

```
<script src="text/javascript" src="bigbundle.js"></script>
```

---

[4] We have done extensive testing on this default. There are ways to modify it in the browser, but by default, two is the limit of simultaneous connections, at least for JavaScript files. See *http://www.w3.org/Protocols/rfc2616/rfc2616-sec8.html* for more details.

Lazy-Load Your Code

Many JavaScript libraries employ a form of "lazy-loading" or on-demand fetching by which code is loaded only when necessary. For example, you might employ this:

```
window.onload = function () {
  lazyCodeLoad(["http://example.com/somelib.js","http://example.com/otherlib.js"]) }
```

where the function defined reads each URI in the array and just creates a `script` tag using the DOM. It then sets its source to the file in question and inserts it into the page to retrieve it.

In addition, you might use a similar pattern to preload objects that are likely to be used later, including images and CSS files. If your browser caches them properly, they will be quickly available when needed later. Of course, you do pay the price of potentially downloading objects that the user may never actually need.

 Lazy-loading and preloading techniques often introduce more HTTP requests. You may want to introduce steps to minimize this effect because extra requests increase overall download time. One approach is to employ a server-side bundling program which, when passed file names as arguments such as *.js* and *.css* files, bundles them up to be downloaded all at once to be later unpackaged by your receiving script.

Pace Yourself

The lazy-load idea should have given you the notion that maybe you could use Ajax to load information just before it is needed. For example, imagine if you had a large amount of content and you wanted to fetch it 50 rows at a time. You could load in, say, 100 rows ahead of time and then, as the user pages forward, prefetch more data to stay ahead of the user. This prefetching would give the user the sense of near-instantaneous loading. Understand, of course, that if the user jumps ahead a few thousand records, he will still pay a loading penalty because such a request will not have been expected.

Monitor User Rendering Time

Although we're all for reducing script size, putting scripts in the right place, and squeezing bytes, the only thing the user cares about is how long pages take to load and how well they run.

Several observers have found that one of the main performance problems facing Ajax developers (at least on the initial load of the application) is too many individual requests for JavaScript files and other dependencies. They cite as much as 50% to 60% of the start-time delay being related to having too many different requests for dependencies.[5]

---

[5] Neuberg, B. August 15, 2006. "Tutorial: How to Profile and Optimize Ajax Applications." Coding in Paradise, *http://codinginparadise.org/weblog/2006/08/tutorial-how-to-profile-and-optimize.html* (accessed February 11, 2008).

Yet, even if you bundle requests to reduce this potential problem, the time the user waits for a page to render may not always be an exact function of the bytes delivered and the requests made. Anything from a brief network hiccup to the fact that the user's local system might be overloaded could slow down the display time of the page. Users won't know where to direct their frustration, so you need to know what they are experiencing. This is particularly true if you are promising them some speedy Ajax-powered experience. You can use JavaScript to see how long it takes a page to load. For example, at the top of an HTML document, start a script timer:

```
<!DOCTYPE html PUBLIC "-//W3C//DTD XHTML 1.0 Transitional//EN" "http://www.w3.org/TR/
xhtml1/DTD/xhtml1-transitional.dtd">
<html xmlns="http://www.w3.org/1999/xhtml">
<head>
<meta http-equiv="Content-Type" content="text/html; charset=UTF-8" />
<title>And they're off...</title>
<script type="text/javascript">
var gPageStartTime = (new Date()).getTime();
</script>
```

Then bind a script to stop the timer upon full-page load to calculate how long it took:

```
window.onload = function ()
{
 var pageEndTime = (new Date()).getTime();
 var pageLoadTime = (pageEndTime - gPageStartTime)/1000;
 alert("Page Load Time: " + pageLoadTime);
}
```

Of course, instead of alerting the page load time as we did here, we could transmit it to our server with an Ajax request:

```
sendAjaxRequest("http://example.com/recordtime.php", "time="+pageLoadTime);
```

Practice Error Awareness

Similar to the preceding point, it would be a good idea to know when users are frustrated or experiencing trouble outside of slow downloads, such as a JavaScript error or a feature problem. In fact, you might want to know that the user even has her JavaScript turned on. This is actually pretty easy to do using the noscript tag. Consider the markup shown here:

```
<noscript>
 <span class="error">Error: This site requires JavaScript.</span>
 <img src="http://example.com/errormonitor.php?scriptoff=true" />
</noscript>
```

The image tag references a server-side script that will record that the user has her JavaScript off. It will be fetched only when the browser has the script off.

If her JavaScript is on but you still encounter an error, you might imagine associating an error handler to `window.onerror` that then makes a call to the server indicating what has happened. Here is the outline of such code:

```
window.onerror = reportJSError;
function reportJSError(errorMessage,url,lineNumber)
{
    /* form payload string with error data */
    payload = "url="+url;
    payload += "message=" + errorMessage;
    payload += "&line=" + lineNumber;
    /* submit error message  */
    var img = new Image();
    img.src = "http://example.com/errormonitor.php"+"?error=scriptruntime&"+payload;

    alert("JavaScript Error - Administrators have been notified.");

    /* return true to suppress normal JS errors */
    return true;
}
```

Please note that we opted not to use an XHR in our code example, but instead invoked an image to issue our request. This is because when errors occur it might just be because something that isn't XHR-aware is running our script!

Clean Up After Yourself

The beauty of using a high-level language such as JavaScript is that you don't have to worry about allocating memory for objects. Or do you? JavaScript uses a garbage collection system to recover memory. It won't do so, however, unless a value is no longer used. In the past, most JavaScript developers were sloppy with memory and didn't take the time to set variables to null or use the delete operator on unused object properties. Their scripts would often leak memory, but they usually didn't know it. In a traditional JavaScript application, you would unload the page relatively quickly and get a new page that would cause the memory to be recovered. In the case of Ajax-style applications, users will generally stay on pages much longer and memory leaks may occur.

Memory leaks and garbage collection in Internet Explorer

Internet Explorer up to version 6 has problems when garbage-collecting circular references. For example, if one object points to another object and that object points back to the first object, neither of those objects will be collected. We see this most often with closures and event handling when the event handler refers back to the DOM object that caused the event. Circular references with event handlers and excessive use of global timers can cause memory leaks and instability in some browsers, so always clean up after yourself. If you want to monitor Internet Explorer for memory leaks, for which some older versions are notorious, you might find the Drip tool useful (*http://outofhanwell.com/ieleak*).

Go Native

Many Ajax libraries introduce various features to make DOM programming easier, such as new methods like getElementsByClassName( ). Given that these methods are indeed quite useful, some browsers such as Firefox 3 are making native versions of them. If you employ a library or write your own version of such helpers, make sure you check for a native version of the library first before using your own code, which may be slower.

```
function getElementsByClassName(class)
{
    if (document.getElementsByClassName( )
     return document.getElementsByClassName(class);
   /* otherwise do my slower version */
}
```

This move to native DOM is not limited to the getElementsByClassName( ) inclusion in Mozilla. The W3C also is developing a selector specification so that methods such as selectElement( ) may in the future become the preferred way to access the DOM rather than $css( ) or $$( ) or getElementsBySelector( ).

Clock Your Runtime

Getting the large amount of JavaScript code down to the end-user in a timely manner is certainly a major objective, but it doesn't address what happens next. When the code executes, it could be slow for a number of reasons. The first step is to profile the JavaScript code to see where the problems might lie. Firebug contains a feature which profiles JavaScript so that you can see where any bottlenecks might arise (see Figure 8-5).

With the profiler in hand you can then focus on the functions that are called frequently or that are slow to execute. You can certainly improve efficiency if you get rid of unnecessary steps or recode algorithms. Be careful, however, when trying to treat JavaScript like some low-level language where you tune it for cycles. First, you'll find that the language and its implementation in different browsers will surprise you. The excessive use of a native DOM method call can be quite slow in one browser but not in another. Second, if you turn to tricks that you learned from a lower-level language such as C, they might actually hurt performance. For example, bitwise operations don't always make calculations any faster in JavaScript. It depends on how they are used. They can actually make things worse. Remember that this is a high-level interpreted language.

Next, understand that when you run the profiler, it is your machine running the code, not the user's machine. The user's experience may be very different. Even if something downloads fast and appears to run decently on your system, it is still possible that it is painful to run on an end-user's system. If you find out that this is the case, you may want to create a diagnostic script to run some calculations to get a sense of how fast,

Google - Mozilla Firefox

File   Edit   View   History   Bookmarks   Tools   Help

http://www.google.com/webhp?complete=1

Web   Images   Video   News   Maps   Gmail   more ▼   iGoogle | Sign in

Google Suggest LABS

Ajax	
ajax tutorial	30,000,000 results
ajax examples	4,680,000 results
ajax tutorials	45,800,000 results
ajax toolkit	1,610,000 results
ajax framework	44,400,000 results
ajax asp.net	9,780,000 results
ajax control toolkit	1,210,000 results
ajax php	89,300,000 results
ajax example	19,600,000 results
ajax.net	850,000 results

Advanced Search
Preferences
Language Tools

As you type, Goo   sults. Learn more

Inspect   Clear   Profile

Console   HTML   CSS   Script   DOM   Net   YSlow   Options ▼

Profile (62.502ms, 456 calls)

Function	Calls	Percent	Own Time	Time	Avg	Min	Max	File
n	80	25%	15.626ms	15.626ms	0.195ms	0ms	15.626ms	vST7u151leI.js (line 6)
Da	4	25%	15.626ms	31.252ms	7.813ms	0ms	15.626ms	vST7u151leI.js (line 13)
va	18	25%	15.625ms	15.625ms	0.868ms	0ms	15.625ms	vST7u151leI.js (line 12)
ca	65	25%	15.625ms	62.5ms	0.962ms	0ms	15.625ms	vST7u151leI.js (line 10)
pa	9	0%	0ms	0ms	0ms	0ms	0ms	vST7u151leI.js (line 7)
da	4	0%	0ms	0ms	0ms	0ms	0ms	vST7u151leI.js (line 12)
y	120	0%	0ms	0ms	0ms	0ms	0ms	vST7u151leI.js (line 12)
Fa	16	0%	0ms	46.877ms	2.93ms	0ms	15.626ms	vST7u151leI.js (line 15)
U	9	0%	0ms	15.625ms	1.736ms	0ms	15.625ms	vST7u151leI.js (line 6)
ma	4	0%	0ms	0ms	0ms	0ms	0ms	vST7u151leI.js (line 7)
ba	4	0%	0ms	15.625ms	3.906ms	0ms	15.625ms	vST7u151leI.js (line 9)
oa	9	0%	0ms	0ms	0ms	0ms	0ms	vST7u151leI.js (line 7)
v	4	0%	0ms	46.877ms	11.719ms	0ms	15.626ms	vST7u151leI.js (line 9)
n	80	0%	0ms	0ms	0ms	0ms	0ms	vST7u151leI.js (line 6)
na	5	0%	0ms	0ms	0ms	0ms	0ms	vST7u151leI.js (line 7)
sa	4	0%	0ms	0ms	0ms	0ms	0ms	vST7u151leI.js (line 10)
wa	4	0%	0ms	0ms	0ms	0ms	0ms	vST7u151leI.js (line 14)
aa	4	0%	0ms	0ms	0ms	0ms	0ms	vST7u151leI.js (line 7)
Ea	4	0%	0ms	46.875ms	11.719ms	0ms	15.625ms	vST7u151leI.js (line 14)
$	5	0%	0ms	0ms	0ms	0ms	0ms	vST7u151leI.js (line 7)
ua	4	0%	0ms	0ms	0ms	0ms	0ms	vST7u151leI.js (line 12)

GET http://www.google.com/complete/search?hl=en&client=suggest&js=true&q=A *(93ms)*   vST7u151leI.js (line 15)

>>>

Done   YSlow   0.172s

Figure 8-5. Firebug's JavaScript profiler in action

medium, and slow computers execute and to get a sense of how many of your users are experiencing slow execution.

Minimizing HTTP Requests

One aspect about web browsers that web developers often misinterpret is the two-connection limit. According to the HTTP specification, browsers are limited to two connections to a fully qualified domain. Conventional wisdom on the Web suggests that some browsers exceed this limit (for images, at least), but this is actually not true unless the end-user has modified them. As one article notes:

Clients that use persistent connections SHOULD limit the number of simultaneous connections that they maintain to a given server. A single-user client SHOULD NOT maintain more than 2 connections with any server or proxy. A proxy SHOULD use up to 2*N connections to another server or proxy, where N is the number of simultaneously active users. These guidelines are intended to improve HTTP response times and avoid congestion.[6]

The reality of the two-connection limit is the primary reason why people host images or other dependent objects such as JavaScript and CSS files on other domains. For example, the site Example.com serving an HTML page containing the following image references:

```
<img src="image1.gif" />
<img src="image2.gif" />
<img src="image3.gif" />
<img src="image4.gif" />
```

would find that using other fully qualified domain names such as those shown here will increase the fetching browser's connection efficiency:

```
<img src="http://images.example.com/image1.gif" />
<img src="http://images.example.com/image2.gif" />
<img src="http://images2.example.com/image3.gif" />
<img src="http://images2.example.com/image4.gif" />
```

Your Ajax programs can make only two connections at a time, so if you make a third or fourth request, it will have to wait until one of the other requests finishes. Now, this can be quite problematic if your requests stall for some reason. You will find that your connection will then choke.

 Internet Explorer 8 introduces the possibility to go well beyond the two persistent connections specified by the HTTP specification. Although this may improve speed and remove some bottlenecks in parallel requests, the impact on servers is yet to be fully understood. Given the likely changes in simultaneous request restrictions, developers should proceed with caution.

Given the previous discussion of utilizing additional domains to increase image request parallelization, you might be tempted to use the same trick here, but it will not work. You see, Ajax falls under the security policy known as the Same-Origin Policy (*http://en.wikipedia.org/wiki/Same_origin_policy*), which limits you to making requests from the same domain name that served the page.

There is currently no way around the two-requests-at-a-time limit to a single fully qualified domain name when making a standard XHR request. Of course, if you use a script tag communication mechanism, you won't have this problem, but as you

[6] Fielding, R. et al. June 1999. *"Hypertext Transfer Protocol—HTTP/1.1."* RFC 2616, *http://www.w3.org/Protocols/rfc2616/rfc2616-sec8.html* (accessed February 11, 2008).

are no longer using an XHR, you won't have as much control over the request and response. In addition, you will be introducing potential security concerns.

Recently, the idea of XHRs being extended to allow for cross-domain requests was introduced in Firefox 3 and Internet Explorer 8. If this concept is adopted, the use of the multiple-domain technique to exceed the two-connection limit may again become viable. At the time of this writing, however, that time is quite a ways off. Given this simultaneous request restriction, we have even more reason to keep our Ajax requests to a minimum and to make sure we time out any stalled requests, lest the two-request limit become a bottleneck.

Choosing Data Formats Wisely

Ajax requests may be small, but there certainly are differences size-wise between the various data formats, especially if you consider the included content versus the structural markup. For example, consider that when we request a simple list of comma-separated values, any returned data will be quite concise:

```
value1,value2,value3,...value N
```

If you encoded the same data in XML, it would be much bulkier:

```
<?xml version="1.0" encoding="UTF-8" ?>
<packet>
  <item>Value 1</item>
  <item>Value 2</tem>
  ...
  <item>Value N</item>
</packet>
```

Fortunately, in the case of an Ajax-style application, the data sent and received is often very small and is textual, so it can be HTTP-compressed transparently for transmission.

The *x* in Ajax is supposed to stand for XML, but we often find that developers are not terribly excited about using XML. First, there is the aforementioned bulkiness. Second, there is the excessive DOM code that is necessary to deal with parsing out the response. Finally, we may find that because browsers generally are not acting as validating XML parsers but instead focus solely on well-formedness, the semantic value of XML is somewhat wasted.

As an alternative to XML, many Ajax developers prefer to use JSON, available at *http://www.json.org*. JSON is a lightweight data-interchange format that is based on a subset of the JavaScript language. Because it is a subset of JavaScript, we can very easily convert a JSON response into something that the receiving script can consume directly.

For example, we may return the following, which is a valid JSON array:

```
["value1","value2","value3","value4"]
```

Or we might return a JSON object literal such as this:

```
{"today": "Wednesday", "planet" : "Earth" , "mood" : "happy" }
```

If this were found in the responseText property of an XHR object, we might quickly make it available for use via this:

```
var result = eval(xhr.responseText);
```

And now you would be able to reference the individual values in the result object, like so:

```
var str = "Today is " + result.today + " and on planet "+ result.planet + " people
are generally " + result.mood;
```

There are some downsides to using JSON. Various security concerns have emerged, particularly with immediate eval( ) of a JSON payload from an untrusted source. Many people have declared JSON to be the *x* in Ajax, given its ease of consumption and the fact that the format is so simple that it is pretty much language-independent. Unless there is some overriding reason to use XML in your Ajax application, don't do it. Use JSON instead.

Consider Ajah

Asynchronous JavaScript and HTML (Ajah) is a pattern whereby you pass back fully rendered HTML responses rather than XML or JSON formats.

For example, with our "Hello World" example, our response with an XML packet would be like this:

```
<?xml version='1.0' encoding='UTF-8'?><message id='message1'>Hello World to user from
63.210.161.190 at 10:54:00 AM</message>
```

In an Ajah style, it might look like this:

```
<h3>Hello World to user from 63.210.161.190 at 10:54:00 AM</h3>
```

Or it might just look like an unmarked-up string, such as this:

```
Hello World to user from 63.210.161.190 at 10:54:00 AM
```

Consumption of an Ajah-style response is simply a matter of setting the innerHTML value of some target element.[7] For example, instead of a callback function handling an XML response packet, like this:

```
function responseCallback(xhr)
{
  if (xhr.readyState == 4  && xhr.status == 200)
    {
      var parsedResponse = xhr.responseXML;
```

---

[7] Note that innerHTML has been added to the HTML 5 draft. See *http://www.w3.org/html/wg/html5/diff/*.

```
        var responseString = parsedResponse.getElementsByTagName("message")[0].
    firstChild.nodeValue;

        var output = document.getElementById("output");
        output.innerHTML = responseString;
        }
}
```

you would simply have one that directly consumes the content, such as this:

```
function responseCallback(xhr)
{
  if (xhr.readyState == 4  && xhr.status == 200)
    {
    var output = document.getElementById("output");
    output.innerHTML = xhr.responseText;
    }
}
```

If you then used chaining, you could further compress the result, like so:

```
function responseCallback(xhr)
{
  if (xhr.readyState == 4  && xhr.status == 200)
     document.getElementById("output").innerHTML = xhr.responseText;
}
```

before applying variable name reductions or other minimization techniques. This
particular callback is so small now that it is probably more appropriate to inline it, as
shown here:

```
if (xhr)
  {
      xhr.open("GET","sayhello.php",true);
      xhr.onreadystatechange = function( ){if (xhr.readyState == 4 && xhr.status ==
200)document.getElementById("output").innerHTML = xhr.responseText;};

      xhr.send( );
}
```

With the reduced code needed from the Ajax pattern and having applied all the techniques discussed previously, our final compressed solution looks like this:

```
<!DOCTYPE html PUBLIC "-//W3C//DTD XHTML 1.0 Transitional//EN" "http://www.w3.org/TR/
xhtml1/DTD/xhtml1-transitional.dtd"><html xmlns="http://www.w3.org/1999/xhtml"><head>
<meta http-equiv="Content-Type" content="text/html; charset=iso-8859-1" /><title>Ajax
Hello World</title><script type="text/javascript">d=document;M="Msxml2.
XMLHTTP";function c( ){try{return new XMLHttpRequest(
)}catch(e){}try{A=ActiveXObject;return new A(M+".6.0")}catch(e){}try {return new
A(M+".3.0")}catch(e){}try {return new A(M)}catch(e){}try {return new A("Microsoft.
XMLHTTP")}catch(e){}}function s( ){var x=c( );if(x){x.open("GET","sayhello.php");x.
onreadystatechange=function( ){if(x.readyState==4&&x.status==200)d.
getElementById("o").innerHTML=x.responseText;};x.send( );}}window.onload=function(
){d.getElementById("b").onclick=s}</script></head><body><form action="#"><input
type="button" value="Say it!" id="b" /></form><br /><br /><div id="o"> </div></
body></html>
```

The very terse code of this page weighs in at a svelte 947 bytes, for a total savings of nearly 37%; with further gzipping you can save even more (as high as 62%). However, continuing our efforts is somewhat foolish because we're already below the minimum packet size we'd typically encounter in TCP. Thus, it really buys us little to continue.

Addressing the Caching Quandary of Ajax

Unfortunately, Ajax and caching don't get along that well. Internet Explorer caches Ajax-fetched URIs, so if you aren't careful, subsequent requests may appear not to work. Interestingly, this may not be inappropriate, as a GET request should be cacheable if you are requesting the same URI. Firefox does not cache Ajax-fetched URIs. That itself is a problem, because you get a different behavior when requesting the page directly through the browser and through the XHR object. In either browser, if you make a POST request, you don't have to worry because the browser won't cache the request. Some Ajax libraries now default to POST requests, although some developers persist in misusing GET requests. The usual reaction to Ajax caching confusion is simply to make sure the browser does not cache Ajax requests. There are three methods you can use to do this.

Method 1: Output No Caching Headers on the Server Side

You can easily keep the browser from caching requests by emitting headers on the server. In PHP, you would use statements such as these:

```
header("Cache-Control: no-cache");
header("Pragma: no-cache");
```

There are many choices, and servers can be quite loquacious in the kinds of headers they stamp on a response to avoid caching. For example, you might set some headers to really let caches know that you mean business:

```
Expires: Wed, 18 Nov 1981 09:12:00 GMT
Cache-Control: no-store, no-cache, must-revalidate, post-check=0, pre-check=0
Pragma: no-cache
```

Method 2: Make Requests with Unique URIs

A common way to bust a cache is to make the URIs different each time in a way that does not affect the actual request. For example, imagine calling *sayhello.php*. This page returns the time as part of the Hello statement, so we need a fresh response each time it is called. Because the URI would be the same on subsequent requests, you might be concerned that it would be cached so that you wouldn't see the new message. To make it unique, you could just append a query string such as sayhello. php?ts=unique-value. A simple way to do this would be to use a timestamp such as the one illustrated in this code fragment:

```
var ts = "ts=" + (new Date()).getTime();
sendRequest("sayhello.php", ts);
```

Method 3: Make Requests with an Old If-Modified-Since Header

Another way to prevent caching is use the XHR object's method, setRequestHeader( ), to set the If-Modified-Since in a request to a date far in the past so that the request will appear to need to be refetched:

```
xhr.setRequestHeader("If-Modified-Since", "Tue, 14 Nov 1995 03:33:08 GMT");
```

Developers tend to prefer this method because it does not rely on changing the URI and you can do it without any server-side modifications. There is one problem with these suggestions, however. They do not optimize Ajax in any way other than making it work. We should want to use the browser cache!

Now, it would seem that for an optimal experience, we ought to take advantage of a browser cache, not fight it. As you'll discover in Chapter 9, you can employ a number of cache control techniques by setting various headers such as Cache-Control and Expires. For example, if we used the Cache-control header to set max-age to be 31,536,000 seconds, which equals one year (60 * 60 * 24 * 365):

```
header("Cache-Control: max-age=31536000");
```

the browser should not re-request that object for quite a while. Alternatively, you could simply set the Expires header far in the future, like so:

```
header("Expires: Sun, 05 Jan 2025 04:00:09 GMT");
```

If you are trying to use a cache on purpose with Ajax, you might be disappointed, because some browsers currently do not seem to respect cache control headers when the request is made with an XHR. Proceed with caution.

Create Your Own Cache

Although the opportunity to use the browser's built-in cache now seems a bit problematic, there is a solution that might work: your own JavaScript-based memory cache. Using a simple JavaScript array, you might create a cache that stores requested URIs and their response packets. When you make another request using your Ajax library, you could consult the custom cache array first before doing another fetch. As the cache is stored in memory, it is good only as long as the user is on the current page. In large-scale Ajax applications, users can remain on the same page as long as they are at the site.

The code to write a custom cache isn't tremendously involved. This is really a feature that should be part of a library, and we encourage readers to adopt a library that supports response caching. Without caching, you are optimizing with one hand tied behind your back. Hopefully, we'll see improvements in the way the browsers handle caching with XHRs in the future so that caching can be more consistent.

Addressing Network Robustness

While we're on the subject of networking with Ajax, one important concern is network robustness: something few developers may want to acknowledge as a potential problem.

Traditional web applications employ a useful form of human-based error correction that we might dub "layer eight" error correction in reference to the seven-layer network model.[8] Users are accustomed to failures with traditional web applications. If a site takes too long to load, they simply click Stop and reload the page. They may even retry this process a few times before timing out and giving up—clicking the Back button or finding another site of interest.

Users are accustomed to doing this because the web browser informs them of the status of a connection with a pulsing logo, flipping cursor, loading status bar, and page painting progress. They even expect failure knowing that when they click on a link (particularly one to another site), they just might have to wait a few moments. With an Ajax application, what will trigger a network connection is not as clear. So, the user may sit by, watching a spinning logo that tells him next to nothing about what is going on (see Figure 8-6).

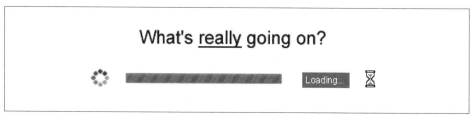

Figure 8-6. It might spin, but is it informative?

Ajax developers are now responsible for making network requests and addressing many issues that users and browsers addressed for them in the past. Optimal Ajax applications acknowledge the fact that bad things happen. They try to mitigate these problems if possible and to inform the user when there are no problems.

Timeouts, Retries, and Ordering

First, consider the simple fact that an Ajax request may not return. Make sure you or your Ajax library employs a timeout mechanism. If you need to do it yourself, just set a timer to fire after a set period of time—say, five seconds—to abort the connection in progress.

---

[8] Zimmerman, H. 1980. "OSI Reference Model—The ISO Model of Architecture for Open Systems Interconnection." *IEEE Transactions on Communications* COM-28 (4): 425–432.

```
var g_abort = false;
var xhr = createXHR();

if (xhr)
 {
   xhr.open("GET","sayhello.php",true);
   var timeout = setTimeout(function (){g_abort=true;xhr.abort();},5000);

   xhr.onreadystatechange = function(){responseCallback(xhr,timeout);};
   xhr.send();
 }
```

You will notice the inclusion of a g_abort variable. This is added in because when the XHR is aborted, the onreadystatechange function will be called with a readyState of 4. It is vital to ensure that the g_abort variable is set to false before processing incomplete data.

Certainly, we shouldn't be using global variables like this. We should instead pass an object wrapper for the XHR that contains useful information to control it and the timer as well, but the code requires enough changes to our "Hello World" example to ruin the simplicity of it. Hopefully, the necessity of applying the inelegance of globals to keep this simple doesn't distract you from handling network problems.

Of course, setting a realistic timeout is important. A smart timeout would actually be related to the network conditions that the user is accustomed to and would adapt as conditions change.

Retrying after a timeout

If your requests time out, you should retry them. Depending on your timeout time and user tolerance, you should retry your Ajax request a few times before presenting an error dialog to the user. If the user does encounter retries, it would be wise to keep track of that situation and, if possible, transmit statistics about network problems back to your site.

```
var g_abort = false;
var g_retries = 0;

function sendAjaxRequest()
{
 var xhr = createXHR();
 if (xhr)
 {
   xhr.open("GET","sayhello.php",true);
   var timeout = setTimeout(function (){responseTimeout(xhr);},5000);

   xhr.onreadystatechange = function(){responseCallback(xhr,timeout);};
   xhr.send();
 }
}
```

```
function responseTimeout(xhr)
{
    g_abort = true;
    xhr.abort();
  if (g_retries < 3)
  {
        sendAjaxRequest();
        g_retries++;
  }
}
```

Out-of-order responses

Finally, you need to acknowledge that your HTTP requests can come back out of order. In traditional web application design, the whole page is the unit of execution, so we tend not to worry about having one image come down before another. If you are using Ajax to issue to a server multiple requests that depend on one another, however, it is quite possible that in some situations you may receive responses out of order. This could cause errors if unaccounted for. It is interesting that, so far, most Ajax developers are unaware of this because they generally do not issue multiple requests at the same time, especially dependent requests. More interestingly, when they do, the two-simultaneous-request limitation often helps to minimize the problem.

Hoping for the best isn't the way to build a robust Ajax application. It's easy to solve the ordering issue if you add a request and/or response queue mechanism to your Ajax application to force sequencing. You can enforce the execution order yourself so that you wait for a dependent request to come back before you move on.

At the time of this writing, you generally need to roll your own queuing mechanism because many libraries currently overlook this problem.

Addressing Server and Content Error

There are more than just network errors to be concerned with in Ajax applications. Just waiting around to get a 200 OK HTTP response isn't going to ensure that you actually have the content you were expecting. Application servers far too often return error messages with such indications, and if you use the basic code such as this:

```
function responseCallback(xhr)
{
  if (xhr.readyState == 4  && xhr.status == 200)
    {
       /* go to work */
    }
}
```

it isn't going to keep you from outputting or consuming an error message as though it were content (see Figure 8-7).[9]

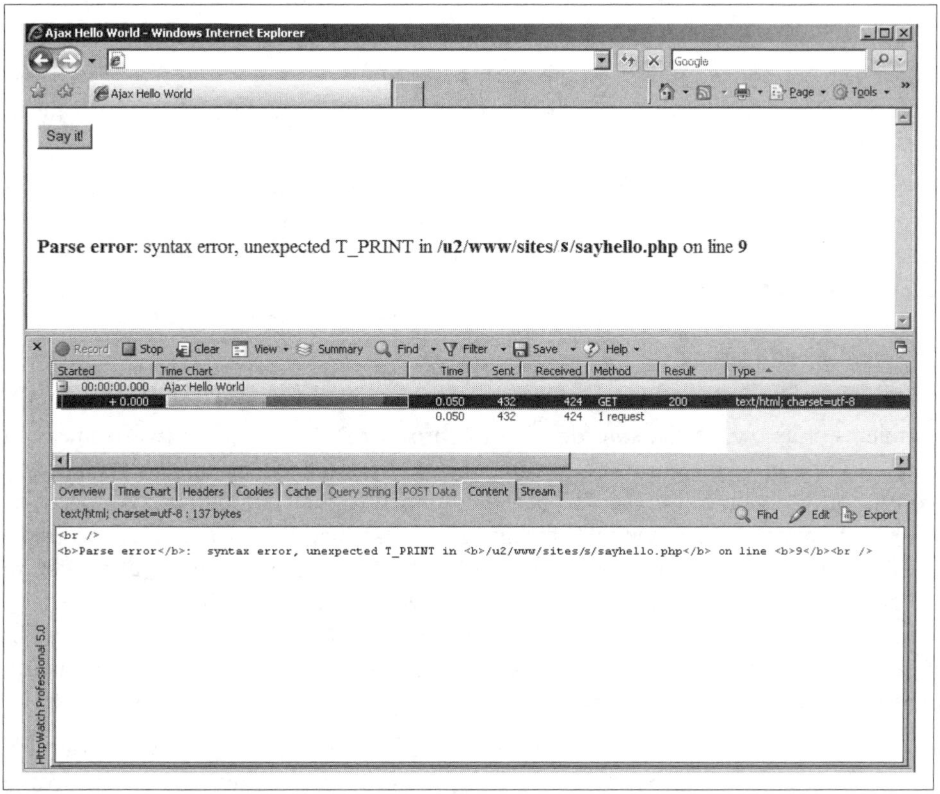

Figure 8-7. OK—it's an error!

Your only protection against server and content errors is careful inspection of each and every response. If you don't see what you expect, bail out.

Polling Carefully

One surefire way to cause trouble with Ajax is to poll a server excessively. Even though your requests may be very small, you need to acknowledge that web servers can get network-bound even with small requests. In fact, if numerous Ajax-enabled clients are continuously polling a server, the server's ability to service other connections can be severely impacted.

---

[9] For more in-depth error correction and prevention, see the "Networking Considerations" chapter (written by T. Powell) in my book, *Ajax: The Complete Reference* (McGraw-Hill Osborne Media).

So, why do people employ such a polling scheme if it can cause such trouble? Usually the answer is that they want to create some type of application that gets updates frequently or in near-real time, like a chat application. Ajax is a poor solution for such a situation, frankly.

If, for some reason, you must poll, poll with a *decay*. This means that as you poll and do not see any changes, you poll less frequently. When you see a change, go ahead and poll more aggressively again.

Instead of polling, you might employ a different communication pattern in which you keep an open connection between the browser and the server and push data down the pipe. This pattern has many names, including "endless iframe," "reverse Ajax," and, most commonly, "Comet."[10]

The problem with polling

Although this push-style architecture can reduce the impact of polling, it has major problems of its own. First, consider that the browser still maintains a two-connection limit so, in employing this architecture, you will potentially tie up one connection continuously. Second, web servers are ill-equipped to handle long-lived connections with each connection potentially forking a process. Because of the stress on traditional web services from the use of the Comet pattern, you often must run a separate helper server to work in conjunction with the web server to handle that push traffic efficiently. Third, even if serving isn't an issue, browsers may not be up to the job. They crash or have memory problems if connections are held too long, particularly when using the endless iframe approach.

If you really need to employ a robust push-style pattern within a browser, you may best be served by using Flash or a Java applet to open a socket connection. In the future, we may see that this binary crutch is no longer required when browsers are extended to listen for server events. Opera 9, for example, already supports the event streaming that follows the emerging What-WG/HTML 5 draft specification (*http://www.whatwg.org/specs/web-apps/current-work*) that includes event streaming, which is a Comet-like interface. Don't blaze too many trails in search of new technology and trouble, because many challenges with the use of Ajax are generally still unmet.

Understanding the Ajax Architecture Effect

Like many rich technologies, you can use Ajax to break the one-URI-equals-one-resource architecture of the Web. Consider entering an Ajax application and performing many different tasks. You will likely stay on the same page with partial

---

[10]The term *Comet* is not an acronym. The general introduction of the term is attributed to Alex Russell from Dojotoolkit.org sometime in early 2006 (see *http://alex.dojotoolkit.org/?p=545*).

screen updates and the URI will probably not change. If you accidentally click the Back button, you will very likely be ejected from the application. There will be no way to actually use the browser's native bookmarking feature to save your position in the application. The application may, however, provide some internal button to generate a URI to bookmark the current state. Finally, because of the complex use of JavaScript and the inability to associate a state or resource with a differing URI, more limited user agents such as search engine spiders and screen readers will simply be locked out of many Ajax applications.

The Location Hash Technique

Using Ajax may not seem as appealing if it keeps your site from being search-indexed, breaks Back buttons, and makes it inaccessible under any less-than-ideal conditions. However, it doesn't have to be that way. You can, indeed, address the problems of saving state by using an idea called the *location hash technique*.

Consider a traditional web application that may have URIs such as these, which perform the simple actions indicated by the URIs:

```
http://example.com/record/add
http://example.com/record/edit
http://example.com/record/delete
```

Now, if this were an Ajax application, we might start with a base URI such as *http://example.com/record*. It would never change as you performed the various add, edit, and delete tasks. You might change the URI so that it looks like *http://example.com/record#add* or *http://example.com/record#delete*, depending on what state you were in. The hash mark in the browser can be added and modified by JavaScript and not cause a page refresh. Unfortunately, we have to hack around a bit to address the Back button and history concerns for all browsers. We can add an invisible iframe into our application and change its state to address that, and suddenly we find ourselves with an application that has a working Back button.

The actual implementation of the history and Back button fix for Ajax is quite ugly and involved, and it's best to rely on a library such as YUI to do the work for you. Understand, however, that many libraries still label such history fixes as experimental, so test early and often.

Adding history and bookmarking capabilities may ease the user's move from traditional to Ajax-style browsing, but you will have to spend time trying to design the site so that it works with Ajax on as well as off. The best way to approach the problem is to start with a simple site that uses baseline technologies such as form posts and links, and then to progressively enhance the site with new features such as CSS, JavaScript, and Flash. As you enhance your site, build it so that if the user disables the technology or simply doesn't have it available, it falls back to what it can handle.

In contrast, you could start with the latest and greatest approach to application development and then try to figure out a way to gracefully degrade in light of less-capable browsers, but that approach tends to be harder. We'll explore progressive enhancement (static content overlaid with dynamic content) in Chapter 9. Although this discussion is a bit philosophical, it serves as a great bookend for the beginning of this chapter. The choice to use Ajax, particularly to make it mandatory, is a significant one. There will be an increase in implementation difficulty and testing, along with serious side effects. User and search robot lockout are indeed real possibilities if Ajax is misapplied.

Summary

The introduction of the Ajax communication pattern into a website or application puts more emphasis on JavaScript and network management. Correct usage of the pattern can result in a richer and faster experience for end-users. However, it is quite easy to misapply the technology. If you add too much JavaScript, issue too many requests, or fundamentally change the way the site or application acts, you may inadvertently frustrate your end-users.

In this chapter, we explored a number of ways to reduce JavaScript code bulk and add robustness so that the application of Ajax doesn't sting.

## CHAPTER 9

Advanced Web Performance Optimization

Now that you've learned how to crunch your content, let's look at some more advanced server- and client-side techniques for increasing web performance.

On the server side, this chapter explores methods that you can use to boost performance by:

- Optimizing parallel downloads
- Caching frequently used objects
- Using HTTP compression
- Deploying delta encoding
- Rewriting URIs with `mod_rewrite`

On the client side, we'll investigate procedures that you can use to improve the speed of content delivery. Although these techniques take some additional effort, they boost both perceived and actual web page speed.

Server-Side Optimization Techniques

This section explores some server-side techniques that you can use to boost your site's performance. Note that some of these techniques are hybrids, combining server-side settings with concomitant client-side modifications. For more on server-side performance optimization, you can also check out *Web Performance Tuning: Speeding Up the Web*, by Patrick Killelea (O'Reilly).

Optimizing Parallel Downloads

The HTTP 1.1 specification recommends that browsers limit downloads to two objects per hostname. This recommendation was created in 1999, in the days of dial-up and less robust proxy servers. Most browsers default to this limit. Although users can change these defaults, most don't bother to do so. For sites hosted on one domain, the result is slower load times with objects loaded two at a time.

Now that bandwidth and proxy servers have improved, you can improve parallelism by using multiple domains (or subdomains) to deliver objects. Yahoo! found that increasing the number of hostnames to two was optimal (see Figure 9-1).[1]

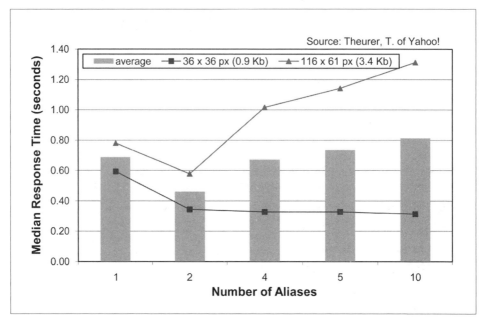

Figure 9-1. Loading an empty HTML document with 20 images using different numbers of aliases

Increasing to four or more hostnames actually degraded performance for larger images, because of the overhead of off-site requests and "CPU thrashing."

Ryan Breen of Gomez reported similar improvements after increasing the number of subdomains to serve objects. He used Domain Name System (DNS) canonical name records (CNAMEs) to create subdomains such as *images1.example.com*, *images2.example.com*, and *images3.example.com*, all pointing back to the main server, *www.example.com*.[2] Then he used code to assign subdomains to images, even though they all point back to the same server.

 You may decrease the potential search rankings of content that is hosted on subdomains, but for external objects such as images and videos this technique can improve performance.

[1] Theurer, T., and S. Souders. April 11, 2007. "Performance Research, Part 4: Maximizing Parallel Downloads in the Carpool Lane." Yahoo! Interface Blog, *http://yuiblog.com/blog/2007/04/11/performance-research-part-4/* (accessed February 11, 2008). Theurer provided the author with an updated figure.

[2] Breen, R. December 18, 2006. "Circumventing browser connection limits for fun and profit." Ajax Performance, *http://www.ajaxperformance.com/?p=33* (accessed February 11, 2008). Figure 9-2 used with permission.

Moving from two to six simultaneous connections improved the load time of a sample page by more than 40% (see Figure 9-2).

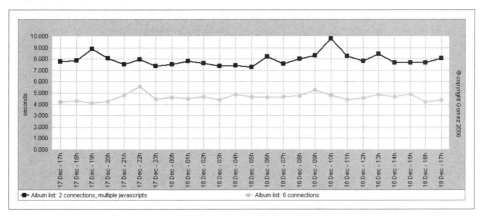

Figure 9-2. Response time improvement from two to six simultaneous connections

When evaluating the maximum number of simultaneous downloads per server, browsers look at hostnames, not at IP addresses. This technique fools browsers into thinking that these objects are served from different domains, allowing more simultaneous downloads. Another way to increase parallelism is to downgrade your object server to HTTP 1.0, which allows up to four simultaneous downloads. See *http://www.die.net/musings/page_load_time/* for some simulations of the effect of multiple hostnames, object size, and pipelining on page load time.

Reduce DNS lookups

The Domain Name System (DNS) maps domain names to IP addresses. DNS gives portability to domain names by allowing sites to move to new servers with different IP addresses without changing their domain name. DNS typically takes 20–120 milliseconds to look up the IP address for each hostname. The browser must wait for DNS to resolve before continuing to download the page components. Therefore, minimizing the number of hostnames per page will minimize the overhead due to DNS lookups.

Minimizing the number of hostnames per page also limits the number of parallel downloads, however. For the average web page with more than 50 objects, the best compromise is to split your objects among two to four hostnames to balance the speedup of parallel downloads with the overhead of DNS lookups, opening TCP connections, and the use of client-side resources. The CNAME trick we discussed before can help to simplify object management.

Caching Frequently Used Objects

Caching is the temporary storage of frequently accessed data in higher-speed media (typically SRAM or RAM), or in media that is closer to the user, for more efficient retrieval. Web caching stores frequently used objects closer to the client through browser, proxy, or server caches. By storing "fresh" objects closer to your users, you avoid unnecessary HTTP requests and minimize DNS "hops." This reduces bandwidth consumption and server load, and improves response times. Yahoo! estimates that between 62% and 95% of the time that it takes to fetch a web page is spent making HTTP requests for objects.[3] Caching helps to reduce costly HTTP requests to improve performance.

Unfortunately, caching is underutilized and often is misunderstood on the Web. A July 2007 survey of Fortune 1000 company websites revealed that 37.9% used cache control headers.[4] What the survey doesn't tell you is that most of these sites use "don't cache" headers. Developers routinely bust caches for fear of delivering stale content.

---

[3] Theurer, T. November 28, 2006. "Performance Research, Part 1: What the 80/20 Rule Tells Us about Reducing HTTP Requests." Yahoo! User Interface Blog, *http://yuiblog.com/blog/2006/11/28/performance-research-part-1/* (accessed February 11, 2008).

[4] Port80 Software. July 2007. "Port80 Surveys HTTP Cache Control on the Top 1000 Corporations' Web Sites." Port80 Software, *http://www.port80software.com/surveys/top1000cachecontrol/* (accessed February 11, 2008).

Browsers have also not helped the situation. To avoid "304" requests that would come from revalidating previously downloaded objects, developers have adopted a check-once-per-session scheme. If a user doesn't shut down her browser, however, she can see stale content. One solution is to cache web objects for longer periods (some developers set their expiry times 20 years into the future), change object filenames for updates, and use shorter expiration times for HTML documents, which tend to change more frequently.

Caching is not just for static sites; even dynamic sites can benefit from it. Caching dynamically generated content is less useful than caching all the dependent objects, such as scripts, styles, images, and Flash, which are often re-requested or at least revalidated by browsers or intermediaries. Dependent objects such as multimedia objects typically don't change as frequently as HTML files. Graphics that seldom change, such as logos, headers, and navigation bars, can be given longer expiration times, whereas resources that change more frequently, such as HTML and XML files, can be given shorter expiration times. By designing your site with caching in mind, you can target different classes of resources to give them different expiration times with only a few lines of code. You can test how well caching is set up on your site using Port80 Software's Cache Check tool (see Figure 9-3).

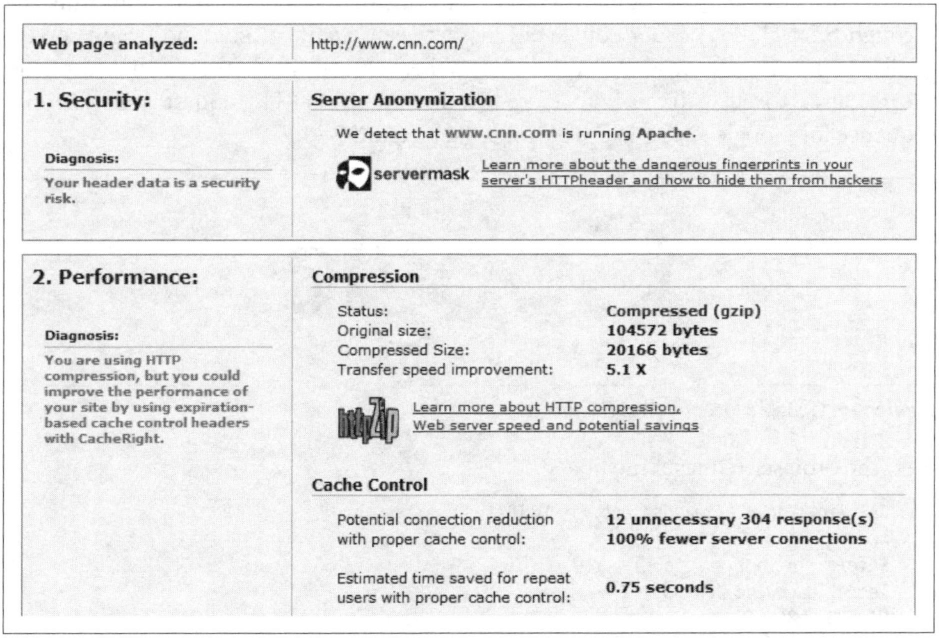

Figure 9-3. Checking the caching on CNN.com with Port80Software.com's Cache Check tool

Three ways to cache in

There are three ways to set cache control rules for your website:

- Via <meta> tags (<meta http-equiv="Expires"...>)
- Programmatically, by setting HTTP headers (CGI scripts, etc.)
- Through the web server general configuration files (*httpd.conf*)

In the section that follows, we'll explore the third method of cache control: server configuration files. Although the first method works with browsers, most intermediate proxy servers don't parse HTML files; they look for HTTP headers to set caching policy, thus undermining this method. The second method of programmatically setting cache control headers (e.g., Expires and Cache-Control) is useful for dynamic CGI scripts that output dynamic data. The third and preferred method is to use web server configuration files to set cache control rules. In addition, we'll explore mod_cache, which provides a powerful caching architecture to accelerate HTTP traffic.

Example cache control conversation. To cache web objects, browsers and proxy servers upstream from the origin server must be able to calculate a time to live (TTL), or a limit on the period of time you can display an object from the cache since the last time it was accessed or modified. HTTP does this digital melon-squeezing primarily through brief HTTP header conversations between client, proxy, and origin servers to determine whether it is OK to reuse a cached object or whether it should reload the resource to get a fresh one. Here is an example HTTP request and response sequence for Google's logo image, *logo.gif* (see Figure 9-4).

Figure 9-4. Google's logo: back to the future

First the browser requests the image:

```
GET /intl/en_ALL/images/logo.gif HTTP/1.1
Accept: */*
Referer: http://www.google.com/
Accept-Language: en-us
UA-CPU: x86
Accept-Encoding: gzip, deflate
User-Agent: Mozilla/4.0 (compatible; MSIE 7.0; Windows NT 5.1; .NET CLR 1.0.3705;
.NET CLR 2.0.50727; .NET CLR 1.1.4322; Media Center PC 4.0)
Proxy-Connection: Keep-Alive
Host: www.google.com
```

One of Google's servers replies with the following:

```
HTTP/1.1 200 OK
Content-Type: image/gif
Last-Modified: Wed, 07 Jun 2006 19:38:24 GMT
Expires: Sun, 17 Jan 2038 19:14:07 GMT
Server: gws
Content-Length: 8558
Date: Tue, 23 Oct 2007 23:21:55 GMT
```

This image was last modified June 7, 2006 and includes an Expires header set to January 17, 2038, far into the future. In its minimalist reply header, Google does not use the Cache-Control header, an entity tag (ETag), or the Accept-Ranges header. The Cache-Control header was introduced in HTTP 1.1 to provide a more flexible alternative to the Expires header. Rather than setting a hardcoded time into the future, as the Expires header does, the max-age setting of the Cache-Control header provides a relative offset (in seconds) from the last access. Here is an example that sets the cache control maximum age to one year from the last access (in seconds):

```
Cache-Control: max-age=31536000
```

The Expires header works for browsers that encounter a server that switches to HTTP 1.0, which should send *only* an Expires header. Of course, because Google doesn't use ETags, once it substitutes one of its patented seasonal logos it would need to change the filename to make sure the logo updates in browsers (see Figure 9-5).

Figure 9-5. Happy Halloween logo from Google

Use a future Expires header. By using an Expires header set far into the future, Google ensures that its logo will be cached by browsers. According to the HTTP specification, the Expires header tells the browser "the date/time after which the response is considered stale." When the browser encounters this header and has the image in its cache, the cached image is returned on subsequent page views, saving one HTTP request and HTTP response.

Configure or eliminate ETags. ETags were designed to be a more flexible caching alternative to determine whether a component in the browser's cache matches the one on the origin server. The problem with ETags is that they are constructed to be unique to a specific resource on a specific server. For busy sites with multiple servers, ETags can cause identical resources to not be cached, degrading performance. Here is an example ETag:

```
ETag: "10690a1-4f2-40d45ae1"
```

In Apache, ETags are made out of three components: the INode, MTime, and Size.

```
FileETag INode MTime Size
```

You can configure your Apache server (in your *httpd.conf* file) to strip the server component out of each ETag, like so:

```
<Directory /usr/local/httpd/htdocs>
    FileETag MTime Size
</Directory>
```

However, most of the websites that we tested don't bother configuring their ETags, so a simpler solution is to turn off ETags entirely and rely on Expires or Cache-Control headers to enable efficient caching of resources. To turn off ETags, add the following lines to one of your configuration files in Apache (this requires mod_headers, which is included in the default Apache build):

```
Header unset Etag
FileETag none
```

The effect of cookies on caching. Cookies are commonly used on the Web for tracking and saving *state* across browser sessions, but they are often overused. Researchers have found that popular sites indiscriminately set cookies for all their URIs, denying themselves the benefits of Content Delivery Networks (CDNs) and caching, both of which are impeded by cookies. For example, one study found that 66% of responses were uncacheable or required cache validation. A significant fraction of these uncacheable responses was due to the use of cookies (47% of all requests used).[5]

Most sites use the Set-Cookie header path of root (/), which sets cookies for every object. If you segregate cookied content, move images to a separate directory or server, and use more specific paths to assign cookies, you can minimize their impact on performance.

A specific caching example

Let's look at a specific example as we build up the caching efficiency for WebSite-Optimization.com's logo, *l.gif*. First we request the image from Internet Explorer:

```
GET /l.gif HTTP/1.1
Accept: */*
Referer: http://www.websiteoptimization.com/
Accept-Language: en-us
```

[5] Bent, L. et al. 2004. "Characterization of a Large Web Site Population with Implications for Content Delivery." In *WWW 2004* (New York: May 17–22, 2004), 522–533.

```
UA-CPU: x86
Accept-Encoding: gzip, deflate
User-Agent: Mozilla/4.0 (compatible; MSIE 7.0; Windows NT 5.1; .NET CLR 1.0.3705;
.NET CLR 2.0.50727; .NET CLR 1.1.4322; Media Center PC 4.0)
Proxy-Connection: Keep-Alive
Host: www.websiteoptimization.com
```

To demonstrate the default Apache configuration, we eliminated the cache control directives from our *httpd.conf* file, and the response was as follows:

```
HTTP/1.1 200 OK
date: Mon, 22 Oct 2007 23:32:20 GMT
server: Apache
last-modified: Sat, 19 Jun 2004 15:25:21 GMT
etag: "10690a1-4f2-40d45ae1"
accept-ranges: bytes
content-length: 1266
content-type: image/gif
```

This image was last modified June 19, 2004 and will not be changed for some time. It is clear from these response headers that this object does not change frequently and can be safely cached for at least a year into the future. Note the lack of Expires or Cache-Control headers, and the inclusion of an ETag header for the image. Next we'll show how to add cache control headers.

Cache control with mod_expires and mod_headers.　For Apache, mod_expires and mod_headers handle cache control through HTTP headers sent from the server. Because they are installed by default, you only need to configure them. Before adding the following lines, first check that they are not enabled. On many operating systems, they are enabled by default. For Apache 1.3*x*, enable the expires and headers modules by adding the following lines to your *httpd.conf* configuration file:

```
LoadModule expires_module       libexec/mod_expires.so
LoadModule headers_module       libexec/mod_headers.so

AddModule mod_expires.c
AddModule mod_headers.c
...
```

For Apache 2.0, enable the modules in your *httpd.conf* file like so:

```
LoadModule expires_module modules/mod_expires.so
LoadModule headers_module modules/mod_headers.so
...
```

Target files by extension for caching

One quick way to enable cache control headers for existing sites is to target files by extension. Although this method has some disadvantages (notably the requirement of file extensions), it has the virtue of simplicity. To turn on mod_expires, set ExpiresActive to on:

```
ExpiresActive On
```

Next, target your website's root HTML directory to enable caching for your site in one fell swoop. Note that the default web root shown in the following code (/var/www/htdocs) varies among operating systems.

```
<Directory "/var/www/htdocs">
    Options FollowSymLinks MultiViews
    AllowOverride All
    Order allow,deny
    Allow from all
    ExpiresDefault A300
    <FilesMatch "\.html$">
        Expires A86400
    </FilesMatch>
    <FilesMatch "\.(gif|jpg|png|js|css)$">
        Expires A31536000
    </FilesMatch>
</Directory>
```

ExpiresDefault A300 sets the default expiry time to 300 seconds after access (A) (using M300 would set the expiry time to 300 seconds after file modification). The FilesMatch segment sets the cache control header for all *.html* files to 86,400 seconds (one day). The second FilesMatch section sets the cache control header for all images, external JavaScript, and Cascading Style Sheet (CSS) files to 31,536,000 seconds (one year).

Note that you can target your files with a more granular approach using multiple directory sections, like this:

```
<Directory "/var/www/htdocs/images/logos/">
```

For truly dynamic content you can force resources to not be cached by setting an age of zero seconds, which will not store the resource anywhere (or you can set Expires to A0 or M0):

```
<Directory "/var/www/cgi-bin/">
    Header Set Cache-Control "max-age=0, no-store"
</Directory>
```

Target files by MIME type. The disadvantage of the preceding method is its reliance on the existence of file extensions. In some cases, webmasters elect to use URIs without extensions for portability. A better method is to use the ExpiresByType command of the mod_expires module. As the name implies, ExpiresByType targets resources for caching by MIME type, like this:

```
<VirtualHost 10.1.1.100>
...
ExpiresActive On
ExpiresDefault "access plus 300 seconds"
<Directory "/var/www/htdocs">
Options FollowSymLinks MultiViews
AllowOverride All
```

```
Order allow,deny
Allow from all
ExpiresByType text/html "access plus 1 day"
ExpiresByType text/css "access plus 1 year"
ExpiresByType text/javascript "access plus 1 year"
ExpiresByType image/gif "access plus 1 year"
ExpiresByType image/jpg "access plus 1 year"
ExpiresByType image/png "access plus 1 year"
</Directory>
</VirtualHost>
```

These *httpd.conf* directives set the same parameters, only in a more flexible and readable way. For expiry commands you can use access or modified, depending on whether you want to start counting from the last time the file was accessed or from the last time the file was modified. In the case of WebSiteOptimization.com, we chose to use short access offsets for text files likely to change, and longer access offsets for infrequently changing images.

Note the AllowOverride All command. This allows webmasters to override these settings with *.htaccess* files for directory-based authentication and redirection. However, overriding the *httpd.conf* file causes a performance hit because Apache must traverse the directory tree looking for *.htaccess* files.

After updating the *httpd.conf* file with the preceding MIME-based code, we restart the HTTP daemon in Apache for Linux using this command from the shell prompt:

```
service httpd restart
```

Red Hat Enterprise, Fedora, and CentOS all make use of the service command. Note that the commands to restart the HTTP daemon vary among operating systems. On most systems, you can use the apachectl command or the */etc/init.d/ apache2* init script to start, stop, or restart Apache. Some administrators choose to do Apache configuration and control entirely through a web interface such as Webmin, or through an OS-specific graphical utility.

HTTP header results. We updated the *httpd.conf* configuration file with the MIME type code in the preceding section. Let's look at the how the headers change when we request the WebSiteOptimization.com logo (*l.gif*):

```
GET /l.gif HTTP/1.1
Accept: */*
Referer: http://www.websiteoptimization.com/
Accept-Language: en-us
UA-CPU: x86
Accept-Encoding: gzip, deflate
User-Agent: Mozilla/4.0 (compatible; MSIE 7.0; Windows NT 5.1; .NET CLR 1.0.3705;
.NET CLR 2.0.50727; .NET CLR 1.1.4322; Media Center PC 4.0)
Proxy-Connection: Keep-Alive
Host: www.websiteoptimization.com
```

The headers for our home page logo now look like this:

```
HTTP/1.1 200 OK
Date: Thu, 25 Oct 2007 12:51:13 GMT
Server: Apache
Cache-Control: max-age=31536000
Expires: Fri, 24 Oct 2008 12:51:13 GMT
Last-Modified: Sat, 19 Jun 2004 15:25:21 GMT
ETag: "10690a1-4f2-40d45ae1"
Accept-Ranges: bytes
Content-Length: 1266
Content-Type: image/gif
```

As a result, this resource has cache control headers. We left the ETag in as we use one server. Note also that the Server field is also stripped down, to save some header overhead. This is done with the ServerTokens command:

```
ServerTokens Min
```

This minimizes the response header from this:

```
Server: Apache/1.3.31 (Unix) mod_gzip/1.3.26.1a mod_auth_passthrough/1.8
mod_log_bytes/1.2 mod_bwlimited/1.4 PHP/4.3.8 FrontPage/5.0.2.2634a mod_ssl/2.8.19
OpenSSL/0.9.7a
```

to the minimal:

```
Server: Apache
```

Our images are now cacheable for one year. We could eliminate other headers, such as Cache-Control, ETags, and Accept-Ranges, but we don't gain as much by doing so.

Cache control with Microsoft IIS. You can do cache control in Internet Information Server (IIS) by accessing the IIS Manager and setting headers on files or folders. First, navigate with the IIS Manager to the file or directory that you want to target (see Figure 9-6).

Right-click Properties and choose the HTTP Headers tab. Check "Enable content expiration" and then set the appropriate time frame (see Figure 9-7). This will land you on the screen that includes the HTTP Headers tags and content cache options.

If your site is not organized in directories for cache control optimization, it can be quite cumbersome to set cache control policies for a large number of files. See *http://www.port80software.com/support/articles/developforperformance2* for more details about IIS cache control. You can't set cache control headers by MIME type settings with this technique, so Port80 wrote CacheRight to deal with this issue. CacheRight is basically "mod_expires plus" for IIS.

Using mod_cache

With Apache version 2.2, mod_cache has become suitable for production use. mod_cache implements a content cache that you can use to cache local or proxied content.

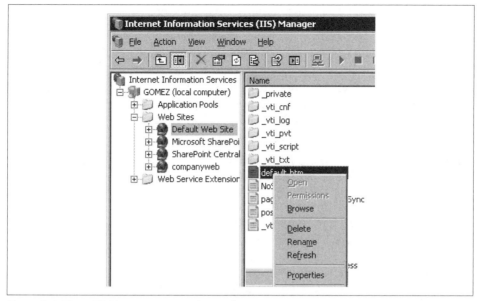

Figure 9-6. Using IIS Manager to set caching policy

Figure 9-7. Setting content expiration in IIS

This improves performance by temporarily storing resources in faster storage. It can use one of two provider modules for storage management:

- mod_disk_cache, which implements a disk-based storage manager.
- mod_mem_cache, which implements a memory-based storage manager. You can configure mod_mem_cache to operate in two modes: caching open file descriptors or caching objects in heap storage. You can use mod_mem_cache to cache locally generated content or to cache backend server content for mod_proxy when configured using ProxyPass (a.k.a. reverse proxy).

Content is stored in and retrieved from the cache using URI-based keys. Content with access protection is not cached. Example 9-1 shows a sample mod_cache configuration file.

Example 9-1. Sample mod_cache configuration file

```
# Sample Cache Configuration
#
LoadModule cache_module modules/mod_cache.so

<IfModule mod_cache.c>
#LoadModule disk_cache_module modules/mod_disk_cache.so
# If you want to use mod_disk_cache instead of mod_mem_cache,
# uncomment the line above and comment out the LoadModule line below.
<IfModule mod_disk_cache.c>
CacheRoot c:/cacheroot
CacheEnable disk /
CacheDirLevels 5
CacheDirLength 3
</IfModule>

LoadModule mem_cache_module modules/mod_mem_cache.so
<IfModule mod_mem_cache.c>
CacheEnable mem /
MCacheSize 4096
MCacheMaxObjectCount 100
MCacheMinObjectSize 1
MCacheMaxObjectSize 2048
</IfModule>

# When acting as a proxy, don't cache the list of security updates
CacheDisable http://security.update.server/update-list/
</IfModule>
```

CacheDirLevels, set to 5, is the number of directory levels below the cache root that will be included in the cache data. CacheDirLength, set to 3, sets the number of characters in proxy cache subdirectory names.

For more details, see the Apache documentation at *http://httpd.apache.org/docs/2.2/mod/mod_cache.html*.

Using HTTP Compression

HTTP compression is a publicly defined way to compress textual content transferred from web servers to browsers. HTTP compression uses public domain compression algorithms, such as gzip and compress, to compress HTML, JavaScript, CSS, XML, and other text-based files at the server. This standards-based method of delivering compressed content is built into HTTP 1.1. All modern browsers that support HTTP 1.1 and PNG files support ZLIB inflation of deflated documents (see the upcoming sidebar "Browsers That Support HTTP Compression"). In other words, they can decompress compressed files automatically, which saves time and bandwidth.

Browsers That Support HTTP Compression

The Portable Network Graphics (PNG) format uses the ZLIB compression algorithm. ZLIB can also decompress gzipped data. So, browsers that can handle PNG files already have the necessary software to decompress gzipped data. Internet Explorer 4 and later (other than IE Mac versions 4.5 and 5), Firefox, and Opera 5.12+ all support HTTP compression. Aren't standards wonderful?

Browsers and servers have brief conversations regarding what they would like to receive and send. Using HTTP headers, they zip messages back and forth over the ether with their content shopping lists. A compression-aware browser tells servers that it would prefer to receive encoded content with a message in an HTTP header like this:

REQUEST

```
GET / HTTP/1.1
Accept: */*
Accept-Language: en-us
Accept-Encoding: gzip, deflate
User-Agent: Mozilla/4.0 (compatible; MSIE 7.0; Windows NT 5.1)
Host: www.webcompression.org
Connection: Keep-Alive
```

An HTTP 1.1-compliant server would then deliver the requested document by using an encoding that is acceptable to the client. Here's a sample response from Web-Compression.org:

RESPONSE

```
HTTP/1.1 200 OK
Date: Sun, 06 Apr 2008 22:38:00 GMT
Server: Apache
X-Powered-By: PHP
Cache-Control: max-age=300
```

```
Expires: Sun, 06 Apr 2008 22:38:00 GMT
Vary: Accept-Encoding
Content-Encoding: gzip
Content-Length: 1168
Keep-Alive: timeout=15
Connection: Keep-Alive
Content-Type: text/html; charset=ISO-8859-1
```

Now the client knows that the server supports gzip content encoding, and it also knows the size of the file is 1,168 bytes (Content-Length). The client downloads the compressed file, decompresses it, and displays the page. Without gzip compression, the home page HTML of WebCompression.org would be 3,183 bytes, about 2.7 times larger in file size (see Figure 9-8).

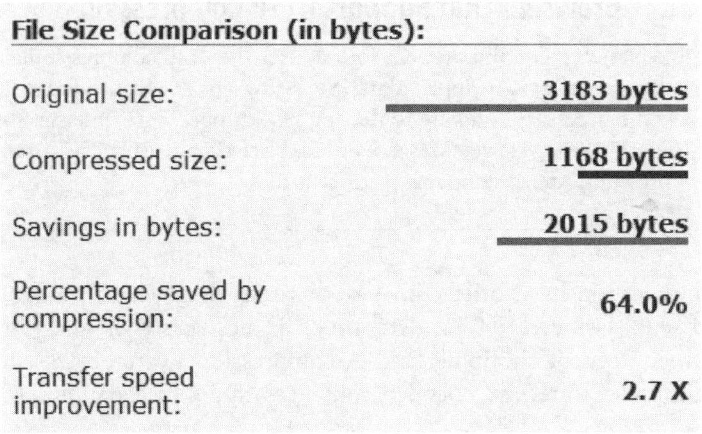

File Size Comparison (in bytes):

Original size:	**3183 bytes**
Compressed size:	**1168 bytes**
Savings in bytes:	**2015 bytes**
Percentage saved by compression:	**64.0%**
Transfer speed improvement:	**2.7 X**

Figure 9-8. File size savings with HTTP compression (from Port80Software.com tool)

Both IIS compression and Apache 2.x's mod_deflate now do compression very well, so the need for add-on compression modules has decreased. Products such as mod_gzip, Vigos's Website Accelerator, PipeBoost, httpZip, and others offer configurable software to enable compression, and some offer hardware solutions to speed response times. Applications servers, such as WebSphere, PHP, and Java, also offer HTTP compression.

Compressing content in Apache

In Apache, you can either precompress content or configure a module to compress content on the fly. Precompressing content requires changing links (*.htmz* or *.html.gz*, etc.) which can be a lot of work. A more elegant method is to compress content on the fly with a module such as mod_gzip (for Apache 1.3+) or mod_deflate (for Apache 2+).

Content Negotiation in Apache

Since version 1.3.4, Apache has supported transparent content negotiation as defined in the HTTP 1.1 specification. To negotiate a resource, the server needs to know about the *variants* of each resource.

Multiviews implicitly maps variants based on filename extensions, such as *.gz*. Multiviews is a per-directory option that you can set within *.htaccess* files or within server configuration files (such as *httpd.conf*) on one or more directories. Setting the Multiviews option within the *.conf* file is more efficient because Apache doesn't have to access an *.htaccess* file every time it accesses a directory. To turn on Multiviews, append it to the Options line in your *httpd.conf* file:

```
<Directory "/usr/local/apache/htdocs">
    Options Indexes FollowSymLinks MultiViews
    AllowOverride None
    Order allow,deny
    Allow from all
</Directory>
```

Apache recognizes only encodings that are defined by the AddEncoding directive. So, to let Apache know about gzip-encoded files, you'd add the following directive:

```
# AddEncoding allows you to have certain browsers
# uncompress information on the fly. Note: Not all browsers
# support this. Despite the name similarity, the following
# Add* directives have nothing to do with the FancyIndexing
# customization directives above.
#
AddEncoding x-gzip .gz .tgz
```

Now, with Multiviews set, webmasters need only create filename variants of resources, and Apache does the rest. So, to create gzip-compressed versions of your *.html* or *.js* files, you zip them up like this:

```
gzip -9 index.html
gzip -9 script.js
```

Then, when you link to the uncompressed *.html* or *.js* files, Apache will negotiate to the *.gz* variant for capable browsers.

Content negotiation can produce significant overhead, on the order of 25% in some cases. But as long as your server's response time is measured in milliseconds, your users won't notice the difference in response times. The net effect will be faster because smaller files are being transferred and decompression times are fast.

Port80 Software created PageXchanger to address content negotiation in Microsoft IIS. For more information on content negotiation, see *http://httpd.apache.org/docs/2.0/content-negotiation.html*.

mod_gzip for dynamic compression. mod_gzip can compress content dynamically and use content negotiation at the server to intelligently serve the appropriate content to capable browsers. Dynamic compression does place an additional load on the server, but the compiled C code is efficient and is an issue only for the slowest of servers. Be sure that you have 1 GB or more of memory to handle the increased demand on your server. Remember that many web servers are provided on low-end hardware with a minimum amount of memory.

Setting up HTTP compression with mod_gzip. To configure mod_gzip, all your server administrator needs to do is install the precompiled package from your package management utility (for Linux and BSD; for Solaris you'll want to download the pre-compiled module), edit the server configuration file, and restart Apache.[6] mod_gzip compresses content after everything else happens at the server, so it is always referenced last in any server configuration list. Here is an example addition to an *httpd.conf* configuration file:

```
# Dynamic Shared Object (DSO) Support
#
# To be able to use the functionality of a module which was built as a DSO you
# have to place corresponding 'LoadModule' lines at this location so the
# directives contained in it are actually available _before_ they are used.
# Please read the file http://httpd.apache.org/docs/dso.html for more
# The order in which these modules load is important...
#
LoadModule rewrite_module        libexec/mod_rewrite.so
LoadModule expires_module        libexec/mod_expires.so
LoadModule php4_module           libexec/libphp4.so
LoadModule bwlimited_module      libexec/mod_bwlimited.so
LoadModule bytes_log_module      libexec/mod_log_bytes.so
LoadModule auth_passthrough_module libexec/mod_auth_passthrough.so
LoadModule gzip_module           libexec/mod_gzip.so
# ...
#  Reconstruction of the complete module list from all available modules
#  (static and shared ones) to achieve correct module execution order.
#  [WHENEVER YOU CHANGE THE LOADMODULE SECTION ABOVE UPDATE THIS, TOO]
ClearModuleList
AddModule mod_env.c
...
AddModule mod_php4.c
AddModule mod_bwlimited.c
AddModule mod_log_bytes.c
AddModule mod_auth_passthrough.c
AddModule mod_gzip.c
```

Note how LoadModule and AddModule mod_gzip are the last commands in the list. Next, configure mod_gzip with the minimum file size (anything less than 1,000 bytes

---

[6] The mod_gzip software for Apache 1.3, and a link to a 2.*x* version, are available from SourceForge at *http://sourceforge.net/projects/mod-gzip/*. A development version of mod_gzip for Apache 2.0 is available at *http://www.gknw.com/development/apache/httpd-2.0/unix/modules/*.

is not worth the overhead), the maximum in-memory size directive (we chose 1,000,000 bytes as a maximum), and the types of files to include in compression:

```
<IfModule mod_gzip.c>
mod_gzip_on yes
mod_gzip_send_vary yes
mod_gzip_dechunk yes
mod_gzip_keep_workfiles No
mod_gzip_temp_dir /tmp
mod_gzip_minimum_file_size 1002
mod_gzip_maximum_file_size 0
mod_gzip_maximum_inmem_size 1000000

mod_gzip_item_include file "\.htm$"
mod_gzip_item_include file "\.html$"
mod_gzip_item_include mime "text/.*"
mod_gzip_item_include file "\.php$"
mod_gzip_item_include mime "jserv-servlet"
mod_gzip_item_include handler "jserv-servlet"
mod_gzip_item_include mime "application/x-httpd-php.*"
mod_gzip_item_include mime "httpd/unix-directory"

mod_gzip_item_exclude file "\.css$"
mod_gzip_item_exclude file "\.js$"
mod_gzip_item_exclude file "\.wml$"
</IfModule>
```

Note that we include text, *.htm/.html*, and *.php* files but exclude *.css*, *.js*, and *.wml* files to simplify this example. Do not HTTP-compress MP3 files (because they are already compressed), or PDF files (Acrobat Reader can have problems reading gzipped PDF files because they are already compressed internally).

Apache 2.0 and HTTP compression. Apache 2.0 includes the mod_deflate module instead of mod_gzip. Setting up mod_deflate is easy because it is already included in Apache 2.0.

To configure mod_deflate, add the following lines to your *httpd.conf* file:

```
LoadModule deflate_module modules/mod_deflate.so
SetEnv gzip-only-text/html 1
SetOutputFilter DEFLATE
```

You can choose to approach configuring mod_deflate slightly differently, depending on your style. You can either explicitly include MIME types, or explicitly exclude file types from the compression routine.

This example, from the *httpd.conf* file, shows explicit inclusion by MIME type:

```
DeflateFilterNote ratio
DeflateCompressionLevel 9
DeflateMemlevel 9
DeflateWindowSize 15
AddOutputFilterByType DEFLATE text/html text/plain text/css text/xml
AddOutputFilterByType DEFLATE application/x-javascript
AddOutputFilterByType DEFLATE application/ms* application/vnd* application/postscript
```

This example shows explicit exclusion by file extension:

```
SetOutputFilter DEFLATE
DeflateFilterNote ratio
DeflateCompressionLevel 9
DeflateMemlevel 9
DeflateWindowSize 15
SetEnvIfNoCase Request_URI \.(?:gif|jpe?g|png)$ no-gzip dont-vary
SetEnvIfNoCase Request_URI \.pdf$ no-gzip dont-vary
SetEnvIfNoCase Request_URI \.(?:exe|t?gz|zip|bz2|sit|rar|Z)$ no-gzip dont-vary
```

Both HTTP-compress your HTML, CSS, and JavaScript files.

From now on, when these text files are requested with the appropriate Accept-Encoding headers, they will be compressed. For compression solutions for different operating systems, see the following URLs:

Apache
   http://httpd.apache.org/docs/2.0/mod/mod_deflate.html

Unix
   http://www.gknw.de/development/apache/httpd-2.0/unix/modules/

Windows
   http://www.gknw.de/development/apache/httpd-2.0/win32/modules/

Average compression ratios for HTTP compression

So, what can you expect to save using HTTP compression? In tests that we ran on 20 popular sites, we found that, on average, *content encoding saved* 75% off text files (HTML, CSS, and JavaScript) and 37% overall.[7] A larger study of 9,281 HTML pages of popular sites found a mean compression gain of 75.2%.[8] On average, HTTP compression reduced the text files tested to one-fourth their original size. The more text-based content you have, the higher the savings.

Joe Lima, COO and head of product development at Port80 Software, said this about HTTP compression:

> HTTP compression provides such a clear benefit that it appeals to all kinds of users. Our customers include consumer sites that want to improve end-users' experience, hosting providers seeking to differentiate their offering, Fortune 500s looking to make a specific extranet application as bandwidth-efficient as possible, and many others. Simply put, compression is easy to deploy, widely supported, and saves money. Who could say no to that?

---

[7] See Table 18.2, "Content Encoding Average Compression Ratios for Different Web Site Categories," in my book *Speed Up Your Site: Web Site Optimization* (New Riders).

[8] Destounis, P. et al. 2001. "Measuring the mean Web page size and its compression to limit latency and improve download time." *Internet Research* 11 (1): 15. Analyzing five popular websites (CNN.com, Disney.com, IBM.com, Microsoft.com, and Netscape.com), Destounis found a mean compression gain of 75.2% across 9,281 HTML pages. The mean web page size was 13,540 bytes.

Improving Compression Efficiency

Compression efficiency depends on the repetition of content within a given file. Smaller files have fewer bytes, and therefore a lower probability of repeated patterns. As file size increases, compression ratios improve because more characters mean more opportunities for similar patterns. The tests discussed in this section ranged from a 13,540-byte mean (Destounis et al. 2001) to 44,582 bytes per HTML page (King 2003). Smaller files (5,000 bytes or less) typically compress less efficiently, whereas larger files typically compress more efficiently. The more redundancy you can build into your textual data (HTML, CSS, and JavaScript), the higher your potential compression ratio. That is why using all lowercase letters improves compression in XHTML.

Typical savings on compressed text files range from 60% to 85%, depending on how redundant the code is. Some JavaScript files can actually be compressed by more than 90%. Webmasters who have deployed HTTP compression on their servers report savings of 30% to 50% off their bandwidth bills. The cost of decompressing compressed content is small compared to the cost of downloading uncompressed files. On narrowband connections with faster computers, CPU speed trumps bandwidth every time.

Use of HTTP compression among the Fortune 1000. Only 27.5% of the Fortune 1000 companies are using some form of HTTP compression, although the percentage of those that compress is increasing at about 11.7% each year (see Figure 9-9).

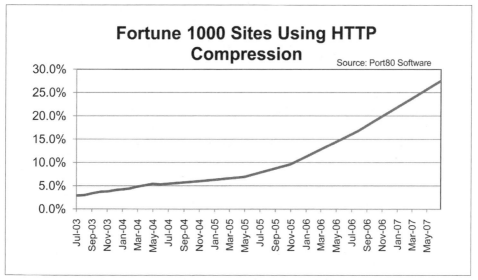

Figure 9-9. Use of HTTP compression among the Fortune 1000 companies

JavaScript optimization and gzip. Gzipping your JavaScript has a more significant effect than minification on file size. However, by minifying your JavaScript before you gzip it, you can realize even more file size savings. In Chapter 10, minification saved an average of 4.8 percentage points (from 73.7% to 78.5% smaller), or 17.6% off the gzipped-only versions of the CSS and JavaScript for seven popular sites. Note that you can realize further savings by concatenating JavaScript files before compressing them, because the efficiency of compressing a single large JavaScript file would be greater than compressing multiple small ones.

Delta encoding (delta compression)

As it applies to web servers, delta encoding is a way to update web pages by sending the differences between versions of a web page. The server (proxy or origin) sends only what has changed in the page since the last access, greatly reducing the amount of data sent (in some cases, on the order of a few TCP/IP packets). As about 32% of page accesses are first-time visits, about 68% of page visits are eligible for delta compression.

There are different ways to implement delta encoding: you can save old versions of pages and send differences, use reference files on the same server that are in the user's cache, and use "value-based web caching" that employs blocks of data already sent to the client, independent of file boundaries.[9]

Same-URI delta compression. Delta compression for pages at the same URI typically achieves higher compression ratios than other schemes, but it has some drawbacks. Sending deltas for the same URI assumes that the client has accessed the page in the past. On the Web, this is true for only 30% of web pages, according to one study.[10] This method also imposes costs to the origin or proxy server to save old versions of the same page to use as reference files.

Different-URI delta compression. Delta compression for pages at different URIs typically achieves more modest compression ratios than the same-URI method, but it does not suffer from the overhead of the same-URI method. Improvements of 1.7 times for all pages to 2.9 times for eligible text or HTML data have been found over gzip compression.[11]

---

[9] Savant, A., and T. Suel. 2004. "Server-Friendly Delta Compression for Efficient Web Access." In *Proc. of the 8th International Workshop on Web Content Caching and Distributing*, 303–322.

[10]Mogul, J. et al. 1997. "Potential benefits of delta-encoding and data compression for HTTP." In *SIGCOMM 1997* (Cannes, France: September 14–18, 1997), 181–194.

[11]Savant and Suel. "Server-Friendly Delta Compression for Efficient Web Access."

Production delta compression. Although delta encoding is part of the HTTP 1.1 specification,[12] it has not been widely adopted among browser and server software. However, some delta compression products use JavaScript instead, generally available through website acceleration appliances. Delta encoding is usually performed as an injected JavaScript that reassembles the differences between a base page and subsequent pages. It can reduce the page load down to a TCP packet or two in some cases, particularly when combined with gzip for text. Cisco and Citrix both offer products that use delta encoding.

Delta encoding and RSS. Although browsers and servers have been slow to adopt delta encoding for websites, the practice has become popular in one area: RSS news feeds. The problem with RSS is that most sites poll feeds for updates. For popular sites, this can add up to a lot of bandwidth use.[13] Delta encoding was proposed as a temporary solution to reduce the overhead of polling while a push-based model is adopted.[14]

Sites that have adopted delta encoding for RSS news feeds report that the average request was reduced by 75% (see Figure 9-10).[15] Bob Wyman estimates that if everyone had adopted the RFC 3229 protocol for RSS news feeds, the bandwidth for his now-defunct news aggregation site PubSub.com would have been reduced by two-thirds.

The Windows RSS platform (Vista) supports this feature, as do a number of other RSS clients. If, unlike WordPress, your blog software provider doesn't already support delta encoding of RSS, ask them to do so, to help save the Web's bandwidth.

Although delta-encoded RSS can save bandwidth, sometimes it can bog down your server. For example, dynamically created feeds such as those in WordPress can cause servers to become overloaded during traffic spikes. That's one advantage of Movable Type. It uses static RSS files, which scale better under higher loads.

The Benefits of a Content Delivery Network

A CDN is a collection of web servers distributed geographically that is designed to speed the delivery of content to users. CDNs such as Akamai (the industry leader with 80% of CDN traffic and 20% of all Internet traffic), Limelight Networks, and CDNetworks deliver content to users from a network of distributed caches.

---

[12]Mogul, J. et al. January 2002. "Delta encoding in HTTP." RFC 3229, *http://www.ietf.org/rfc/rfc3229.txt* (accessed February 11, 2008).

[13]Scoble, R. September 8, 2004. "Full text RSS on MSDN gets turned off." Scobleizer, *http://radio.weblogs. com/0001011/2004/09/08.html#a8195* (accessed February 11, 2008).

[14]Wyman, B. September 13, 2004. "Using RFC3229 with Feeds." As I May Think, *http://www.wyman.us/ main/2004/09/using_rfc3229_w.html* (accessed February 11, 2008).

[15]Wyman, B. October 3, 2004. "Massive Bandwidth Savings proven!" As I May Think, *http://wyman.us/main/ 2004/10/massive_bandwid.html* (accessed February 11, 2008).

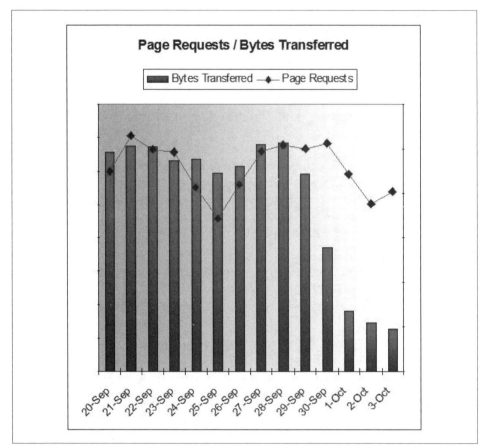

Figure 9-10. Bandwidth savings by adopting delta encoding at PubSub.com

When you distribute your content over a CDN, sophisticated software routes requests to cache servers based on where the user is located on the Internet. According to Steve Souders' *High Performance Web Sites* (O'Reilly), tests conducted by Yahoo! showed an overall 20% reduction in response times for the Yahoo! Shopping Network after moving static components to a CDN. (Yahoo! uses Akamai.) Although the price of large CDNs limits their use to larger companies, some low-cost academic-based CDNs are available, including the Coral Content Distribution Network (*http://www.coralcdn.org/*) and CoDeeN from Princeton University (*http://codeen.cs.princeton.edu/*).

Rewriting URIs with mod_rewrite

For the Apache web server, `mod_rewrite` can map URIs from one form to another. You can use `mod_rewrite` to abbreviate URIs to save bytes or create more search-friendly URIs. For example, you can substitute URIs such as *r/29* for longer ones such as *http://travel.yahoo.com* to save space.

Apache, IIS, Manilla, and Zope all support this technique. Yahoo! and other popular sites use URI abbreviation to shave off 20% to 30% of HTML file size. The more links that you have within your pages, the more effective the abbreviation.

How mod_rewrite works

As its name implies, `mod_rewrite` rewrites URIs using regular expression pattern matching. If a URI matches a pattern that you specify, `mod_rewrite` rewrites it according to the rule conditions that you set. Essentially, `mod_rewrite` works as a smart abbreviation expander. For example, to expand r/pg into /programming Apache requires two directives: one turns on the rewriting machine (`RewriteEngine On`) and the other specifies the rewrite pattern matching rule (`RewriteRule`). The `RewriteRule` syntax looks like this:

```
RewriteRule <pattern> <rewrite as>
```

The preceding code snippet becomes:

```
RewriteEngine On
RewriteRule ^/r/pg(.*)  /programming$1
```

This regular expression matches a URI beginning with `/r/` (this sequence would signify a redirect to expand) with pg following immediately afterward. The pattern `(.*)` matches one or more characters after the pg. So, when a request comes in for the URI `<a href="/r/pg/java/">Programming Java</a>`, the rewrite rule expands this abbreviated URI into `<a href="/programming/java/">Programming Java</a>`.

Note that you can also use `mod_rewrite` in the same manner to map search-friendly URIs to database queries:

```
/keyword1+keyword2 /index?cat=153
```

RewriteMap for multiple abbreviations. The preceding technique will work well for a few abbreviations, but what if you have a lot of links? That's where the `RewriteMap` directive comes in. `RewriteMaps` group multiple lookup keys (abbreviations) and their corresponding expanded values into one tab-delimited file. Here's an example map file snippet from the Yahoo.com home page:

```
r/4d    http://answers.yahoo.com/
r/2h    http://autos.yahoo.com/
r/25    http://finance.yahoo.com/
r/26    http://sports.yahoo.com/
r/29    http://travel.yahoo.com/
...
```

The *MapName* file maps keys to values for a rewrite rule using the following syntax:

```
${ MapName : LookupKey | DefaultValue }
```

MapNames require a generalized RewriteRule using regular expressions. The RewriteRule references the MapName instead of a hardcoded value. If there is a key match, the mapping function substitutes the expanded value into the regular expression. If there's no match, the rule substitutes a default value or a blank string.

To use this MapName we need a RewriteMap directive to show where the mapping file is, and a generalized regular expression for our RewriteRule:

```
RewriteEngine    On
RewriteMap       abbr    txt:/www/misc/redir/abbr_yahoo.txt
RewriteRule      ^/r/([^/]*)/?(.*)    $(abbr:$1}$2    [R=301,L]
```

The new RewriteMap rule points the rewrite module to the text version of our map file. The revamped RewriteRule looks up the value for matching keys in the map file. The permanent redirect (301 instead of 302) boosts performance by stopping processing once the matching abbreviation is found in the map file.

Binary hash RewriteMaps. For maximum speed, you should convert your text map files into a binary *DBM hash file, which is optimized for maximum lookup speed. To create a DBM file from a source text file, use the *httxt2dbm* utility:

```
$ httxt2dbm -i abbr_yahoo.txt -o abbr_yanoo.map
```

As such, the earlier RewriteMap line would look like this:

```
RewriteMap       abbr    txt:/www/misc/redir/abbr_yahoo
```

Yahoo! saves nearly 30% off its home page HTML with this technique. Yahoo! also uses subdomains, which helps to redistribute the load. For more details on using mod_rewrite, see the Apache documentation at *http://httpd.apache.org/docs/2.2/mod/mod_rewrite.html#rewritemap*.

Client-Side Performance Techniques

Beyond optimizing your content so that it is as small as possible and loads more efficiently, you can delay the loading of some types of content to boost the initial display speed of web pages. You can defer certain types of JavaScript to execute after the page loads. You can employ progressive enhancement to layer more advanced functionality over HTML elements. You can stage Flash, Ajax, and JavaScript to load only on demand or asynchronously. You can cache offsite files on your server to load locally. Finally, inline images can reduce HTTP requests for the browsers that support them.

Delay Script Loading

You can improve page load times by delaying the loading of your scripts until some or all of your body content has displayed. For nonessential services (advertising, interface enhancements, surveys, etc.) this technique can boost the initial display speed of your pages. You can also load scripts, such as Ajax, on demand via document object model (DOM) methods, or by using iframes.

One problem with JavaScript is that it is a single-threaded language: it executes scripts linearly. There are exceptions to this with extensions such as Google Gears.[16] When there is a slowdown in loading or executing a script, it delays the rest of the objects in a page from loading and rendering.

Scripts in the head of HTML documents must be processed before the body content is parsed and displayed. Including multiple external CSS and JavaScript files in the head of HTML documents can delay the download and display of body content due to the connection limit default that is present in browsers that follow the HTTP 1.1 specification. (Refer back to Chapter 8 for more details on simultaneous connection limits; servers with HTTP 1.0 allow up to four simultaneous connections per hostname.)

Even after placing external scripts at the end of the body element, your users can experience delays caused by slow server response. Late-loading scripts can have adverse effects, including stalling any events attached to the onload event. So, be sure to initialize as soon as possible and don't use onload for the fastest initialization. In this section, we'll explore the following ways to delay or accelerate script loading to combat JavaScript load lag:

- Use progressive enhancement.
- Load JavaScript on demand or onload.
- Use an iframe for external widgets to simulate asynchronous JavaScript.

Use progressive enhancement

Progressive enhancement (PE) is a web design strategy that uses layers of standards-based technology (XHTML, CSS, and JavaScript) to deliver accessible content to any browser regardless of its capability. By providing static HTML content and overlaying dynamic content with CSS, JavaScript, or Flash, Java, or SVG, PE provides basic content for all browsers, and an enhanced version of the page for browsers with more advanced capabilities. PE improves performance by separating data (XHTML) from presentation (CSS) and behavior (JavaScript), allowing for better caching. PE uses the following techniques:

- Sparse, semantic XHTML for basic content accessible by all browsers
- Enhanced layout provided by external CSS

---

[16] Google's "Gears" API includes the ability to run scripts asynchronously in the background. Available at *http://code.google.com/apis/gears/*.

- Enhanced behavior provided by external JavaScript
- JavaScript to add/subtract objects from the DOM
- JavaScript to add advanced functionality

One early example of PE was WebReference.com's News Harvester Perl/DHTML news flipper.

News Harvester: Overlaying static HTML with DHTML. The simplest method of delaying the loading of external JavaScript is to place the script at the end of your body element, and provide empty stub functions in the head to avoid script errors. This technique requires that core HTML functionality be present upon page load, and that enhanced functionality be layered on top after the script loads. We used this technique for our Perl/DHTML news flipper at WebReference.com (see Figure 9-11).

Figure 9-11. DHTML news flipper at WebReference.com

First we used a Perl script to grab an XML feed, and then we inserted two or three headlines as an HTML include. These headlines displayed even with JavaScript turned off. We then overlaid a DHTML news flipper on top to replace the headlines. Once the core feature was in place, we created empty stub functions to avoid JavaScript errors if users had rolled over the element (to stop the flipping) before the JavaScript loaded:

```
<script type="text/javascript">
    function newsflipper(){};
</script></head>
```

At the end of our body tag, we redefined the DHTML news flipper function like so (delayed load):

```
<script src="/scripts/newsflipper.js"></script>
</body>
```

Empty stub functions allow users to interact with the page without generating "undefined" JavaScript errors. Another method would be to add the event-based triggers to the elements with JavaScript after defining the functions. The script loads just before the closing body tag to redefine the stub function once the body content has displayed. Because the script is small and on the same server, users experienced little or no delay with this approach. See *http://www.webreference.com/dev/evolution/* for more information.

Be careful with this approach, however. Large JavaScript files, especially those that execute slowly, can bog down your page's response time after it has loaded.

Progressively enhanced tabs. David Artz, leader of the AOL Optimization team (and coauthor of Chapter 10), has developed a suite of accessible rendering technologies, which are demonstrated at his site, *http://www.artzstudio.com/artz/*. He invented a technique for disassembly of the "enhancement" on the fly, saving the user's preference with a cookie. What follows is a brief review of this technique.

A tab box example. Tabs are a common form of navigation on the Web. You can avoid loading a new page when selecting a new tab by using Ajax, DHTML, CSS, and Flash. Artz used lightweight CSS and JavaScript to toggle tab (and matching content box) visibility using multiple CSS classes (class="tab on"), setting a cookie to remember user preferences, and standards-based XHTML (see Figure 9-12). He invented two improvements to PE to toggle the visibility and position of the elements by dynamically assigning a class with JavaScript, and to toggle attaching the artz_switch( ) function and text to the "Enable AOL Accessibility" link.

Figure 9-12. Example PE tabs from Dave Artz

Clicking on one of the tabs instantly flips to the next set of headlines. With Java-Script turned off, the same page looks like Figure 9-13.

Figure 9-13. PE example with JavaScript turned off

Without JavaScript, the page is still accessible, showing the default content. Artz starts with the default content using standard XHTML to define the content module and uses CSS to style and position the presentation:

```
<link rel="stylesheet" href="/artz/a.css" type="text/css" media="screen" />
</head>
...
<div id="main"><h2>tab box</h2></div>
<div class="module-container">
<script type="text/javascript" src="tab-box.js"></script>
<p><a href="javascript:void(0)" class="artz-switch"></a></p>
<div id="sports-bloggers-live" class="artz-tb">
    <div class="head"><h2>SPORTS BLOGGERS LIVE</h2></div>
    <div class="desc">
        <a href="#"><img class="photo" src="i/sasha.jpg" alt="image of snowboarder
width="75" height="75" /></a>
        <h4>'If He Wants to Ski Drunk, Then Let Him'</h4>
        <p>SBL previews Turin with figure skaters Johnny Weir and Sasha Cohen,
snowboarder Shaun White and many more.</p>
```

```
        <p><a href="http://sports.aol.com/bloggerslive">Hear Sports Bloggers Live</
a> | <a href="http://journals.aol.com/dcsportsguy/mrirrelevant/entries/2262"
target="new">Watch the SBL Video</a></p>
        </div>...
```

Next, Artz inserts the tabs dynamically with JavaScript. The code is commented here for reference when styling, but these elements are created with JavaScript based on the text of the <h3>s in the document (the real function is abbreviated). Here is the HTML:

```
<!-- DYNAMICALLY INSERTED HTML (artz_tabbox_init)
    <ul class="dtabs">
        <li onclick="artz_tabbox_set(e)" class="on">SBL Audio Clips</li>
        <li onclick="artz_tabbox_set(e)">Blog Buzz</li>
        <li onclick="artz_tabbox_set(e)">Top Blogs</li>
        <li onclick="artz_tabbox_set(e)">Podcasts</li>
    </ul>
END DHTML -->
```

The JavaScript to add these tabs follows:

```
for (var i=0;i<l;i++){
  var li=ce('li');               // create a new list item (<li>) element
  li.className = c;              // assign the class name to the <li> element
  c='';                         // clear the class name for the future
  ac(li,ct(h3s[i].firstChild.data))  // grab the text of the <h3> element and append
it to the <li>
  ae(li,'click',artz.tb.set);   // assign the tb.set() function to the <li>'s
click event
  ac(f,li);                    // append the <li> to the unordered list <ul>
}
```

Next, he displays the default tabs and matching content all within a single unordered list item (<li>) like so:

```
<ul class="tabs">
        <li class="tab on">
            <h3>SBL Audio Clips</h3>
            <p>Five recent guests on AOL's Sports Bloggers Live podcast:</p>
            <ul>
                <li><a href="http://us.video.aol.com/audio.full.
adp?pmmsid=1462037" target="_blank">Dave's Football Celebrates 'One for the Thumb'</
a></li>
                <li><a href="http://us.video.aol.com/audio.full.
adp?pmmsid=1462036" target="_blank">The 12th Man Complains About Refs and Detroit</a>
</li>
                ...
            </ul>
        </li>
```

Note the <li class="tab on"> here to set visibility to "on" for this list item with CSS. Next, Artz includes the code for the other three tabs in a similar fashion. The only difference is the lack of an "on" class to hide these tabs.

```
            <li class="tab">
            <h3>Blog Buzz</h3>...</li>
```

Now when a user clicks on another tab, JavaScript toggles the selected tab to be visible, and turns the other tabs off, completing the effect:

```
<li onclick="artz_tabbox_set(e)">Blog Buzz</li>
```

One tricky part is the "Enable AOL Accessibility" link:

```
<p><a href="javascript:void(0)" class="artz-switch"></a></p>
```

This link is dynamically updated with JavaScript to an "on" or "off" state. When accessibility is switched on with a click on the link, the following code finds the element associated with the artz-switch a(nchor) with getElementById and a class (using the custom function getElementsByClassName to manipulate elements by class and tag) and removes and adds the event listener from the accessibility links:

```
if (artz.toggle == null || typeof(artz.toggle) != "object") artz.toggle = new Object(
);

artz.toggle = {

    init: function () {
        var on='Enable AOL Accessibility', off='Disable AOL Accessibility';
        var s,sw;
        artz.on()?s=off:s=on;
        sw = gc('artz-switch','a',' ');
        for (var i=0,l=sw.length;i<l;i++) {
            re(sw[i],'click',artz.toggle.set);
            ae(sw[i],'click',artz.toggle.set);
            !sw[i].hasChildNodes()?ac(sw[i],ct(s)):sw[i].firstChild.data=s;
        }
    },
```

Another tricky thing that Artz did was dynamically apply an outer class, artz, to the tab box module with JavaScript. This turns on the following styles:

```
/* Dynamically enabled classes (artz_tabbox_init) */
.artz .artz-tb .tabs h3, .artz .artz-tb .tabs .tab {display:none;}
.artz .artz-tb .tabs .on, .artz .dtabs {display: inline;}
```

So, if you do not have JavaScript, the artz class never gets applied, and thus these styles never get applied. The beauty of this technique is that all of the CSS stays in the CSS, and JavaScript toggles accessibility and applies the artz class that controls visibility. The following code does that trick:

```
tb.parentNode.className+=' artz';
tb.className+=' artz';
```

For a working example and other accessible progressive enhancement techniques, see *http://www.artzstudio.com/artz/* and *http://en.wikipedia.org/wiki/Progressive_ enhancement*.

Load JavaScript on demand (remote procedure calls)

A common Ajax pattern is to load resources on demand as they are needed. You can do the same using only JavaScript without the need for Ajax. Using the DOM you can create a script element and append it to the head element, like this:

```
function include_js(file) {
    if(document.getElementByTagName) {
        var html_doc = document.getElementsByTagName('head')[0];
        var js = document.createElement('script');
        js.setAttribute('src', file);
        js.setAttribute('type', 'text/javascript');
        html_doc.appendChild(js);

        js.onreadystatechange = function () { // for IE
            if (js.readyState == 'complete') {
                alert('JS onreadystate fired');
                // return true;
            }
        }

        js.onload = function () { // for non-IE
            alert('JS onload fired');
                // return true;
        }
        return false;
    }
    else alert('getElementsByTagName not supported');
}
...
```

Now the function `$include_js('http://domain.com/myfile.js')` will add a `script` element to the head of your XHTML document. Note that Opera spawns an error when appending a `script` element to the body element, so it is best to append scripts to the head element.

Improvements to JavaScript on demand. You can make a few enhancements to the script in the preceding section. First, to avoid caching, you can add a random seed to the script name, like so:

```
function include_jsNoCache {
    var ms = new Date().getTime().toString();
    var seed = "?" + ms;
    include_js(src + seed);
}
```

This function will import the script with a random query parameter to avoid caching. Unfortunately, Safari doesn't spawn an onload event with the preceding code.[17]

---

[17]Chipman, S.G. September 26, 2005. "09.26.2005—Safari & createElement('script')." slayeroffice, *http://slayeroffice.com/archives/?p=172* (accessed February 11, 2008).

It turns out that setting the onload and src attributes *before* loading the script will spawn an onload event in Safari. The preceding script also does no housecleaning to conserve memory. Once a script has been added to the DOM and used, it can be removed to save memory. Here is the revised script:

```
include_js = (function(){
    var uid = 0;
    var remove = function(id){
        var head = document.getElementsByTagName('head')[0];
        head.removeChild( document.getElementById('jsInclude_'+id) );
    };
    return function(file,callback){
        var callback;
        var id = ++uid;
        var head = document.getElementsByTagName('head')[0];
        var js = document.createElement('script');
        js.setAttribute('type','text/javascript');
        js.setAttribute('src',file);
        js.setAttribute('id','jsInclude_'+uid);
        if( document.all )
        js.onreadystatechange = function(){
            if(js.readyState == "complete"){ callback(id);remove(id); }
        };
        else
            js.onload = function(){
                callback(id); remove(id);
            };
        head.appendChild(js);
        return uid;
    };
})();
```

For more details on this technique by Stoyan Stefanov, see *http://www.phpied.com/javascript-include-ready-onload/*.

Consider JavaScript libraries to avoid problems. You could make other improvements with this technique. For example, namespaces are not supported, and previously loaded scripts will be loaded again. You could address these issues, or turn to a library designed to import scripts in a cross-browser manner. Ajile by Mike Skitz is one solution, and it is available at *http://ajile.iskitz.com/*.

LazyLoad from Ryan Grove is another cross-browser solution that supports multiple scripts and callbacks. For more, visit *http://wonko.com/article/527*.

Use an iframe for external JavaScript

One solution to fixing slow-loading JavaScript problems is to use an iframe to load the external script or data. If there is any delay in loading the script, only the iframe will be delayed, not the entire web page. Because JavaScript can access variables from an HTML file to an embedded iframe and vice versa, this effectively makes a synchronous HTML page asynchronous by breaking it up into iframes.

First, create a function to process the data once the iframe loads:

```
function mainPageFunction (data) {
    // code that uses the iFrame data
}
```

Next, create the iframe to load the external JavaScript file. Note that iframes can cause layout problems, so the easiest way is to use a hidden iframe, like so (some browsers don't like positioned iframes):

```
<div style="position:absolute;left:0;top:0;visibility:hidden;" id="datadiv">
    <iframe height="0" width="0">
        <script src="http://www.example.com/scripts/widget.js"
        type="text/javascript"></script>
    </iframe>
</div>
```

Or you could load the data with an empty iframe, like so:

```
<iframe src="about:blank" height="0" width="0" name="dataframe"></iframe>
<script type="text/javascript">
window.frames['dataframe'].window.location.replace('loadData.html');</script>
```

Now, once you fill up JavaScript variables with data in the iframe, you can pass them to the main HTML page using the following code:

```
parent.mainPageFunction (data);
```

Cache Off-Site Files on the Server and Load Locally

The Web has experienced a proliferation of third-party web services (ad software, surveys, web analytics, etc.), with most relying on JavaScript to accomplish their tasks. We've found that even after placing these scripts near the end of the body element, unexplained delays can occur when waiting for overloaded servers. One method you can use with non-real-time content is to cache the off-site file locally. In Unix-like operating systems, you can use a cron job to grab the file periodically and load it locally to avoid any delays for overloaded external servers.

With more real-time content, such as stock quotes, you can use the following strategy. Every time you grab the data, cache the previous entry. If you get a bad result, use the previous entry. After a certain number of bad results, spawn an alert.

Example RSS cache

To localize an external RSS feed, you can use a conversion script such as Jonathan Eisenzopf's *rss2html.pl* script to grab an RSS feed and convert it to HTML or text on your server.[18] Once the feed is on your server, you can display it locally to avoid any off-site delays. The format for a cron job file is as follows:

```
[min] [hour] [day of month] [month] [day of week] [program to be run]
```

---

[18]Eisenzopf, J. September 1, 1999. "Using RSS News Feeds." *Mother of Perl* column, WebReference.com, *http://www.webreference.com/perl/tutorial/8/* (accessed February 11, 2008).

where:

```
field = allowed values
min = 0-59
hour = 0-23
day of month = 1-31
month = 1-12 (or names, see below)
day of week = 0-7 (0 or 7 is Sun, or use names)
```

Here is an example cron job to grab The Daily Sucker from Vincent Flanders' site once a day at 3:10 A.M. (it is created around midnight PST):

```
# grab the day feed for flanders' web pages that suck site
10 3 * * * /www/yourdir/cgi-bin/rss2html.pl
http://www.webpagesthatsuck.com/dailysucker/rss.xml > sucker.html
```

To save an HTTP request, you could merge this file within the destination page with a CGI script or a content management system (CMS). Alternatively, you could use a server-side include (SSI) to include it within your page, like this:

```
<!--#include virtual="/news/feeds/sucker.html" -->
```

In Microsoft IIS, you can use the AT command for the Schedule service to achieve a similar effect. The syntax is as follows:

```
at \\computername id / delete | /delete/yes
at \\computername time /interactive | /every:date,... /next:date,... command
```

For example, to back up the sales server at 11:30 P.M. every weekday, create a batch file that contains the backup commands in *Backup.bat*, and press Enter to schedule the backup:

```
at \\sales 23:30 /every:M,T,W,Th,F backup
```

JavaScript Optimization and Packing

A number of JavaScript packers remove whitespace and comments and abbreviate variable names. Some packers remap object names. (See Chapter 8 for more details on object remapping and other JavaScript-specific optimization techniques.) Rhino, compliments of the Mozilla Project, analyzes your code with a JavaScript parser, minimizing the possibility of errors. Java-based Rhino compresses JavaScript with the aforementioned techniques, plus it is scriptable.

First, install Rhino. Next, run it from the command line, like this:

```
java -jar rhino.jar -c orig.js > opt.js 2>&1
```

This code optimizes orig.js and outputs opt.js. Rhino removes spaces and comments, and shortens variable names. The Dojo Project and Yahoo! also offer compressors based on Rhino. Dojo offers ShrinkSafe, available at *http://dojotoolkit.org/docs/shrinksafe*.

Julien Lecomte offers the YUI Compressor, also based on Rhino. Lecomte claims higher compression ratios than Dojo's ShrinkSafe. For more information, visit *http://www.julienlecomte.net/blog/2007/08/13/introducing-the-yui-compressor/*.

Another JavaScript, CSS, and XHTML optimizer is w3compiler from Port80 Software, available at *http://www.w3compiler.com*.

W3compiler safely removes whitespace and comments, replaces entity and color values, removes unnecessary meta tags, abbreviates variable names, function names, and filenames, and remaps built-in JavaScript objects. W3compiler is smart enough not to remap names to ensure that the relationship between the XHTML, CSS, and JavaScript stays intact.

W3compiler also does dead-code removal, curly-brace removal on statements such as if/while with only one inner statement, and expression condensing (e.g., x=x+1 becomes x++). Once you've optimized your JavaScript, you can then gzip it for additional savings. We explored HTTP compression earlier in this chapter.

Extreme optimization not advised

Note that some optimization tools will remove quotes from attributes, DOCTYPE tags, and closing tags, and will substitute shorter but less semantic tags (e.g., <b> for <strong>). We don't recommend violating web standards, even if you do it for the sake of a marginal increase in download speed. In fact, practices such as omitting closing tags can actually slow down the rendering of your pages by making the browser work harder to parse your page by switching to "quirks" mode.

Inline Images with Data URIs

You can embed images directly into your web page markup without the need to reference an external file using the data URI scheme. Although data URIs were detailed in RFC 2397 back in 1998,[19] Internet Explorer versions 5 through 7 do not support them. Internet Explorer 8 reportedly does support data URIs.[20] Other standards-compliant browsers such as Opera 7.2+, Firefox, Safari, and Mozilla do support data URIs, so at least you can save HTTP requests for these browsers. Workarounds are available for older versions of Internet Explorer.

You've no doubt seen other URI schemes in your travels around the Web, such as http:, ftp:, and mailto: schemes. The data: URI scheme is a way to embed "immediate data" as though it were included externally. Data URIs use the following syntax:

```
data:[<mediatype>][;base64],<data>
```

---

[19]Masinter, L. August 1998. "The 'data' URL scheme." RFC 2397, *http://www.ietf.org/rfc/rfc2397.txt* (accessed February 11, 2008).

[20]Lawson, B. December 19, 2007. "IE8 passes Acid2 test." The Web Standards Project, *http://www.webstandards.org/2007/12/19/ie8-passes-acid2-test-2/* (accessed February 12, 2008).

In the case of an image, you'd use a MIME type identifying the image (e.g., image/gif) followed by a Base64 representation of the binary image. To create a Base64 representation of a binary image you can use the online data URL generator at *http://www.sveinbjorn.org/dataurlmaker*.

Here is an example:

```
<img src="data:image/gif;base64,R0lGODlhEAAOALMAAOazToeHhOtLS/7LZv/0jvb29t/f3//Ub//
ge8WSLf/rhf/3kdbW1mxsbP//mf///
yH5BAAAAAAALAAAAAAQAA4AAAAARe8L1Ekyky67QZ1hLnjM5UUdeOECwLJoExKcppVOaCcGCmTIHEIUEqjgaORC
MxIC6eOCcguWw6aFjsVMkkIr7g77ZKPJjPZqIyd7sJAgVGoEGv2xsBxqNgYPj/gAwXEQA7" width="16"
height="14" alt="embedded folder icon">
```

The resultant image is a folder icon (see Figure 9-14).

Figure 9-14. The folder icon

Disadvantages of inline images

The Base64 textual representation of image data also takes up more bytes than the binary image. In our tests, the Base64 data was 39% to 45% larger than the binary image, but with gzip compression the difference was reduced to only 8% to 9% larger.[21] Optimizing the images before converting to Base64 reduced the size of the string proportionally.

There are size limitations for inline images. Browsers are required to support URIs of up to only 1,024 bytes in length, according to RFC 2397. Browsers are more liberal in what they'll accept, however. Opera limits data URIs to about 4,100 characters.[22] Firefox supports data URIs up to 100 KB, so this technique is best used for small, decorative images.

CSS and inline images

Embedded in XHTML files, data URI images are not cached for repeated use, nor are they cached from page to page. One technique to enable caching is to embed background images in external CSS files. CSS is cached by browsers, and these images can be reused with a selector. For example:

```
ul {list-style:none;}
ul > li {
    margin:0 0 .1em;
```

---

[21]For our inline image size comparison, the folder image was 526 bytes for the Base64 code, versus 409 bytes gzipped, versus 377 bytes for the folder image GIF.

[22]Mozilla Developer Center. February 12, 2007. "The data URL scheme." Mozilla Foundation, *http://developer.mozilla.org/en/docs/The_data_URL_scheme* (accessed February 11, 2008).

```
    background:url(data:image/gif;base64,R0lGODlhEAAOALMAAOazToeHhOtLS/7LZv/0jvb29t/
f3//Ub//ge8WSLf/rhf/3kdbW1mxsbP//mf///
yH5BAAAAAAALAAAAAAQAA4AAARe8L1Ekyky67QZ1hLnjM5UUde0ECwLJoExKcppV0aCcGCmTIHEIUEqjgaORC
MxIC6eOCcguWw6aFjsVMkkIr7g77ZKPJjPZqIyd7sJAgVGoEGv2xsBxqNgYPj/gAwXEQA7) top left no-
repeat; )
    height:14px;
    text-indent:1.5em;
}
</style>
```

Now the folder image is repeated for each instance of the li (or you could use a class or ID here as well):

```
<ul>
<li>Testing one</li>
<li>Two</li>
<li>Three</li>
</ul>
```

Figure 9-15 shows results in the page in Firefox.

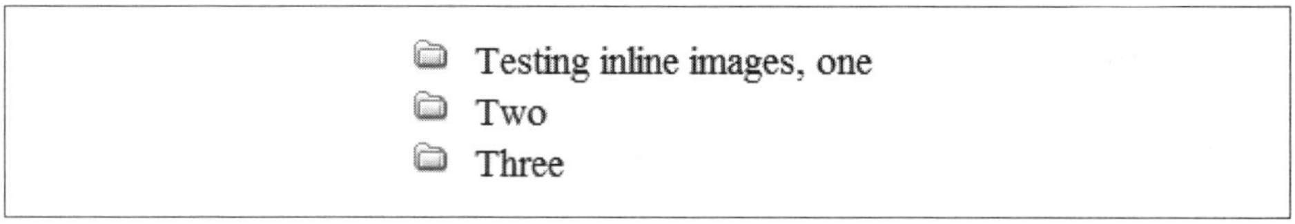

Figure 9-15. Caching an inline image with CSS

There is one issue with this approach. You must recalculate the Base64 data and edit the CSS file every time the image changes. The problem has a simple PHP solution:

```
<?php echo base64_encode(file_get_contents(" ../images/folder16.gif")) ?>
```

This code reads the image and converts it to Base64 automatically at the server. You pay for this editing convenience with some server-side processing.

Internet Explorer workarounds. There are two ways around the lack of data URI support in Internet Explorer versions 5 through 7. Using browser sniffing, you can simply show the external image for Internet Explorer and the embedded images for other browsers. Or you can use JavaScript to simulate data URI support in Internet Explorer, but this method requires a fair amount of JavaScript code.[23] The earlier PHP code makes insertion of the Base64 equivalent of an image easy:

```
ul {list-style:none;}
ul > li {
    margin:0 0 .1em;
```

---

[23]Herrera, B. March 25, 2005. "A Cross-Browser Method for Embedding Images in Self-Contained HTML Documents." BennHerrera.com, *http://www.bennherrera.com/EmbeddedImage/EmbeddedImageArticle.html* (accessed February 12, 2008).

```
    background: url(data:image/gif;base64,<?php echo base64_encode(file_get_
contents("../images/folder16.gif")) ?>) top left no-repeat;
    height:14px;
    text-indent:1.5em;
}
</style>
```

Now when your server parses the CSS file, it will automatically encode the binary image file into Base64 and send the encoded inline image data directly within the CSS file.

Next you need to add browser sniffing to deliver the image for Internet Explorer and the inline image for all others. You could do this within the CSS file with PHP or with conditional comments, like so:

```
<!-[if gte IE 5]>
<link type="text/css" rel="stylesheet" href="ie.css">

<![endif]-->

<!--[if !(IE)]>
<link type="text/css" rel="stylesheet" url="notie.css">
<![endif]-->
```

where the ie.css would have a normal image reference:

```
ul > li {
    margin:0 0 .1em;
    background: url("/images/folder16.gif") top left no-repeat;
...
```

For more information on this technique, see *http://en.wikipedia.org/wiki/Data:_URI_ scheme*.

Summary

This chapter highlighted some of the most effective server- and client-side techniques you can use to speed-optimize your website. You learned about optimizing parallel downloads using multiple hostnames, targeting frequently used objects for caching, and using HTTP compression to reduce text file sizes by 75%. We explored using delta encoding for RSS XML feeds, and using mod_rewrite to abbreviate and map search-friendly URIs. On the client side, we explored progressive enhancement to improve accessibility and performance, loading JavaScript on demand, caching off-site resources locally, and inlining images with data URIs.

You can use other techniques to shrink your content and improve server response times. To learn more, see the Speed Tweak blog at *http://www.websiteoptimization.com/speed/ tweak/*.

## CHAPTER 10

Website Optimization Metrics

What gets measured gets managed.

—Peter Drucker

Without quantifiable metrics, website optimization (WSO) is a guessing game. But with hundreds of billions of e-commerce dollars at stake, most companies cannot afford to guess.[1]

With web metrics, you can progressively improve your search engine marketing (SEM) campaigns, conversion rates, and website performance. The results of using these controlled experiments[2] are more profits, happier customers, and higher return on investment (ROI). The folks at Amazon.com have a saying that nicely sums up the gist of this chapter: "data trumps intuition."[3]

 Web analysts are a special breed. They're people who measure everything. They know how many miles per gallon their cars get, the expense associated with each mile, and which routes to take to increase efficiency. According to Jim Sterne, founder of the eMetrics Summit (*http://www.emetrics.org*), good web analysts are in short supply.[4]

---

[1] Eisenberg, B. November 26, 2007. "Future Now's 2007 Retail Customer Experience Study." Future Now, *http://www.grokdotcom.com/2007/11/26/cyber-monday-future-nows-2007-retail-customer-experience-study/* (accessed February 21, 2008). Forrester Research projects that U.S. online retail sales will grow to $316 billion by 2010.

[2] Kohavi, R. et al. 2007. "Practical Guide to Controlled Experiments on the Web: Listen to Your Customers, not to the HiPPO." In *KDD 2007* (San Jose, CA: August 12–15, 2007), 959–967. Don't listen to the Highest Paid Person's Opinion (HiPPO), but rather pay attention to experimental data. The researchers stress the importance of statistical power and sample size.

[3] Kohavi, R., and M. Round. 2004. "Front Line Internet Analytics at Amazon.com." In *eMetrics Summit 2004* (Santa Barbara, CA: June 2–4, 2004), *http://ai.stanford.edu/~ronnyk/emetricsAmazon.pdf* (accessed February 21, 2008).

[4] As of May 2008, there were 2,199 open jobs for "web analytics" at *http://www.simplyhired.com/a/jobs/list/q-%22web+analytics%22*.

Nevertheless, website owners are awash in a sea of data. With such a surfeit of statistics the variety of metrics available to analyze can be overwhelming. You can use web analytics software such as WebTrends to analyze server log data and provide standardized reports. But how do you choose the best metrics to measure website success? How do you best run controlled experiments such as A/B split tests, multivariate tests, and parallel flights? What is the best Overall Evaluation Criterion (OEC) for your particular goal?

This chapter will boil down this statistical tsunami to highlight the most effective metrics and techniques that you can use to optimize the effectiveness of your website.

What follows is a summary of the most effective metrics, including some you may have not yet seen. For each subject area (SEM and performance), we will then highlight the metrics that have the most impact on website success. Next, we'll show some examples of select metrics in action. Finally, we'll highlight some of the best tools you can use to measure and tweak websites. Let the optimization begin!

Website Success Metrics

Although website content optimization is basically common sense—who doesn't want a fast, easy-to-find site with engaging content?—it helps to know the real impact that it can have on your audience growth, engagement, and ultimately, conversion and monetization. The following are generally accepted, simple metrics that you can change through the optimization techniques detailed in this book. Figure 10-1 shows some of them in action.

Unique visitors
> Hits are not what you think. A server hit is an HTTP request for a single web object. One web page view can require many hits to the server. The true mark of how you should measure your audience is in unique visitors. You want to increase your unique audience by providing fast, engaging, relevant, and navigable web pages. Tracking new unique visitors can help you track audience growth.

Average time on site (ATOS) and length of visit
> How long are your users sticking around? According to ClickTracks, ATOS is one of the best measures of user engagement and the propensity to buy.[5]

Pages per visit
> The number of pages that were consumed during a visit is a broad and simple measure of user engagement. Pages per visit and ATOS are two measures that can indicate possible flow states of high engagement.

---

[5] Eisenberg, B. et al. 2006. *Call to Action: Secret Formulas to Improve Online Results* (Nashville, TN: Thomas Nelson), 218.

Controlled Experiments: Powerful Change

In isolation, human intuition is poor at predicting the value of novel or radical ideas. We are bad at assessing changes that are not incremental. We often confuse ourselves with the target audience. We bias our intuitive decisions with anchoring, or rely too heavily on one point of reference. Experts can experience overconfidence and can be influenced by office politics.[a] Controlled experiments, however, are immune to these drawbacks. To find the best alternatives, controlled experiments can confirm or refute our intuitive judgment of proposed website changes.

Controlled experiments are tests in which users are randomly shown one of several variants (e.g., control and treatment in a simple A/B test). User interactions are instrumented, and an Overall Evaluation Criterion (OEC) is computed for each variant. Any difference in the OEC between the control and the treatment can be explained by only one of two things: the change itself, or random chance. Everything external to the system impacts both factors in the same way. Statistical tests are made to rule out the possibility that the change is due to chance, so if the difference is statistically significant, what remains is that the change is responsible for the difference in the OEC. This establishes causality.

Even small changes can have significant effects. Amazon found that every 100 ms increase in the load time of its pages decreased sales by 1%.[b]

Microsoft has done extensive research on this topic, and Ronny Kohavi, general manager, is in charge of Microsoft's Experimentation Platform (*http://exp-platform.com*). After performing numerous web-based controlled experiments, Kohavi offered the following advice:

- Conduct single-factor tests to study decoupled incremental design changes.
- Make bold bets on different designs and iterate the winner.
- Use factorial designs when you suspect that several factors may interact.
- Watch out for the primacy effects of new features; new users can be utilized to avoid this effect.
- Integrate controlled experiments into your system to avoid coding errors and allow fast failures.
- Lower the cost of experimentation and thus increase the number of experiments.

Ideally, companies create a controlled experimental platform where they can run experiments faster. This will reduce the cost of failure and encourage iterative improvement. Optimost.com, Offermatica from Omniture, and Google Website Optimizer all offer the ability to run controlled experiments. Because these products depend on Java-Script modifications to call services, they are platform-independent.

---

[a] Kohavi, R. 2005. "Focus the Mining Beacon: Lessons and Challenges from the World of E-Commerce." In *PKDD 2005* (Porto, Portugal: October 3–7, 2005). Invited keynote.

[b] Kohavi, R., and R. Longbotham. 2007. "Online Experiments: Lessons Learned." *Computer* 40 (9): 103–105. This is an Amazon statistic taken from a presentation by Greg Linden at Stanford: *http://home.blarg.net/~glinden/StanfordDataMining.2006-11-29.ppt*, November 29, 2006.

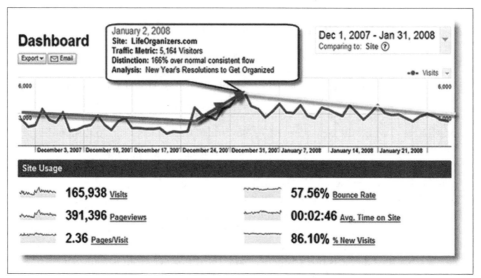

Figure 10-1. *Google Analytics dashboard showing site usage trends*

Bounce rate

The bounce rate is the percentage of users who left your site without browsing to another page or terminating by some means within a certain period of time. You should examine pages with high bounce rates closely for improvement to content or technical impediments.

Conversion rates

The ratio of the number of objectives accomplished (i.e., sales, cart additions, opt-ins, etc.) when compared to unique visitors is your conversion rate. You can boost your conversion rate in myriad ways, all of which you can test. See Chapter 5 for more information on increasing conversion rates.

Primary content consumption

Every site visit has to have an entry point. This is the percentage of times that a page constitutes the first impression of a site.

PathLoss

PathLoss is the percentage of times that a page was seen within a visitor's navigation path where the visit was terminated without bouncing. PathLoss can indicate attenuation, distraction, incomplete information, faulty navigation, or a misguided search marketing tactic.

ROI by keyword or campaign

Which keywords or campaigns are making you the most money? ClickTracks and other analytics software can track these metrics.

Cost per conversion

> If the cost per conversion for a particular campaign, ad group, or keyword is larger than the average sale value for the associated item, you'll lose money. Find a better way to do it with an ROI calculator.

Popular Web Metrics

How are companies measuring website success? According to JupiterResearch, companies use metrics to track the basic measures of click-throughs, impressions, site interaction, and engagement, as well as rich metrics such as online registration (66%), online purchases (55%), revenue per order (37%), and profit per order (23%). Advertisers using cross-tactic optimization techniques have shown higher usage of each of these metrics.[6]

Measuring SEM success

How do companies measure the success of their SEM campaigns? According to a survey by the Search Engine Marketing Professional Organization (SEMPO), the most popular metrics used to track the success of companies' SEM campaigns are to:

> Report overall traffic levels (73%)
> Determine conversion rates (71%)
> Determine click-through rates, or CTRs (68%)

Tracking ROI comes in fourth at 62% (see Figure 10-2).[7]

In Figure 10-2, you can see that the top two reasons for using website metrics are related to traffic measurement. Knowing how your unique visitors and impressions are growing is a good start, but what *types* of visitors are visiting your site? What fraction of users is on broadband? Where are they coming from? Is your traffic organic search engine, PPC, bookmark, or link-driven traffic? Are users aborting page loads partway through or are they engaged? How much revenue are you generating per order? What is the average amount of time spent on your site? As you delve deeper into the metrics matrix, you'll find that with more sophisticated analytics software you can glean more of this type of detail.

Next, we'll explore the different types of metrics tools that are available, including server-side, client-side, a hybrid of both, and user experience testing software that acts as a virtual usability lab.

---

[6] Riley, E., I. Mitskaviets, and D. Card. 2007. "Optimization: Maximizing ROI Through Cross-Tactic Optimization." JupiterResearch, *http://www.jupiterresearch.com* (accessed February 12, 2008).

[7] SEMPO. December 2006. "Search Engine Marketing Professional Organization survey of SEM agencies and advertisers, December 2006. Global Results." SEMPO, *http://www.sempo.org* (accessed February 12, 2008).

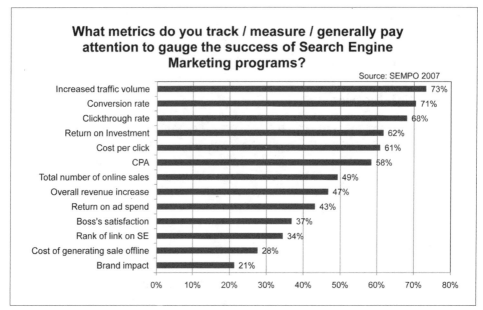

Figure 10-2. *Metrics used to measure SEM campaign success*

Types of Web Analytics Software

There are two common types of analytics technologies to be aware of: *web server log analysis* and *JavaScript page tagging*. Individually, these methods each have their pros and cons. Taken together, they provide a holistic view of what is going on with your website from both server-side and client-side perspectives. A brief overview of each method, as well as a hybrid of the two, follows.

You'll learn how you can use these methods to track the success metrics outlined earlier with the recommended tools. You'll also read about two more advanced analytics tools, namely Google Website Optimizer and the user experience tool WebEffective from Keynote Systems.

Web Server Log Analysis

Web servers record every single HTTP transaction in text files known as *logs*. This includes every image, Cascading Style Sheet (CSS), JavaScript, HTML page, and any other file served to your visitors.

Because this data is already available on the web server, there is no need to modify your pages to start receiving data. Thus, there is no decrease in performance. You need only install a log analysis tool, configure it (consolidate browser IDs, eliminate internal traffic, exclude bots, etc.), and point it to the logs. However, installation is not as simple as in JavaScript page tagging, and is typically performed by a system administrator.

Webalizer, AWStats, and Analog are three of the commonly supplied logfile analysis tools. They are all free. Because server logs are usually in a standard format, they will work across all platforms and web servers. For more details on these packages, see the following sites:

- Webalizer, *http://www.mrunix.net/webalizer/*
- AWStats, *http://awstats.sourceforge.net/*
- Analog, *http://www.analog.cx/*

Commercial Web Analytics Packages

Commercial web analytics packages feature either logfile analysis, client-side tagging, or both. Two popular packages are WebTrends and ClickTracks.

WebTrends Analytics
> An online marketing analytics solution available for both software and hosted implementations. It supports both logfile analysis and client-side data collection via JavaScript tagging. The product provides predefined reports for measuring and optimizing the performance of online marketing campaigns, organic and paid search engine traffic, pages and content groups, Web 2.0 content, paths and conversion funnels, products and merchandising, visitor segmentation, and geographic analysis.

ClickTracks web analytics
> Available as a hosted web service. Part of Lyris's marketing suite, Lyris HQ, Click-Tracks features intuitive reports that overlay behavior data on top of each web page. Using client-side JavaScript, ClickTracks users can analyze site visitors by PPC campaign, email campaign, search keyword, search engine, purchase behavior, or other measures. ClickTracks shows visitors' behavior—from their entry point into the site through their purchase, lead generation activity, or exit—in the context of the actual website. It provides predefined reports on site navigation patterns, page views over time, ATOS, ROI, return on advertising spend (ROAS), click fraud, and funnel reports.

AWStats, for example, breaks out humans from search robots in its summary traffic report (see Figure 10-3). The behavior of web robots, spiders, and crawlers is something that JavaScript-based analytics tools cannot show you, because search engines cannot execute JavaScript and send data back to the tracking server.

Server hits and an accurate count of bytes sent are also information that you will not get from a JavaScript-based solution. These two metrics can help you benchmark the performance of your web server. Log analyzers can also show you reports on 404s (Page Not Found errors) along with the referring page to help you track down broken links. You can also find this type of information through Google Webmaster Central's Sitemaps tool, at *http://www.google.com/webmasters/*.

Summary					
Reported period	Month Sep 2007				
First visit	01 Sep 2007 - 00:54				
Last visit	30 Sep 2007 - 22:56				
	Unique visitors	Number of visits	Pages	Hits	Bandwidth
Viewed traffic *	1593	2288 (1.43 visits/visitor)	11158 (4.87 Pages/Visit)	57934 (25.32 Hits/Visit)	1.03 GB (469.91 KB/Visit)
Not viewed traffic *			17235	27909	678.71 MB
* Not viewed traffic includes traffic generated by robots, worms, or replies with special HTTP status codes.					

Figure 10-3. AWStats breaking out viewed and not viewed traffic

The drawback to log analyzers is that they will not see transactions that do not take place on the server, such as interaction with DHTML on the page, or web pages that are cached by the user's web browser. For busy sites that see heavy traffic, logfiles can become huge over a short period of time. For these reasons, as well as the desire to centralize and outsource analytic data services, JavaScript page tagging was born.

JavaScript Page Tagging

Analytics tools based on JavaScript page tagging are popular for their ease of installation and for their ability to track cached page views and non-HTTP interactions within Flash movies, DHTML, or Ajax, assuming the analytics code is in the cached page.

The technology works by adding a bit of JavaScript to a page, or *tagging* it. When a user loads the page in a browser, the code is executed and sends a 1×1-pixel transparent GIF image back to a web server with information collected about the page view.

Installation is easy and is typically a cut-and-paste operation. To install Google Analytics, a developer need only include this bit of code on every page in the site by means of a site-wide footer:

```
<script type="text/javascript" src="http://www.google-analytics.com/ga.js"></script>
<script type="text/javascript">  var pageTracker = _gat._getTracker("UA-xxxxxx-x");
pageTracker._initData();   pageTracker._trackPageview();</script>
```

Unlike with log analysis tools, you can also track JavaScript or Flash events caused by widgets that don't necessarily call the server. In Google Analytics, you can do this through the trackPageview function.

Say we want to count a page view every time a user clicks the Next button in a photo gallery without refreshing the page. We could write the following bit of JavaScript:

```
<input type="button" onclick="getNextPhoto(); pageTracker._trackPageview('/photo-
gallery/next/');" value="Next" />
```

Now when users interact with our photo gallery, even though the page does not fully refresh, we will record a page view. You can find more instructions on this level of tagging at *http://www.google.com/support/googleanalytics/bin/answer. py?answer=55597&topic=10981.*

JavaScript tagging can also provide more information about the user's browsing capabilities, whereas log analyzers rely on the `User-Agent` header sent with the browser to gather insight in this area (which can be and sometimes is forged, especially in Firefox and Opera):

```
User-Agent: Mozilla/4.0 (compatible; MSIE 6.0; Windows NT 5.1; SV1; .NET CLR 1.1.
    4322; .NET CLR 2.0.50727; .NET CLR 3.0.04506.30)
```

JavaScript-based analytics solutions can give you information about screen size, color support, and installed browser plug-ins (e.g., Flash, Java) in addition to browser and operating system types. Unlike server-side logfile analysis, JavaScript tagging incurs a performance hit from both downloading and executing the JavaScript and the overhead of the image beacon. Improperly coded, external resources can grind your pages to a halt if the tracking server goes down or becomes unresponsive.

Multivariate testing with Google Website Optimizer

Google's Website Optimizer is a free A/B testing tool that allows developers to run controlled experiments. Released in late 2006, Website Optimizer has revolutionized the testing of multiple variations to optimize conversion rates. Now there is no need to purchase specialized software run by white-coated lab technicians to run multivariate tests. Website Optimizer packages the mathematics of statistical power, sample size, and random variation into an intuitive integrated system. Figure 10-4 shows an overview of how Website Optimizer works.

You can use Website Optimizer as an A/B split testing service for sites with lower page traffic (less than 1,000 page views per week) that want to test alternatives, or as a multivariate testing platform for busier sites that want to test multiple content changes simultaneously.

Using Google's interface, developers take the following steps to run a multivariate test:

1. Choose the elements to test.
2. Set up the experiment by inserting JavaScript in various places in the target pages.
3. Launch the variations.
4. Analyze the results.

Step 2 uses JavaScript to randomly display and monitor content variations. A header script, page control script, and tracking script do the heavy lifting. The greater the number of combinations, the more traffic or time will be needed to have enough statistical power to achieve a significant result. Google Website Optimizer is a great way to try out different ideas to maximize your conversion rates. For more information about Website Optimizer, see *http://www.google.com/websiteoptimizer/*.

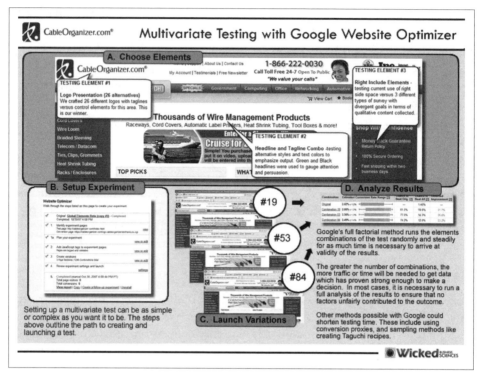

Figure 10-4. Multivariate testing with Google Website Optimizer

Hybrid Analytics Systems

By combining logfile analysis with client-side tracking, you can harness the best features of both. UsaProxy is a hybrid analytics system developed by University of Munich researchers that can track both client-side interaction and HTTP activity.[8]

The UsaProxy architecture is HTTP-based. It has a proxy server that automatically injects JavaScript into web pages to track client-side behavior. It also improves logfile functionality by recording both HTTP requests as well as client-side activity such as mouse movements and document object model (DOM) interaction within the same logfile. Here is a sample from an actual logfile showing mousemove and keypress activity:

```
127.0.0.1 2007-12-02,23:04:46 httptraffic url=http://mail.google.com/mail/ sd=624
127.0.0.1 2008-00-02,23:04:48 sd=627 sid=Adn1KROHr8VT event=load size=0x0
127.0.0.1 null httptraffic url=http://mail.google.com/mail/?ui=2 ik=ae8caaf240
view=cbj sd=632
127.0.0.1 2008-00-02,23:04:48 sd=627 sid=Adn1KROHr8VT event=load size=300x150
```

---

[8] Atterer, R. et al. 2006. "Knowing the user's every move: User activity tracking for website usability evaluation and implicit interaction." In *WWW 2006* (Edinburgh, Scotland: May 23–26, 2006), 203–212.

```
127.0.0.1 2007-12-02,23:05:02 httptraffic url=http://mail.google.com/mail/ sd=649
127.0.0.1 2008-00-02,23:05:06 sd=627 sid=Adn1KROHr8VT event=mousemove offset=75,27
coord=84,54 dom=abaaaaaaaaaababcaaa
127.0.0.1 2008-00-02,23:06:24 sd=627 sid=Adn1KROHr8VT event=keypress key=shift+H
127.0.0.1 2008-00-02,23:06:25 sd=627 sid=Adn1KROHr8VT event=keypress key=m
```

The combined logfile allows finer-grained analysis, timings, and overlays of client-side interaction on web pages (see Figure 10-5).

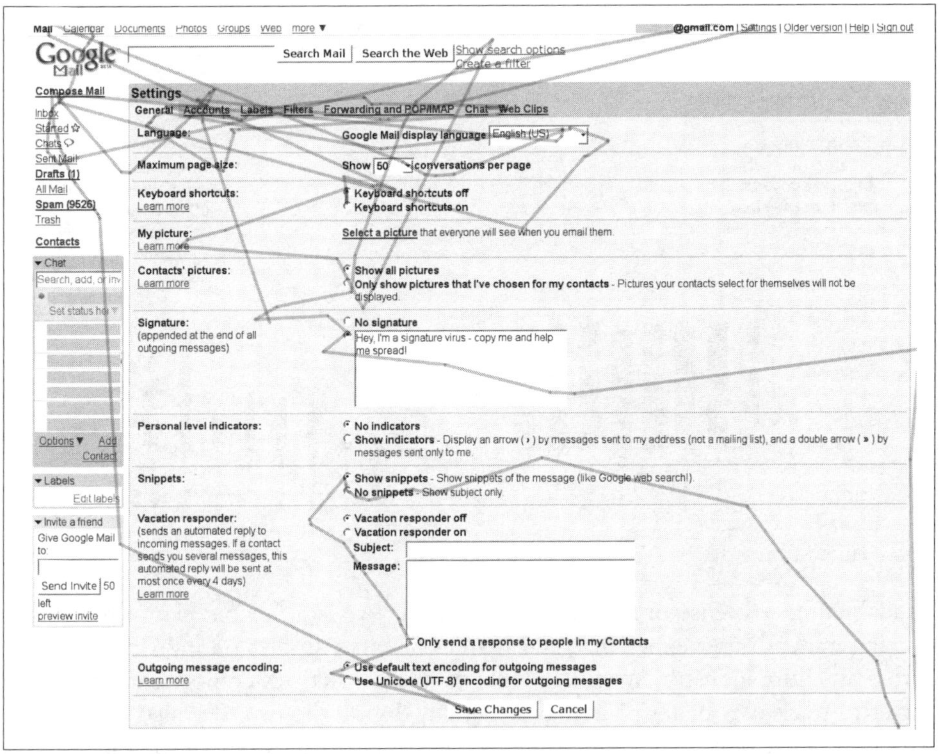

Figure 10-5. Mouse trails recorded by an HTTP proxy overlaid onto a screenshot

The advantage to the HTTP proxy technique is that there is no need to tag pages. One disadvantage is that HTTP compression is disabled while gathering data. You should run UsaProxy only for logging on a live website when site visitors have agreed to it, because the high level of detail raises some privacy concerns, such as login identifiers and passwords. The UsaProxy software is available at *http://fnuked.de/ usaproxy/*.

User Experience Testing Software

What if you want to track metrics across multiple sites, including those of your competitors? Or compare task completion success to user attitudes? That's where User Experience (UX) testing software comes into play. UX testing was once the exclusive domain of usability labs. Now UX software semiautomates user experience testing with specialized software for running usability tests and capturing results. Keynote Systems' WebEffective software is one such UX testing platform (see Figure 10-6).

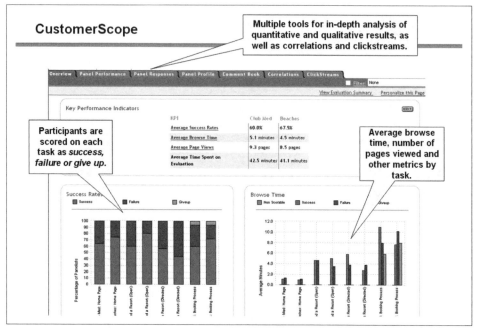

Figure 10-6. Keynote Systems' WebEffective output

Available under license or as a service, WebEffective is a flexible platform for conducting in-depth user experience and market research studies on individual sites or across an entire industry. WebEffective uses a small ActiveX component or a proxy server to track user behavior and gather input during the test. Detailed clickstream data is available only through Internet Explorer and the ActiveX control, but you can use WebEffective with all other browsers for task-based testing. Researchers design and deploy tests that include screening panelists and running tasks on one or more sites, while at the same time gathering detailed information on user activity and success rates. The tool provides a window into the real-world attitudes, behaviors, and intentions of users. For instance, users tend to overestimate success rates when compared to actual drop-off rates (see Figure 10-7).

The significance of Figure 10-7 is that 70% of testers said they completed the task, but only 20% of those actually completed the task as it was designed to be completed.

The software provides robust reporting tools, showing success rates, browsing time, page views, stay and load times, and other metrics. More important, it integrates user feedback with results (shown in Figure 10-7). So, not only do you find out *what* happened, but you can also learn *why* it happened. Figure 10-8 shows some sample results from a comparison between the Club Med and Beaches websites.

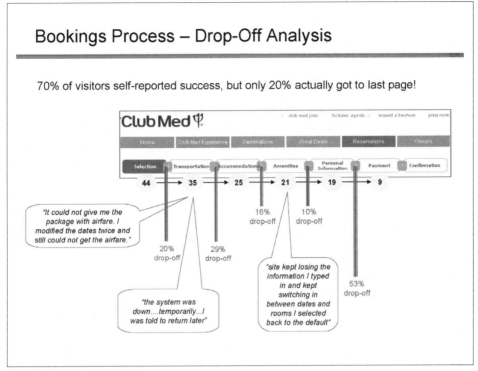

Figure 10-7. Conversion funnel with drop-off rates and comments

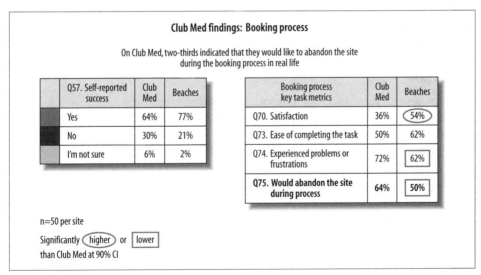

Figure 10-8. Club Med findings: booking process

This kind of integrated approach to usability testing can boost conversion rates significantly without the need for an expensive usability laboratory. Think of it as a global usability lab without walls.

Search Engine Marketing Metrics

Search metrics help marketers improve website PR campaigns and conversion rate optimization (CRO) efforts. By tracking your progress over time or against the competition, you can optimize the effectiveness of your advertising budget. By running controlled experiments to compare alternatives, you can quickly determine higher return strategies. The type of analytics software that you choose to use is less important than which metrics you choose to measure.

Search Marketing Strategy

Search marketing is all about strategy. It's thinking about moves, trying them out, measuring, making predictions, testing, and going back and trying them over and over again until you find what works for your site.

Let's face it. The mechanics of setting up PPC campaigns and site submission can be successfully taught to relatively inexperienced personnel. The true work in search marketing is in developing theory and testing it with enough statistical power, by which we mean *validity*, to realize significant change. Web analytics information can tell marketers the language and specific word combinations that are most frequently used on a per-page basis within their sites. That information is the key to making good decisions on where and at what level to expend financial resources for the benefit of the company.

Optimal paths

Think of your website as a digital informational organism composed of smaller subordinate organs or pages. The relationship between a page and its purpose is directly correlated to its value (you value your heart more than your appendix, right?). Every major goal for a site has an optimal path for navigation from the home page and popular, or valued, landing pages. The notion of a page within an optimal path is where measurement should begin, but this is the most common omission made by analysts.

Classes of Metrics

Now that you're collecting and analyzing SEM metrics data, how do you use it? To better explain how metrics fit into the big picture, the Web Analytics Association (WAA) categorized them through counts, ratios, and key performance indicators (KPIs).[9]

---

[9] Burby, J., and A. Brown. August 16, 2007. "Web Analytics Definitions." Web Analytics Association, *http://www.webanalyticsassociation.org* (accessed February 5, 2008).

Research conducted by Wicked Business Sciences argues that website metrics can be categorized into four basic functional classifications: volume, content, means, and objectives.[10] In some descriptions, the words *means* and *content* may appear to be a part of the same grouping. Regardless of how you categorize metrics, by placing any metric into one of these groupings you can more easily find the context and relevance of each of the numbers and how they relate to your overall goals.

Volume

Volume is, quite simply, "How many?" Volume is any metric that deals with percentages of the whole. Metrics such as unique visitors, sessions, and page views are volume measures.

Content

Content refers to the quantified behaviors exhibited on a site. Content metrics help to gauge how users respond to the presentation, layout, and persuasiveness of the materials on the page as it relates to the site's primary purpose. When the goal is optimization, content should be valuable to search engines and engaging to your human audience. Messages need to be carefully crafted to entice users and help them find the action areas of the page easily. Content is the primary area for experimentation for both quantitative and qualitative analysis. We discussed it in more detail in Chapter 5.

Objectives

Objectives are the actions that you want users to take. These are exhibited behaviors indicative of the primary purpose of the site. In some sites, this might be a visit resulting in a sale. In others, it might be something like a user signing up for a newsletter or commenting on a blog post.

Means

The means are the aggregated paths into and away from the objectives. These are the most qualitatively rich and contextually fulfilling metrics of a website. The class of means includes page-based metrics, contributions, and compositions. It also represents the multitude of opportunities to optimize the site's messages at their most influential position. This area speaks directly to marketing.

---

[10]Shields, D. December 15, 2007. "Definitions of Web Analytics Metrics by Classification of Function." Wicked Business Sciences, *http://wickedsciences.com/research/white-papers/5163,0512,1215,2007.pdf* (accessed February 4, 2008).

You can break down each general metric class into sets of specific metrics that comprise the widely used measures of the Web. By organizing them by function, we can show their relationships to each other, to the larger classifications, and to the world of people and behaviors that create them.

The remainder of this section will clearly illustrate these metrics in action.

Volume Metrics

Volume is primarily broken down into traffic metrics or numbers, independent of any operations. The WAA refers to this as *count*. These metrics house the building blocks that are the most familiar to members of your optimization team. Some basic volume metrics include page views, visits or sessions, and unique visitors.

Page views

A page view is the act of calling a single, completely loaded URI from a server. With the increasingly volatile adoption of new technologies to provide useful content—things such as Flash, Ajax, RSS and XML—this volume term is becoming increasingly fuzzy. The page views metric is still in use, but it has become somewhat less useful.

Visits or sessions

A visit or session is the act of requesting one or more pages from within the defined parameters of a specific site. Each subsequent page view, as long as it remains within the agreed length of inactivity prior to session termination, counts as part of that single session. A common standard is to view 30 minutes of inactivity (or lack of tag collection) from a single site. Sessions also terminate when the browser is closed.

Unique visitors

Ideally, a unique visitor count would be the number of real people who have visited your site within a specified time frame. This is actually not the case for log-based analyzers. With JavaScript-based systems each user gets a unique cookie, which ensures that each person accessing from the same IP (e.g., an office LAN) counts as a unique visitor. Unique visitors refer to the unique browsers that have acquired their first tag in a solution per IP in a given time frame. Cookie deletion can cause issues in this realm.

 The WAA remains attached to the idea that unique visitors are, in fact, people.

The metrics we just discussed detail the packaged volume metrics of most enterprise solutions. For WSO purposes, these metrics are used as denominators in equations to get a sense of the ratios where objectives are posed as the numerator. Analysts at events such as the eMetrics Summit (*http://www.emetrics.org*) and the Semphonic XChange (*http://semphonic.com/conf/*) frequently discuss the need for new metrics. Based on those venues and on publications presented by the WAA, some additional standardized metrics might be included in this publication's volume classification. These include the following.

New visitors

The WAA defines new visitors as "The number of Unique Visitors with activity including a first-ever visit to a site during a reporting period." *New visitor* is a useful alternative term for *first-time visitor* because it addresses the idea that the user is not only a unique visitor, but also that her first actual visit to the site occurred within the time frame of the report. This fundamental volume term can be extremely useful in gauging marketing and optimization efforts.

 Some vendor tools may handle the *new visitor* designation differently.

You can test new users to eliminate the *primacy effect* that sometimes occurs for new features. For example, a new navigational system may be better, but may initially show lower usability for existing users.

Repeat visitors

A repeat visitor is a unique visitor who visits more than once in a given time frame. This, of course, is dependent on the cookie deletion rate for tag-based solutions, multiple browser use, and the percentage of unique IPs experienced over the same time period. The numbers associated with this metric can be tricky. As stated earlier, it is important to consult the definitions in your particular analytics solution to adjust this metric to fit into the confines of the tool.

Instances

Although Omniture SiteCatalyst uses the term *instances* rather ambiguously, it is a handy metric. Instances refer to the number of times an event occurs. It may be used to quantify searches on a site, or for the execution of some page behavior. As more sites begin to transition to live-writable data tables updated by Ajax or off-site XML, this most likely will become a more important metric of consideration.

Content Metrics: Measuring Each Component

Content metrics deal with specific functions of web pages. Content has virtues based on function within a hierarchy of overlapping dimensions. Content is defined by its purpose within the structure of a website to supplement the primary goal.

Entry page
> The page on a website where the visit originates.

Landing pages
> Entry pages that are specifically designed to convert users for marketing campaigns.

Segue pages
> Pages that exist for the purpose of taking a user from a general informative state of gathering information into an actionable state. Segues may be subcategory pages or a topic cloud.

Action pages
> Pages that are meant to elicit a response from the user. Examples are product pages with an "Add to Cart" action function or any blog page where the author invites users to comment. Bloggers have so few valuable metrics by which to truly measure their success that a major conversion metric for a blog might be the number of comments per post or article.

Fulfillment pages
> Pages whose primary function is the exchange of information.

Content is evaluated and measured on a page-by-page basis. Each page is taken as a single entity for the purpose of its improvement. In addition, each page should conform to the actionable goals of the entire site. As such, each page comes with a set of metrics that help to evaluate a subset of purposeful valuations.

Each page is potentially a landing page as well as a page within a path to the ultimate goal. This tension between *destination* and *path* creates the duality of page design. Optimization efforts, then, must prepare the page for the best results of each world. This encompasses principles of:

- Search engine readability and relevance
- Clear and visible navigational cues
- Persuasive and engaging content

Entries

Entries are the origination of a visit. This might be perceived as a volume metric, but because entries are typically used in making determinations for a single page of content, it can be argued that they are most applicable to content metrics. Because this term is frequently used in the context of content valuation, this metric is defined as content by virtue of its primary function.

Single-access visits

Like entries, single-access visits are a building-block volume term used to build out calculated metrics for content. A single-access visit is literally a bounce.

Bounce rate (and simple engagement)

> Bounce rate = single-access visits / total entries

The bounce rate is the percentage of people who arrive on a page and leave it within a defined period of time without performing any action that shows engagement. This is actually a packaged metric in Google Analytics and a calculated metric in other solutions. It is an inherently negative metric.

For reporting purposes, consider using simple engagement, the formula for which follows:

> Simple engagement = 1 − (single-access visits / total entries)

Simple engagement is the reciprocated percentile created by subtracting the bounce rate from 1. In other words, it is an *inversion* of the "bounce rate" metric. It is a great metric for quickly determining whether visitors find content immediately relevant and engaging. It can point to major deficiencies in a page's design or content. You also can use it to measure the effectiveness of a new ad campaign.

Killer Keywords

Bounce rate or simple engagement can give an analyst a quick means to identify fundamental issues with a page. Usually a very high bounce rate indicates that there is a loading problem with a server or script on a page, or a major keyword flaw. One client provided this example with the search word *clutter*. After looking into pages where *clutter* was a frequently sought-after term, we noticed traffic coming in from their paid campaigns using that word in the context of results for "Clutter Family Murders."

The murders of the Clutter family were described in the book *In Cold Blood* by Truman Capote (Random House). This was not exactly what they were looking for in traffic. Therefore, with the high bounce rate, we decided to flag *family* and *murder* as negative keywords, thus reducing the likelihood of getting inadvertent traffic. Using these negative keywords reduced our client's bounce rate on those pages, as well as their costs on those campaigns.

Figure 10-9 illustrates the bounce rate per search engine referring visits to CableOrganizer.com during a given time period. Baidu and Yandex appear to give the highest bounce. This should not be surprising, as CableOrganizer.com provides no content in the dominant languages of those search engines.

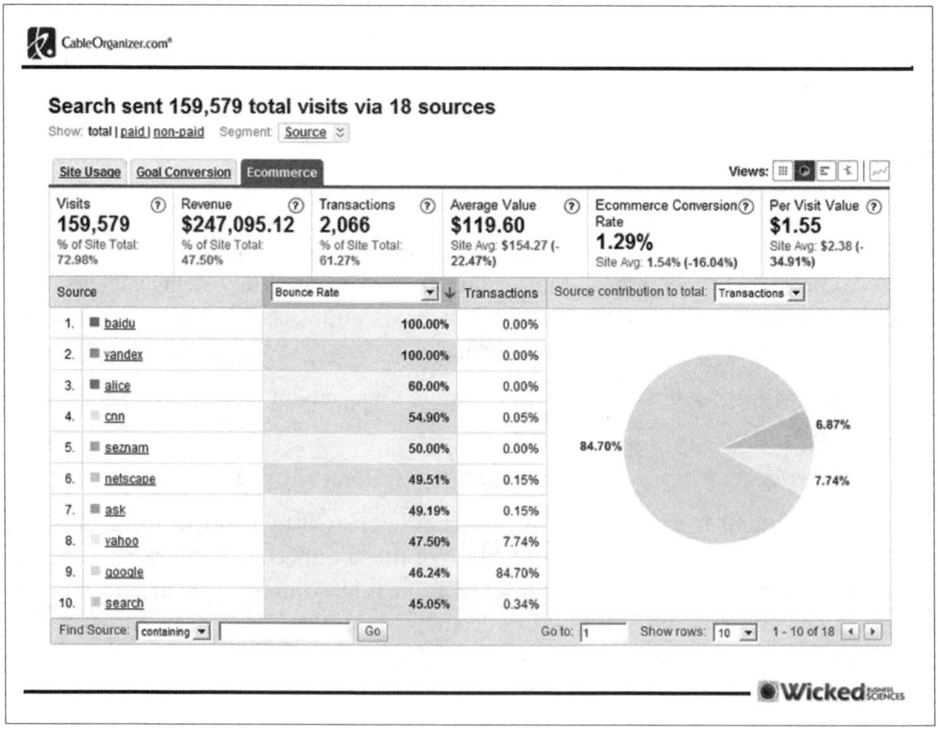

Figure 10-9. Bounce rate per search engine referring visits

Google Analytics also provides pie charts, comparative charting, and trending to show metrics assigned to certain timelines and composition models.

Revenue per visit(or)

On a content basis in e-commerce, it is important to understand how each page contributes to the site's success. The amount of revenue per visit or per page view can be a very important metric to note when optimizing a site.

Page attrition

1 – (primary objective / immediately preceding step of primary objective)

Page attrition is a reciprocated metric. It is similar to bounce rate in that it is inherently a negatively connotative metric and it indicates an action that is undesirable. This metric shows the percentage of people exposed to a single page and who do not act on the content of that page in a positive way.

PathWeight and ProxyScoring

PathWeight is a metric CableOrganizer.com invented to identify the importance of each page within the optimal path to conversion. This algorithm is based on inputs associated with each of the important components of a page. PathWeight indicates its value in comparison to pages of the same tier in relation to the primary objective. When sorted by PathWeight, pages of equal characterization and hierarchy should be isolated together (see Figure 10-10).

ProxyScoring is the idea that, when going into testing and optimization scenarios, you need to present success metrics within the specific context of the page's purpose. Developing a series of powerful calculated metrics, it is possible to employ surrogate conversion metrics. In doing so, the relative success of a page becomes clear against the backdrop of otherwise indirect conversion metrics. A pleasant side effect is that using proxies based on this system, testing to optimize a page based on alternative objectives shortens the time needed to achieve statistically sound results.

We find that this is an excellent proxy scoring metric as well. When running a multivariate test, we often have to create a means to indicate proxies to conversion to speed up testing times. When a page is undesirably far away from the primary objective in terms of hierarchy and characterization, choosing pages with a high PathWeight or ProxyScore can bring the virtual conversion up as an objective and can cut testing time significantly.

Primary content consumption

PCC = [(page views) * (entries / visits)] / (total page views)

Primary content consumption is the percentage of each page as a portion of those aggregate first impressions. This percentile helps to sort pages based on the number

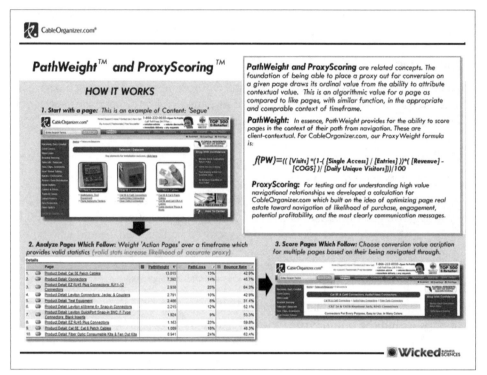

Figure 10-10. PathWeight and ProxyScoring in action

of times each is the first page representing your site. How important is this? If you consider that every page is a possible spokesperson for your brand, this metric can be the single most important metric by which to sort everything else.

PathLoss

PL = (exits – single access) / (page views – entries)

PathLoss[11] is the percentage of times a page was seen within a visitor's navigation path where the visit was terminated without bouncing. In other words, it is the percentage of times in which a potentially valuable visit ended prematurely. It might indicate attenuation, distraction, or the possibility of incomplete information (see Figure 10-11).

Exit rate (or page exit ratio)

ER = exit ratio = exits / page views

---

[11]PathLoss is a metric developed by Paul Holstein of CableOrganizer.com.

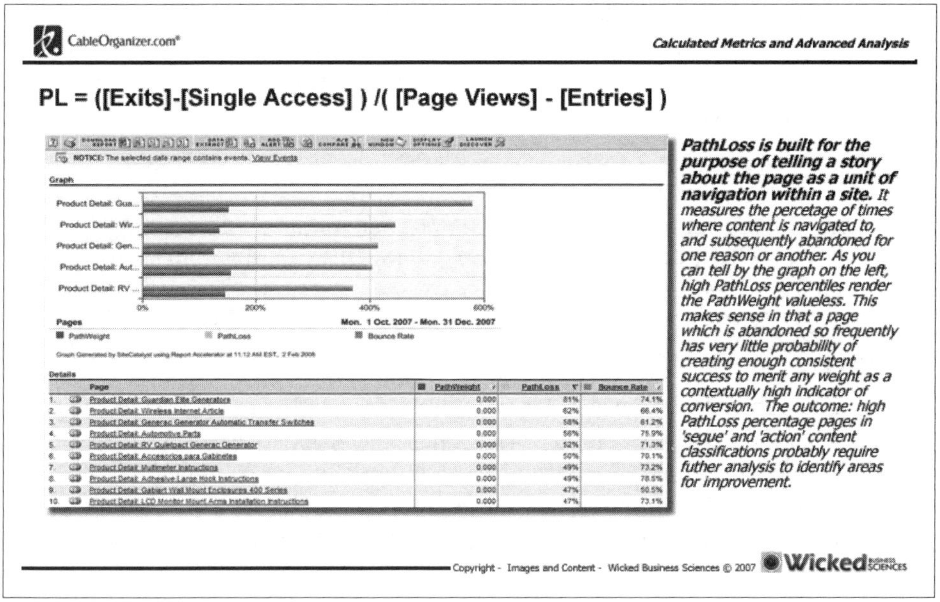

Figure 10-11. PathLoss metric showing path abandonment

Exit rate is the percentage of times a particular page acts as a means to exit the site. With the sole exception of the "Thank You" page for your shopping cart or other post-conversion closure, a high rate of exit means the page content has properties that are causing attrition.

By looking at a cross section of your website through the exit ratio, you can quickly identify where problems might exist or where language might be confusing or ambiguous.

Objectives

Optimization and analytics help you to understand the processes and behaviors of your users to get a sense of how to improve your site. They help you present the appropriate stimuli to evoke the desired impulse. By creating a system of objectives or checkpoints, a website becomes easier to build or improve. The checkpoints ultimately build a path or pattern up to and following through to a primary goal.

Understanding objectives

The objectives are the goals of your site. For some sites, the goals are sales or sign-ups. For other sites, they might be simply to engage the audience in viewing content such as videos or a blog. Whatever your site's purpose, you have goals. The number of times those goals are reached is a percentage of the number of opportunities the user was given to perform them. Objectives are made up of performance check-points and primary success metrics. Often, to create conversion metrics or ratios, we would place the objective in the position of the numerator and the count or volume in the place of the denominator.

Ad clicks

For informational pages that seek to build a revenue model on advertising, ad clicks are the primary goals. Collecting and analyzing this data can be difficult because all of the information has to come from diverse sources.

Goal pages

If the primary objective of a website is to provide information to the user, some pages can meet that objective better than others. That objective may need to be a page that is set up solely for that purpose. It could be a link off-site, or to some other page. Be sure to properly tag the location of your goal to ensure that you can collect, aggregate, and appropriately quantify it in relation to the volume metrics of your navigation activity.

Comments

For the benevolent bloggers who seek to inform and garner discussion, an appropriate objective might be to see commentary or trackbacks as the primary goal.

Orders

Orders are the single most important objective for any online retailer. Every business function is measured, in some way, on the ability to produce orders. A wise man once said that anything multiplied by zero is zero. If you have zero orders, revenue is a secondary consideration. However, once you can begin to accumulate orders, more interesting metrics become valuable, and eventually, a system of measurement and key performance indicators can be sifted from your silos of data.

Sign-ups

Sign-ups include signing up to a newsletter, subscribing to an RSS feed or blog community membership, and signing up to receive "Coming Soon" promotional ticklers. For example, Chumby.com marketed a cool alarm clock radio that plays a dashboard piped in from a Wi-Fi connection. For months, you couldn't get the product, but you were able to sign up so that when they started selling it you could "Be the First in YOUR neighborhood with a Chumby." It worked. We signed up.

Cart additions

Retailers view cart additions as a secondary metric. However, cart additions can be valuable for the purpose of looking into bigger problems that might exist on the site.

Your shipping calculator might be a persistent problem area. Your cart-addition-to-orders ratio is a great metric to monitor to show the impact on your conversion performance.

Conversion

CV = objective / opportunity

Conversion is essentially the number of times you reach a goal divided by the number of times where it was possible (see Figure 10-12).

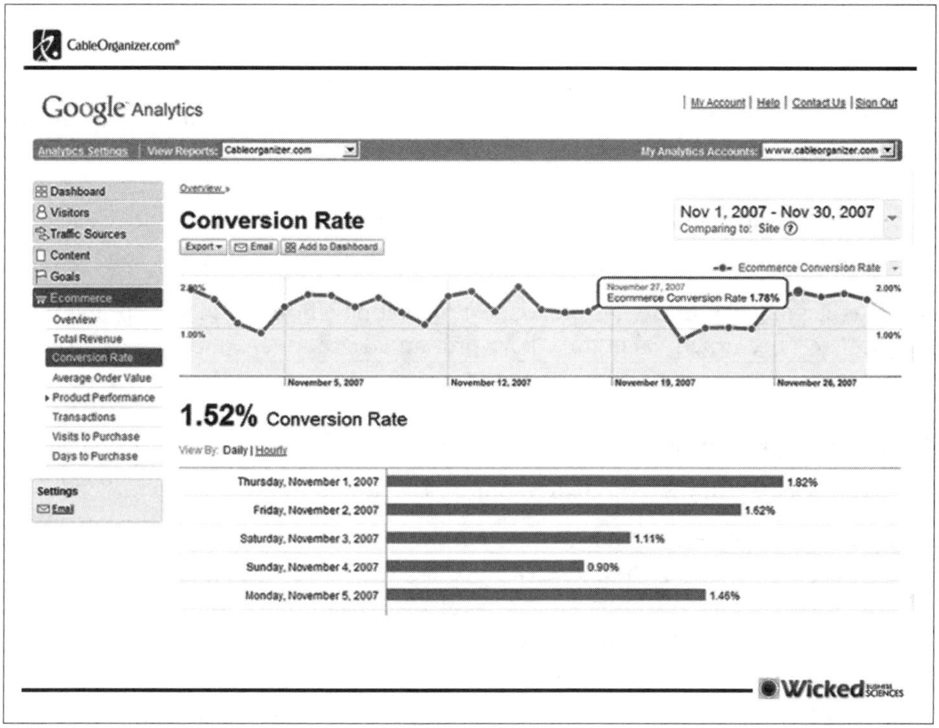

Figure 10-12. Conversion rate graph from Google Analytics

Measuring the Means

The means refers to the way in which a site visitor reached the objectives. The means are the previous sites, search engines, ad creatives, and campaign metrics. These measure the performance of efforts in advertising and marketing, and encompass search marketing and targeted content. In multiple types of analyses, you can use these metrics to make channels and functions accountable. You also can use them to alter strategies to increase the likelihood of success.

CPC: Cost per click

CPC = clicks / ad spend

CPC is the cost of each click on a banner or text ad. Search marketing bases this on a "bid" price, which is determined by the venue used and the terms described. Banner and graphics advertising can work on either a fixed CPC or with a bidding system. Generally, CPC is the preferred form of measurement over CPM (cost per 1,000 impressions) because it is more measurable and tangible than the CPM alternative.

CTR: Click-through rate

CTR = clicks / impressions

This is the rate at which users click on a displayed ad when starting a visit. Click-through is useful as a metric for multivariate tests of text or alternative creative advertisements.

ROAS: Return on ad spend

ROAS = revenue / cost of means

ROAS is a simple metric applicable to most marketing efforts. It is useful primarily as an estimate of returned value for a keyword, an ad group, a campaign, or a search engine.

ROI: Return on investment

ROI = yield – COGS – (human resources + ad costs)

ROI is a more complete version of the ROAS metric. Whereas ROAS only calculates return based on the keyword or creative costs by whichever incremental they are reported, ROI is valuable in its ability to calculate based on resource consumption, cost of goods sold (COGS), and holding costs. A solid program to maximize campaign value should track this metric.

Omniture has the ability to add what is called a VISTA rule (visitor identification, segmentation, and transformation architecture) to your campaign. VISTA rules correlate the cost of goods, per uniquely defined product, to product SKU or another variable from a hosted shopping cart solution (e.g., product ID). Being able to focus on the keywords that yield the highest ROI is much more valuable than a potentially problematic and incomplete metric such as ROAS.

Success Metrics = Reaching Goals

Improving your search engine marking success is all about reaching your goals. Web metrics quantifies those goals so that you can measure and improve your online marketing campaigns. Rather than measure simple volume metrics such as impressions and unique visitors, savvy analysts measure the value of each page within the context of how it contributes to the site's success. In other words, they measure how effective and engaging pages are within optimal paths, and how well they retain and attract users. Metrics such as primary content consumption, PathWeight, and Path-Loss proactively help you to locate these problem areas for improvement before they become trends in monthly reports.

Web Performance Metrics

At first glance, measuring the speed of a web page seems straightforward. Start a timer. Load up the page. Click Stop when the web page is "ready." Write down the time.

For users, however, "ready" varies across different browsers on different connection speeds (dial-up, DSL, cable, LAN) at different locations (Washington, DC, versus Mountain View, California, versus Bangalore, India) at different times of the day (peak versus off-peak times) and from different browse paths (fresh from search results or accessed from a home page).

Also, what's ready for one user may not be ready for another. Some users wait until the page is fully loaded before interacting with it. Others begin scrolling right away. Some users will bail out of the page if they do not see a response in a few seconds. For them, "ready" does not come soon enough. As you learned in the introduction to Part II, the old 8- to 10-second rule has split into faster response guidelines for broadband users and slower ones for dial-up users.

In reality, a web page is ready at a variety of different times. Performance optimization, therefore, serves to reduce the variability of those times despite all conditions. Consistent response times make it easier for users to attune to a website's performance characteristics.[12]

As a result, the speed of your web pages can have a profound impact on conversion rates, on user engagement, and on the overall experience of your web site.

In this section, we will establish a working vocabulary in the metrics that impact load times. We will show how to baseline your pages using the best tools available today, and we will leave you with some advice in managing the numbers.

---

[12]Roast, C. 1998. "Designing for Delay in Interactive Information Retrieval." *Interacting with Computers* 10 (1): 87–104.

Keeping Score

One thing you'll take away from this section is that you need to keep score. You need a *big board* to point to. Maintain a tracking spreadsheet or scorecard. This lets you effectively manage the progress of your changes. You can then do some competitive analysis and see how much you have improved.

Effective management
> The analytics numbers and their trends will seed actionable tasks for improvement and will keep all eyes in the room focused on the prize.

Competitive analysis
> The cost of switching between similar sites and content is small; use speed as a competitive advantage and beat your competitors' numbers.

Historical reference
> Quickly seeing where you were and how much you have improved enables you to validate and learn from past decisions. You can give rightful credit for the gains and account for the losses.

Feel free to create your own scorecard based on the information provided here, or you can download the one from this book's companion website, *http://www. websiteoptimization.com/secrets/metrics/scorecard.xls*, and follow along.

You can divide the metrics we will be tracking, analyzing, and inserting into three categories:

- Speed checklist
- Request statistics
- Load times

The benefit of this method is that one category impacts the next. Improving your speed checklist score improves request statistics, which in turn improves load times.

Speed checklist

Thanks to the advancement of performance optimization tools, we can now see whether web pages leverage basic speed optimization techniques and track them as metrics. We covered implementation of these techniques in Part II of this book, but here we will briefly describe why they are important to track:

Cache static objects
> All static objects (images, JavaScript/CSS, SWF, etc.) should have cache headers (max-age, Expires) specified, because this minimizes Not Modified (304) requests on repeat page views. Ideally, set the expiration time to 30 days or more. Streamline your workflow to rename the objects when they need to be updated.

Combine JavaScript/CSS files

You should combine JavaScript and CSS requested from the same server to reduce the number of requests, a key influencer of load times.

Use a Content Delivery Network (CDN)

Using a CDN improves the time to first byte (TTFB) of individual objects, directly improving load times (more on this shortly).

Gzip

Modern web browsers support HTTP compression using primarily the gzip algorithm. Think of it as WinZip (PC) or StuffIt (Mac) for the Web. Turning on gzip reduces kilobytes received of text-based files (HTML, JavaScript, CSS, XML, etc.), typically by 70% to 75%.[13] We reduced the JavaScript and CSS files of seven popular sites by 73.7% using gzip compression (see Table 10-1).

Compress images

You should store graphics in a format (typically, GIF, PNG, or JPG) that results in the smallest possible file size at the best possible quality. Although this is as much a subjective art as it is a science, you should monitor it closely to reduce kilobytes received.

Keepalive or persistent connections

Web servers configured with HTTP keepalive enable browsers to reuse and conserve socket connections. A socket connection takes as much load time as an object request, and can also bog down servers as more and more are opened and served. Although in general this is not a large issue anymore on the Web (ad servers seem to be the only ones without a clue), you should account for and watch it.

Cookies

Never set cookies to a domain or path from which static objects are served. The cookies will be sent out with the request on every CSS, JavaScript, or image object on that domain, or within that path. Moving these objects to a CDN is a common technique for stopping unwanted cookie stowaways.[14]

Minify JavaScript/CSS

Minifying is the process of removing unnecessary comments and whitespace from code, at the cost of making the code less maintainable. We recommend keeping a fully commented development copy of your JavaScript and CSS files and minifying only for the live server. Although gzip compresses code quite well,

---

[13]Balashov, K., and A. King. 2003. "Compressing the Web." In *Speed Up Your Site: Web Site Optimization.* Indianapolis: New Riders, 412. A test of 25 popular sites found that HTTP gzip compression saved 75% on average off text file sizes and 37% overall.

[14]Bent, L. et al. 2004. "Characterization of a large web site population with implications for content delivery." In *WWW 2004* (New York: May 17–20, 2004), 522–533. In a 2004 trace, 47% of requests used cookies; 34% of all requests were for cookied images; and 73% of all cookied requests were for images, showing that judicious use of cookies would cut their use by half and enable caching.

you can squeeze even more bytes from gzip when you combine it with minifying. The impact can be surprisingly large on reducing kilobytes received (see Table 10-1).

Table 10-1. Minification and gzip savings

Site	Original	Minified	Gzipped	Minified and gzipped
CNET	100 KB	78 KB (22%)	27.8 KB (72.2%)	21.6 KB (78.4%)
Travelocity	45.5 KB	37 KB (18.7%)	12.4 KB (72.7%)	9.9 KB (78.2%)
WSJ	211.4 KB	180.2 KB (14.8%)	45.4 KB (78.5%)	38.8 KB (81.6%)
ESPN	168.5 KB	164.8 KB (2.2%)	52 KB (69.1%)	45.5 KB (73%)
Digg	179.4 KB	148.1 KB (17.4%)	52.8 KB (70.6%)	41.3 KB (77%)
CNN	297.9 KB	231.2 KB (22.4%)	73.7 KB (75.3%)	59.1 KB (80.2%)
Amazon	223.4 KB	190.7 KB (14.6%)	50 KB (77.6%)	42.7 KB (80.9%)
Average	**175.2 KB**	**147.1 KB (16%)**	**44.9 KB (73.7%)**	**37KB (78.5%)**

On average, minifying reduced the file size of the home page JavaScript and CSS of these seven popular sites by 16%. Compressing them with gzip reduced them by 73.7% on average, with a small performance penalty for decompressing the files at the browser. Combining minifying with gzip compression reduced them by 78.5% overall. So, minifying buys you 16% without compression and 4.8 percentage points more than gzip compression alone. Note also that using *lowercase text and markup* improves the efficiency of gzip compression by increasing the likelihood of string matches. The speed checklist metrics make it easy for us to determine that fundamental optimization techniques have been implemented: our goal is 100% compliance.

Request statistics

These metrics are positively correlated to load time. To illustrate this fact, we took a load time sampling of the top U.S. web sites and correlated their kilobytes and object requests (see Figure 10-13).

The higher these metrics are, the greater the chances of high load times. You will want to work to reduce these:

Kilobytes received

The size (or weight) of the objects in the page, including HTTP headers (cookies, etc.), images, scripts, advertisements, and so on. The slower the user's Internet connection, the more strongly kilobytes received influences load times.

Kilobytes sent

The total weight of the outbound object request headers (user-agent, cookies, etc.) sent by the browser. Cookies are the source of excess weight here, and they affect the speed with which the browser is able to make requests.

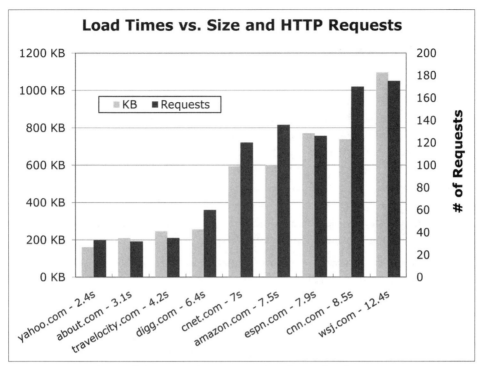

Figure 10-13. Load times, kilobytes, and requests are directly correlated

Number of requests
> The number of objects called by the page. Each object called has a *speed tax* associated with it for simply existing (refer back to Part II's introduction for more details). On faster connections such as fiber optic, the number of objects becomes the key influencer of load times.

Socket connections
> Before requesting an object, the browser must establish a connection to the web server. Because of the advent of persistent connections (covered in the preceding list, in the entry for keepalive or persistent connections), sockets are less of a factor but are still worth watching and improving when necessary.

Domain Name System (DNS) lookups
> For every domain or hostname referenced by your markup, a DNS lookup occurs. These can be dangerous because you cannot predict how much time they will take. Although the user's Internet service provider (ISP) and browser typically cache them, it is not uncommon to see these take seconds or longer if a DNS server is acting up. It is best to reduce as much as possible the chances of this occurring.

Not Modified (304)

The 304 response code indicates a request for an object that existed in the user's browser cache. In other words, the request did not need to occur in the first place, but it impacted load time.

Redirects (301/302)

A 301 or 302 response code indicates that a server redirect has occurred. For example, if a user accesses *http://www.example.com* and she is redirected to *http://www.example.com/main*, this adds an additional request/response and increases load time as well as potentially harming search engine rankings if done improperly. For fast performance, it is best to reduce the number of redirects.

Not Found (404)

Sometimes HTML code references images or scripts that no longer exist. Although nothing is downloaded, the request is still made and it impacts performance, making this metric important to watch.

Improving these metrics will have a direct impact on your load times, and we will be tracking and analyzing them all very closely.

Load times

Yes, load times, *plural*. Instead of working on one master load time, we will be looking to improve four points of time critical to the user experience:

TTFB

The time period measured from when a user requests the HTML document until it is processed on the server and content starts to download.

Start Render

The point at which the screen begins to draw. Until this point is reached, the page is blank for users.

Document Complete or "Web 1.0" time

This event fires when all images and scripts called by the HTML and CSS have been downloaded. It is a great load time indicator for basic content sites such as blogs.

Fully Loaded or "Web 2.0" time

Images and scripts called by JavaScript or Flash can be loaded after the onload JavaScript event fires. This behavior makes it necessary to have a measurement for content that is dynamically pulled into the page. Flash-enabled websites such as *http://www.disney.com* typically initialize their content after the onload event, illustrating the need for a metric capturing the elements loading thereafter.

We break load times into four parts to make each piece more actionable. For example, a long TTFB could indicate server or network congestion. Tracking only the Fully Loaded time metric would not give you enough information to allow you to act on this problem immediately, or to even know whether there *was* a problem to begin with.

We recommend tracking all of these times, and reporting either Document Complete (Web 1.0) or Fully Loaded (Web 2.0) for the sake of simplicity for those who insist on only one load time metric.

Scorecard tips

If you haven't yet downloaded our sample scorecard, there are a few final requirements that we should mention:

Dates
> We should make these metrics easy to track over time and calculate percentage gains for reporting progress.

Multiple pages
> The scorecard should support multiple pages. Tabs in Excel come in handy here.

Multiple paths
> Because page performance can be different depending on the path users take to access it, we need to account for this. At a minimum, we recommend showing the first view versus the follow-up, or repeat view.

Armed with our speed metrics and scorecard in hand, we can move on to measurement.

Designing a Sample Test

Because of the many conditions in which users may access our page, we need to standardize on a few things.

Find your audience

Your analytics software can tell you the dominant browser and connection speed that the majority of your visitors are using. For our purposes, we will assume Windows XP, Internet Explorer 7, and a 1.5 Mbps connection speed.

Analytics software can also tell you what browse paths are common. For example, if it turns out that a common path to the product details page is from a search engine and from the home page, this might be an important path to baseline in your scorecard.

We are also going to capture two types of page loads: the first view and the repeat view. The first view simulates the first impression experience of a user who has never visited the site before. The return experience metric tests the speed of the page should the user return to the page within the hour.

Clear cache and cookies

Recent research by Yahoo!'s performance team suggests that the empty cache page view is more common than one would assume. Their study concluded that 40% to 60% of Yahoo!'s users have an empty cache experience and about 20% of all page views are done with an empty cache (see Figure 10-14).[15] Possible explanations are that browser caches fill up quickly and that users have been trained to clear their cache and cookies to fix issues with slow performance and other problems.

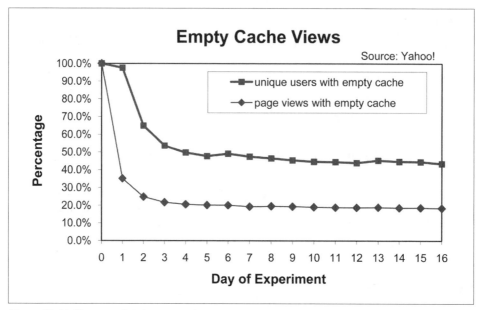

Figure 10-14. Empty cache views over time

You should also clear cookies. Cookie traffic can have an impact on load times because the extra bytes piggyback onto the outbound request. To delete your browser cache and cookies, follow these steps:

For Internet Explorer 7:

1. Select Tools → Internet Options → Delete → Delete Files and then click Yes.
2. Select Tools → Internet Options → Delete → Delete Cookies and then click Yes.

For Internet Explorer 6:

1. Select Tools → Internet Options → Delete Cookies and then click OK.
2. Select Tools → Internet Options → Delete Files and then click OK.

For Firefox:

1. Select Tools → Clear Private Data → Check Cache, Cookies → Clear Private Data Now.

---

[15]Theurer, T. January 4, 2007. "Performance Research, Part 2: Browser Cache Usage—Exposed!" Yahoo! User Interface Blog, *http://yuiblog.com/blog/2007/01/04/performance-research-part-2/* (accessed February 22, 2008).

Flush DNS

Every time a browser encounters a new domain during page load, it performs a DNS lookup to the ISP to determine the IP address of the domain name. The speed of the lookup varies by ISP, but it is generally 10 to 20 ms.[16]

Because we are aiming to simulate users who have never looked up the domain before, we should clear this as well.

For Windows XP:

1. Select Start → Run.
2. Type `ipconfig /flushdns` and then click OK.

For Mac OS X:

1. Select Open Terminal.
2. Type `lookupd -flushcache`.

Simulate connection speeds

Bandwidth and network latency are the two biggest factors that influence a page's load times. We will use a tool called Charles, available at *http://www.charlesproxy.com/*, to simulate the common broadband speed of 1.5 Mbps, as well as to induce a latency of 80 ms (see Figure 10-15).[17,18] Typical end-to-end latencies in the United States are from 70 to 80 ms for the average web surfer. Analog modem or ISDN connections add 30 to 150 ms of latency. You can see how latencies will vary with connection speed. Narrowband latencies average about 250 ms whereas broadband connections average about 100 ms.[19] Satellite connections have longer latencies on the order of 250 to 500 ms.

Charles is a web debugging proxy. Among its other features, it can throttle bandwidth. The tool is shareware and is fully functional for 30 days. A license costs about $50 (at the time of this writing) and is well worth it if you are serious about optimizing for performance on all types of connection speeds and network latencies.

[16]Bent, L., and G. Voelker. 2002. "Whole Page Performance." In *WCW 2002* (Boulder, CO: August 14–16, 2002), 11. The average DNS lookup in the United States takes about 7.1 milliseconds.

[17]Cardwell, N. et al. 2000. "Modeling TCP Latency." In *INFOCOM 2000* (Tel Aviv, Israel: March 26–30, 2000): 1742–1751. Found that 70 ms is a reasonable round-trip time (RTT) for web objects.

[18]Habib, M. A., and M. Abrams. 2000. "Analysis of Sources of Latency in Downloading Web Pages." In *Web-Net 2000* (San Antonio, TX: October 30–November 4, 2000), 227–232. Round-trip times range from 20 to 90 ms across the United States. Overseas RTT ranged from 140 to 750 ms for a satellite link to Bangladesh. About 40% to 60% of total web page latency is from the initial request to receiving the first byte, due mainly to overhead, not server delay.

[19]Touch, J. et al. December 1998. "Analysis of HTTP Performance." USC/ISI Research Report 98-463.

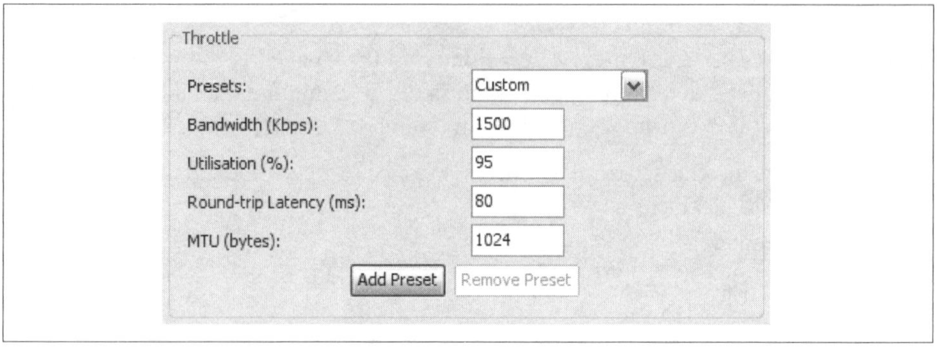

Figure 10-15. Charles throttling bandwidth

Charles comes with presets for dial-up, ISDN, and low DSL connection speeds (as shown in Figure 10-15). We will configure Charles to the typical U.S. DSL broadband connection speed in 2008: 1.5 Mbps or 1,500 Kbps.

In addition to bandwidth threshold, you can set the utilization percentage to simulate users who don't get the fully advertised speed, who download files at the same time, or who share a connection with a neighbor. You can also adjust round-trip latency to simulate poor network conditions (satellite Internet, Wi-Fi) or geographic issues. For example, a round trip to India from the United States takes about 400 to 750 ms.

We will configure Charles with an 80 ms round-trip latency as our standard with 95% utilization and start our tests. Your browser needs to be configured to properly use Charles for repeatability (see the installation steps for auto-configuration at the Charles website).

It's Measuring Time

With our cache, cookies, and DNS cleared and with Charles throttling our connection to a common broadband speed, we are ready to roll. We are going to baseline Digg (*http://www.digg.com*), a popular social bookmarking service, starting from a blank page (`about:blank`).

> If you have a machine dedicated to performance analysis, use `about:blank` as your home page.

IBM Page Detailer

IBM Page Detailer is a Windows tool that sits quietly in the background as you browse. It captures snapshots of how objects are loading on the page behind the scenes. Download it from *http://www.alphaworks.ibm.com/tech/pagedetailer/download*.

IBM Page Detailer captures three basic performance metrics: load time, bytes, and items. These correlate to the Document Complete, kilobytes received, and number of requests metrics we are tracking.

We recommend capturing three to five page loads and averaging the metrics to ensure that no anomalies impacted performance in the data, such as a larger ad. It is important, however, to note the occurrence and work to mitigate such anomalies. Table 10-2 shows our averaged results.

Table 10-2. IBM Page Detailer metrics for http://www.digg.com

	Load time (sec.)	Bytes	Items (requests)
First view	8.7	421,102	64
Repeat view	3.9	82,363	25

Under the hood: Waterfall reports

The real power of IBM Page Detailer is in its detailed "waterfall reports." These charts show the sequence and timing of web page objects as they download for a requested web page (see Figure 10-16). They can illustrate common web performance issues, such as blocking JavaScript files and the browser limitation of "two simultaneous connections per hostname" on HTTP 1.1 servers. We covered the perils of parallelism in the introduction to Part II.

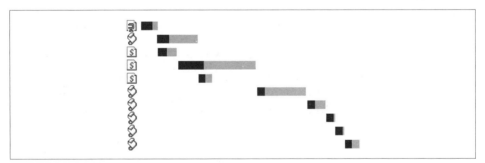

Figure 10-16. IBM Page Detailer waterfall report

The Chart tab of IBM Page Detailer shows a graphical view of all objects loading on the Digg.com home page (as shown in Figure 10-16). Page Detailer shows how each request breaks down between Server Response (time associated with the request) and Delivery (time to download all of the object's kilobytes). This is also shown in Figure 10-16. The darker bar represents the time waiting for the server response, and the lighter bar is the delivery time of all the bytes.

IBM Page Detailer also has a Details view that helps you understand more about the impact of each object on the page. Here you can sort by load time to see the big offenders. Be sure to check out the additional columns (right-click the column name, and then select Add Column), especially Item Start Offset, to understand when each object loads into the page. In Figure 10-17, you can see that on this page load, *jquery.js* took one second and *label.js* didn't start to load until 4.16 seconds.

Item	Item Duration	Item Size	Graph - Item Duration	Item Start Offset
/	0.421722	13359		0.0
prototype.js	0.767034	71976		0.320362
global.css	0.438479	38698		0.482127
lightbox.css	1.690460	9591		0.944668
ie6.css	0.267410	13826		1.103370
jquery.js	1.022308	85605		2.684870
digg.js	0.394479	24277		3.740146
label.js	0.213490	2726		4.167971
lightbox.js	0.206830	4246		4.396250

Figure 10-17. IBM Page Detailer Details tab

IBM Page Detailer works with both Internet Explorer and Firefox, but you must load it separately from the browser as a standalone application. For performance analysis tools that load right in the web browser, read on.

Firebug: A simple alternative

Firebug is an add-on for Firefox that adds a cross-platform measurement tool to your belt. Though not as detailed as the aptly named IBM Page Detailer, you can use it to dig in to what's happening in Firefox.

Like IBM Page Detailer, Firebug provides a waterfall report, as well as the basic speed metrics such as requests, kilobytes, and load time in seconds (see Figure 10-18). Notice that CSS has the same blocking effect as JavaScript in Firefox. This is one of the differences in the way files are handled between Internet Explorer and Firefox. Another difference that you may encounter is that JavaScript files pulled dynamically (via DOM methods) block objects in Firefox, whereas in Internet Explorer they do not.

If you mouse over any of the images, you will get a preview of the image to quickly identify fat graphics (also shown in Figure 10-18).

Unlike IBM Page Detailer, Firebug doesn't show detail regarding server response and delivery. It combines everything into one time. It also includes JavaScript execution time. Keep this in mind when using this tool! For example, on the Repeat view, you'll see objects pulled from cache (not 304s) show up in the report. You aren't crazy: this is how Firebug works and why Yahoo! patched it in its YSlow tool (more on YSlow shortly).

The fact that Firebug can measure execution time can also be a good thing; you can profile your JavaScript functions to see where your holdups are. To profile execution time, click Console and then Profile. Load the page, and then click the Profile button again to see a detailed report of all the functions executed by the page and how long they took (see Figure 10-19).

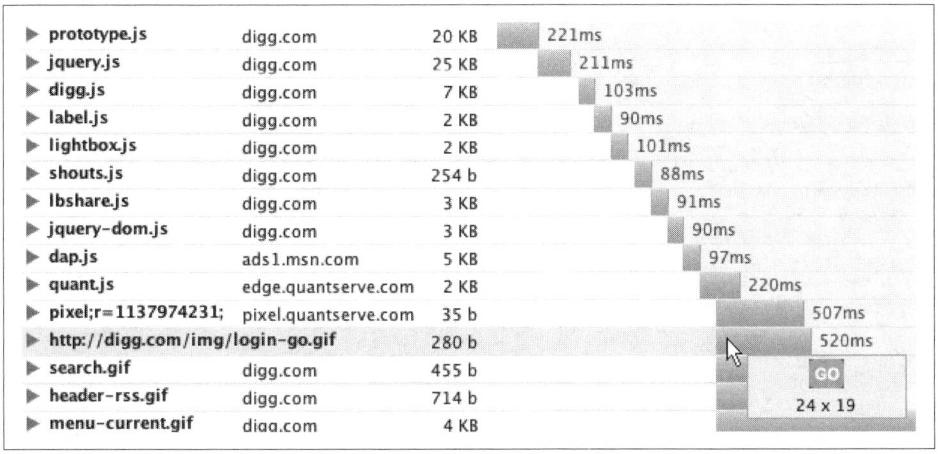

Figure 10-18. Firebug output display of Digg.com, first view

Profile (360.517ms, 6560 calls)

Function	Calls	Percent	Time	Avg	Min	Max	File
tt_HideSrcTagsRecurs	1696	19.44%	70.101ms	0.041ms	0ms	70.101ms	tooltip.js (line 458)
merge	7	13.89%	50.072ms	7.153ms	0ms	30.043ms	jquery.js (line 753)
tt_GetDivW	1	11.11%	40.058ms	40.058ms	40.058ms	40.058ms	tooltip.js (line 195)
displayAd	2	11.11%	40.057ms	20.029ms	20.028ms	20.029ms	dap.js (line 101)
_D	114	5.56%	30.044ms	0.264ms	0ms	10.015ms	hbxdigg.js (line 35)
classFilter	2	5.56%	20.029ms	10.015ms	10.014ms	10.015ms	jquery.js (line 1243)
_IL	1321	5.56%	20.028ms	0.015ms	0ms	10.014ms	hbxdigg.js (line 38)
_EV	294	2.78%	10.015ms	0.034ms	0ms	10.015ms	hbxdigg.js (line 104)

Figure 10-19. Firebug JavaScript profiler

Remember that JavaScript blocks pages from rendering until they are requested, downloaded, *and executed*, so optimization here can prove worthwhile.

What about keeping score? So far, we have seen two popular tools for performance analysis, but none that quickly summarize the metrics outlined early in this section. A new tool called AOL Pagetest allows a finer-grained performance analysis than previously possible.

AOL Pagetest

AOL uses Pagetest, a homegrown performance measurement tool recently released to the open source community. At the time of this writing, Pagetest has more features than any other tool, free or otherwise.

In addition to the waterfall reports you have seen so far, Pagetest adds a timeline across the top, numbered objects down the side, and vertical bars marking key points in time in the page load process (see Figure 10-20).

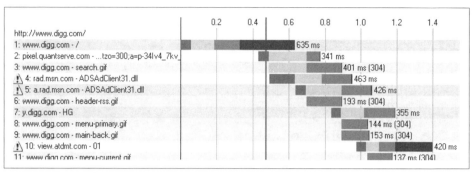

Figure 10-20. AOL Pagetest waterfall report, Digg.com cached view

The first vertical bar (shown as green on this book's companion site) represents when the browser window has a width and height greater than zero: in other words, when the document starts to render. This correlates to our Start Render metric identified earlier in this section.

The second vertical bar (blue) represents when the browser fires the Document Complete JavaScript event, and is a good indication of when the page is ready for Web 1.0 or progressively enhanced sites that don't rely on Flash and Ajax.

The black line at the end represents the *fully loaded* time. It captures any additional requests made after the previous event, such as objects requested through JavaScript and Flash. The fully loaded time fires after two seconds of network inactivity.

Each object request is numbered, which makes it easy to discuss performance problems. Notice, for example, that objects 8 and 9 in Figure 10-20 are highlighted and are returning 304s. This is a ripe opportunity for cache headers!

Inside an HTTP request. Notice that in Pagetest, each object request is broken down into different colors (or shades of gray in Figure 10-20). Recall that in Firebug, all we get to see is the overall time of the object, but here we have more details within each request. These colors correlate to the different parts of an HTTP request with more granularity than IBM Page Detailer. Figure 10-21 shows the HTTP request breakdown.

As we covered in our overview of request statistics, DNS lookups occur when accessing new hostnames. The operating system then stores them for about 30 minutes in the user's local cache. It is important to reduce lookups, as times will vary.

After getting the IP, the browser opens a socket connection with the server. Two simultaneous socket connections stay open at any given time, assuming persistent connections (keepalives) are enabled. If persistent connections are not enabled, the browser opens a socket connection for every request.

Once the socket is opened (or reused), the browser makes another request to the web server (e.g., Digg.com). The TTFB, as described earlier, is the period between when the browser makes the request and when the server processes the request and then sends the first byte of the page (or object) back to the browser.

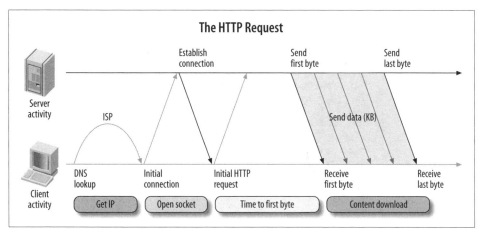

Figure 10-21. Anatomy of an HTTP request and correlation to Pagetest legend

Finally, the server responds with the content the browser requested. This period is where the object's kilobytes and the user's bandwidth, or throughput, impact the time it takes to download.

Special responses. If the user already has the object in his cache, a Not Modified (304) response is returned and the content download is avoided. One study found that 29% of objects requested from servers were not modified.[20] Pagetest highlights these in yellow, so you can quickly spot them and address them with the proper cache headers.

If the object wasn't found on the server, a Not Found (404) response is returned. The problem here is that the browser still went through all the time and trouble to request it. What a waste!

Finally, Pagetest will also highlight requests that were redirects. As you may have guessed, 301/302 redirects also count as requests, so we want to be sure we really meant for them to happen.

Summarizing load time and request statistics. We have kept you waiting long enough. Now that you understand how HTTP requests work and why reducing them is important, it is time to update our scorecard.

In Pagetest, go to File → Save Optimization Report. At the top of the saved file, you will find a summary with all of the metrics we want to track (see Figure 10-22).

Scrolling down, you will also find an organized summary of all objects that failed to meet the items in our speed checklist. Pagetest is available for download at *http://pagetest.sourceforge.net*. It is also available as an online tool at *http://www.webpagetest.org*.

---

[20]Bent, L. et al. "Characterization of a Large Web Site Population with Implications for Content Delivery," 511.

```
Optimization Report : 11/20/07 at 11:32:24

Results for 'http://www.digg.com/':

Page load time: 8.474 seconds
Time to first byte: 0.354 seconds
Time to Start Render: 4.175 seconds
Time to Document Complete: 7.763 seconds
Time to Fully Loaded: 8.474 seconds
Bytes sent out: 13.872 KB
Bytes received: 402.702 KB
DNS Lookups: 11
Connections: 12
Requests: 50
   OK Requests:  50
   Redirects:    0
   Not Modified: 0
```

Figure 10-22. AOL Pagetest Optimization Report summary

Speed Up Your Site

Now you know how fast your site is loading and how to measure website performance and the various request statistics that impact speed. Next, it is time to improve performance and track it via our speed checklist metrics.

Pagetest provides a chart that shows a quick analysis of all the optimization checklist metrics outlined earlier in this chapter. The chart is at the page object level. To check it out, in Pagetest select File → Export Checklist. Each heuristic is scored individually, making them great metrics to track and improve (see Figure 10-23).

http://www.digg.com/	Cache Static 32%	Use a CDN 0%	Combine CSS/JS 13%	GZIP text 28%	Compres 10
1: www.digg.com - /				✓	
2: www.digg.com - prototype.js	✓	✗	✗	✗	
3: www.digg.com - global.css	✓	✗	✗	✗	
4: www.digg.com - lightbox.css	✓	✗	✗	✗	
5: www.digg.com - ie6.css	✓	✗	✗	✗	
6: www.digg.com - jquery.js	✓	✗	✗	✗	
7: www.digg.com - digg.js	✓	✗	✗	✗	
8: www.digg.com - label.js	✓	✗	✗	✗	
9: www.digg.com - lightbox.js	✓	✗	✗	✗	
10: www.digg.com - shouts.js	✓	✗	✗	✓	
11: www.digg.com - lbshare.js	✓	✗	✗	✗	
12: www.digg.com - jquery-dom.js	✓	✗	✗	✗	
13: ads1.msn.com - dap.js	⚠	✗	✓	✓	
14: edge.quantserve.com - quant.js				✓	
15: pixel.quantserve.com - ...tzo=300;a=p-34lv4_7kv					

Figure 10-23. AOL Pagetest Optimization Checklist Report

The optimization checklist tests each object against eight techniques that we recommend for every page on the Web (cache, CDN, gzip, compress images, minify, combine JavaScript/CSS, keepalives, and cookies), with few exceptions. Pagetest calculates a score based on the number of passing objects versus failed objects. This is translated into an overall percentage score. To get a good read, make sure you run the checklist on the first view (cleared cached) experience.

We can transfer these numbers directly into our scorecard, so we can watch how they impact load times.

Note that Pagetest includes this chart in text format in its Optimization Report (select File → Save Optimization Report) in a more actionable format. At AOL, this is the start of a performance action plan for product teams. All that's missing are owners and dates for when offending objects will be fixed.

Enhance Firebug with YSlow

YSlow is a great companion to Firebug. It was designed to check web pages against Steve Souders's rules for speeding up your site (see Figure 10-24). It uses Firebug's Net Panel and traverses the HTML DOM to develop a thorough list of objects to score the page.

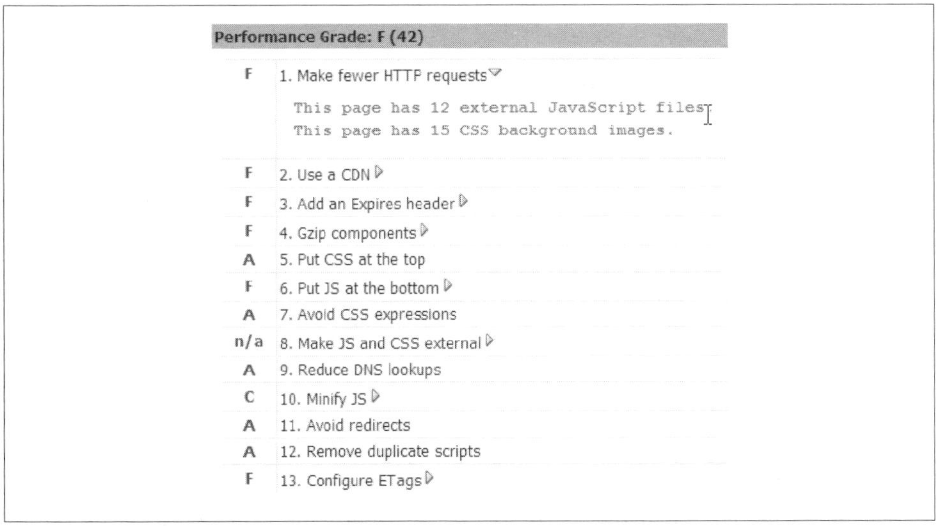

Performance Grade: F (42)

F	1. Make fewer HTTP requests ▽
	This page has 12 external JavaScript files This page has 15 CSS background images.
F	2. Use a CDN ▷
F	3. Add an Expires header ▷
F	4. Gzip components ▷
A	5. Put CSS at the top
F	6. Put JS at the bottom ▷
A	7. Avoid CSS expressions
n/a	8. Make JS and CSS external ▷
A	9. Reduce DNS lookups
C	10. Minify JS ▷
A	11. Avoid redirects
A	12. Remove duplicate scripts
F	13. Configure ETags ▷

Figure 10-24. YSlow Performance tab

Using Digg.com as our example, we see that it gets a failing grade compared to several important best practices, especially #1: make fewer HTTP requests.

Clicking the arrows will give you actionable information on what caused it to fail. For example, to address Rule #1, the 15 CSS background images might be good candidates for using a CSS sprite map (covered in Chapter 7). The 12 external JavaScript files should be combined into fewer files, directly improving our number of requests and start render metrics.

YSlow patches the Net panel of Firebug, adding an option to get rid of objects that were pulled from cache from the waterfall chart (remember, Firebug shows execution time, unlike Pagetest and IBM Page Detailer). Be cautious of this patch, however. In our testing, it sometimes did not show scripts loading on the first view, mistaking them somehow for cached objects. The YSlow team is good about quickly releasing patches, so be sure to keep it up-to-date and cross-check it with IBM Page Detailer or Pagetest's results.

On YSlow's Stats tab, we see that it further breaks down the total kilobytes and HTTP requests and categorizes them so that they are more actionable. For a nice summary report, select Tools → Printable View (see Figure 10-25). It makes a punch list of things to fix.

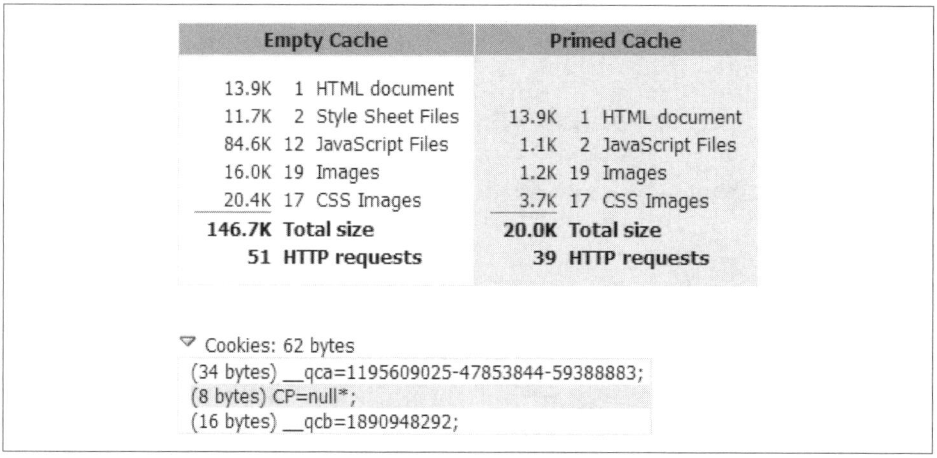

Empty Cache		Primed Cache	
13.9K	1 HTML document		
11.7K	2 Style Sheet Files	13.9K	1 HTML document
84.6K	12 JavaScript Files	1.1K	2 JavaScript Files
16.0K	19 Images	1.2K	19 Images
20.4K	17 CSS Images	3.7K	17 CSS Images
146.7K	**Total size**	**20.0K**	**Total size**
	51 HTTP requests		**39 HTTP requests**

▽ Cookies: 62 bytes
(34 bytes) __qca=1195609025-47853844-59388883;
(8 bytes) CP=null*;
(16 bytes) __qcb=1890948292;

Figure 10-25. YSlow Stats tab

Reporting the Numbers

By now, you have a scorecard that holds the key metrics for web performance optimization. We went ahead and baselined Digg.com a month later, to check on its progress and to show you our metrics in action (see Figure 10-26).

Let's examine what Digg did to improve its site between November 2007 and December 2007.

Performance Scorecard

Page http://www.digg.com

	Date	11/20/07	12/21/07	Change	%
Load Times					
First	TTFB	0.354	0.329	-0.025	-7.1%
	Start Render	4.175	2.878	-1.297	-31.1%
	Document Complete	7.763	6.355	-1.408	-18.1%
	Fully Loaded	8.474	7.86	-0.614	-7.2%
Repeat	TTFB	0.329	0.329	0	0.0%
	Start Render	0.475	0.481	0.006	1.3%
	Document Complete	2.033	3.107	1.074	52.8%
	Fully Loaded	2.839	4.342	1.503	52.9%
Request Statistics					
First	KB Received	402.702	255.804	-146.898	-36.5%
	KB Sent	13.872	17.08	3.208	23.1%
	# of Requests	50	60	10	20.0%
	Socket Connections	12	14	2	16.7%
	DNS Lookups	11	13	2	18.2%
	Not Modified (304)	0	0	0	0.0%
	Redirects (301/302)	0	0	0	0.0%
	Not Found (404)	0	0	0	0.0%
Repeat	KB Received	62.513	79.336	16.823	26.9%
	KB Sent	11.975	16.078	4.103	34.3%
	# of Requests	28	39	11	39.3%
	Socket Connections	14	11	-3	-21.4%
	DNS Lookups	9	8	-1	-11.1%
	Not Modified (304)	16	31	15	93.8%
	Redirects (301/302)	1	0	-1	-100.0%
	Not Found (404)	0	0	0	0.0%
Speed Checklist					
	Cache	32	21	-11	-34.4%
	Combine	13	18	5	38.5%
	CDN	0	0	0	0.0%
	GZIP	28	78	50	178.6%
	Compress Images	100	100	0	0.0%
	Keep-Alive	100	100	0	0.0%
	Cookies	100	100	0	0.0%
	Minify	72	72	0	0.0%
	Doctype	100	100	0	0.0%

Figure 10-26. Digg.com performance scorecard

Looking at our speed checklist metrics, we see that Digg improved in two areas, that is, in the "Combine" and "GZIP" items. These metrics typically impact start render, as they address CSS and JavaScript files in the head of the document. Digg's score improved 178.6% for "GZIP" in particular, so we can expect big savings here.

On the downside, we see that Digg.com's Cache score dropped by 34.4%. We can almost certainly expect more Not Modified (304) responses and longer load times on the Repeat view to be reflected in the metrics in Figure 10-26.

Turning our attention to our request statistics, we see a big improvement in "KB Received"; Digg reduced it by 36.5%, or 146.9 KB. This was no doubt caused by the savings we had due to the gzip win.

However, Digg bumped its requests up from 50 to 60, and also appears to be making more DNS lookups and socket connections. This hints at ad issues. We will see how this plays out in Digg's load time metrics. Finally, as predicted, we see a 93.8% rise in Not Modified (304) responses, something that will guarantee a slower Repeat view.

Finally, we arrive at Digg's load time metrics. Digg made major headway in its "Start Render" time, engaging its users 31.1% faster than before! This illustrates the power of gzip. Its poor caching issues and increased 304s are impacting its Repeat view load times, rendering them more than 50% slower than before.

In its next release, Digg should apply cache headers to its static template images, and after celebrating its already big win in start render time, should work to combine its JavaScript and CSS files to engage its users even sooner and to serve a near immediate first impression.

A movie is worth a thousand scorecards

Clients can sometimes be overwhelmed by numbers, but a visual aid can help. If you are really trying to sell web performance, you'll want to have movies in your arsenal. To illustrate how compelling this can be, we have a video of Digg.com's load time for download at our companion site (see Figure 10-27).

The most basic way to measure performance is simply to give it a good look and time some of the key points visually:

Start render
> The first sign of feedback to the user

Useful content
> The time when content is usable, that is, navigation or search appears, the window is scrollable, and so forth

Graphics loaded
> The time when the experience is visually complete with all logos and icons in place above the fold

Ads loaded
> The time when advertisements on the site have loaded and impressions have been registered

Let's look more closely at each key visual performance metric.

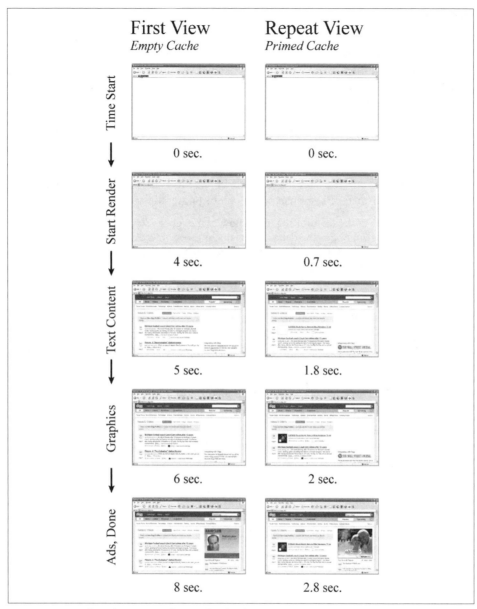

First View
Empty Cache

Repeat View
Primed Cache

Time Start

0 sec.

0 sec.

Start Render

4 sec.

0.7 sec.

Text Content

5 sec.

1.8 sec.

Graphics

6 sec.

2 sec.

Ads, Done

8 sec.

2.8 sec.

Figure 10-27. Video of Digg.com showing key load times

Start render

Up to this point, users are staring at the page where they started. Before a page is displayed, it must download all the elements called from the <head> HTML element. This is typically all the JavaScript and CSS needed by the web page. The start render time is arguably the most important, because at this point we are at the greatest risk of a user bailing out before she experiences the content.

You can improve the start render time by optimizing the JavaScript and CSS in the HTML head by combining files, reducing their weight, moving the JavaScript to the end of the HTML document, or loading them on demand.

Ideally, you want your start render time to be within one second, which would be perceived as a near-instant response on the Web. Jakob Nielsen wrote:

> 1.0 second is about the limit for the user's flow of thought to stay uninterrupted, even though the user will notice the delay. Normally, no special feedback is necessary during delays of more than 0.1 but less than 1.0 second, but the user does lose the feeling of operating directly on the data.[21]

Useful content display

After the page is visible, HTML text typically displays first in the load order. The more text there is on the page, the more a user has to interact with. Be sure to set important headers, navigation, and readable content as HTML text to give the best "useful content" time.

Pages that are designed correctly, with CSS at the top and JavaScript at the bottom, display content progressively. This page-loading behavior is a form of feedback that makes users more tolerant of delays. You can improve useful content times by simplifying HTML markup (de-nesting divs and tables) and by converting graphical text to CSS text. See Chapter 6 for details on progressive rendering and optimal placement of CSS and JavaScript files.

Your target for useful content display should be in the range of one to two seconds over broadband. According to research, that is the threshold for retaining a user's attention. See the introduction to Part II for details on attention thresholds.

Graphics loaded

Images and graphics will paint in after the text has loaded. This time is important, especially if the graphics contain critical information to users accomplishing a task. In Digg's case, most of the important content is conveyed as text. Digg does a good job here. Only user icons and some background gradients make up Digg's design.

---

[21]Nielsen, J. 2007. "Response Times: The Three Important Limits." Useit.com, *http://www.useit.com/papers/ responsetime.html* (accessed January 18, 2008).

Keep in mind that some users do wait for all graphical elements to load before proceeding to browse, so it is important that we improve the graphics load time.

Improving graphics load time involves using CSS sprites, and using more text and CSS-based design treatments.

As for time limits, if there is useful content in graphics, we will want the graphics to display in one to two seconds; otherwise, we recommend a threshold of 3 to 4 seconds for broadband-targeted content and 8 to 12 seconds for dial-up. The key word here is *targeted*. Examine your audience and ensure that your site appeals to your users for their respective bandwidth thresholds. Optimizing for dial-up will enable you to better monetize their traffic, as well as make your broadband users even happier.

Ads loaded

It is important to note the time when ads are loaded because in most cases that is when your money is made. If ads are taking too long to load, you may not be getting those impressions because of user bailout. It is important to fully monetize your website and load ads as quickly as possible.

The best solution we have found for advertisements is to compromise and stick them in iframes so that they will load sooner. Although they eat up bandwidth, iframes load asynchronously and they ensure early impressions. If you head down this path, be sure to test extensively across browsers to ensure that the ads still function properly.

Our target time for loading advertisements should be as soon as possible to gain impressions. To improve performance, offload any video or extended interactive creative until the end of the page load.

Commercial Monitoring Tools

Although we have detailed how to measure web performance metrics on your own, several commercial services are available. These services provide measurements of your site's performance from different geographic areas, as well as more detailed transaction reports for e-commerce sites.

Keynote is a leader in end-user experience testing, and can track your key pages under a variety of configurations. Keynote has the ability to script tests using a real Internet Explorer browser, and collect metrics from all over the globe. One of its newer capabilities that sets it apart is its mobile testing, where it can do speed testing across an array of mobile devices and carriers. Keynote claims to have the market-leading infrastructure for testing, measuring and monitoring website performance, streaming downloads and live streaming, mobile content quality, VoIP, and online customer experience.

To accomplish all this, the company maintains an infrastructure of more than 2,400 measurement computers and real mobile devices representing actual end-user experience from more than 160 metropolitan areas worldwide. Additionally, it maintains a panel of more than 160,000 people who perform interactive website studies that assess online user experience with the goal of improving overall online business effectiveness.

Gomez also does end-user testing, using both a browser and an emulator. The combination provides the deep data needed to analyze performance and a window into how your website's performance is perceived across multiple browsers and operating systems. Gomez's claim to fame is that its software can run on any machine, and can serve as a peer that reports performance data back to its data centers where it is then aggregated and analyzed. Gomez claims it has 38,000 such peers around the globe. It has also developed a solution that actually reports how users experience a website by using a JavaScript tag and reporting data back to the Gomez mother ship. Finally, we can see how our users truly experience our content!

Overlooked Web Performance Issues

We talked to Ben Rushlo, senior manager of Service Level Management Consulting at Keynote Systems, to get his input on performance metrics for his Fortune 100 clients. We asked Rushlo, "What performance issues do you find that clients overlook?" He replied:

> Typically, customers have pet metrics—metrics such as average download time or average availability. While these can be great for long-term trending and, in some cases, SLA management,[22] they are very imprecise for understanding the actual technical quality of a site. In fact, just using the term *technical quality* is a stretch for folks who are entrenched in the idea of uptime or speed (as key metrics).
>
> For Keynote, technical quality is a holistic way of looking at the site and gauging if all the pieces and parts are working together to create a good technical experience for site visitors.
>
> In order to measure technical quality, you have to look beyond simple averages. Averages hide the real interesting data, data that indicates site health.
>
> We suggest that our customers look not only at averages, but also at variability. That is, variability over hour, over time, and over geography. You might have a site whose search process downloads in three seconds on average (acceptable for our standards). However, the average is hiding the fact that off-peak the process takes one second and on-peak (when users want to use the site) it slows down to five seconds. This variation (we call it *load handling*) indicates a significant issue on the site. The average would never tell you that.

---

[22] A service level agreement (SLA) is a formally negotiated agreement between two parties that records a common understanding of the level of service.

Finally, just as variability gives shape to the averages, we suggest customers use tools to measure their site that can give them details about each part of the download time of the page. If all you have is the total page download time, or even large "buckets" of time (like content download versus network), you won't be able to improve performance. This is especially true in the more complex world of the Web where application calls are hidden within the content portion of the page and third parties are critical to the overall download time. You need to have a view into every piece of the page load in order to manage and improve it.

Summary

Website optimization requires using web metrics. With the right metrics and analytics tools, you can pinpoint potential problem areas for improvement and progressively improve them. To optimize your SEM campaigns and conversion, analysts should track measures of engagement such as pages per minute, PathLoss, and, of course, conversion.

Performance metrics let you sleep well at night, knowing your audience is happily and efficiently flowing through your content without unnecessary delays. Watching and reducing key metrics such as 304s, requests, and kilobytes received will have a direct effect on improving load times. Using tools such as Pagetest, Firebug, and YSlow can be a cost-effective way to quickly identify trouble spots and achieve 100% scores in your speed checklist. As we demonstrated with our scorecard, tracking and visualizing improvements over time helps to sell the value of web metrics, and ensure management buy-in.

Index

Symbols

$ selector, 201
$$( ) method, 242
$( ) function, 229
* selector, 201
, (comma), 23
^ selector, 201

Numbers

301 response code
    AOL Pagetest support, 337
    resource moved, 39
    server redirects, 328
302 response code
    AOL pagetest support, 337
    resource moved, 39
    server redirects, 328
304 response code
    AOL Pagetest support, 336, 337
    caching static objects, 324
    object in browser cache, 328
404 response code
    AOL Pagetest support, 337
    HTML reference errors, 328
    log analyzer support, 303
    resource moved, 39

A

A records, 259
A/B tests
    controlled experiments, 299
    multivariate testing, 305

about attribute, 43
Accept-Encoding header, 276
Accept-Ranges header, 263
ActiveX controls, 222, 308
ad campaigns
    BodyGlove.com case study, 105–106
    differences in bulk editing, 58–59
    duplicate keywords, 70
    importance of metrics, 297
    metrics tracking ROI by, 300
    PPC recommendations, 63
    SEM metrics, 310
    setting up, 56
    targeting, 55
    tracking phone call conversions, 90
ad clicks, 320
ad copy, 55–56, 76–79
ad groups
    defined, 56, 71
    grouping guidelines, 72
    optimizing after launch, 74
    optimizing bids, 91
    PPC optimization and, 55, 56
    recommendations, 55
    themed, xxiii, 71, 72, 73
ad spend, 59
AddEncoding directive, 273
Adepoju, Samson, xxiii
Adobe Creative Suite, 140
Adobe ImageReady, 10
Adobe Photoshop, 168, 169, 176
ads, 56, 345
    (see also PPC advertising/optimization)
AdWords (see Google AdWords)

We'd like to hear your suggestions for improving our indexes. Send email to *index@oreilly.com*.

JavaScript (*continued*)
  garbage collection, 241
  HTTP compression, 276, 277, 278
  iframe support, 290
  index limitations, 10
  lazy-loading code, 239
  loading on demand, 289–290
  loading wisely, 184–185
  localized functions, 235
  logfiles, 302
  minifying, 325, 326
  monitoring rendering time, 239–240
  name collisions and, 235
  optimization and packing, 292
  PE strategy, 283, 285–288
  placement considerations, 156
  reducing whitespace, 231
  refactoring, 180
  remapping built-in objects, 234
  removing comments, 230–231
  SEO considerations, 10
  shortening names, 233
  shorthand statements, 231, 232
  speed considerations, 325
  staging loading, 282, 283
  Start Render time metric, 344
  string constant macros, 232
  XSSI support, 180
  (see also Ajax)
JavaScript includes, 166
JavaScript Object Notation (JSON), 216,
    245
JavaScript page tagging, 302, 304–305
Jordan, Lawrence, xxiii
JPEG format, 167, 168, 169
jQuery library, 226, 227
.js file extension, 237, 273
JScript, 211
JSON (JavaScript Object Notation), 216, 245
Jung, Carl, 117
Juon, Catherine, xxiii
JupiterResearch, 147, 301

K

Kaiser, Shirley, xxiii
Kanoodle, 58
keepalive connections, 325
KEI (keyword effectiveness index), 15, 17, 67
Kenkai.com, 36
key frames, 173, 174
Keynote Systems, 308, 345

keyphrases
  in anchor text, 26
  baking into domain names, 26
  baking into site URIs, 29
  creating tag clouds, 32–34
  CRO discovery considerations, 129
  deploying strategically, 11
  determining, 13–15
  finding, 15
  keyword-focused content, 28
  long tail keywords, 69
  optimum length, 19, 20
  placement in headlines, 25
  rankings and, 11, 13
  refining, 18–21
  re-sorting, 18–21
  right-sizing, 18–21
  targeting multiple, 21
  in title tags, 21, 22
  writing title tags, 21–22
  (see also primary keyphrase)
keypress event, 306
keyword effectiveness index (KEI), 15, 17, 67
keyword matching, 66
keyword phrases (see keyphrases)
keyword research, 67–68
keyword stuffing
  defined, 5
  optimization and, 5, 22
  ranking factors, 16, 22
Keyword Universe (Wordtracker), 68
KeywordDiscovery, 67
keywords
  adding tactically, 25–27
  baking in, 26
  calculating minimum bid, 60
  content focused on, 27–34
  deploying strategically, 11
  duplicate, 70
  embedding in graphics, 10
  in headline summaries, 29
  keyword suggestion tool, 13
  long tail, 69
  metrics tracking ROI by, 300
  negative, 68, 316
  paid links, 38
  PhillyDentistry.com case study, 47, 53
  placement in headlines, 122
  PPC optimization and, 55, 56, 69–71
  pruning unrelated, 18–21
  ranking factors, 16
  sorting by popularity, 16–17

About the Author

Andrew B. King is the president of Website Optimization, LLC, a web performance and search engine marketing firm based in Ann Arbor, Michigan (*http://www.websiteoptimization.com*). Since 2002, the WSO team has helped firms optimize the effectiveness of their websites to improve their ROI. Their clients include Bank of America, AOL, Time Warner, Net Zero, WhitePages.com, and Caravan Tours.

Andy is the author of *Speed Up Your Site: Web Site Optimization*, a highly regarded book on web site performance tuning and search engine optimization. He holds a BSME and MSME from the University of Michigan, specializing in design optimization of structures. He was recruited by NASA after graduation, but chose instead to join the fast-paced world of engineering consultants.

Since 1993, Andy has worked full time as a web professional applying and teaching web optimization and creation techniques. He is the founder and former managing editor of WebReference.com and JavaScript.com, two award-winning developer sites owned by Jupitermedia. (WebReference.com was acquired by Mecklermedia—now Jupitermedia—in 1997.) His license plate reads OPT1MIZ. His hobbies include photography, hiking, and skiing.

Colophon

The animal on the cover of *Website Optimization* is a common nighthawk (*Chordeiles minor*). Members of the nightjar family, nighthawks are medium-size birds, measuring 9 inches long and 2.2–3.5 ounces, with a wingspan of roughly 21 inches. They have large heads and tiny bills disguising a cavernous mouth. Like its nearest relative, the owl, the nighthawk's plumage comprises well-camouflaged shades of black, brown, and gray.

Common nighthawks inhabit all of North America, and are known by several other names depending on region. In many parts of the U.S. and particularly in the south, they are called bullbats; "bull" is believed to derive from the bellowing sound the male makes during the breeding ritual, and "bat" because nighthawks' erratic flight resembles that of a bat. Nighthawks are also known as "goatsuckers" due to an ancient belief that they fed on goats' milk at night. (In actuality, any evidence of the birds' presence near goats is likely attributable to the flying insects in the surrounding fields, which constitute much of the nighthawk diet.) Other names include the Louisiana French Creole *crapau volans* ("flying toad"), "pick-a-me-dick" (an imitation of one of the bird's notes), pisk, pork and beans, will-o'-wisp, burnt-land bird, and mosquito hawk.

Nighthawks are quite beneficial to humans, as they eat many of the insects that destroy vegetation or are otherwise harmful, such as beetles, boll-weevils, and mosquitoes. The nighthawk opens its beak as it flies through clouds of insects, scooping them into its enormous mouth. It can eat more than 2,000 insects at a time, and as many as 50 different species have been found in the stomach of one nighthawk.

The cover image is from Wood's *Animate Creation*. The cover font is Adobe ITC Garamond. The text font is Linotype Birka; the heading font is Adobe Myriad Condensed; and the code font is LucasFont's TheSansMonoCondensed.

Related Titles from O'Reilly

Web Authoring and Design

ActionScript 3.0 Cookbook

Ajax Hacks

Ambient Findability

Creating Web Sites: The Missing Manual

CSS Cookbook, *2nd Edition*

CSS Pocket Reference, *2nd Edition*

CSS: The Definitive Guide, *3rd Edition*

CSS: The Missing Manual

Dreamweaver 8: Design and Construction

Dreamweaver 8: The Missing Manual

Dynamic HTML: The Definitive Reference, *3rd Edition*

Essential ActionScript 3.0

Flex 8 Cookbook

Flash 8: Projects for Learning Animation and Interactivity

Flash 8: The Missing manual

Flash 9 Design: Motion Graphics for Animation & User Interfaces

Flash Hacks

Head First HTML with CSS & XHTML

Head Rush Ajax

Head First Web Design

High Performance Web Sites

HTML & XHTML: The Definitive Guide, *6th Edition*

HTML & XHTML Pocket Reference, *3rd Edition*

Information Architecture for the World Wide Web, *3rd Edition*

Information Dashboard Design

JavaScript: The Definitive Guide, *5th Edition*

JavaScript & DHTML Cookbook, *2nd Edition*

Learning ActionScript 3.0

Learning JavaScript

Learning Web Design, *3rd Edition*

PHP Hacks

Programming Collective Intelligence

Programming Flex 2

Web Design in a Nutshell, *3rd Edition*

Web Site Measurement Hacks

O'REILLY®

Our books are available at most retail and online bookstores.

To order direct: 1-800-998-9938 • *order@oreilly.com* • *www.oreilly.com*

Online editions of most O'Reilly titles are available by subscription at *safari.oreilly.com*

Try the online edition
free for 45 days

70502